Moir's Guide North

THE OTAGO SOUTHERN ALPS

a tramping and transalpine guide from the Hollyford to Lake Ohau

Dedicated to the people who look after our environment, the people who maintain the basic huts, tracks and bridges in the hills and those who have fought for over a century to keep the backcountry free, public, and open.

Seventh Edition
2005
Edited by Geoff Spearpoint

Published by the New Zealand Alpine Club 2005

Although every effort has been made to ensure that the information contained in this guide book is accurate at the time of publication the editor and publishers accept no responsibility for any accident, misadventure or injury associated with its use. The sketch maps are designed to give an overview of each region, and relevent track, park, or NZMS 260 maps will be required in the field.

It would be very much appreciated if details of errors, omissions, or clarifications for the routes are sent to the editor to help in the update of future editions. Write to:

Geoff Spearpoint
49 Hillview Rd, Birdlings Flat
Little River 8162.
E-mail geoffspearpoint@paradise.net.nz
Ph 03 329 0008.

SEVENTH EDITION 2005.

Successor to:

Guide book to the Tourist Routes of the Great Southern Lakes. George M Moir, 1925.

Second Edition: Revised and enlarged by W Scott Gilkison and Arthur H Hamilton as *Moir's Guide Book,* 1948, 1950.

Third Edition: Revised by Gerard Hall-Jones (Southern Section) 1959, and Peter M Chandler (Northern Section) 1961.

Fourth Edition: Revised by Gerard Hall-Jones (Southern Section) 1969, 1973; Peter M Chandler and Ronald J Keen (Northern Section) 1968.

Fifth Edition: Revised by Gerard Hall-Jones (Southern Section) 1979, 1986; Lawrence D Kennedy (Northern Section) 1977, and reprinted with limited revision, 1984.

Sixth Edition: Revised by Robin McNeill (South) 1995; Geoff Spearpoint (North) 1998, updated and reprinted, 2000.

Seventh Edition: Revised by Geoff Spearpoint (North) 2005.

Printed by Saxon Print, Christchurch

Jacket Photographs

Front cover: View south along the Haast Range from near Waiatoto Saddle. Waiatoto Valley to the left, and the Arawhata Valley to the right.

Inside front cover: Trampers descending Destiny Ridge, Joe Valley. Main Divide (Barrier Range) in background.

Back cover, clockwise from top left: Approaching Arawhata Rock in the upper Arawhata Valley. Camp on the ridge to Mt Ansted. Mt Aspiring to the right, Dart Peaks to the left. Newland Stream from the Main Divide, Wilkin Catchment. Billy and fire, upper Arawhata Valley.

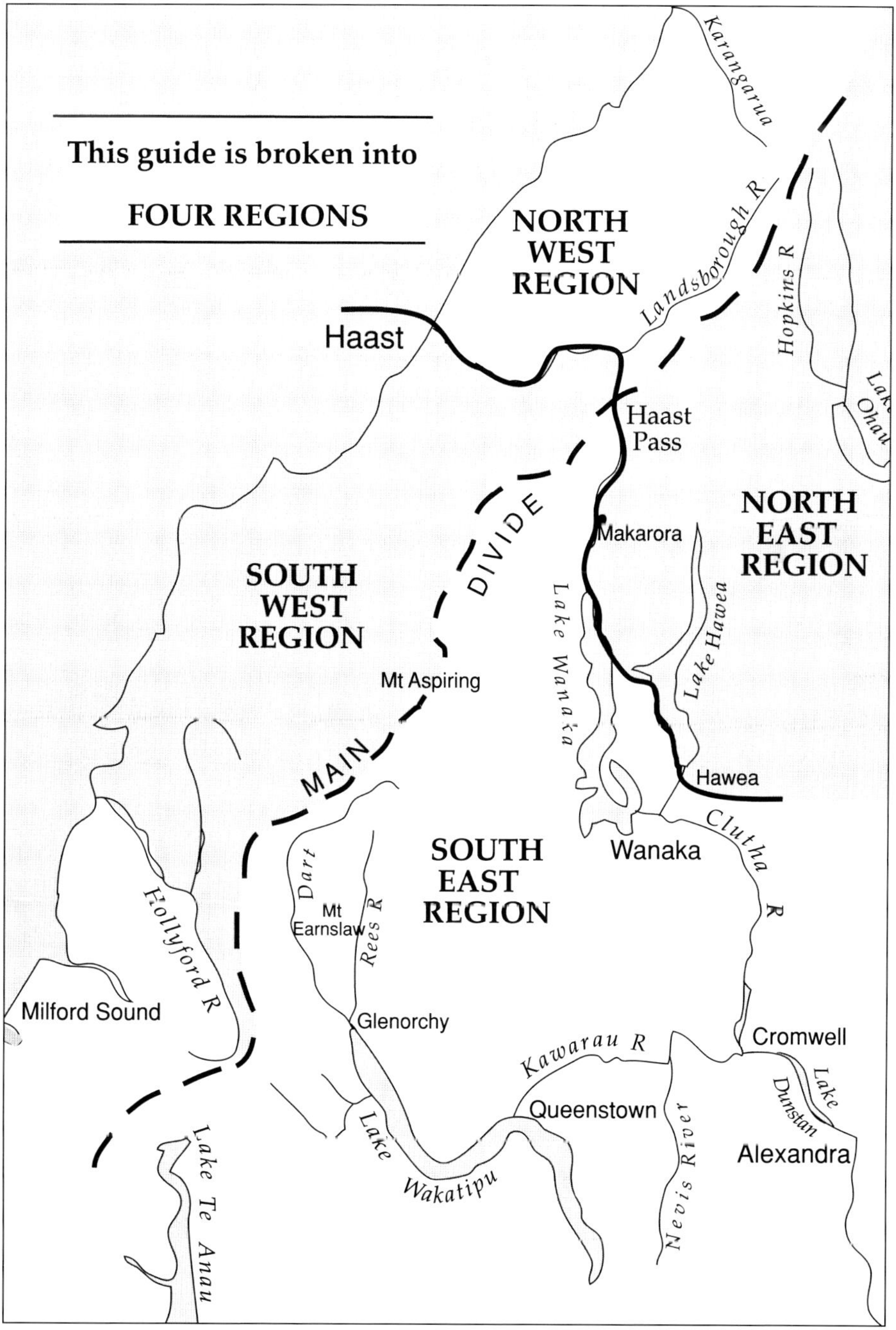
This guide is broken into
FOUR REGIONS
NORTH WEST REGION
NORTH EAST REGION
SOUTH WEST REGION
SOUTH EAST REGION
MAIN DIVIDE
Karangarua
Landsborough R
Hopkins R
Lake Ohau
Haast
Haast Pass
Makarora
Lake Wanaka
Lake Hawea
Hawea
Wanaka
Clutha R
Mt Aspiring
Dart
Rees R
Mt Earnslaw
Hollyford R
Milford Sound
Glenorchy
Kawarau R
Cromwell
Lake Dunstan
Queenstown
Nevis River
Alexandra
Lake Wakatipu
Lake Te Anau

CONTENTS

PART 2: THE SOUTH WEST REGION

ILLUSTRATIONS

MAPS

PHOTOGRAPHS

All uncredited photographs taken by the editor.

FOREWORD

This is the seventh edition of *Moir's Guide Book (Northern Section).* The first edition, called *Guide Book to the Tourist Routes of the Great Southern Lakes* was written and published by Dr George Moir in 1925, and ran to over 3000 copies. In the late 1940's, long after this had gone out of print, discussions were held between JA Sim of the NZAC and George Moir about reprinting the guide. W Scott Gilkison and Arthur Hamilton edited this second edition, which was published by the NZAC in 1948. Initially, 3000 copies were sold, and a further 2000 with supplementary notes were issued in 1950. The third edition was divided into two sections. *A Southern Section* edited by Gerard Hall-Jones was printed in 1959. The *Northern Section* was edited by Peter Chandler in 1961. Since then, both sections of the Guide have been regularly updated with new editions being issued at roughly ten yearly intervals. I was encouraged to edit the sixth edition of the *Northern Section* by John (Bouncer) Stevenson. This sold out, and it was updated and reprinted. This too is now out of print, and it was decided to do a new edition, the seventh, which is in your hands.

Very good NZMS 260 series metric maps cover the area, and it is assumed that parties will be using them, particularly off tracks. Obvious deer trails, blaze lines and now permolat tracks are less able to be followed in many places. Consequently, more detail gives trampers at least a fighting chance of staying on old routes. This can be far from easy and maintaining cairns will be appreciated by those who follow (but not indiscriminate cairning). It is great to see though that a lot of maintainence on quintessentially Kiwi basic huts, tracks and bridges in less visited areas has also been done recently. On the other hand, on chosen tracks, the standards are becoming so high as to convert them from tramping trips to Great Walks, with some very large new 'huts' in already crowded areas. One can't help but wonder where such planning is going. There are now many guides to the more developed routes. In comparison, *Moir's* strength has always been its comprehensive nature and this edition builds on that foundation.

On a personal note, I would have loved to add more about the mosses and lichens and trees, the birds and insects, and the magnificent landscapes. Finding *Peripatus* high in the tussock under the OSONZAC Twins and the like. They are my interest just as much as the routes through these hills. However, *Moir's* has always been primarily about where to go, and it still is. On another note, like thousands of other outdoor New Zealanders, men and women, young and old, my life is scattered throughout the hills. Home is where the heart is; much of my home is in the hills. Returning on trips to 'our place' is something to continue to cherish. It has also been wonderful to have the continued strong support from the tramping and climbing fraternity for *Moir's*. That helps the task of editing and has been much appreciated. I hope you all find the result well worthwhile. See you in the hills.

Geoff Spearpoint
Birdlings Flat
Canterbury.

ACKNOWLEDGEMENTS

Just like all good trips, revising *Moir's* has truely has been a team effort. First and foremost, I'd like to thank Barb Brown, for being great company and very supportive through the revision process. We've had quite a few trips into *Moirs* country since the last edition, and there are more to come. Secondly, to John (Bouncer) Stevenson, thanks for getting me going in the first place on the last edition. And thirdly to all the people out there who feed stuff back to me. There are more people out there sneaking around enjoying the backcountry than some might think. A good many of them have club affiliations, while others work for DoC, are guides, farmers or transport service operators to the hills.

For all sorts of help, I'd like to sincerely thank Nick Atkinson, Dave Bamford, Shaun Barnett, Simon Beale, Arthur Borrell, Sven Brabyn, James Broadbent, Chris Brown, Rob Brown, Dave Campbell, Mauryne Cannell, Paul Chapman, Warren Chinn, Lionel Clay, Taff Cochrane, Tony Condon, Helen Cooper, Ross Cullen, Mike Dunn, Barry Dunnett, Peter Dymock, Bob and Evelyn Entwistle, Mark Farrell, Jane Forsyth, John Fox, Don French, Tony Gates, Martin Gledhill, David Glenny, Noel Gray, Adrian Grierson, Jeff Hall, Chris Haslett, Mark Hassleman, Danilo Hegg, Arnold and Jan Heine, Warren Herrick, Lloyd Homer, Franz Hubman, Andrew Jackson, Simon Johnston, Kim Landreth, Simon Lewis, Kelvin Lloyd, Andrew McLellan, Robin McNeill, Karen Marinkovic, Stephen Martin, Colin Monteath, Johnny Mulheron, Stanley Mulvany, John and Maurice Nolan, John Ombler, Tony Perrott, Mark Pickering, Anne Relling, John and Marion Rhodes, John Robinson, John Rundle, Sandy and Jennifer Sandblom, Morgan Saxton, Bob Scott, Cathy Staples, Paul Elwell-Sutton, Bev Thorne, Ian Turnbull, Geoff Wayatt, Grant Wheaton, Paul Wopereis, and James Wright.

DoC staff have been very helpful keeping me up to date on changes in the hills. Grateful thanks to DoC staff: Richard Kennett and Sue Scott (Glenorchy), Emily Anderson (Makarora), Paul Hellebrekers (Wanaka), Glen Newton (Haast), Richard MacNamara (Twizel), Ian Thorne (Te Anau), and Paddy Driver (Fox Glacier) for their ready and open support.

Lynette Hartley drew the wonderful new sketches scattered throughout this edition. I especially like the robin, boots and Tunnel Gully Hut drawings. Thanks Lynette, they are absolutely superb. Neville Jones of Mapworld in Christchurch who sells maps, guidebooks and navigational equipment also assisted. Craig Potton Publishing over the years have continued to do a great job of distributing *Moirs*, and last, but definitely not least, I'd particularly like to thank Mark Watson and Victoria Mackay (NZAC) for their hard work, tolerance and an inspiring, superb layout. You guys are fantastic. Despite all that help, any mistakes remain mine. But you already knew that!

Sincere thanks, guys.

Geoff.

GENERAL INFORMATION

Extending north from the Hollyford Valley and Lake Wakatipu through the West Otago Mountains and the Southern Alps as far up as Mt Cook National Park's southern boundary, this guide is divided into two unequal blocks by the Haast Pass Highway. Each block is further split by the Main Divide into east and west, providing a natural framework of four regions. Each region is then divided into river catchments, beginning with a route description up the main valley and over the pass in the head, followed by major tributaries and side routes.

Times are included in most cases, but these are only meant to be a general guide. Large variations in times can occur, particularly off track, due to fitness, experience, familiarity with an area, party size, the weather, the season, etc. Times given tend to be on the generous side. Times are averages of those reported for the routes, therefore less experienced people on a hard trip may find the times too short, while for experienced people, times on popular tracks like the Routeburn may seem unnecessarily generous. Do the editor a favour and think 'approximately' when reading times.

WHO FOR

The guide is designed for all, but as with previous editions, many routes require a high standard of experience and fitness to use. There are now many guides catering for routes that the Department of Conservation (DoC) has put resources into, such as the Routeburn, Rees/Dart, Matukituki, Siberia/Young, etc. and these too are covered.

However, the main focus is routes in the back country, and consequently, as with previous editions, this guide has been written with the traditional New Zealand outdoor user in mind.

HOW TO USE THE GUIDE

Many tramping guides today focus on specific trips. *Moir's*, however, remains as an overview of all the region, requiring parties to use their own initiative, common sense and ability to plan their route. It is strongly recommended that the first journeys should be better known trips with facilities provided on them. The Greenstone/Caples, the Routeburn Track, Rees/Dart, Matukituki Valley, and Siberia/Young are all ideal. But whatever the choice of trip in this block of country, *Moir's* should provide relevant and useful route information.

Route notes, especially those off track, are intended to be read in conjunction with the metric NZMS 260 series, 1:50,000 maps, on which a route should be able to be established. Lightly marking the route in pencil on the map may help in tricky areas. Many shorter distances and heights are approximations only to give parties a scale to work to and will contain a subjective element on the part of both editor and user. Grid references are often given to define specific points along routes, particularly in more remote areas. However, despite the detail, *Moir's* far from covers everything. Instead, it should continue to provide a springboard for those who are keen and have already visited some of this country to try other routes: there are all sorts of good lines waiting to be used by those who want challenge.

In untracked country, routes other than those described may work and in some cases be better because of various factors including the party, personal preference and conditions. Please be mindful of this. *Moir's* is neither omnipotent nor a substitute for careful observation, initiative, experience and personal judgement. It is just a guide.

ALPINE ROUTES

Some route descriptions are qualified by comments like 'climbing parties only', or 'transalpine skills and equipment required'. These mean what they say, and the route will require an ice axe, crampons, rope and general moutaineering skills. A careful study of the map should indicate the seriousness. Be prepared for crevasse travel on glaciers for instance and steep hard snow on many higher, south facing slopes.

Some standard tramping routes may also become alpine during winter, and parties must use their own common sense. Routes described as 'difficult' or 'for capable parties only' are likely to be very steep, rough, or densely bushed. Such routes will only suit those with extensive experience.

MAPS

This edition refers to the NZMS 260 series (1:50,000) maps throughout, including named features, unless specifically mentioned in the text. Frequently map heights, contours, and grid references are used to describe a route.

For interests sake, the current grid system on the NZMS 260 map series is based on the NZ Geodetic Datum 1949, which in turn is based on the old Hayford (International) ellipsoid model of the earth. This is inconsistent with GPS technology. Mapmakers Land Information New Zealand (LINZ) have therefore adopted a new grid for a new map series, based on a more accurate NZGD2000. This is based on the newer GPS compatible GRS80 ellipsoid model of the earth. Which means that in the future, a new map series incorporating the newer grid will supersede the current NZMS 260 series map. The old and new map grid positions will differ by roughly 200m, but by then a new edition of *Moir's* should be out anyway.

NZMS 260 SERIES MAP REFERENCES are used frequently. The first letter and 2 numbers refer to the map sheet number e.g. E40 (Earnslaw). The following 6 numbers are the grid reference. The first 3 refer to blue numbers along the top or bottom (north and south) of the map. Only the first 2 numbers are printed on the maps. The third is an estimate in tenths between the grid squares. The last 3 numbers refer to the blue numbers marked on the east and west margins of the map, with the last number estimated in tenths also. So, for instance, in either axis, if the reference point is midway between the 38 and 39 grid lines, then the 3 numbers given would be 385.

To remember the order in which to refer to the axes, there is a little mnemonic that can be helpful. You go along the street before you go up the stairs. Read the numbers off the bottom or top of the map before you go up the sides. Convention runs all 6 grid numbers together with no break between them. In *Moir's* there is a break between the numbers on each axis for easier use in the field.

For parties visiting the more popular routes, the Mt Aspiring National Park map may be sufficient. There are also some specialised *Track Maps* for some of these routes. Maps may be purchased at most DoC Visitor Centres and some outdoor shops. Mapworld, specialists in navigation, have a comprehensive selection of maps and also sell GPS's and locator beacons. They are based at 173 Gloucester St in Christchurch, ph 0800 627 967. For members of Federated Mountain Clubs (FMC), which includes NZAC and most tramping clubs, maps may be purchased at a discount. See the *FMC Bulletin* for further information. The maps included in this guide are only intended as an overview of each region

LAND OWNERSHIP

Most of the country covered by the guide is public land, currently managed on behalf of New Zealanders by the Department of Conservation. Much of it is in Mt Aspiring National Park. The Conservation Act and park bylaws apply. Practice the conservation code and there should be no problem. DoC has a useful website, www.doc.govt.nz, and offices at:

TE ANAU	Ph (03) 249 7921	PO Box 29, Te Anau
QUEENSTOWN	Ph (03) 442 7933	PO Box 811, Queenstown
GLENORCHY	Ph (03) 442 9937	PO Box 2, Glenorchy
WANAKA	Ph (03) 443 7660	PO Box 93, Wanaka
MAKARORA	Ph (03) 443 8365	Private Bag via Wanaka
HAAST	Ph (03) 750 0809	PO Box 50, Haast
ALEXANDRA	Ph (03) 448 8874	PO Box 176, Alexandra
FOX GLACIER	Ph (03) 751 0807	PO Box 9, Fox Glacier
TWIZEL	Ph (03) 435 0802	Private Bag Twizel
MT COOK	Ph (03) 435 1819	PO Box 5, Mt Cook

ACCESS to some areas lies through farm country, and permission to cross this must be sought from the runholder. Phone numbers are included to assist in seeking permission, but it should not be assumed that permission will always be granted. Parties with firearms should be particularly mindful of their obligations. Pastoral lease country east of the Main Divide is currently in a state of flux as a result of an ongoing Tenure Review Process. This has brought new land under DoC, with some very good outcomes for recreation, such as the purchase of Birchwood Station in the Ahuriri. In the future, more land will come under DoC management with access corridors to it, while in the front country, some land will be freeholded to farmers. DoC will be able to update the current situation for most areas.

AIR ACCESS is officially prohibited for all recreational use in Wilderness Areas. Outside Wilderness Areas, permits are required by those landing aircraft. This can normally be arranged by the aircraft operator through DoC. When supplies are flown in, most parties prefer to have them landed rather than dropped, as packages are easily lost or burst open. If packing for an airdrop, there are several points to note: pack in plastic, then something stronger, then a double sack with plenty of packing material stuffed around it at each stage. A net of cord will also help. Do not use straw, as it is impossible to avoid introducing seeds of noxious weeds. It is also absolutely essential that parties carry out all items that cannot be burned. This is a condition of flying supplies in, and there is no acceptable alternative.

HUNTING PERMITS

These are available from the relevant DoC office. For private land, permission must be obtained from the runholder.

HUTS

All of the huts mentioned belong to somebody. For private huts, permission should be sought before using them. Huts are valuable items and expensive to replace. Please take care of them. Fire is a particular hazard. It is never acceptable to leave a fire burning with no one in attendance. Before leaving, spend 10 mins preparing the hut for how you would like to find it. Replace firewood, (dead wood only), clean out pots, leave billies upside down, remove food scraps, wipe the benches and sweep the floor. Shut windows and secure the door. Carry out any rubbish. This is just good traditional hut sense. Mention of a hut in this guide is no guarrantee of its continued existence.

Hut information in the text is included in brackets. It generally covers sleeping space, whether there is an open fireplace or some form of enclosed fire (referred to in the text as a stove) and ownership.

All Department of Conservation huts are now graded into 4 categories, abbreviated 'cat'.

Cat. 1 huts in this guide are virtually all on the Routeburn Track and must be booked in advance.

Cat. 2 huts are maintained to a high standard, with mattresses and often flush toilets. A warden is usually in residence during summer. Parties will normally need to carry their own cooking stove and fuel though gas stoves may sometimes be provided. Cost, $10/person/night or 2 tickets.

Cat. 3 huts are the more traditional tramping huts offering good basic accommodation in the hills, usually with mattresses, and either an open fire or stove. Parties using these huts need to carry their own cooking stove and fuel however. $5/person/night or 1 ticket.

Cat. 4 huts, are basic and of varying standards, but all are very welcome in bad weather. There is no charge.

Hut tickets, paid for in advance, is DoC's system of charging. Each ticket costs $5, and can be bought from DoC offices.

ABBREVIATIONS

MAPS Spot height or point in metres marked on the map; e.g. pt 1562m.

COMPASS POINTS The full word is given for north, south, east and west. Intermediate points are abbreviated to their capital initials. For instance, north west is referred to as NW.

TIME AND DISTANCE Throughout the guide, the following abbreviations are used:
Kilometre (km); metre (m); hour (hr); minute (min).

SOME DEFINITIONS

BIVVY ROCK; a dry natural space, usually under a big boulder, that offers shelter from the rain. Some are large, dry and spacious, while others are small, cramped and prone to flooding in very wet conditions.

PERMOLAT; track markers made from cut pieces of venetian blind material. Made of thin aluminium, they are almost always coloured red or white. Where DoC maintains a marked route permolat is replaced by orange plastic triangles.

4WD TRACK; or road denotes anything from almost 2WD to a bulldozed track that has long since ceased to be useable by vehicles, even 4WD ones.

TRACK; only applies to cut and marked maintained routes that are clear and easy to follow. In almost all cases there will be a ground trail and markers. The ground trail may be up to a benched standard, but not necessarily. With common sense and care, tracks should be followable by anyone.

MARKED ROUTES; are just that. Each marker should be visible from the last enabling a route to be followed with care, according to a nationally recognised cutting and marking standard set by DoC. However, markers can be a bit intermittent, due to such factors as windfall, regrowth etc, and lack of maintanence priority. There may be little or no discernable ground trail. Some marked routes take a fair bit of skill and care to follow.

ROUTES; assume no marking on the ground at all. It is up to each party to find their way. A route description simply offers a way to go from one place to another. On some routes there may be the odd strategic cairn on a pass or at some junction, but frequently there is not. By their nature, routes require more knowledge and bush skill to negotiate, and range up to the very demanding and complex.

TRAIL; is only used to indicate an unmarked animal track in this guide. These are generally deer trails and stock trails. Their path may be continuous or discontinuous, and their usefulness will vary.

TRUE LEFT AND RIGHT IN RIVERS

This convention is now well established in the outdoors, and is used throughout this guide. If you are standing in the middle of the river FACING DOWNSTREAM, the true left bank is on the left and the true right bank is on the right. Imagine the river has eyes as it swims its way to the sea. Rivers and other watercourses may swing to all points of the compass, but the true left is always the true left and the true right is always the true right. Once the concept is known, it is simple and unambiguous.

SEARCH AND RESCUE

INTENTIONS AND SEARCH AND RESCUE (SAR)

Leave intentions with a friend, stating party names, phone numbers and with an agreed plan what to do if you are late out. A capable party might agree that action should begin promptly after waiting one day beyond their due date out of the bush (panic date). Where DoC has intention cards or books on the route in, please fill them in. Equally, they must be signed out again. Filling in log books in huts and updating party intentions will considerably simplify search efforts.

Land Search and Rescue in New Zealand is under the final control in most cases of the Police. In the event of a search being necessary, DoC staff will often be the first people involved. They may seek funding approval for helicopter time from local police and usually have a close working relationship with them. In most cases DoC or local SAR volunteer groups with expertise carry out the search. This is a good system. There is no charge for bona fide emergencies. SAR, however, is not a taxi service. Frustration at searches begun due to a party returning and travelling on without signing out has led to some calls for charging. It is in each party's interest to sign in and everyone's interest that they sign out.

FIRST AID AND EMERGENCIES

Take the time, once the initial first aid has been applied and an assessment has been done, to write down:

1. party members names and addresses or phone numbers,
2. who has sustained what injury,
3. where the party is, both a grid reference and description,
4. what experience, equipment and food the party has, and
5. intentions of the injured party, if moving.

If there are sufficient party members, send out two with this information (or radio if contact can be made). Although this seems simple, there have been cases in New Zealand of people struggling hard to get out to notify SAR only to be unable to accurately say where the injured person is or what is actually wrong. And days have been spent relocating them.

Being lost is only a matter of degree. You probably know the catchment you are in already. Sit down, eat something and consider what you know. Write it down if you can; it will help the thought processes. Before you leave the site, build a cairn, leave a note or something obviously yours but not important, and indicate the direction of travel. Use more cairns. Break fern fronds. Leave bootprints in mud. Wear bright clothing. If you don't have a plan don't move, except a few hundred metres to somewhere more visible and obvious like a riverbank or clearing. Remember that the sun is roughly north at midday. With water, and not rushing around, you'll just be very hungry for the first week. The SAR Organisation in New Zealand is very efficient, and something will have sorted itself out by then, especially if you actively help to attract their attention.

MOUNTAIN RADIO SERVICE

Two way Mountain Radios (High Frequency Single Side Band transceivers) for outdoors people are small, lightweight, and easy to use. They can be hired from several South Island locations, most of which are outlets for the **Canterbury Mountain Radio Service.**

Many of the **Canterbury Mountain Radio Service** (CMRS) radios include sophistocated technology to enable direct dialling into the phone system 24/7, as well as the more conventional daily voice scheds for the weather etc. Hence their slogan that help is only a phone call away. They can be contacted at their main base in Christchurch on Ph/Fax 03 366 5241, E-mail www.mountainradio.co.nz, or PO Box 22342 Christchurch. Their other locations and contacts are:

Dunedin phone 03 434 3262, Nelson phone 03 544 7085, Hokitika phone 03 755 6135 and DoC Wanaka phone 03 443 7660. The CMRS operates on the 3261 kHz frequency and offers three daily sched times of 8.30am, 12 noon, and 7.30pm all year. Their radios are also equipped with the Fiordland/Aspiring DoC 3336 kHz channel. Rates are reasonable at $30 for one or two days, and $40 for three to seven days. Professional businesses are charged a slightly higher rate.

Southland Field Radio also offers standard portable two way radios for hire at $25 per week. Direct dialling through to the telephone system is not available. However, their radios do have the Fiordland Aspiring DoC 3336kHz channel fitted. Their contact is Ray Philips in Invercargill, ph (03) 216 3751 (evenings). Call(sched) times are 6.30pm in winter and 8.30pm during daylight saving time in summer. They also hire out GPS's for $10 per week.

Radios brought down from the North Island will not nomally have the Fiordland 3336 kHz DoC channel fitted.

Personal Emergency Locator Beacons can also be hired from many outlets. They are light and compact. In an emergency, an alerting signal can be released, pinpointing the location of a party for SAR. Check batteries. If beacon is activated, keep outside rock bivvys in the open. For more information, contact the Locator Beacon Trust in Southland, ph (03 226 6341).

WEATHER FORECASTS, WEATHER AND CLIMATE

Weather forecasts can be heard on National Radio: The 5 day forecast at 12:30pm daily; Mountain forecast at 4:05 pm daily; and the coastal forecast at 3:03 and 5:03am daily. Several websites offer weather maps and other information. Eg. The New Zealand Metservice at www.met.co.nz and NZ Satellite images at www.oneweather.nzoom.com/index.html . South Island snow stability information can be found at www.avalanche.net.nz .

The DoC morning radio schedule (8am on) from October to May also includes the weather forecast.

The Mountain Radio Service also offers a forecast at the start of scheds at 8.30am and 7:30pm.

The Southland Field Radio forecast starts at 6.30pm in winter and 8.30pm in summer daylight saving time.

Weather is a major subject beyond the scope of this guide. Watch the weather for a week or more before the trip to get an understanding of the prevailing pattern and trends. Fast moving westerlies? Slow moving highs and lows stagnating over the hills? What happens in the hills won't necessarily follow the forecast, but the forecast may give a moderately useful overview. Remember that generally the weather will be much wetter and less predictable west of the Main Divide. January, February and March are usually the best months in the hills for trips. The period from April to June is often dry too, but will unpredictably turn very cold, with snow and storms from time to time blanketing the ranges. July to October is a time of winter snow with avalanches frequently sweeping paths across valleys well down into the bush in most areas. There can also be fine, settled, frosty spells at this time, despite the short daylight and the cold. November and December are frequently months of turbulent, unsettled weather often with considerable rain. They are also a time of high rivers and streams fed by the melting winter snow. These are all factors to consider in trip planning.

BUSH SKILLS

Look for the best fords in a river, even if you are never likely to have to cross it; keep your eye open for good campsites …

Note the character of ridges and valleys, and especially note prominent objects so that you will recognise them when you see them again; taking it by and large, observation is the foundation stone of bushcraft.

—AP Harper.

Bushcraft begins with being aware in nature: What the seasons mean—about eight hours half light in winter, and 16 hrs of bright daylight in summer and the myriad of implications that can have. Like, how far one can comfortably travel in a day; dampness of campsites and wood; and the length of the night if the weather is bad and one is at an exposed campsite. The NZ Mountain Safety Council produces a series of manuals covering bushcraft, mountaincraft, hypothermia and first aid. These will be very useful to those new to tramping. What is in these manuals should already be known by people heading into remoter areas. Some topics in them are briefly covered below.

GEAR

Tramping gear doesn't have to be new or flash, but it does have to fulfill its function. For instance, a parka must be waterproof. A light but inexpensive PVC parka a size larger than normal to minimise condensation will do that. Wool or polypropylene next to the skin is recommended. Buy boots that are a little loose and need two pairs of socks, because feet swell when tramping all day, and almost all leather boots shrink a little with age. Tight boots will wreck a trip more quickly than anything else.

A pack should shed water well and be comfortable. Pack everything inside it into a large plastic liner and plastic bags, keeping items such as a sleeping bag and spare clothes off the bottom, because any water that creeps in will pool there. A simple personal first aid kit, maps, matches…the lists and details go beyond this guide. There is plenty to learn to remain comfortable and secure in the bush. See the publications put out by the NZ Mountain Safety Council, including *Bushcraft* and *Mountaincraft* for further information.

FOOD

A huge variety of instant dried food is available. Take advantage of it. Up to four or five days food should not be too hard to plan. Beyond that, requires care and focus to keep the weight down. As a guide to use, most people will be okay with about 700 gms per person per day, dry weight. This can be broken down approximately as follows:

Breakfasts, about 150 gms, lunches, about 150 gms and dinners about 200 gms.

Ready to eat snack material, scroggin, etc, about 150 gms, and hot and cold drink materials, about 50 gms.

These figures can be varied according to individual preferences, but remember that people burn 3000 to 7000 calories per day in the hills and that energy is only derived from food. Weight watching food simply wastes pack space. Try to keep a balance between sweet and savoury items, and a balance between carbohydrate, fat, sugar, protein, vitamins and minerals. Take a variety of what you like. For shorter trips of two to four days, be more lenient on yourself, and indulge in a bit of fresh fruit and vegetables, though the bulk may remain dried. Pack food in plastic bags or containers.

TRIP PLANNING

Like other things in life, trip planning and then the trip itself is a continuous process of risk assessment. Competent assessment requires knowledge. For this reason, it is stressed that parties build their knowledge base with better known established routes to begin with, seeking advice from DoC staff, local outdoor people, tramping clubs, guides, etc.

When planning trips there are some basic things to keep in mind.

1. Add another day for bad weather on trips longer than three days.
2. Plan to avoid major or difficult river crossings. If possible, use bridges instead.
3. If river crossings cannot be avoided, arrange the trip to get them over with early on, so that problems get smaller as the trip progresses.
4. The same applies to high passes or tops traverses. This precaution means that unexpected bad weather one day from being due out won't hold the party up for a week.
5. This may at times require some creative and smart thinking in the planning process. Good trips require this forethought so that some of the potential to produce 'accidents' is reduced.
6. Take some care to plan where campsites will be each night to maximise enjoyment from the trip and minimise risk.
7. Check out escape route options.
8. Know something about the people in your party, their fitness, experience and medical problems. A party can only travel as fast as its slowest member.

ROUTE FINDING

Competence at finding good routes through difficult country in the bush and on the tops is not something one can learn from books. However, there are some useful pointers. Keep a continuous note of where you are in relation to the map until it becomes second nature. Look for repeating patterns in the landscape. This continuous comparison between the map and landscape gives you a feel for the country and a basis from which to make decisions and extrapolations on the best route ahead. It will also show map usefulness and limitations. Deer numbers are now low throughout the area described. However, those deer left still travel around, maintaining light trails. These are well worthwhile persisting with if they are going in your direction, particularly in places such as gorges. Deer have a tendency to pass an obstacle (such as windfall) on the uphill side.

Many marked routes have existed for 50 years or more, however maintenance varies, and considerable time and skill is required to follow some of them. Tracks crafted in the past by competent bushmen seldom had sudden sharp bends and didn't duck and dive left and right all the time. Instead, they tended to flow. Consequently, if markers disappear, the best bet is to initially search ahead for clues, using any markers visible from the opposite direction as a guide.

In valleys, gorges excepted, the fastest travel is frequently along the riverbank, on gravel or boulders. Where this is not feasible, better travel may exist on the riparian strip in the bush beside the river, or higher up on a terrace overlooking the river. The most defined deer trail in a valley will frequently be along here too.

Ridges and spurs usually provide best access between the tops and valley floors. Look for well defined and consistent spurs, both going up and down. Streams, unless they consist of fresh gravel, are frequently slow, greasy and best avoided as routes. Falls, guts, and bluffs, not necessarily visible on the map, may make travel in some creeks virtually impossible.

Speed at which parties travel will depend on many factors, but a stuff-up in the scrub may reduce speed to a few hundred metres an hour, for hours and hours, at which point Sods Law usually takes over and rain begins! It always pays to observe and plan carefully. Intelligent persistence is required, rather than any superhuman strength.

AT CAMPSITES

Water, shelter and a site that will remain dry in rain are campsite requirements. Choose for the conditions you have, erring on the side of caution. Avoid islands in river channels. Remember that one of the first effects of rain is to fill up hollows. The tent site should be on a rise rather than in a depression. Good bushcraft skills mean that when parties leave campsites in the morning, the site should be restored as close as possible to its natural state, and all rubbish removed (carried out).

STOVES AND FIRELIGHTING

Whatever the stove carried, check out carefully how it functions. Hut ethics and safety make it essential to fill and connect new fuel cannisters outside. Use metal top benches, where available, to cook on. Be aware that stoves frequently give off carbon monoxide in enclosed spaces. Avoid using stoves inside tents, especially closed ones. Carbon monoxide is a tasteless, odourless, invisible gas, and haemoglobin in the bloodstream forms a stable bond with it in preference to oxygen. As more haemoglobin becomes tied up like this, the body becomes progressively starved of oxygen. The result is increasing drowsiness and sleep, followed by death.

Firelighting tends to be discouraged on maintained, popular routes, but it is still a useful skill, particularly in remote areas. Before lighting a fire, check first that there is water handy to put the fire out completely. Avoid fires in windy places. Using a gravel riverbed and driftwood minimises disturbance to the environment.

Good preparation pays off. For instance, choose the bush edge that receives the sun on a flat. In wet conditions, keep an eye out for dry twigs under a boulder. Start with only a few twigs, and specifically set them above the flame to catch alight. Once alight, in damp, calm conditions, stack twigs up on top of each other in a small column, keeping the sides open for air to be drawn in. A tower of twigs helps draw air upwards and also allows the column to dry with the heat. Lack of air is a frequent cause of fire failure in the bush. Avoid the temptation to put big pieces on too soon. Fire size will depend on conditions. In dry conditions, keep fires small. In wet conditions, there is a minimum critical size that has to be reached before the fire will become easily self sustaining. Fires must always be attended and completely put out when left. This will involve copious quantities of water followed by the complete dismantling of any stonework, the dispersal of wet charcoal and covering of the site in local litter, to leave the site looking as it did beforehand.

RIVER CROSSING

The key to successful river crossing is observation, forethought and planning. Observe where the force of the river is going, how fast it is going, how deep it is and in each case relate this information to your party and their ability. Check your observations against other sections of the river to increase the accuracy of your assessment. Every observation helps. Filter this information and take time to formulate a crossing plan.

Generally, where the river widens above rapids, it is shallower and slower. Gravel, too, usually provides the best crossings. Beware of deep hollows around boulders and where channels join. All crossings have a point at which the current and depth create the greatest challenge. Be very careful assessing this point and clearly identify it. Rivers cannot be fought. Plan to work with and use the river forces on the crossing. Cross diagonally downstream with the current. Allow for that before entering the water.

Crossing technique will usually be by mutual support, preferably in groups of two to five. Hold onto the pack shoulder straps of the person beside you either at the top or between the straps and their back lower down. The important thing is to get a good comfortable grip that reinforces the group into one unit. Have the strongest river crossing person, who directs the crossing, upstream. During the crossing, that person should continue the assessment made earlier with what the party finds in the water. Be prepared to back out again if the comparison is unfavourable.

If a party is bowled over, the assessment has failed, and the river has taken control. Much can be done to lessen the danger at this point. Turn to face downriver, with your feet out in front, stay together if at all possible and use any opportunity to ferry glide or push towards the bank the current is trending towards. Use, don't fight, the river. Be patient with flooded rivers. After rain ceases, they usually fall as rapidly as they rose.

A couple of associated points: When decision making, keep in the equation that the chances of losing one's life by not crossing a flooded river are almost zero. Drowning in a river is probably the greatest hazard faced in the hills. It is never essential to cross a river. To test the validity of this, imagine being in a coroner's court giving reasons for why the crossing was attempted. One year on, all reasons sound trivial. The second point is that river crossings change with time. That includes all crossings mentioned in this book. Never plunge in blindly relying on a description in *Moir's*.

The competent New Zealander 'tramper' is a highly qualified outdoor person, with a hardiness and discipline gained from years of bivouacking in wet forest and navigating in misty conditions, contending with all types of flooded rivers, strenuously 'pass hopping' between alpine valleys ... with the added hazard of snow in winter.

—Rod Hewitt and Mavis Davidson, 1954.

NEW ZEALAND ENVIRONMENTAL CARE CODE

The aim of this code is to minimise your impact on the environment and on other users.

- Protect plants and animals
- Remove rubbish
- Bury toilet waste
- Keep streams and lakes clean
- Take care with fires
- Camp carefully
- Keep to the track if there is one
- Consider others
- Respect our cultural heritage
- Enjoy your visit
- Leave the land undisturbed (Toitu te whenua), taking nothing but photographs, leaving nothing but footprints.

TRANSALPINE TRIPS

Versatile gear and flexible plans are keys to successful transalpine trips, as are timing and good mobility, ie. light packs, fitness, and weather. Seizing opportunities, but on the other hand, not pushing it when things aren't right, either. Commonly, a climbing trip approach is applied to transalpine trips, but really they require a focus of their own. The priorities are different. Transalpine trips are about flowing with the landscape, finding good routes that allow interesting journeys through an alpine environment, rather than climbing over it with weighty technical extras. However, this will depend on trip aims.

The wilder the landscape, the more challenging it is to find good lines from place to place. It is about getting a feel for an area, discovering alternate routes, (*Moir's* really only offers the tip of the iceberg), and new places that spark further adventures. 'I wonder if…' It is about living in the land, day and night, self sufficient, with strategies to cope with the unexpected. When things go well, the experience is wonderful, but when they don't, things can be very, very unpleasant. There is usually a bit of challenge involved somewhere along the way. For successful transalpine trips good all round alpine skills are necessary, and a good appreciation of what the weather and other conditions will and won't allow. Beyond that, the limits are up to you.

FURTHER INFORMATION

DoC produces many pamphlets for recognised tracks, including a more substantial booklet *Tramping Guide to the Makarora Region. Moir's Guide South* (McNeill) covers Fiordland and mutual ground in the Greenstone, Routeburn and Hollyford areas. Other tramping guides include *101 Tramps in NZ* (Pickering and Smith), *South Island Weekend Tramps* (Groves), and the more glossy *Classic Tramps in NZ* (Barnett and Brown). *Adventure* and *Wilderness* magazines often feature tramps in the region.

NZAC also offer two very good climbing guides to the region. *The Mt Aspiring Region* (Uren and Watson), and *Barron Saddle—Mt Brewster* (Cullen). NZAC's quarterly magazine *The Climber* sometimes features articles on the area, and the annual *NZ Alpine Journal* likewise, particularly those from the 1930s to the 1960s. Other tramping, hunting and mountaineering club journals also have trip accounts and features about the region. More general publications cover aspects such as flora, fauna, geology and history. These will enrich the journeys of those who seek them out.

AND FINALLY...

It is to be expected that the information in this guide will become progressively less accurate with time. Seek information from DoC staff to keep your knowledge up to date. While the editor hopes that this guide approaches the ideal of complete accuracy, errors no doubt remain. If you have comments to make about routes mentioned in this edition, write to tell the editor, who will tell everybody else, who can then write in and comment on your comments ... and so *Moir's* continues. That's partly how we've got what we've got. And while every attempt has been made to provide as accurate information in this guide as possible, neither the NZAC nor the editor accepts any liability arising from the use of it. Take care out there.

I will lift my eyes to the hills, from whence cometh my help

—Psalm 121.

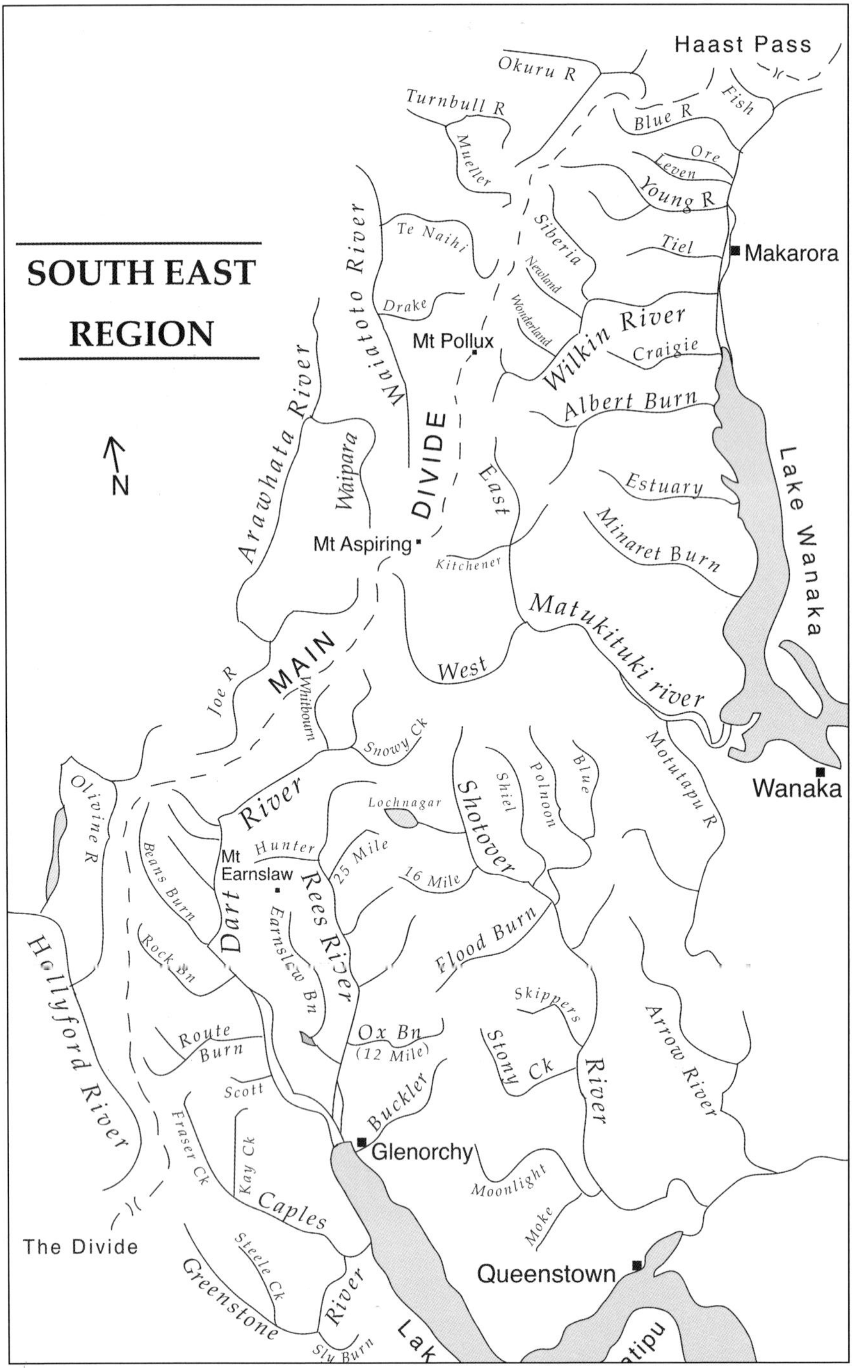
SOUTH EAST
REGION
N
Haast Pass
Okuru R
Turnbull R
Blue R
Fish
Ore
Leven
Young R
Mueller
Siberia
Newland
Wonderland
Te Naihi
Tiel
Makarora
Drake
Mt Pollux
Wilkin River
Craigie
Waiatoto River
Arawhata River
Albert Burn
Lake Wanaka
Waipara
DIVIDE
East
Estuary
Minaret Burn
Mt Aspiring
Kitchener
Matukituki river
MAIN
West
Joe R
Whitbourn
Snowy Ck
Motutapu R
Wanaka
Olivine R
River
Lochnagar
Shiel
Polnoon
Blue
Shotover
Beans Burn
Mt
Earnslaw
Hunter
25 Mile
16 Mile
Rees River
Dart
Earnslaw Bn
Hollyford River
Rock Bn
Flood Burn
Skippers
Arrow River
Route
Burn
Ox Bn
(12 Mile)
Stony
Ck
River
Scott
Buckler
Fraser Ck
Kay Ck
Glenorchy
Moonlight
Caples
Moke
The Divide
Steele Ck
Greenstone
River
Queenstown
Sly Burn

PART 1: THE SOUTH EAST REGION

The Otago Alps, from the Greenstone to the Makarora

INTRODUCTION

Routes in each catchment begin with a description up the main valley and over the pass at the head, followed by the major tributaries and side routes.

Wonderful river flats surrounded by mature beech forest and capped by high alpine peaks make this probably the most appealing of the four regions in this guide. This is a very pleasant area to tramp in. DoC facilities are also concentrated in this region, reflecting the long and popular tramping use of the area. Trips include the Routeburn, Greenstone/Caples, Rees/Dart, Matukituki Valley, Wilkin, and Siberia/Young. These are all ideal trips for those new to the area. DoC Visitor Centres are located at Queenstown, Glenorchy, Wanaka, Makarora and Alexandra.

The weather is generally drier, being east of the Main Divide. There have been some spectacular exceptions, however, such as the storms in the summer of 1994 and early 1995. November to April is the popular time for trips in this area. Snow effectively closes many routes in winter, including the Routeburn, because of avalanche danger.

Throughout the region, the bedrock is predominantly schist, a metamorphic rock. Mt Earnslaw and Mt Aspiring are the dominant peaks. Relatively open beech forest extends throughout the region, consisting of red, silver, and mountain beech in the Glenorchy and Matukituki valleys, and almost entirely silver throughout the Makarora Catchment. Subalpine scrub is often dominated by *Dracophyllum* species. The region is a stronghold for endangered yellowheads, and there are reasonable populations of other birds such as parakeets, bush robins and rockwren. For further information, see the bibliography.

Other trip possibilities include;

- Rock Burn/Lake Nerine/North Routeburn, 3 days, and an ice axe usually necessary.
- Beans Burn/Fohn Saddle/Fiery Col/Cow Saddle/Park Pass/Rock Burn/Sugarloaf Pass, 5 days.
- Matukituki/Dart (or Rees), 4 days.
- Wilkin/East Matukituki, 4 days.
- Albert Burn/East Matukituki, 5 days.
- Kea Basin in the Rees, 2 days.
- Earnslaw Burn, 2 to 3 days.

SE Region

GREENSTONE VALLEY

This has long been a popular valley for tramping. Combined with the Routeburn or Caples, it offers a variety of relatively easy round trips from 4 to 6 days long. The grassy river flats are private farmland owned by Ngai Tahu. Note that the footbridges over the Greenstone River above and below the Caples/Greenstone confluence (E41 410 757 and E41 419 755) marked on Ed.1 no longer exist and a large new hut (Greenstone Hut) has been built at the old Sly Burn Hut site to replace Mid Greenstone Hut, which is now a locked hunting hut. The main track in this valley, like the Caples, is well maintained and signed by DoC.

Follow the Routeburn road across the Dart bridge and turn left along the western shore of Lake Wakatipu to the Greenstone carpark, where there are toilets and a shelter. Daily transport (including boat) from Glenorchy, services the Greenstone from November to April inclusive. (Backpacker Express, Ph 03 442 9939).

CARPARK TO GREENSTONE HUT

Follow the signposted benched track up valley, past the Lake Rere stockbridge. Stay on the true left of the Greenstone river. In less than 30 mins the Caples bridge will be seen. Cross here, and continue along the track on the true left of the Greenstone up through the gorge to Slip flat. Enroute, a signposted side track leads down to a Greenstone footbridge at E41 389 739, offering alternative access to Lake Rere. There are great campsites at the top end of Slip flat, but grazing cattle can make that a bit unpredictable. Slip Flat Bivvy (sleeps 3, DoC cat 4) and painted green at E41 373 729 on the true left of Slip Stream is tucked at the bushedge about 300m above the emergency bridge. It is popular with hunters. Streams at E41 385 738 and E41 370 721 are also bridged. Continue through the bush to the Greenstone Hut junction sign, and follow the track down over a bridge across a dramatic gorge in the Greenstone River and up to the new Greenstone Hut (20 bunk, coal stove, DoC, cat 2) on the old Sly Burn Hut site at E41 365 702.

Time: Road to Greenstone Hut, 4 hrs.

GREENSTONE SADDLE Greenstone Hut to Lake Howden Hut

Cross the bridge back over the Greenstone River and follow the main valley track on the true left upvalley. Old Mid Greenstone Hut is now a locked hunters base. A swingbridge crosses Steele Creek and the track continues to another swingbridge back across the Greenstone near McKellar Hut. (20 bunks, coal stove, DoC cat 2). Travel is mostly in bush and sometimes on tussock flats, while a little beyond Steele Creek, the river runs through an impressive little canyon.

To continue to Lake Howden Hut from McKellar Hut, follow the track upvalley on the true right of the Greenstone, and sidle Lake McKellar on the west side to the head. The McKellar Saddle track junction is on flats at a signpost shortly beyond the lake. The valley track continues along the western side of Lake Howden to Lake Howden Hut. See the Routeburn Track for further notes.

Times: Greenstone Hut to McKellar Hut, 5 to 7 hrs; McKellar Hut to Lake Howden Hut, a good 2 hrs.

LAKE RERE

About 5 mins from the Greenstone carpark, cross the stockbridge over the Greenstone. Turn left, and follow orange triangles outside the fenceline at the edge of a terrace directly across to pt 351m. Markers continue along the cliff top before descending to the Elfin Bay Jetty and tin shed at E41 436 736. From a DoC sign about 40m before the jetty, a track, originally bulldozed but now grassy and overgrowing, climbs diagonally SW then crosses the stream that saddles with Lake Rere. On the true right of this stream it joins a track leading up to the lake. (This track leads on down to Elfin Bay Station. Although signposted, look out for this turnoff coming the other way, as it is not obvious. A red permolat has 'car park' scratched on it, indicating the way back to the Greenstone). Continue up the 4WD track, which is spartanly marked with orange triangles, staying on the true right of the stream (not the true left as marked on E41 Ed 1) into magnificent red beech forest. At the lake, the 4WD track continues through forest along the northern shoreline. There is a pleasant picnic area at the NW end of the lake, but the hut marked here on some maps no longer exists. Poles and orange triangles continue in grassland and beech forest along the 4WD track up the true right of the Greenstone Valley, over the toe of a big slip, to a footbridge at E41 389 739. This crosses the Greenstone River. On the true left, a gate leads off the cattle track up to the Greenstone Track.

Times: Carpark to Lake Rere, 2hrs; Lake to Greenstone track, 1hr.

HOME HILL SADDLE Slip Flat to Mid Caples Hut

A variety of unmarked routes cross one of several optional saddles, all about 1300m high, west of Home Hill. From Slip Flat the starting point is usually a fairly large stream carrying quantities of serpentine rock 100m east of the bivvy. Enter the bush and climb steadily up the spur on the true left of this stream. Choose and cross one of several easy saddles on the range, then sidle east above Reids Creek and a private hut at the bushline to descend the main spur off Home Peak to the old Birchdale Homestead and Mid Caples Hut.

Times: About 6 hrs in either direction.

STEELE CREEK Greenstone Track to Upper Caples Hut

A relatively good marked route leads up Steele Creek, with carpets of *Dicranaloma* moss under wonderful beech forest in the lower reaches, and aromatic celery pine (*Phyllocladus* sp) on the flats further up. Suitable for moderately experienced trampers, this marked route begins at a signpost about 50m west of the Steele Creek bridge and heads up an open spur. Markers are easily followed upvalley from the bushedge on the spur, sidling through open beech forest to Steele Creek Bivvy (sleeps 3, DoC, cat 4), still on the true right. The bivvy is quite basic, but a very functional alternative to a night in the rain. Please look after it. It is at the forest edge about 25m from the creek at the lower end of an open scrubby flat that continues upvalley and turns into an extensive gravel flat. There are also good campsites both on this flat and on little grass flats 10 to 20 mins downvalley from the bivvy by the track.

From the bivvy, push through the scrub (no defined track) to the top of the flat and follow up the shingle streambed. At E41 324 779 pick up the marked track again on the true right. The track leads through open bush, descending to the West Branch Stream just above the forks at the foot of Tongue Spur. Cross the West Branch Stream to more markers and continue up around the toe of Tongue Spur, sidling into the East Branch (which drains the pass). Markers stop shortly after at the bushedge at E41 322 795, near the creek on the true right. Follow the creek banks on up towards the pass. Most of the route above the bushline is marked with poles and cairns.

On the Caples side, follow marker poles to the NE, sidling tussock slopes across, then down, to the spur running north from pt 1611m. These slopes can be slippery when wet. Markers continue at the bushline on this spur. The track forks partway down through the bush, one branch leading to Upper Caples Hut, and the other to Top Flat lower down the Caples. The East Branch of Steele Creek is subject to winter avalanche danger.

Times: Greenstone track to Steele Creek Bivvy, 2 hrs; Bivvy to Saddle, 4 hrs up or 3 hrs down; Saddle to Upper Caples Hut, 2 hrs down or 3 hrs up.

MAVORA WALKWAY

This track is an easy but long tramp through mainly open tussock country, and although lightly grazed by cattle, is scenic with a good variety of bird and plant life. It can be quite exposed to southerly weather, even though it crosses only a low saddle from the Greenstone River to the Mararoa River and the Mavora Lakes. From these lakes, 45km of gravel road leads out to the Te Anau Mossburn Highway. Part of the walkway (north of Boundary Hut) passes through Elfin Bay Station, and is closed in winter between May and Labour weekend at the end of October. Bits of iron in the grass under a collapsed silver beech are all that remains of a small hut in the upper Sly Burn.

GREENSTONE HUT TO MAVORA LAKE ROADEND

Greenstone Hut (20 bunk, coal fire, flush toilet, DoC cat 2) is 4 hrs from the Greenstone Road. The track shown on E41 from the Greenstone valley to the Mararoa is the old cattle track. DoC's marked track (not shown on E41 Ed. 1.) follows a slightly different line. From Greenstone Hut in the Greenstone, the track sidles through the bush to the Pass Burn, crosses to the true left and follows the Burn up staying inside the bush to the saddle. The cattle track offers a pleasant alternative through open country on the true right of the Pond Burn, and rejoins the poled track at the pond, E41 354 645. Pond Burn Hut (4 bunks, private, Elfin Bay Station) at E41 352 644 is tucked at the bushedge above the pond. The markers continue directly across at the base of the hill to meet the Mararoa at Taipo Hut.

Taipo Hut (8 bunk, DoC cat 3) is at E41 339 622, 1km up the Mararoa from the Pond/Mararoa forks on the true left, not at the forks as marked on E41. A swingbridge crosses the Mararoa River by the hut and poles lead down the true right on terraces at the base of the hill to roughly E41 341 607 before swinging towards the river and following close to it for about 1km. Alternatively, a 4WD track crosses the terrace above here. The poled route then follows along the base of the hill, still on the true right, (passing a locked station hut) to another swingbridge about 5km upstream from North Mavora Lake.

Cross to Boundary Hut, which is on the true left. Boundary Hut (8 bunk, DoC, cat 3) is accessible to 4WD vehicles. Follow the 4WD track on the true left downstream from Boundary Hut, sidling up to 50m above North Mavora Lake (good views) and descend to Careys Hut (DoC cat 3, sleeps 7, fire with wetback and shower but no wood!). Careys Hut is about 1km along the lakeshore from the river inlet, and is popular with fishermen. The 4WD track continues to the gravel road and DoC campsite (with toilets) between the lakes. This is a very popular campsite in summer. There is no hut at the northern edge of the beech forest on the eastern side of North Mavora Lake as marked on some maps.

Times: Greenstone Hut to Taipo Hut, 4 hrs; Taipo Hut to Boundary Hut, 4 hrs; Boundary Hut to Careys Hut, 2 hrs; Careys Hut to the DoC campsite between the Mavora Lakes, 2 hrs.

CAPLES VALLEY

Although a smaller valley than the Greenstone, the Caples is in some ways more attractive. It is more parklike, compared with the long tussock flats of the upper Greenstone. The valley offers a number of 2 to 6 day trips connecting with the Greenstone and other valleys.

CARPARK TO UPPER CAPLES HUT

From the Greenstone Carpark follow the track on the true left of the river up past the Greenstone/Caples confluence without crossing. Continue on the true left of the Caples along the

■ Lake McKellar in the Greenstone Valley from the Livingstone Mountains.

bush edge and up flats to a bridge over a spectacular chasm just before Mid Caples Hut (12 bunks, coal stove, DoC Cat 2). The hut is on a terrace on the true right at E41 368 800. Historic old Birchdale Homestead, slightly less than 1.5km downstream, is over 110 yrs old. The track to Upper Caples Hut is all on the true right, passing through beech forest and open flats. Upper Caples Hut (20 bunk, coal stove, DoC cat 2) is on Tent Flat, a small bush clearing roughly opposite Kay Creek, on the true right of the Caples River, 20 mins beyond Top Flat.

Times: Road to Mid Caples Hut, 2.5 hrs; Mid Caples Hut to Upper Caples Hut, 2.5hrs.

SLEEPY HOLLOW can be approached up an unmarked spur beginning at E41 352 825. The spur swings back east above the bushline. About 200 or 300m before pt 1742m is reached, sidle east onto a bench beside the lake.

MCKELLAR SADDLE Upper Caples Hut to Greenstone Track

The track up valley beyond Upper Caples Hut is considerably closer to the river than that shown on E41 Ed.1. Also, the bridge giving access to marked routes up Kay and Fraser Creeks is about 300m upstream from the hut, not by it. To approach McKellar Saddle, follow the track up the true right from the hut, climbing to a basin at the 640m contour. Beyond, the track climbs to the bushline and crosses wonderful tussock basins and fragile subalpine bogs (on boardwalk) to the saddle. From the bushline on the Greenstone side, the track drops steeply to the valley floor and crosses it to the signposted Greenstone track junction at the top end of Lake McKellar. McKellar and Lake Howden Huts are each an hour away.

Times: Upper Caples Hut to McKellar Saddle, 3.5 hrs; Saddle to Greenstone track, 2 hrs.

FRASER CREEK

The access into Fraser Creek is incorrectly shown on E41 Ed.1 and storm damage in the valley during the 1990's severely affected the marked route. However, the valley is pleasant, and a mix of river travel and the old marked route provide fairly good going. The valley will be kept at a marked route standard.

About 300m upvalley from Upper Caples Hut cross the Caples on a swingbridge and go another 300m to a signpost where two marked routes begin, one downstream to Kay Creek and the other upvalley to Fraser Creek. This sidles over a spur at the 600m contour before descending to near Fraser Creek at about the 560m contour. Less than 500m upstream, the marked route crosses Fraser Creek to the true right. Eroded banks and lost markers make it essential to keep a sharp lookout, but the lightly marked route on the true right now goes for some distance upvalley, leading to several crossings, some river travel and open flats at about E41 311 892. From here to the next flats at E40 308 916 use good going in the streambed where practical, and pick up markers on the true left upstream when it becomes more practical to sidle. From the top of these next flats, near the stream, follow up gravel debris under the trees to approx E40 308 923, where markers lead on up the true left directly from the stream, giving reasonable travel to the upper limit of the beech forest and another small flat. Follow up rough travel in the creekbed beyond here. A bivvy rock exists on the true right near the head of the valley, upstream from the one marked.

If descending Fraser Creek, look for markers where the beech forest begins, close to the stream on the true left at the bottom of a small flat at the 840m contour. Further down, at the lower end of the main flat (E40 308 915), pick up the marked route on the true left, close to the stream (a marker on the true right just indicates to cross). There is a small rock bivvy (max 2) on the true left here.

Time: Upper Caples Hut to bushline, 6 hrs; Bushline to Routeburn Track, 3.5 hrs.

FRASER COL (pt 1544m) east of Emily Peak, can be crossed to Emily Stream and the Routeburn. On the south side, hard snow often lies well into summer; once gone, the route is on moderately steep scree. On the north side, cross tussock slopes heading NNW to a gravel stream hard on the true left of the Emily Basin before descending this rocky gully to the Routeburn Track bridge. A low point on the ridge west of Fraser Creek and south of Emily Peak at 1440m separates Fraser Creek from Lake Mackenzie. This is very steep on the Fraser Creek side and is not a practical route.

KAY CREEK

This pleasant valley also suffered 1994 storm damage, especially the middle section where the marked route becomes patchy and travel in the riverbed is sometimes better. The valley will be maintained to marked route standard. The access into Kay Creek is inaccurate on E41 Ed.1. Instead, cross the bridge 300m upstream of Upper Caples Hut to a signpost 300m beyond in the bush and follow markers up to a small saddle (580m contour) overlooking Kay Creek. About 45 minutes from the bridge, markers reach Kay Creek and shortly after, a section eroded by the river. However, the marked route continues on the true right, and in less than an hour reaches an extensive gravel flat. Go up the flat (at approx E41 335 880), and continue on a mix of the old track (still on the true right) and river gravel upvalley until the stream begins to climb at about E41 338 892 and the forks are visible not far ahead. Here, less than 30 mins from the hut, the marked route crosses to the true left, and sidles upvalley to the bank of Kay Creek opposite Kay Creek Hut. However, the hut is not visible from the bank. Cross Kay Creek and climb 10 to 20m up onto the scrubby open terrrace between the forks of Death Valley and Kay Creek. Kay Creek Hut (sleeps 3) is an old musterers hut in delapidated condition, about 100m north of the forks.

KAY CREEK TO SCOTT CREEK. From the hut, follow a short, ill-defined track up into beech trees, cross open scrubby flats and descend to the streambed after about 300-400m where gravel flats begin. Follow up Kay creekbed to forks at the 1160m contour, and continue up the true right fork to within about 100m of the falls ahead. Climb the tussock and boulder slopes to the north on the true right of Kay Creek then swing right (looking up) to ascend an easy tussock gully through bluffs at E40 354 920, only about 100m from the stream. On the tussock bench above, sidle across to tarns at the 1380m contour and climb up to the pass. The Scott Creek side is straight forward; sidle down the creek to the bushline. Then either descend open beech on the true right or follow a narrow tussock rib between two streams on the true left to the hut flat. **In reverse**, from Scott Creek, be careful to pick up the southern tributary leading to the pass and the tussock gully leading through bluffs at E40 354 921 on the Kay Creek side.

Times: Upper Caples Hut to Kay Creek Hut, 3.5 hrs; Kay Creek Hut to Scott Creek Hut, 4 to 5hrs.

OTHER ROUTES. Two crossings can be made from Death Valley. A pass at the 1660m contour south of pt 1960m offers a relatively straight forward route in late summer to join the Kay Creek/Scott Creek crossing. A higher pass between pt1951m and pt1933m requires an iceaxe but is also reasonably straight-forward in good conditions to Double Barrel Falls Creek. Double Barrel Falls Creek is best travelled to bushline in the stream itself, to avoid scrub in the tussock. At the bushline there are good campsites. However, this valley ends in complex bluffs that are quite difficult to descend past Double Barrel Falls. This route is not recommended, except for experienced parties, and a rope could be helpful. Accounts indicate to sidle on the true left from about the 840m contour, keeping up initially, then working down through bluffs generally within about 250m of the stream. Do not under estimate the difficulty of bypassing these falls.

SCOTT CREEK

Combining Scott Creek with Kay Creek makes an interesting 2 to 3 day round trip. The marked route in Scott Creek (entirely on the true right) is variable, but quite followable with care. A washout gully (from 1994 storms) halfway up has resulted in the track being rerouted in at least one place.

From the sign at the Routeburn Road edge on the true right of Scott Creek, cross farmland (stiles over fences) towards bracken covered hill slopes and pick up orange marker poles. They lead onto a spur, reaching the bush edge at about the 600m contour E40 385 945. From here, initially sparse markers are followed in the beech forest upvalley, sidling into the streambed, following it awhile (without crossing) then sidling higher in the forest to the washout gully roughly halfway. The marked route now descends along the lower lip of the gully, crosses the slip near Scott Creek and climbs back up to the marked route on the other side of the slip. The markers lead on up to small flats. A final climb through beech forest, still on the true right, leads to almost directly opposite Scott Creek Hut. Here, the marked route dips, crosses Scott Creek and climbs 20 to 30m to the hut on the true left, which is tucked in at the bushline. Scott Creek Hut (damp, no door) is an old musterers hut in poor condition.

Times: Road to Hut, 4 hrs; Hut to road, 3 hrs.

GLACIER BURN (WAKATIPU)

This is a pleasant daytrip. Follow the marked route from the road up into Glacier Basin, mostly on the true left of the Burn. It reaches the bushline, where a campsite can be found, 2 hours from the road, and snow can usually be reached a good hour beyond that, depending on conditions.

THE ROUTEBURN TRACK

The Routeburn Track runs from the Routeburn road end north of Glenorchy to The Divide on the Milford road. The mix of scenery is superb, the Otago Alps blending into Fiordland, producing a landscape rich in flats, forests, craggy mountains and deep canyons.

The Routeburn Track is in a different category to all other tracks in this guide because of the higher facility standard, the requirement to book in advance, the higher number of users and the cost. It is designated by DoC as a Great Walk, and this it surely is. It is managed by DoC to cater for those with minimal or no previous tramping experience, and about half the users are overseas visitors. Most people walk the track in 2 to 3 days. A long established private company (Routeburn Walk Ltd., Ph. 03 442 8200) also offers a 3 day guided walk using their own huts at Routeburn Falls and Lake Mackenzie. Camping within 500m of the Routeburn Track is prohibited outside of the track campsites.

It should be noted that the track is neither an all season route nor an all weather one. Snow on the bluffs around Lake Harris, Harris Saddle and on the track between Howden and Mackenzie creates a significant avalanche hazard in winter and spring. All the tops, especially the Hollyford side of Harris Saddle, are exposed in bad weather. Outside of the main season, generally May to October inclusive (exact dates vary), there is no booking requirement and hut tickets and backcountry passes can be used. There is also no gas cooking provided, the water is turned off to prevent frost bursting pipes and the toilet facilities change. See the DoC website www.doc.govt.nz for current information.

BOOKING

Those staying overnight in huts or track campsites between November and April inclusive, the summer season, need accommodation passes. Bookings are accepted from the beginning of July each year at the bookings desk, Fiordland National Park Visitor Centre, Te Anau Ph 03 249 8514 and DoC Visitor Centres at Queenstown Ph 03 442 7935 and Glenorchy Ph. 03 442 9937. Passes need to be collected from one of these centres on the day of departure before 2pm. 20% discounts for families, and 30% for school and youthgroups can apply. Day users on the track do not need to book at any time and there is no charge.

COSTS

Hut fees are $40 per night per adult. The youth (14 and under) rate is $20 per night. Those who arrive at the huts unbooked pay a penalty charge of double the standard rate. Campsites are $15 per adult (and $7.50 per youth) per night. Camping is restricted to two sites near Routeburn Flats Hut and Lake Mackenzie Hut. Hut facilities are not available for campers.

FACILITIES

Wardens are in residence at the huts all season. They are there to help, but respect their right to privacy too. Gas cookers, a coal fire, cold running water, mattresses and flush toilets are provided at each hut. The track is mostly benched and graded, well defined and signposted, and all significant streams are bridged.

ACCESS

Many transport operators service the track. The DoC website lists several with contact details. At the **GLENORCHY** end of the track Backpacker Express Transport, Ph. 03 442 9939 operates a twice daily service all season from Queenstown to the Routeburn Roadend and return. Upper Lake Wakatipu Tours Ph. 03 442 9986 also offer daily services all season from Queenstown to the Routeburn and return.

Transport to **THE DIVIDE** on the Milford Road generally leaves Queenstown between 7 am and 9am to arrive at The Divide between 11am and 1pm. Transport leaves the Divide between 3.30pm and 5.30pm to return to Queenstown by 8.30pm. Operators providing this service include Kiwi Discovery Ph 0800 505 504, Inter City, Milford Explorer and Mt Cook. Fiordland Tracknet Ph 03 249 7777 also run a daily service to The Divide from Te Anau.

ROUTEBURN VALLEY Routeburn Roadend to Routeburn Falls Hut

The Routeburn Track begins at the carpark, 200m before the roadend Routeburn Shelter and crosses the Routeburn on a suspension bridge. The track leads through magnificent stands of red beech forest on the flats, crosses Sugarloaf Stream and begins to climb more steeply. After Bridal Veil Stream, the track cuts across a line of bluffs to sidle above the impressive Routeburn gorge. Further up valley the track crosses the Routeburn on a suspension bridge and leads through silver beech forest slopes just above grassy Routeburn Flats. Routeburn Flats Hut (20 bunk, DoC cat 1) and 15 campsites are a few hundred metres beyond the track turnoff sign to Routeburn Falls Hut. The track sidles steadily up through the forest towards Routeburn Falls Hut, crossing a recent slip on the way. Routeburn Falls Hut (48 bunks, DoC cat 1) was built in 1996 to replace an older much loved National Park hut on the same site, and is the larger of two huts here, the other belonging to Routeburn Walks Ltd.

Times: Roadend to Flats Hut, 2.5 hrs; Flats Hut to Falls Hut, 1.5 hrs.

HARRIS SADDLE Routeburn Falls Hut to Lake Mackenzie Hut

The track over the tops is exposed to bad weather. In bad conditions, parties need to be equipped and experienced to continue. Seek guidance from the warden, and find a companion to travel with. Snow can be expected at times, even in summer. The track continues above Falls Hut through tussock, and then climbs scrubby slopes towards the falls draining Lake Harris. Beyond here, the track is benched into bluffs above the lake and may be impassable if covered with snow. In late winter and early spring there may be significant avalanche hazard. Some avoid the bluffs by crossing the ice on Lake Harris in winter. Though this can be quite practical, be aware that the lake water level may be well below the ice level, making the chance of recovery from breaking through virtually zero. Harris Saddle is a short distance further. The emergency shelter and toilet 200m SW of the saddle are designed for day use only.

CONICAL HILL, 250m to the north above the saddle, is accessible via a good side track. It offers a much more extensive view than the saddle itself.

On the Hollyford Face side of the saddle, the track goes down a gully and sidles south well above the bushline. After a short distance a sign marks the junction with Deadmans Track. See the note below for more information on this side route.

The track to Lake Mackenzie continues to sidle, and a little over half way along the face, a large square rock may be seen a short distance below. This may provide limited shelter in an emergency, but is no longer signposted. After sidling further, the track turns abruptly and climbs a short distance over a shoulder beyond which Lake Mackenzie and the hut can be seen. The track then passes through a line of bluffs to the left, zig zags down to bushline and crosses the bush covered moraine near the lake outlet to Lake Mackenzie Hut close by. (48 bunks, DoC cat 1). There are 10 campsites here. The hut 350m south is owned by Routeburn Walks Ltd. In the **reverse direction**, the track is clearly marked.

Times: Routeburn Falls Hut to Harris Saddle, 1.5 to 2 hrs; Harris Saddle to Lake Mackenzie Hut, 3.5 to 4 hrs, depending on direction.

DEADMANS TRACK leads from the Routeburn Track directly down to the Hollyford Valley. This marked route is steep. Orange painted poles lead down to the bush, then orange triangles continue to the valley floor. In the **reverse direction**, the lower end of the marked route at Deadmans Bluff is signposted on the Hollyford Road.

Times: Routeburn Track to the road, 3 hrs; coming up, allow 4.5 hrs.

LAKE MACKENZIE HUT TO THE DIVIDE

From Lake Mackenzie Hut, the track crosses a small flat through hebe scrub then climbs for about an hour to the bush edge. Earland Falls is less than an hour further on with a gradual descent most of the way. Lake Howden Hut (28 bunk, DoC cat 1) is an hour further down the well graded track. There is a campsite 20 mins from Lake Howden Hut at the SE end of Lake Howden, and tracks from here lead into the Greenstone and Caples Valleys. See those valleys for further notes. From Lake Howden Hut, the Routeburn Track remains benched to the shelter at The Divide roadside. En route, take advantage of the short, signposted side track to Key Summit. It leads to a fragile subalpine parkland, and offers wonderful views in all directions. A rougher alternative route out from Lake Howden Hut is the Pass Creek Track to the Hollyford Valley. This is marked and takes about 1 hour to reach the Hollyford Road.

Times: Lake Mackenzie Hut to Lake Howden Hut, 3 to 4 hrs; Lake Howden Hut to The Divide (Milford Road), 1 to 1.5 hrs, depending on direction.

EMILY PASS Routeburn to Lake Mackenzie

This route is recommended for experienced parties only as it entails steep scree and snowgrass. The route is not marked and is not obvious in poor visibility. Snow slopes can last until February south of Emily Pass. Emily Creek is named where the Routeburn Track bridge crosses it. Leave the track and follow the straight rocky gully SW under bluffs. This is the extreme true left gully of several creeks that join Emily Creek above the bridge. Straight-forward boulder travel leads to the 1200m contour. Here, leave the stream and sidle into the snowgrass basin.

To the east of Emily Peak is an obvious pass at pt 1544m (Fraser Col) which leads steeply down to Fraser Creek. This pass is often mistaken for Emily Pass. Further to the right, north of Emily Peak, are two rocky guts leading to two depressions on the ridge. The northern one is Emily Pass at pt 1607m. Cross steep snowgrass on the near side of a small waterfall and then climb up the gut to the pass. The descent to Lake Mackenzie is straight-forward. To avoid the last scrubby section stay in the streambed. Follow the rough track around the eastern shore to Lake Mackenzie Hut.

In the **reverse direction**, Emily Pass is the northern depression on the ridge and is easily gained. Be aware that the lower ridge to the east at the 1440m contour overlooks Fraser Creek not the Routeburn. It is extremely steep on the Fraser Creek side. From Emily Pass, descend the gut until snowgrass slopes lead out to the left (north). Continue down across tussock then a scree slide towards the stream bed gulch NW at E40 305 970. Descend this streambed to the bridge on the Routeburn Track.

Times: 3 hrs up and 2 hrs down in either direction as described.

NORTH BRANCH ROUTEBURN Flats to North Col

The route up this valley is straight forward if rough in places. Cross the Routeburn in front of Routeburn Flats Hut and follow up the open flats on the true right (west) bank of the North Branch. A little over 500m from the Routeburn Track, there is a bivvy rock (sleeps 2) on the true left of the North Branch Routeburn near the river just inside the bush edge.

■ The North Branch of the Routeburn from Routeburn Flats.

The track remains on the true right. Towards the end of the flat it crosses a small creek and heads up into the beech forest. Once in the bush it is easily followed up onto an old moraine, before passing the hill side of a tarn to grass flats again, 30 mins from the hut. At the end of the flats, the track re-enters the bush and climbs to further open flats upstream, still on the true right.

At E40 302 021 there is a rock bivvy (called Hobbs Bivvy, sleeps 4) about 200m from the river beside a small stream which sometimes runs dry. Further upvalley on the true right, there is a route through scrubby boulders on the flats close to the stream, using a dry channel in places, and crossing to tussock on the true left near the upstream side of the boulders. Beyond these flats, at the 900m contour, a band of scrub crosses the valley and the river climbs again. Cairns at D40 299 036 indicate a marked route climbing up through this scrub on the true left, sidling back in tussock to the stream. From here on it is mainly open travel to the rock walls in the head of the valley.

A long gully leads up to North Col. Partway up, at the 1240m contour (D40 290 055), there is a fairly good bivvy rock but it is not always weatherproof. Campsites exist nearby. Snow and avalanche debris in the gully leading up to North Col is semi-permanent, and parties continuing to North Col may need ice axes and some alpine knowledge. For those with the skills, there is an excellent classic trip sidling along the Divide from here to Lake Nerine, Park Pass and the Rock Burn, taking 3 days. See the Rock Burn (Dart Valley) for more notes.

DESCENDING. Look for the cairned route through scrub on the true left of the North Branch just above the 900m contour when the river steepens. From partway down the flats below, the true right is used to Routeburn Flats Hut. The track through the last main forest begins over near the hillside, at least 200m from the river.

Times: Routeburn Flats Hut to North Col, 6 hrs; Descending, 4.5 hrs.

DART VALLEY

This is one of the classic tramping valleys of Otago. Together with the Rees it offers a wonderful round trip of about 4 days. Add more time for side trips and bad weather. The tracks are generally well marked and Rees Saddle is not difficult in normal summer conditions, posing little problem for average fitness trampers. Crossing Cascade Saddle to the Matukituki however, is more difficult, due mainly to the steepness of the route from the saddle to the Matukituki Valley. Most other routes out of the Dart watershed cross the Main Divide and will often require alpine skills and equipment. Considerable avalanche hazard exists in the upper Rees and Snowy Creek areas in winter and spring.

The Dart is also pleasant and easy tramping country in its own right. The track follows the true left (east) bank throughout the valley. Hut wardens are usually present in the valley from November to April. An area on the true right (west) bank, centred on Slip Stream, has been designated a Special Area because of the archaeological significance of greenstone discoveries there. Entry to the Special Area requires a permit from DoC.

The lower Rock Burn and Beans Burn are usually approached on the true right (west) bank of the Dart from the Lake Sylvan carpark. Parties visiting true right (western) tributaries of the Dart should note that there are 3 footbridges across the Dart, as marked on E40 Ed.1 and E39 Ed.1; one at the top of Daleys Flat, one at Cattle Flat, and one just above the Whitbourn confluence. Fording the Dart should never be taken lightly and is often impractical.

PARADISE ROAD TO CHINAMANS BLUFF

In 1997 Queenstown Lakes District Council metalled and graded the Glenorchy-Paradise Road to the top of Mill Flat for 2WD vehicles, and has since extended this to Chinamans Bluff. However, bridges over Dundas and especially Chinamans Creek will be required before there is reliable 2WD access to Chinamans Bluff.

From Mill Flat, a rough 2WD road continues through beech forest to Dans Paddock, a 2km long clearing. The road then crosses Chinamans Creek, passes through a band of forest and continues to more grass flats. It then follows down these flats by Chinamans Creek to the Dart River bed at Chinamans Bluff. There are some wonderful campsites and scenery in this area, but as with the rest of the Dart, the sandflies can be very bad. There is a small shelter and toilets here at the roadend.

Backpacker Express (Ph 03 442 9939) runs a daily service for trampers from the beginning of November to the end of April from Queenstown and Glenorchy to Chinamans Bluff.

Time: Mill Flat to Chinamans Bluff on foot, 1 hr 15 mins.

CHINAMANS BLUFF TO DALEYS FLAT HUT

Recent changes in the river course have made a sidle track necessary at the bottom end of CHINAMANS BLUFF. From the carpark, a benched track enters the bush at about E40 385 065 near the river edge. It climbs about 20m above the river, sidles and descends to a flat at the base of the bluff. Further up this flat, there is a bivvy rock situated just back into the bush. The main benched track around Chinamans Bluff begins at a sign near the top of this flat, climbing about 40m above the river before descending and sidling along bush flats, bypassing the small grassy Borer Flat at E40 393 088.

The bush track continues through attractive forest to the stream draining Spaniard Valley at E40 399 103. From the Dart confluence with this stream, follow the riverbed for 100m to the start of grass flats. This is Survey Flat, where there are excellent campsites and across which Survey Stream flows at

■ Looking down Cattle Flat in the Dart Valley. *Lloyd Homer*

Daleys Flat Hut
Quinns Flat
Cattle Flat
Rock Biv
Route to Key Dome
from Whitbourn

E40 400 112. Follow markers across the flat. Beyond Survey Stream the track re-enters the bush and continues to Bedford Stream (bridged). It continues past Cathedral Rocks (or The Sisters), a group of huge bushclad boulders in the river, to emerge beside the river on Sandy Flat at E40 401 132. There are great views of the Cosmos and Bride Peaks from here.

The track sidling SANDY BLUFF starts near the head of Sandy Flat at E40 401 141. It steadily climbs 100m and is benched into the rock bluff on three sides in places, forming a spectacular viewing gallery overlooking Dredge Flat. It then continues across and down to Dredge Flat at E40 412 154. While this track is not especially difficult, care is required. Follow up the gravel riverbed until the river cuts in again. A good bush track sidles along the river bank through to the rest of Dredge Flat.

Whatta Creek at the top of Dredge Flat was once the site of Dredge Hut, built in 1900 for the crew of the Dart Valley Dredge, an unsuccessful attempt at commercial goldmining. All the material (except timber) for a complete sawmilling plant including boiler and steam engine was hauled in wagons from Glenorchy. This historic hut was removed by park staff in the 1970's, but the remains of the dredge are still in the hole at the top end of Dredge Flat on the true right with a beech tree growing out of them at E40 417 180. There isn't much to see, and crossing the river here is definitely not advised in normal conditions. Opposite the Dredge Burn, beech forest returns to the river edge, and a marked track leads up to Daleys Flat Hut (20 bunk, coal stove, DoC cat 2), at the SW end of Daleys Flat.

Descending to the roadend. A good bush track leads to opposite the mouth of the Dredge Burn and open flats. When the river cuts in again, the track reappears and sidles through bush to the rest of Dredge Flat. The track around Sandy Bluff begins at bush edge E40 412 154. This marked track initially sidles in the bush before climbing up to 100m above the river and then sidling through a rock gallery cut in the bluff. Below Sandy Bluff, as each flat finishes, look for the track again at the bush edge by the river. The marked track around Chinamans Bluff begins at Spaniard Stream at the bottom end of Survey Flat, E40 399 104. Below Chinamans Bluff, from the shelter and toilet block, follow the 4WD track away from the river up a flat before swinging right, crossing two creeks and entering Dans Paddock. The road continues out to Mill Flat.

Times: Chinamans Bluff to Daleys Flat Hut, about 5 hrs.

DALEYS FLAT HUT TO DART HUT

As marked on the map, the track leaves Daleys Flat at the eastern corner well away from the river, crosses a low saddle, and descends to cross Quinns Flat. Beyond here the track climbs gradually then levels off to emerge on the terrace at the lower end of Cattle Flat.

CATTLE FLAT isn't really a flat— it's a series of of overlapping grass terraces sloping towards the Dart, along which the track goes up and down. A ground trail winds along the flat, touching the bush edge once or twice. Cattle Flat (Veints) bivvy rock is signposted, and about 300m back up in the bush. At the upper end of the flat the track enters the bush near the river and is well marked. The track now remains in the bush to Dart Hut, (apart from the scrubby Whitbourn Slip between Dart Hut and the Whitbourn Valley,) mostly sidling high above the river. A signposted side track down to the river just beyond Whitbourn flats gives access to the Whitbourn Valley via a swingbridge across the Dart. The new Dart Hut (32 bunks, coal stove, flush toilets, DoC cat 2) at the bush edge above the Snowy/Dart confluence, replaced an earlier DoC hut built in 1976, which in turn replaced the NZ Alpine Club hut built there in 1937. There are excellent campsites just across Snowy Creek.

Descending. The track from Dart Hut enters the bush just past the woodshed and is well marked to Cattle Flat. A new track has been benched more or less level across the scrubby Whitbourn Slip.

At the bottom end of Cattle Flat, the track marking begins at a gate at the bush edge, 200m back from the river, and leads through to Daleys Flat Hut.

Times: Daleys Flat Hut to Dart Hut, about 7 hrs; in the reverse direction, about 6 hrs.

REES SADDLE Dart Hut to Shelter Rock Hut

This route traverses open tussock and speargrass scrubland, and is exposed to bad weather. The upper Snowy bridge is removed during winter, to save it from avalanche damage. In winter and early spring, there is significant avalanche danger in Snowy Creek and the upper Rees. From Dart Hut cross the bridge to the track sign on the true right of Snowy Creek. Climb gradually through scattered scrub, crossing creekbeds, to the foot of the ridge off Headlong Peak. The ground trail, cairns and orange poles continue straight up the ridge for 60m then traverse out to the right, sidling and climbing, keeping roughly 100m above the Snowy. From a shallow basin at the 1200m contour, climb again following poles to 1300m, sidle across to the upper bridge and cross. Beyond the bridge, a reasonable ground trail marked with orange poles on the true left of Snowy Creek leads along a shelf past tarns then climbs to Rees Saddle, which is the lowest saddle ahead. Water can usually be found in small tarns a little to the SE, along the ridge.

From the orange poles on the saddle, follow scree down steeply below a bluff into the Rees Valley. Travel in the valley below is easy but marking disappears for about 1km. From E40 562 191, pick up the foot track, poles and cairns on the true left as they lead through taller tussock and bands of scrub across to a marshy grassland at the 1100m contour. Follow the foot track as it sidles through *Dracophyllum* scrub and across creeks, keeping its height, while the Rees River continues to descend below. Then the track loses about 200m height, descending to the riverbed and following it to Shelter Rock Hut, still on the true left (20 bunks, coal stove, DoC cat 2). **Reverse direction**. See Rees Valley notes.

For moderately capable people there is a very worthwhile side trip from Rees Saddle up scree slopes to the ridge overlooking Lochnagar.

Note. Above Rees Saddle, Snowy Creek flows through an easy basin with another fairly low saddle above it leading to Lochnagar. Although it is unlikely, make sure this is not mistaken for Rees Saddle. This much more difficult crossing is mentioned (in reverse) in the Shotover Valley notes.

Times: Dart Hut to Shelter Rock Hut, 4 to 6 hrs in either direction.

CASCADE SADDLE Dart Hut to Aspiring Hut

From Dart Hut, a day trip to the Dart Glacier and Cascade Saddle is popular and generally straightforward. From Cascade Saddle, the views of the West Matukituki Valley and Rob Roy Peak are spectacular, while a few minutes along the ridge to the south brings Mt Aspiring into view. However, the full crossing is not easy. Virtually the whole route is above bushline and exposed to the weather. The descent on the West Matukituki side (the Cullers Route) is unrelentingly steep and exposed, leading down steep snowgrass and rockbluffs to the bushline. This descent is particularly dangerous when the snowgrass is wet and it becomes an alpine undertaking when covered in snow.

The route to Cascade Saddle is on the true left of the Dart all the way and is generally well defined with ground trails and cairns along the flats. From Dart Hut, cross the Snowy Creek bridge to the sign on the true right. A new track leads from here through a small tongue of bush and across undulating tussock slopes, cutting the corner and dropping 20m to the Dart river bed and flats just upstream from a small bluff at E39 575 225. Up near the glacier, streams cutting down into the gravel terraces near the snout of the Dart Glacier make it necessary to descend to the glacial flats.

Follow cairns up the ablation valley beside the glacier. Beware of old cairned routes at high levels as they lead nowhere.

From the 1080m contour in the ablation valley, E39 604 267, a line of cairns climbs diagonally up the gravel slopes to the 1420m contour at about E39 615 272 where orange poles begin in a stable tussocky moraine-wall trough. The section from the valley to this moraine-wall trough is actively sliding, albeit slowly and a new line is cairned across it by park staff each year. Follow the trough along to a fine little gravel flat, where there is usually water. Camping is encouraged here to avoid impacts in the main Cascade Basin. From here, the marker poles climb again, bypassing Cascade Saddle and following a small gully up to the Cascade Creek Basin. Although there are great campsites here, they can be very exposed in bad weather.

The poles cross Cascade Stream and climb to the ridge overlooking the West Matukituki Valley. The start of the descent to the Matukituki Valley is marked on the ridge by a small pylon, at 1800m. It is ESSENTIAL that parties find this pylon before descending. A gully immediately below the pylon on the east side of the ridge can hold snow until late in the season.

The route down is marked with orange poles which, along with a light ground trail, should be followable all the way to the bushline. There are three rock steps to descend in the middle section of the route. These require care, especially in wet conditions, but narrow ledges provide reasonable footholds. Below the last step the snowgrass is longer and the slope less steep. A track cut through the scrub on the southern side of the ridge leads into the bush. Markers replace orange poles and lead on down to cross the stream to the north at the 940m contour, below a fork. There is a small campsite near this stream. Another smaller stream is crossed in 10 mins and the track leads NE to finish beside Aspiring Hut. The **reverse direction** is described in the West Matukituki Valley notes.

Times: Dart Hut to Cascade Saddle, 4 hrs; Saddle to Pylon, 1.5 hrs; Pylon to Aspiring Hut, 3 to 4 hrs; Cascade Saddle to Dart Hut, 3 hrs.

WHITBOURN VALLEY Dart Hut to Whitbourn Glacier and Key Dome

The Whitbourn Glacier also makes a great day trip from Dart Hut, but this valley is more enclosed than the Dart. The marked route is as shown on E39 Ed.1, except that, once across the footbridge, the route sidles closer to the Dart River bank. The route up the Whitbourn Valley is entirely on the true left.

From the sign by the Dart track, descend steeply, following markers to the bridge across the Dart River. On Whitbourn Flat follow a tongue of grass due north into an alcove at the bush edge to E39 548 231. A marked route enters the bush to the right (looking up) and climbs for about 200m, then sidles out to the left along a fairly even grade. The bush does not last long, and 45 mins from the Dart the marked route emerges from the bush into a patch of fern and scrub. The Whitbourn River is about 100m below. Beyond here follow the cairned route, keeping about 100m above the river until the same height as the flats, then sidle horizontally across to where they begin.

Beyond the main flats there is a bivvy rock at E39 546 252. It is at the upstream end of a heap of boulders on the true left, but the bivvy rock is not part of the rock fan. It is about 40m from the river under a boulder up a gully between rockwalls. Sleeps 3, just.

TO WHITBOURN GLACIER. To continue to the glacier, walk up the flats through a bouldery section and cross the stream draining the Giekie Glacier. Still on the true left of the Whitbourn, a cairned route back from the river now leads up a rock gully through a small bluff onto a rocky knoll, bypassing the river which is enclosed in a slit gorge. Sidle along scree slopes up valley, where there may be further cairns. Keep your height where the slopes are steeper as the glacier is approached and watch for loose stones. Access to the ice may be gained at about the 1200m contour. For further information, see Arawhata Valley.

Descending. Remember the route down off the rocky knoll to the flats. Below the flats follow river boulders on the true left and at about E39 547 239 pick up the cairned route leading back to the bush.

Times: Dart Hut to footbridge, 45 mins; Footbridge to upper flats, 1.5 hrs; Upper flats to the glacier, 1.5 hrs; Dart Hut to Whitbourn Glacier, about 4.5 hrs, and 4 hrs in reverse.

KEY DOME

Follow the directions above to the start of the upper Whitbourn flats. Opposite the flats, (on the true right), a big broad tussock covered slip descends from small bluffs high on the Key Dome ridge. Cross the Whitbourn and find a route through lower scrub bands, at about E39 546 240, to the tussock. Ascend tussock slopes, almost to the base of the bluffs. The bluffs above are very steep, loose, greasy and have little to offer.

Look left for a small ledge covered in tussock that cuts diagonally out through the bluffs to the ridge at E39 539 237. (See the photo on pg 39). The ledge has an old deer trail on it and is reasonably easy, though it requires care in either direction. It should be avoided in wet or frosty conditions, and when it is under snow. There are numerous tarns on the ridge and the flats in Blue Duck Creek are quite accessible. Key Dome is a fast route, with few crevasses, to the Marion Plateau. Follow the ridge, and sidle east under Mt Amundsen to Boys Col. This route is for climbing parties only.

Descending. There should be a cairn on the ridge to indicate where the ledge begins. Check out the descent to the top of the slip without a pack to be sure before descending. It is only about 100m along the ledge from the ridge to the easier tussock slopes below.

MIDDLE DART TRIBUTARIES

Access to the slopes below O'Leary Pass is by the bridge across the Dart at Cattle Flat. The broad spur leading up to trig D is covered in open beech forest offering easy travel. Aim to meet the bushline 1km east of the Pass Burn, then sidle easy undulating tussock slopes to the upper Pass Burn, at about the 1400m contour. There is a bivvy rock about 60m distance due east of where the Pass Burn meets the bushline and another at the foot of Cattle Flat on the north bank of the Dart. Crossing O'Leary Pass and Desperation Pass are described in the Joe River section of the Arawhata, P 146.

Routes crossing the Barrier Range to Forgotten River Flats (Margaret Glacier, Seal Col) are described in the Pyke Valley (Forgotten River), P 126. These are approached on the Dart side across the swingbridge over the Dart at Daleys Flat. A natural rock bridge across the Margaret Burn, near the Dart confluence, gives access up a spur east of the Margaret to the Barrier Range, near Seal Col.

DREDGE BURN

Very few people visit this valley. An unmarked route leads in on the true left from near the mouth of the stream and climbs high to avoid bluffs. This route climbs to about the 1000m contour and sidles up valley to the flats in the head. Alternatively, after climbing for a good hour, the first prominent clearing should be seen across the stream, and a crossing is made to the true right. From here, the route continues through clearings and tongues of bush or scrub to the flats. There is a bivvy rock reported in the beech forest at E40 418 191, at approx the 720m contour.

Time: Dart to the valley head, 6 hrs.

BRIDE BURN

The Bride Burn is also seldom visited. Gain the prominent bush terrace at the 500m contour on the true left of the Bride Burn, 500m north of its confluence with the Dart. Cross the terrace then follow along the brink of this terrace overlooking the stream until the terrace runs out. Climb about 250m to the 760m contour, sidle, then descend steeply to an easy ford and reasonable going along the true right to the bush edge. It is also feasible to cross from the head of the Bride Burn to the Beans Burn by climbing tussock slopes to the west, and crossing the spur running north from Cosmos Peaks to a pleasant basin. Descend to the Beans Burn on the true left of the stream draining this basin. Allow a reasonable day for the crossing.

Times: Dart to the bush edge, 6 hrs; Bush edge to the valley head, a further 3 hrs.

BEANS BURN

The Beans Burn offers one of the easiest approaches to the Olivines, and is the start of an excellent 4 or 5 day journey called the 5 pass trip. This crosses Fohn Saddle, Fiery Col, Cow Saddle, Park Pass, and Sugarloaf Pass.

Access to the Beans Burn is usually by one of three ways:

1. From the Lake Sylvan Carpark, follow the track past Lake Sylvan to the Rock Burn. (See Rock Burn notes). Cross the Rock Burn. Alternatively an old stockbridge (recently upgraded by DoC) 10 mins above the hut crosses an impressive canyon over the Rock Burn if the river is up. Continue up open flats beside the Dart, then sidle in forest along the eroding river edge where the river sweeps against the trees. The clear water of the Beans Burn joins the silty Dart River on gravel flats, and at present, crossing the Beans Burn is mostly straight forward at normally flows. This is the usual foot access.
2. From Paradise via Chinamans Flat. This route is seldom used due to the need to cross the Dart River. This is not recommended, particularly with summer snowmelt, but it may be a useful (but freezing) option in winter.
3. Jetboats operate in summer on a regular basis up the Dart, beyond the Beans Burn. This eliminates river crossings to the Beans Burn Track.

   Contact www.dartjet.co.nz, Backpacker Express, Ph 03 442 9939.

DART TO THE FIRST FLAT

The beginning of the track upvalley is not obvious. It starts at the bush edge by a wire exclosure plot on the true left of the Beans Burn by the Dart confluence, as marked on E40 Ed.1. Ignore the foot trail along the riverbank itself; it is used by jet boat passengers and leads nowhere. The track upvalley is well defined and marked with white permolat. It leaves the river and crosses a bush terrace before returning to the river and footbridge. Across the bridge, on the true right, the track climbs away from the river to cross a small saddle before descending to the first flat at E40 366 099. This section of the track above the bridge is actually about 200m west of the trackline marked on E40 Ed.1.

To find a bivvy rock near here, go 100m downstream from the track entrance at E40 366 099 onto the first flat. Head into the bush (thick) for 50m, and climb about 40m above the river. The bivvy is dry, sheltered, sleeps about 4, faces north and the overhang, although disguised, can be seen from the flat. Other, poorer bivvy rocks also exist.

Times: Dart to footbridge, 45 mins; footbridge to flat, 45 mins.

FIRST FLAT TO HEAD

The track finishes at the first flat, but a route marked with red and white permolat, not shown on E40 Ed.1, is in reasonable condition and followable with care to near the bushline. The true right bank is followed all the way. At the top of the first flat, the marked route stays close to the bank through stands of large red beech trees for 30 mins. At E40 357 115, the markers begin to climb in the bush, crossing a creek at the 600m contour and continuing on to a deep avalanche gully slightly above the 700m contour at E40 351 123. Despite large cairns marking the re-entry to the bush on both sides, and sometimes markers, the re-entry points remain a little obscure. The marked route now gently descends on a long sidle, crossing more chutes and open fans. Look for cairns marking re-entry points.

River level is reached again at about E40 351 129. Travel up valley from here is generally close to the river, following markers through forest and cairns in open scrub areas. Persistence to stay on the marked route here will usually pay off, but if it is lost, return to the river edge, particularly in scrubby sections. Travel along the upper flats is easy. The bivvy rock marked on E40 is a huge split boulder at the top of the flat. The main bivvy under it (sleeps 6) is on the north side, but there are several chambers under this rock.

Descending. From the end of the gravel flat below the bivvy rock, boulder hop for about 600m distance on the true right to pick up the marked route at a large rock jutting into the river at the bush edge. Although it may be lost in scrubby areas, the marked route is generally faster, and care should be taken to return to it downstream. From approx. E40 351 129 the marked route climbs steadily away from the river to cross a deep open avalanche gully at the 700m contour before descending again to the river and the first flat.

Time: First flat to the split boulder bivvy rock, 5 or 6 hrs.

FOHN SADDLE Beans Burn to the Olivine Ledge

From the bivvy rock in the head of the Beans Burn, either side of the river can be used until under Fohn Saddle. On the true left, when the river climbs, follow up swampy tussock and scrub along a rib overlooking the river. Climb directly up tussock to Fohn Saddle. Descend to the stream below, which drains the largest of the Fohn Lakes, cross it at the 1350m contour and follow the true right bank to the Olivine Ledge. See the Olivine River, Pyke Valley for more notes.

Time: Beans Burn bivvy rock to Olivine Ledge bivvy rock, 4 or 5 hrs; In the reverse direction, 3 hrs.

ROCK BURN

This valley is a gem, and has long been popular with trampers. Routes lead from it to the North Routeburn, the Olivine River and the Beans Burn. **Access** to the lower Rock Burn is usually from the Routeburn.

1. SUGARLOAF PASS A few minutes from the carpark, the Routeburn Track crosses a clay/talc slip opposite Routeburn Shelter. Approx 180m beyond this slip, the track to Sugarloaf Pass begins unobtrusively as a light ground trail, leading to the north. It is not signposted. After about 100m markers will be found and these are continuous to the bushline. On the tops, orange poles lead up over the tussock saddle to the Rock Burn side, bearing left to the highest tongue of bush and about 100m on the true left of the creek. (The map shows the track incorrectly here). The track descends steeply in bush and crosses this creek to the true right. The track continues down to a junction at the 820m contour, where it joins tracks from up and down valley. Signs indicate tracks to Theatre Flat, Rockburn Hut, and Sugarloaf Pass. East along the ridge from Sugarloaf Pass there are wonderful tarns and views, making a great day trip from Routeburn Shelter.

The head of the Rock Burn.

2. VIA LAKE SYLVAN. From the Lake Sylvan Carpark and campsite, cross the Routeburn bridge and follow the track to the lake, taking the shorter, direct track to the left (west) when the track forks. Follow the lake edge track past the next junction (also signposted) to the top of the lake. The track continues near a stream feeding the lake (not as shown on E40) and then follows a bush ridge close to pt 572m, before descending to the Rock Burn near Rock Burn (McIntyres) Hut (sleeps 8, open fire, DoC cat 4) on the true right.

Times: Routeburn Track to Sugarloaf Pass, 2 hrs; Sugarloaf Pass to Theatre Flat, 3.5 hrs; Sylvan Carpark to Rockburn Hut, 2.5 hrs.

ROCK BURN HUT TO THEATRE FLAT

A marked track leads from Rock Burn Hut up the true right of the Rock Burn. (A turnoff from it near the hut also leads to a short stockbridge, recently upgraded by DoC, across the spectacular Rock Burn chasm and this is sometimes used by parties heading to or from the Beans Burn). Continue along the track on the true right, which leads up onto and along high terraces above the river before descending to an open flat with campsites at E40 374 038. Beyond here, the track climbs high to avoid a wild gorge, and sidles up valley to the Sugarloaf Pass track junction.

The track then sidles across two streams and through a swampy valley at the 820m contour. Beyond, it drops steeply down a spur to cross a confined creek (quickly impassable after rain) at about the 760m contour, about 100m above the river. On the true left of this creek, a little below the crossing point, there is a 2 person bivvy rock between the track and the stream. The track reaches the valley floor above the main gorge and from now on is never far from the river. Keeping to the true right, the track leads across two open flats.

From the top of the second flat, the track continues past river flood debris and sidles up across steeper forested slopes through prickly shield fern under pt 905m to the bridge across the Rock Burn just below Theatre Flat. Cross the DoC maintained bridge to the true left and continue along the bank to Theatre Flat. A huge rock near the centre of Theatre Flat (on the true left) provides a sheltered campsite, but doesn't always keep out the rain.

Descending. From Theatre Flat, follow along the true left for a few hundred metres to the swing-bridge and cross the Rock Burn to the true right. Markers continue intermittently from here. Be sure to pick up the track again after the mid flats, because at E40 347 041 the track swings away from the river across beech slopes and climbs 200m to avoid the main gorge. The track is well marked over both Sugarloaf Pass and down the valley.

Time: Rockburn Hut to Theatre Flat, 4.5 hrs.

THEATRE FLAT TO PARK PASS

From Theatre Flat, the route up the Rock Burn is all on the true left. A marked route crosses a low saddle at 870m on the spur off Minos Peak. It leads up a gully, follows through a trough beside pt 908m and descends to the flat upstream by the river. The short walk up to pt 908m is rewarded with wonderful views and a natural rock garden setting. A strip of bush breaks the next flat into two. Beyond, at the 840m contour, the valley begins to rise sharply. A marked track on the true left crosses a small creek by the river and climbs through a narrow tongue of bush to avoid a cataract and finishes at the bushline upvalley. The tussock basin beyond leads to a final rib, which has a ground trail on it, up to Park Pass. There is a good bivvy rock (sleeps 5) at the 1000m contour, E40 306 113, about 20 mins below the pass, though it is exposed to the south. See the Pyke Valley for crossing to Hidden Falls Creek.

Descending. From Park Pass, follow the ground trail down a rib to tussocky flats. Continue down them to a creek at about E40 308 102. The river can be seen starting to gorge below. Pick up a ground trail, cross a creek here and pop up onto a swampy scrub and tussock terrace on the true left. Follow along this to the bush edge and the start of a good ground track marked with old blazes and orange tape which leads down through bush to a flat, just over an hour from the pass. Continue down flats to E40 317 085 and locate markers in the bush that lead up a gully to a trough east of pt 908m. Follow markers on down to Theatre Flat.

Times: Theatre Flat to Park Pass, about 3 hrs; 2.5 hrs in the reverse direction.

PARK PASS GLACIER can be approached from Park Pass. Ascend tussock slopes north of the pass, leading through bluffs at E40 305 121. There should be some cairns visible on the route. Only this one line on the spur above Park Pass works, as elsewhere there are lines of bluffs. The glacier now has a terminal lake and is a great place to visit.

LAKE UNKNOWN is accessible for experienced parties from several points. An approach has been made from the bottom end of Theatre Flat. Another route begins at E40 340 058 on a flat lower down the Rock Burn. Both routes climb through steep bush, some scrub, and traverse tussock slopes to converge at E40 345 084 on the ridge overlooking the lake, about 4 hrs from the valley. A steep westward sidling descent, threading through bluffs, gives access to Lake Unknown. Alternatively, follow the ridge towards Minos Peak and just north of pt 1760m look east for a route to the lake shore, threading down steep snowgrass and a series of bluffs. These descents are tricky and should only be attempted in good conditions. Other very steep and bluffed approaches to Lake Unknown have also been used from the first flat in the Beans Burn and the Dart/Beans Burn Confluence, but are not recommended.

A good bivvy rock (sleeps 4) exists 50m back from the lake shore at E40 346 097, and another poorer one exists at E40 338 104, near a tarn. With some alpine skills and equipment, the range from Park Pass via the Park Pass Glacier can also be traversed on snow and rock slopes just below the crest to Lake Unknown. There are some wonderful basins between Amphion and Minos to camp in. From the SW face of Mt Chaos descend to the NW end of Lake Unknown or continue SW to pt 1760m and descend to the Rock Burn.

LAKE NERINE Park Pass to North Col and the Routeburn

From the tarns on top of Park Pass, follow up the long snowgrass ridge to the south. Just before the ridge begins to rise steeply at the 1260m contour, leave it at about D40 300 108 and sidle unpleasantly steep snowgrass and hard earth slopes on the Rock Burn side, climbing steadily until a small lakelet is reached at E40 301 092. Cross the low ridge to the south to a tiny basin and tarn at E40 302 090. From the south side of this tarn, climb south up a gully to a spur 100m west of pt 1594m. Cross this spur at its lowest point (1590m) and drop the relatively short distance down rock and snow slopes (often snow-covered in summer) to a lakelet NE of Lake Nerine. Conditions will dictate the best line. Lake Nerine, with its rock knolls and wonderful views, is a very special place. Go north around the lake and climb back to the main range, 100m north of pt 1580m. From here, either:

1. descend a gully/trough/bench past two tarns and campsites near pt 1444m, then traverse and sidle up the gully to North Col (the best option), or
2. sidle across scree and snowgrass on the Hidden Falls side of Nereus Peak, maintaining an even height until North Col.

On North Col there are 2 or 3 campsites and a poor, small bivvy rock. Pt 1796m above North Col offers great views.

A snow couloir leads from the col to the head of the North Branch of the Routeburn. There is a fairly good bivvy rock at the 1240m contour D40 290 055 in the gully off North Col. See the Routeburn North Branch for further notes. In the **reverse direction,** avoid the temptation to walk around to the outlet end of Lake Nerine, and do not lose too much height immediately after leaving the last lakelet.

Caution. The snowgrass slopes between Park Pass and Lake Nerine are extremely dangerous under snow. With good conditions on a fine day, with dry tussock and no fresh snow on the slopes above Park Pass, the crossing is suitable for capable tramping parties. Under snow it is an alpine crossing. Parts of the route are bluffy.

Times: Park Pass to Lake Nerine, 3 hrs; Lake Nerine to North Col, 2.5 hrs; North Col to Routeburn Flats Hut, 4.5 hrs.

FORBES AND EARNSLAW MOUNTAINS Access from the Dart

Kea Basin and Hunter Creek routes are described in the Rees notes, P54, 56.

BEDFORD VALLEY is approached up Survey Stream from E40 400 111. Follow up open gravel to the 540m contour then gain the ridge on the true right of Survey Creek. Climb the ridge to bushline and continue into the tussock. At the 1260m contour, sidle right (looking up) for 100m to bypass bluffs on a minor spur between two creeks marked on E40. A wide tussock bench at the 1500m contour, with tarns on it at the Bedford end, now leads north towards the chasm of Bedford Stream. Sidle up valley on the true left of Bedford Stream to cross SE of pt 1602m.

There are only alpine routes out of the basin, none of them easy or straight forward. Climbing parties only.

1. **Crossing into the West Hunter Valley** via the col south of Mt Cerberus. This is an easy ascent on the Bedford side, but the descent on the Hunter side is bluffy and less obvious. Sidle to the right through bluffs on steep scree slopes and descend the true right side of the stream marked on E40. There are at least three lines of bluffs to negotiate. The last one can be descended down an unobvious minor tussock gully on a corner at E40 452 150, still on the true right.
2. **Shepherds Pass.** Again, reasonably straight forward on the Bedford side, but is much more difficult and requires climbing skills on the South Hunter side. Either descend a steep confined snow couloir (access to which is frequently cut off from above in summer), or sidle to the right from the pass on steep broken slopes before descending a small snowfield. More steep ground leads to the basin. From the saddle, a traverse of Leary Peak may be easier than the descent to the South Hunter.
3. **To Wright Col.** Head up the Bedford tributary draining Wright Col (South Branch) and bypass a small waterfall on the true right. Above it, easy going up scree and then rock bluffs leads towards Wright Col. A small detour towards East Peak on a scree shelf at about the 2100m contour gives easier going to the gentler slopes SW of the col. Watch for falling stones.

SPANIARD VALLEY is the tussock basin SW of Pluto Peak at the 1340m contour, above Valpys Pass. At E40 423 095 there is a bivvy rock in this basin. Access is usually via a long traverse through the bush from Chinamans Creek, or ascending the ridge from Valpys Pass.

Climb the mountains and get their good tidings. Nature's peace will flow through you as sunshine flows into trees; the winds blow their freshness into you and the storms their energy, while cares will drop off like autumn leaves.

—John Muir.

REES VALLEY

This lovely valley with its easy access and drier climate than the country further west is very popular and offers pleasant tramping. Combined with the Dart, it offers a great round trip of 4 or 5 days. A gravel road runs up the valley to a carpark and toilet at Muddy Creek, about 20 km from Glenorchy. Muddy Creek drains an active slip. The creek bed continually changes its course, depositing fresh gravel and cutting channels in temporary tracks even without rain. Taking cars beyond here is not recommended. Backpacker Express (Ph. 03 442 9939) runs a daily service from the beginning of November to the end of April from Glenorchy to the Muddy Creek Carpark and may also offer a 4WD service by arrangement to 25 Mile Creek.

On the way up the road, just across the McDougalls Creek ford, a signposted track leads up a spur for 40 mins to the historic **INVINCIBLE MINE** remains. There are excellent views of the Rees, Mt Earnslaw and the Forbes Mountains from here.

MUDDY CREEK CARPARK TO SHELTER ROCK HUT

Follow the 4WD track up valley from the carpark. There are locked farm buildings, the property of Rees Valley Station, on both sides of Arthurs Creek. Beyond Arthurs Creek, the 4WD track crosses a channel of the Rees and continues indistinctly up the flats on the eastern side of the valley. If the river is low, this is the easiest option. Alternatively, orange poles sidle up to 20m above the river along the bank, avoiding any need to cross any river channels.

Twenty Five Mile Hut (6 bunks but only 3 kapok mattresses, open fire, Rees Valley Station and OTMC) is about 70m above the valley floor and not visible from it. About 200m south of Twenty Five Mile Creek a sign at the edge of the flats indicates a foot track up to the hut. To continue up the Rees, cross Twenty Five Mile Creek (the largest unbridged creek on the Rees Dart circuit) and sidle, following the orange poles. Continue across terraces as marked on E40 to the bush edge where a good, marked track begins. Alternatively from Twenty Five Mile Creek, in low flow, bomb up the river and rejoin the poled route when flats begin again.

Just inside the bush cross a footbridge to the true right of the Rees River. This is 200m downstream of the old bridge site marked on E40. The track climbs a little then descends after 20 mins and follows through small clearings to the foot of Clarke Slip. There are pleasant campsites here, but numerous small streams cross the flat after heavy rain. A minor lake formed at the top end of the flats during 1996. The track climbs to the bush edge and crosses extensive slopes of subalpine vegetation. These slopes get blasted each winter/spring with snow avalanches and are best avoided at that time. A footbridge leads back to the true left where Shelter Rock Hut (20 bunk, coal stove, DoC cat 2) is situated in a small grassy clearing.

Times: Muddy Carpark to Twenty Five Mile Creek, 2.5 hrs; Twenty Five Mile Creek to Shelter Rock Hut, about 4 hrs.

REES SADDLE Shelter Rock Hut to Dart Hut

From Shelter Rock Hut, the flats and riverbank are followed on the true left for 500m to a cairn and track marker. Here a good track climbs away from the river, gaining 200m altitude through low *Dracophyllum*. It then sidles, before descending slightly to a swampy grass patch at the 1120m contour not far above the river. Waratah poles and cairns continue across to the riverbank at about the 1140m contour where the tussock basin becomes easy travel and the markers become more intermittent. Follow the river, utilising a long, narrow tussock rib between two tributaries at the 1200m contour, then follow the creekbed directly towards the pass. Rees Saddle, the lowest point on the ridge ahead, is easily reached. The last 100m of height is cairned up fairly steep snowgrass and scree at the base of a bluff to the orange poles on the pass. Scrambling up the ridge to pt 2185m from the saddle on a fine day will take about 2 hrs, but the views are magnificent and include Lochnagar, 1100m below in the head of the Shotover.

From the saddle, follow a few orange poles down to the tussock bench below. A trail and cairns continue along the bench and as the gorge begins to close in they lead down to the upper Snowy Creek bridge. From the bridge, the track on the true right climbs about 30m then traverses around to the north. It is marked with cairns and poles most of the way. Little height is lost until the Dart River can be seen, when the track leads down more steeply to a scrubby stream fan at the 1000m contour. There are good campsites on the true right side of the lower Snowy Creek bridge and Dart Hut (32 bunk, coal stove, flush toilets, DoC cat 2) is on the true left. See Dart Valley notes.

Times: Shelter Rock Hut to Rees Saddle, 3.5 hrs; Rees Saddle to Dart Hut, 2.5 hrs.

TWENTY FIVE MILE CREEK

Much of this valley is in Rees Valley Station. Permission will be required for access (Scott Family, Ph 03 442 9908, e-mail: rees.valley@xtra.co.nz). Big Devil Hut (Rees Valley Station) is locked. From Twenty Five Mile Hut, follow sheep trails up valley on the true left and cross Little Devil Creek. Continue to Big Devil Creek where a bridge spans a chasm about 2m wide and 30m deep. From here, turn uphill and skirt around 100m or more above Twenty Five Mile Creek, using a high terrace. The animal trails lead on around and through bush to the hut, which is on a small flat, high above the main stream. Old trails continue up valley, through bluffs at the bush edge and then on up Twenty Five Mile Creek in open going. Upper Twenty Five Mile Creek is pleasant, if a little barren, and there

The head of Twenty Five Mile Creek in the Rees Catchment.

are good campsites. When the valley closes in beyond Rough Creek, tussock on the true right provides easier travel than *Dracophyllum* scrub on the true left. Climb a short steep tussock bank on the true right to a knoll and sidle across to Twenty Five Mile Creek, then repeat the process, sidling back to Twenty Five Mile Creek again at the 1200m contour.

To reach **TWENTY FIVE MILE SADDLE** from Twenty Five Mile Creek. Climb to the 1400m contour up a tussock slope south of the creek draining the saddle. At this height, an animal trail leads horizontally through a line of bluffs to the southern corner of a basin under the saddle. Alternatively, a second trail leads through these bluffs at the 1500m contour. The saddle is now easily crossed to a wonderful clear, spring-fed tarn on the Rees side at the 1460m contour.

To approach the Rees, sidle north between the 1500m and 1400m contours and descend a spur to meet the Rees Valley track at approx. E40 546 187 (The track line marked on E40 Ed 1 is incorrectly shown here). Scrub on this route down to the track is minimal and very short. Alternatively, Twenty Five Mile Spur can be descended along tussock tops on the Rees side, although this is a long and dry traverse. None of these routes are marked.

Times: Rees Valley to Big Devil Hut, 1.5 hrs; Big Devil Hut to Rough Creek, 4 hrs; Rough Creek to Saddle, 2.5 hrs; Saddle to Rees track, 2 hrs.

TWELVE MILE CREEK (OX BURN) Rees Valley Road to Cashs Flat

Sometimes used for difficult crossings to the Shotover, this valley is partly in Temple Peak Station (Mark and Amanda Hasselman, Ph 03 442 9942), and partly in Rees Valley Station (Iris Scott, Ph 03 442 9908). Permission is required to cross their land. Parties crossing any of the high saddles will need to be equipped and capable of traversing steep snowslopes until January. None of these routes are marked.

At E40 470 924 on Rees Valley road there is a turnoff to Temple Peak Station. Follow it to the implement shed, which is only 100m before the homestead. Cross Davidsons Creek here and pick up an at times vague, 4WD track on the true right which zig zags up the spur through grass and beech forest. Climb to the top of the forest, then sidle across left at the 1000m contour, reaching the spur overlooking Twelve Mile Creek (Ox Burn) at the 1060m contour. Cross the fence and sidle down slightly on steeper grassland. Find an animal trail through a bluffline at the edge of an old slip. Aim for the base of beech trees in the slip at the 1020m contour, E40 509 934. Then sidle from the trees at this contour, with an occasional cairn in the tussock marking stream crossings, to the spur down which the fenceline runs at E40 523 931, a point 140m above the Ox Burn. Descend to Cashs Flat. Cashs Flat Hut (sleeps 3, open fire) is on the true right.

To descend to the Rees Valley, from Cashs Flat cross the creek entering from the south and climb the spur to a gate in the fence and follow a sheep track which sidles around the hillside to the slip. Head SW and descend the bulldozed track to Temple Peak implement yard and the Rees Valley road.

Time: Temple Peak Homestead to Cashs Flat, about 3.5 hrs.

OX BURN SADDLE (1734m) is at E40 556 963 and leads to the Flood Burn. There is a gorge to avoid in the North Branch of the Ox Burn. From Cashs Flat Hut, go 300m upvalley to a creek. Follow up the creek a little, and climb out onto a spur at E40 530 934. Follow a good stock trail up the spur to the 1460m contour. Sidle across at about this height on a trail until E40 538 944, when an easy gully descends to the upper basin. Ox Burn Saddle is easily gained on this side, but the descent to the Flood Burn is quite steep.

From the saddle, follow a strong old trail across to a spur at E40 558 964 at the 1700m contour. Descend NE down the tussock spur and open gully system to reach Prince of Wales Flat in the

Flood Burn at E40 565 965. Follow the stream to Duncans Flat, and Flood Burn Hut (2 bunk, DoC) on the true right of the Flood Burn, as marked on E40 Ed.1. See the Shotover Valley for more notes.

DISMAL SADDLE is just that, and not recommended. There are extremely steep snow grass slopes on the Stony Creek side of it.

STONY SADDLE offers the least difficult crossing to Upper Stony Creek. From Cashs Flat, sidle up the true left branch. Keep on the true right, sidling about 100m above a gorge, before returning to the stream at the 1160m contour. Continue up the open valley, boulder hopping most of the way and ascend shingle slides to the saddle. On the Upper Stony Creek side, head 500m south on a bench at roughly the 1800m contour and descend the spur heading SE to forks at the 980m contour in the scrub zone in Stony Creek. This spur is steep and broken in places. The slopes directly below Stony Saddle on the Stony Creek side are not recommended. See Shotover notes.

TEMPLE PEAK can be climbed from Temple Peak Homestead (Mark and Amanda Hasselman, Ph. 03 442 9942 for access permission) by following up the bulldozed track on the true right of Davidsons Creek then continuing up the spur. Alternatively, Temple Peak can be approached from Cashs Flat by climbing the entire spur on which the fence is found. There is a tiny hut on the ridge of Temple Peak at about the 1750m contour with water available on the north side. During 1914 1918 scheelite was mined near the summit of Temple Peak and a tunnel runs right through it 100m from the top. Provided this tunnel is still open, it is possible to go in from the north end and peer straight down into Pulpit Basin, about 120m below the southern portal.

Times: Cashs Flat to Ox Burn Saddle, 3.5 hrs; Ox Burn Saddle to Prince of Wales Flat, 2 hrs; Cashs Flat over Stony Saddle to Stony Creek forks at 980m, about 6 hrs; Allow a full day for the ascent of Temple Peak.

BUCKLER BURN—Glenorchy Road to Buckler/Wallers Forks

The Buckler Burn catchment is still in tenure review. This should lead to some form of public access, but it may bypass the roadline in the lower reaches. However, the present situation (2004) is that permission for access up the Mt Judah Road is required from Wyuna Station (Manager, A Wallace, Ph. 03 442 6046). A difficult loop trip is feasible for strong, fit parties in a long summer weekend, up the Buckler Burn, over into Stony Creek and back via Stony Saddle to the Ox Burn. Parties should be prepared to cope with steep snowslopes until mid summer. None of these routes are marked. The Buckler Burn has a long and rich mining history, particularly for scheelite ore (tungsten).

From the Glenorchy Road, the Mt Judah 4WD track shares the Wyuna Homestead access for the first 150m. Then, at a gate marked private road, the Mt Judah 4WD track continues on up the hill through masses of broom. With permission, follow the Judah Road for about 3.5km then turn left off it onto a 4WD track, passing a disused mine and leading to a collapsed old high level cableway at E41 498 856. This was once used to transport scheelite ore from the slopes of Mt McIntosh. Continue past the old cableway anchor down a 4WD track that stops at a small bluff 10m vertically above Bonnie Jean Creek. An old horse track leads left for 150m down to the gravel and grass in Bonnie Jean Creek, still about 150m distance from the Buckler Burn confluence. (There is also a bulldozed track up the hill right from the forks on the true right of the Buckler Burn).

The gorge leading to Wallers Creek is best traversed on the true left. To continue up the Buckler Burn from the Bonnie Jean Creek forks, stay in the riverbed for the first 300m distance to at least E41 502 859, passing under a high scrubby bluff en-route. Then, as travel in the river becomes difficult, sidle up through beech forest and generally keep about 25m above the river on old trails, inside the bush edge. Intermittent bluffs and steep ground, such as at E41 514 861 make travel awkward in places, requiring climbs into the grass and scrub above. High level options from the end of the Judah Road also exist, but matagouri above the beech forest is very thick in large areas. The hut at the Wallers/Buckler Burn junction has gone, buried in gravel in the mid 1990s, but there are good campsites in the forks here. **Monument Saddle** is not recommended, as the stream on the eastern side is very rough.

Times: Glenorchy Road to Wallers/Buckler Forks, 5 hrs.

PT 1793M SADDLE Buckler Burn to Stony Creek

This saddle is 1km south of Mt Buck and leads to Stony Creek. However, do not attempt to descend into Stony Creek from the lowest point. From the Wallers Creek forks, ascend open grass at the bottom end of Wallers Spur and sidle just above the beech forest, returning to the Buckler Burn at large shingle flats upvalley, E41 528 869. When the creek at E41 548 887 is reached, ascend tussock slopes on the true left to forks above. Continue east up tussock slopes then shingle to the range crossing point at E41 570 885.

From here, sidle down tussock slopes to E41 574 884. Descend to the spur at E41 577 885 at the 1500m contour and the valley floor at E41 579 889. Travel down this valley (locally known as Speargrass Creek) is easy until an 80m waterfall is reached. This is easily bypassed on goat trails down a steep gully on the true right of Speargrass Creek, behind a knoll at E41 583 885. Once in the gully, stay on the true right of this gully too. From the foot of the falls, boulder hop down the gravel and boulder creekbed between confined beech slopes to reach Stony Creek. Excellent little Stony Creek Hut (sleeps 2, open fire), is found on a small grass flat about 2km and 50 mins downstream on the true right. See Stony Creek in the Shotover Valley for further notes.

Times: Forks to Stony Creek Hut via 1793m saddle, 8 to 10 hrs.

MT LARKINS can also be approached up the Judah Road. Follow the road to above the 900m contour in Bonnie Jean Creek. Continue up the bulldozed track across the northern slopes of Mt Alaska to the head of Larkins Creek and a derelict but habitable scheelite miners hut. There is also a more recent hut, used by skiers, on the slopes of Mt Larkins. Continue up to the end of this steep bulldozed track. Gain a ridge and follow it SE to the west ridge of Mt Larkins, where an ice axe may be required. The west ridge gives a good scramble to the summit. Allow a full day.

CLARKE SLIP Rees Valley to Hunter Creek North Branch

This slip occurred shortly after the turn of the century following very heavy rain, but is now well consolidated. It gives reasonable travel to Clarke spur and the Hunter North Branch. Climb up the slip from the Rees. Towards the top of the slip swing north (right). Trails lead through the scrub around the head of the slip, then out to the left, into a tussock basin. Ascend this basin to the main ridge. Hunter Creek North Branch is accessible directly below down a tussock gully at E40 506 153 or else at E40 506 160. Between them is a line of slabs. There is also some scrub to contend with in the North Branch above the flats. There is a bivvy rock (sleeps 2) near the ridge at about the 1360m contour, E40 509 151. Those with alpine aspirations and equipment, ice axes at least, may continue to Mt Clarke.

HUNTER CREEK Rees River to the North Branch forks

From the Rees, an overgrown marked route leads up to the forks of the North and West branches. It is quite hard to follow in some places through windfall and snowbreak. Hunter Creek is crossed half way up on a confined bouldery crossing that will be impassable if the stream is up, but a natural rock bridge (steep on the true right, and pack hauling may be necessary) exists across Hunter Creek 100m downstream. A variation that avoids this crossing altogether is also described.

About 600m up the Rees from the Hunter confluence at E40 504 122, two white strips of permolat will be found on a beech tree at the bush edge. Follow markers up onto and across a bush terrace. These markers then sidle up a gully, briefly cross a tiny slip clearing north of pt 683m and pass back into the bush again.

At E40 498 128 a high level variation marked with one or two red permolat discs splits off the main route and climbs to bushline on the true left, avoiding the need to cross Hunter Creek in the gorge. (The variation heads uphill marked with an occasional blaze and permolat through the bushed gully at E40 497 137 to pt 1114m. From pt 1114m, sidle at about the 1100m contour to about E40 496 147 then descend steeply down a blazed shoulder to the forks. If the river is above normal, this route is preferable to the valley route to avoid the poor crossing in the gorge).

The old main marked route from E40 498 128 sidles on upvalley, crossing a bush terrace NW to the edge of the gorge. The marked route now sidles down to cross Hunter Creek at E40 495 132 in the gorge, about 100m distance before the high prominent bluff up valley. The crossing is only reasonable in low/normal flow. Downstream 100m there is an awkward but useable rockbridge. The marked route then climbs out up a bank diagonally downstream on the true right for 100m to another terrace. The bank is steep to clamber up here, but the route has old permolat markers on it. At the terrace, the markers head up valley again, but are immediately lost under a mess of broken trees. These can mostly be avoided by circling around the back, moving up valley about 200m to relocate the markers without climbing too much.

The marked route now sidles through a slot gorge under the big corner bluff and only about 50m above the river. Take care, then sidle up to a pleasant flat at E40 490 136 where there are campsites and a natural rock bridge. Staying on the true right, the markers sidle up valley, climbing 30 to 60m above the river beyond the flat, sometimes in prickly shield fern (*Polystichum* sp) and windfall, but mostly on reasonable going under beech trees. At the North/West Branch flats, the marked route finishes by the river, 100m beyond the boulders at E40 491 145, still on the true right. It is marked with two bands of white permolat on a tree at the bush edge. The West Branch joins the North Branch through a forbidding waterfall gut. The North Branch has easy travel up flats to the scrub, then the true left bank provides the easiest going as the scrub thickens.

When descending Hunter Creek, use the high level variation if there is any uncertainty about crossing in the gorge. However, if using the overgrown main marked route, make sure to pick up the markers at the bush edge on the true right and again at the small flat 40 mins down river from the main flats. The markers here too, are on the true right, 100m upstream from the natural rockbridge at the bottom of the flat and 5m up the bank into the trees. Likewise, further down where Hunter Creek is crossed, find the white markers where they leave the windfall at the edge of the terrace on the true right of Hunter Creek. From the terrace, they descend 100m up valley along the side of a steep 30m high bank to the river edge. Cross to the true left of Hunter Stream, (an awkward rock bridge 100m downstream) and climb out up a bank heading down valley to another bush terrace, now on the true left.

Time: Rees to the flats at the North and West Branch forks, 3.5 hrs.

The **WEST BRANCH** is most easily approached in summer from Kea Basin via the South Branch. See South Branch notes below. The route to the **West Branch from the North Branch** climbs to the 1460m contour over a shoulder and passes above high bluffs to the NW of the North and West Branch forks. In dry, fine conditions it is a reasonable route, mostly in tussock. This route begins up a fan between two creeks marked on the map at E40 491 152. It then crosses the northern creek and heads up a ramp NE, before climbing more directly up to the 1200m contour. Here, it is necessary to sidle back left, SW, across an unpromising line between bluffs at E40 491 155 on a goat trail, crossing a branch of the same creek crossed earlier, to gain tussock slopes beyond. This is the first key. Reasonably easy tussock slopes now lead slightly south but mainly west, climbing steadily up across streams and a spur, to the 1460m contour where there are a couple of cairns at E40 486 154. Sidle horizontally across to the ridge overlooking the Grant Glacier Lake. This is the second key. Descend easy tussock west to a creek, a low moraine ridge and the West Branch flats beyond.

In the reverse direction, climb to E40 484 153, sidle, then descend tussock slopes diagonally left. When they run out above bluffs at the 1200m contour, E40 491 155, sidle on a goat trail across a stream under a prow to easier slopes of tussock beyond. Descend tussock amongst scrub and sidle down valley to the valley floor.

(A variation on this route traverses about 50m above the West Branch stream down the true left to the corner above the waterfall. There is a giant dry overhang here formed by the bluffs above. This route now swings round at the base of bluffs onto a shelf above big bluffs overlooking the North Branch and climbs up tussock slopes swinging left and right to join the much easier previously described line at about the 1340m contour. This variation is included for completeness, but is not recommended.)

There is a reasonable bivvy rock (sleeps 2 to 3) at E40 464 154 under some bluffs at the edge of the flat in the West Branch. The route to the Bedford Valley over a col south of Cerberus is described in the Bedford Valley, Dart Valley notes, P 48.

The **SOUTH BRANCH** can be approached from Kea Basin. With good visibility in summer, this is the simplest access to both the South and West Branches. See Kea Basin for initial route notes. From Kea Basin, follow the ridge towards Esquilant Bivvy up to the tussock line. At a large cairn in gravel on the ridge at the 1720m contour, sidle across under bluffs, generally staying at the 1700m contour to the tarn studded shoulder overlooking the South Branch. Be aware of snow avalanche hazard from above. Avoid the route when fresh snow lies on it. Access to the South Branch and the West Branch from the shoulder is easy.

The South Branch can also be approached directly from the West Branch flats. Either follow the streambed or head up an alcove of tussock on the true left of the South Branch, about 100m distance from the stream. A grassy old flood channel here leads up through scrub to the base of a cataract in the South Branch. Follow up this gully through open scrub then climb onto boulders by the stream. Follow up the stream bank, sidling about 20m above the stream and cross the South Branch in open tussock country. The extensive gravel flat in the head is now easily accessible up a tussock gully at E40 470 138, amongst other routes. Shepherds Pass at the top of the South Branch can be crossed by climbing parties. See Bedford Valley, Dart Valley notes.

Times: Flats at the North and West Branch forks to West Branch flats, 3 hrs; West Branch to Kea Basin, 4 hrs.

KEA BASIN and Esquilant Bivvy

This delightful place, with interesting vegetation and a small gorge at the back of the basin, can be visited on an easy day trip from the Rees Valley. From Twenty Five Mile Creek, cross the river and the flats, aiming for the terrace 800m north of Lennox Falls. Look for an orange triangle on a red beech tree at the bush edge here, E40 496 103, where a small gully cuts back into the terrace. Once the benched formation back in the trees is found, follow it up as it zig zags to the south end of a terrace. Follow the track north along the terrace until it swings left and climbs again. Shortly, a rudimentary sign indicates a turnoff to the right to historic Earnslaw Hut (sleeps 3, no mattresses, DoC) which was renovated in the 1980s by the Varcoe family. It is 3 mins from the main track in a forest gully. Continue up the track to an excellent bivvy rock (sleeps about 8) at the lower rim of Kea Basin, E40 488 108.

Beyond the basin, the route to Esquilant Bivvy and Mt Earnslaw climbs through scrub and tussock (where the route is not very obvious) to the ridge to the north. Continue up this ridge, where cairns and a good ground trail develop again. At the 1400m contour there is a basin with a tarn in it. Although not entirely weatherproof, there is a bivvy rock (sleeps 3 or 4) on the slopes above the basin at the 1440m contour, E40 481 119, with a great view out over the lower Rees Valley. The route to Esquilant Bivvy (NZAC, sleeps 6, no mattresses or cooker) continues up the ridge then sidles south diagonally up across moderate snow slopes above bluffs, crossing the Birley Glacier to Wright Col. For alpine parties only from the snowline.

When descending from Kea Basin, be careful not to lose the track on the bench at the 760m contour where the real track swings right and a false ground trail (roughly following the trackline on E40 Ed.1) heads on down.

Note that both bivvy rocks in the basin are wrongly positioned on E 40 Ed.1.

Time: Twenty Five Mile Hut to Kea Basin, 2.5 hrs.

EARNSLAW BURN

Comparatively few parties visit the Earnslaw Burn, even though it is easily accessible and the views of Mt Earnslaw and its glacial icefalls in the head are dramatic. Normally a two day trip will be required. From the head of the valley, there is a choice of several routes for the return journey. In addition to the burn itself, the ridges to the west or east may be crossed to the lower Dart or the Rees respectively. Or simply follow the track up the valley and return down the ridge on the true left.

PARADISE ROAD TO THE BIVVY ROCK

The track up the true left of the Earnslaw Burn can be approached from the Glenorchy -Paradise Road on either side of the river.

1. From Glenorchy, cross the Earnslaw Burn bridge, turn right and follow a rough vehicle track for 500m on the true right beside the burn at the bush edge. Vehicles left here are shaded, but may be subject to flooding in bad conditions. Ford the river just below an old bridge site to a cairn and climb up to a grass terrace visible through the trees and look for markers on a tree at the edge of the terrace against the hill, along an old double fenceline.
2. Alternatively from Glenorchy, 1km before (south of) the Earnslaw Burn bridge, turn right through a gate and follow a side (public) road to within 200m of the river and bush edge. Park here on the true left of the Earnslaw Burn. Cross the grass terrace and pick up red markers where the terrace butts against the hill, overlooking the river at the bush edge.

The track climbs up from the Earnslaw Burn on the true left following markers along the edge of the bushed spur. It then sidles through open areas following orange poles and re-enters the bush. About halfway to the head of the valley, the track goes straight across a major slip. The last stream to

The view from Mt Alfred.

cross is also heavily slipped. The track, still on the true left, comes to a clearing by the river. Cross the river here to approach the bivvy rock (sleeps 4), which is uphill on the true right under bluffs as marked. This is your basic track and there may be an odd tree windfall, but trampers shouldn't have too much problem with it.

Camping upvalley, with better views and possibly fewer sandflies, may be preferable to staying in the bivvy rock. Gilkison Falls and stream, directly under the south face of Mt Earnslaw, are correctly labelled on E40 Ed.1. The comment in the 6th edition of Moirs placing them down valley was based on incorrect information.

Time: Glenorchy-Paradise Road to bushline bivvy rock, about 4 to 5 hrs.

ROUTES OUT OF THE UPPER EARNSLAW BURN

There are several alternative routes out of the upper Earnslaw Burn, listed below, that make nice two day round trips.

TO DESCEND THE RIDGE TO LOVERS LEAP on the true left of the Earnslaw Burn. Go 500m down the Earnslaw Burn from the bivvy rock to the first creek on the true left, where there are open flats in the bush. Ascend the spur on the true left of this creek and climb to the ridge before descending along it. Travel on the ridge, although unmarked, is easy and leads back to the track at the mouth of the Earnslaw Burn. There are great views along here.

LENNOX PASS from the Earnslaw Burn to the Rees. Follow the true left of the Earnslaw Burn up valley to the stream draining Lennox Pass. Climb up the stream to Lennox Pass. Steep scree near the top may be more easily bypassed on the true right (north) from the 1500m contour. From the pass, descend tussock to the basin below. Cross the stream draining the pass at the 1400m contour, and head generally in a straight line to cross Lennox Creek at the 800m contour. Lennox Creek is in a gut and impassable above and below this point, E40 491 097. The creek crossing is not obvious. Tussock and scrub on the true right lead to an easy crossing, but a trail on a small bluff on the true left is hidden behind a beech tree. Cairns should be found here coming from the opposite direction. It is essential to locate this crossing. Continue on the same diagonal descent as before and after entering the bush meet the Kea Basin track zig zags at the 620m contour. Descend to the Rees Valley.

Two main routes lead to Paradise in the Dart over the ridge running south from Turret Head.

TURRET RIDGE TO DANS PADDOCK. From the Earnslaw Burn, follow the creek draining pt 1640m. Climb the spur on the true left of it, and at about the 1100m contour, sidle NW over a small spur to a larger basin above falls. Ascend to the pass at pt 1676m. Do not descend west from here. Instead, sidle north on a scree ledge for about 800m at the 1700m contour to a spur descending off Turret Head. Follow this to the bushline at E40 424 053 where permolat markers should be found leading down to the 580m contour at the top of a grass and gravel fan feeding Dans Paddock from the east.

TURRET RIDGE TO RIVER JORDAN. From the bivvy rock in the Earnslaw Burn, go 200m up valley, climb and then sidle south on the tops above the bush and bluffs. Cross Turret Ridge at E40 456 018. Descend the spur on the true right of the river Jordan all the way to the Dart. While there is no track through the bush, the bush is easy, there is no scrub, and access to the ridge is also easy from both east and west. This is a better route than the last edition describes.

MT ALFRED

The summit of Mt Alfred offers wonderful views of Mt Earnslaw and the Glenorchy District. About 5km beyond the Rees bridge, a small carpark is set back off the Routeburn road at E40 425 925. Markers will be found at the bush edge, across a narrow strip of grass. Follow the markers till they finish about 1.5 hrs up and then continue to follow bits of red tape and a ground trail for 45 mins further to the bushline. Take careful note of this point, as it is not well marked. Once in the tussock it is best to gain the summit ridge as quickly as possible, heading up steep gullies to the north or even heading south, where access is easier. Grassland above the bushline is pastoral lease belonging to Earnslaw Station, (Mr Thomson, ph 03 442 5268) from whom permission should be sought for access.

Time: Road to Mt Alfred, 3 hrs.

AROUND QUEENSTOWN

DoC has developed a range of walks and tramps in the hills behind Queenstown. Visit their office at 37 Shotover Street Queenstown, (Ph 03 442 7933) for up to date information and pamphlets. There is also a very good guide to walking tracks around Queenstown available, called Wandering the Wakatipu, by Becky Reid, published in 1994 by the Information and Track Centre in Queenstown. As well as the scenery, this is a region of great historical interest where the tramper may retrace the steps of early miners. Many of these sites are within Goldfields Park or are at least on DoC land, and are protected. It should also be noted that fire is a major hazard in this area of dry windswept tussock and all parties should take special care.

BEN LOMOND AND BOWEN PEAKS

Ben Lomond Peak (1748m) in fine weather is a deservedly popular daytrip, with the upper sections especially scenic. But be aware that from lake level to the summit involves about 1500m climbing. The normal approach from Queenstown is through pine forest up the gravelled Skyline access road beginning at Lomond Crescent. A shorter option using the Gondola leads to this gravel track from the Skyline Complex. A second track beginning at One Mile Creek on the Glenorchy road also links into the Skyline access road. A good benched track, originally to access the Moonlight and Skippers goldfields in the 1860s and 1870s, climbs through tussock beyond the Skyline to the saddle. The track to the left leads to the top of Ben Lomond.

From the summit plane table, the extensive ranges of North West Otago, culminating in Mts Earnslaw and Aspiring, spread out in view. Bowen Peak is also easy to climb from the saddle, but the view is less extensive. In summer, start early and don't forget a drink bottle. Binoculars and a map will make the view much more interesting. For those who want to do something different, try setting out very early in the morning, do the climb in the chill morning air and see the sun rise over the Remarkables.

To Moke Lake. From the Ben Lomond-Bowen Peak saddle, a poled route, which follows an old mining pack track, leads north to the village of Sefferstown which lies amongst mature poplar trees at E41 648 736. The houses of Sefferstown are private. A 4WD road leads from Sefferstown to the DoC recreation camping reserve at Moke Lake outlet, where there is a locked gate across this road. Although there is public access, this route crosses Ben Lomond Station. For walks about Moke Lake, including crossings to Lake Dispute, 12 Mile Creek and the Glenorchy road, see DoC pamphlets available in Queenstown.

The Moonlight Track. Alternatively from Sefferstown, follow down the road a few mins towards the school house and turn right at the sign. Although there is public access, this route crosses Ben Lomond Station. (Be careful to avoid following another private, no exit road that heads up the Moonlight Valley). Follow a 4WD track that quickly leads to the old Moonlight track. (Avoid a no exit road that goes down to a stockbridge). The Moonlight track is then followed to Arthurs Point. Here, the track finishes at a sign on McChesneys road, which joins the Arthurs Point road right beside the Arthurs Point Pub. Sounds like a good finish to me.

Times: Lomond Crescent to Bowen Saddle, 2.5 hrs; Saddle to Ben Lomond peak, 45 mins; Saddle to Moke Lake, 2.5 hrs; Saddle to Arthurs Point, 3 hrs.

TWELVE MILE CREEK - LAKE ISOBEL - MT CRICHTON

This is a wonderful but demanding summer day trip. However, most of the route is unmarked and untracked, so it is really only suitable for the experienced and fit, armed with a copy of map E41. Alternatively, there is a good walking track along the true right of Twelve Mile Creek to the big sluice cut and Sam Summers Hut that loops back to the the Glenorchy Road along a spur overlooking Lake Dispute. Above the hut, Twelve Mile Creek itself is choked with windfalls and quite gorgy. An interesting feature of this area is a deep tailrace cut into solid rock which leads from the head of the sluiced cutting down to Twelve Mile Creek.

To reach Lake Isobel, leave the track just beyond the first side creek (Maori Gully) on the way in, and climb up above the top edge of the big sluice cutting. Pick up an old stock track and follow it through heavy burnt manuka scrub leading up the spur to the open tussock. Continue NW up this spur through a steep bluffy area. The ridge flattens out. Leave the ridge where it turns west and starts to climb again at E41 566 640. Sidle up through tussock slopes and basins above Twelve Mile Creek to gain the slopes directly below Lake Isobel on the true right of the creek. Continue up the creek to the lake outlet. Mt Crichton is an easy climb up a spur from about 1km SW of the outlet. There is a wonderful view of the Lake Wakatipu country from the top. A round trip can be made by dropping steeply through bracken fern directly west to reach the Glenorchy Road a few km south of Bennetts Bluff. However, this is more difficult than the ascent route, and permission should be sought from Creighton Station (Manager, Bruce Douglas, Ph 03 442 9934) to cross the lake-facing slopes.

Times: Road to Sam Summers Hut, about 45 mins; Twelve Mile Creek to Lake Isobel, about 4.5 hrs; Mt Crichton to the Glenorchy Road, 3 hrs down.

THE SHOTOVER CATCHMENT

The Shotover routes are arranged slightly differently. Initially, routes on the true right are described, then the upper Shotover Catchment, then tributaries on the true left. The upper Shotover and its tributaries are infrequently visited, but the area has a wild desolate appeal of its own. Cattle are farmed in more accessible valleys, and the area is one of windswept tussock and scrub. Special care must be taken to prevent fire.

WESTERN TRIBUTARIES AND ROUTES

ARTHURS POINT - MOONLIGHT - STONY CREEK - SKIPPERS

From the end of McChesneys Road, which begins at Arthurs Point Pub, DoC signs indicate a popular walking and cycling track that leads to Sefferstown. Just before Sefferstown, the track turns into a gravel road which then branches. To continue on up Moonlight Creek, permission is required from Ben Lomond Station (Manager John Foster, ph. 03 442 8893). Descend the branch that crosses Moke Creek and then runs along a series of sluiced terraces above the true right bank of the Moonlight. Huts at Butchers Creek are private. Just before these huts a gravel road branches off and crosses Moonlight Creek to the Moonlight Lodge (Private, Ben Lomond Station).

Moonlight Creek is actually a substantial river. There is a stock bridge across it just downstream of the Moke Creek confluence. The Moonlight gorge upstream is wild, rugged and very scrubby. From the Moonlight Lodge, a 4WD track leads past a locked station hut at E41 647 791. Follow this track on to a saddle a few hundred metres west of pt 1085m. Climb to pt 1085m and follow a faint old pack track along the ridge crest, overlooking the Shotover Gorge, to Mt Selwyn. Mt Selwyn is a great view point. The pack track can be followed north from Mt Selwyn into a tussock basin, then along the ridge leading to Stony Creek Terrace over pt 1008m, pt 941m, then pt 966m.

From the terrace, a shingle gut leads to a crossing of Stony Creek at E41 684 856. Either head downstream about 100m, cross and ascend another shingle gut to the low level sluicings on the true left, or alternatively head upstream about 300m, where an overgrown pack track zig zags up through a patch of beech forest on the true left to the high level terrace at E41 683 857. A 4WD track leads from here to Skippers.

UPPER MOONLIGHT CREEK is normally accessed from Mt Creighton Station and Twenty Five Mile Creek on the Glenorchy Road. Permission is required from Mt Creighton Station (Manager Bruce Douglas Ph 03 442 9934). The route follows farm tracks in past Lake Luna, before descending to the upper Moonlight Valley.

STONY CREEK

Stony Creek contains wild gorges in the lower reaches. However, there are routes into the mid Stony and from there crossings can be made to the Glenorchy Road. Good route finding skills and sure feet are required in this wild, isolated country, which can suffer from extremes of weather. Passes across the Richardson Mountains are all likely to have snow on them until at least mid January.

ROUTES INTO MID STONY CREEK

VIA MURPHYS SADDLE. A 4WD track is followed all the way to Murphys Saddle from the Moonlight Lodge. Then from Murphys Saddle, follow the 4WD track north for almost 2km to E41 635 833 and sidle west to gain a spur at E41 629 835. Follow this spur up towards the 1500m contour and sidle as practical under Mt Gilbert onto a spur to the north at E41 617 837. Follow this spur down towards Upper Stony Creek, keeping over on the western side of the spur below the 1100m contour. The last section of the spur is steep and bluffy and it will be necessary to swing left towards the bottom down a grassy basin, descending into Gilbert Creek (local name) at about E41 609 853. Beginning right at the forks, there is an old permolat marked route along the true right bank of Stony Creek upstream to the ex-NZFS Stony Creek Hut (2 bunk, open fire). This marked route stays within 20m of the river all the way.

Alternatively, continue down the 4WD track from Murphys Saddle to the mining hut on a terrace above Stony Creek. Upvalley, look for a rock like a thumb and follow an animal trail at the base of it, at about the 650m to 700m contour, through bluffs. This then leads onto a scrubby manuka face. Sidle down across this towards the edge of the beech forest upvalley, reaching the riverbed at about E41 612 854, 10 mins below the big bend. Beginning a few hundred metres below the Gilbert Creek confluence at the bend, a permolat marked route continues up the true right of Stony Creek to Stony Creek Hut. Alternatively, pick up this marked route at the Gilbert Creek confluence.

LOW LEVEL ROUTE FROM SKIPPERS. This is steep in parts and requires Stony Creek to be low. From the Skippers Schoolhouse, follow a walking track along terraces down the true right of the Shotover to the Pleasant Creek Terrace. Cross Stony Creek to the south (true right) bank, involving steep scrubby climbs on both sides. See notes on the crossing place under Arthurs Point/Moonlight/Stony/Skippers above.

Climb to the prominent water race on the true right above Stony Creek. Fluming carries the race around a bluff at the start and it is necessary to follow animal tracks over this bluff and back down to the race. The race is then followed to Murphys Creek South. Descend into Murphys Creek South beginning about 100m above its junction with Stony Creek, where a route will be found through a patch of bush and down a narrow spur. Follow Murphy Creek South down to Stony Creek.

From this confluence, despite being in a canyon, travel upstream in the bed of Stony Creek is easy for about 3km until a bluff, pool and falls in a steepsided gorge blocks the way at E41 625 848. Keeping to the true right, climb about 150m over this bluff. Now gradually descend, following animal trails on the edge of the beech forest above the river. An old cut and permolat marked route can be found near a large slip beside the river a few hundred metres below the big bend, or alternatively pick it up at the Gilbert Creek confluence. Follow this marked route to the hut.

Note that travel in Stony Creekbed is impossible in high flows. In the vicinity of the miner's hut at E41 634 847, there is a bulldozed ramp out of the Stony Canyon on the true right.

Time: Skippers to Stony Creek Hut, at least 5 hrs.

UPPER STONY CREEK

Although the surrounding country is wild and rugged, travel in Upper Stony Creek above Stony Creek Hut is straightforward if the river is low. Keep to the riverbed all the way except for a 20 min section immediately upstream from the hut. Here, the river drops rapidly and a partially cut, but otherwise unmarked route, sidles through bush above the river as necessary on the true right. There is also a lightly confined section for 500m below approx E40 602 914, which is easily travelled in normal conditions. Good campsites exist from E40 605 908 downstream with some wonderful flats. Beech forest ceases upvalley at E40 608 904. A good campsite exists in the upper valley at E40 601 934.

Routes exist to the Flood Burn (see below), Ox Burn and Buckler Burn (see Rees Valley notes).

Time: Stony Creek Hut to top forks, 3 hrs.

CROSSING INTO STONY CREEK FROM THE FLOOD BURN

A reasonably straightforward but high route exists up Duncans Creek from the Flood Burn and over the range west of Mt Aurum into Stony Creek. The crossing point and upper basin are not visible from lower Duncans Creek, but are hidden to the right (looking up). From Duncans Flat, follow up Duncans Creek. Climb up past a cataract at E40 627 979 on the true right, taking a line to avoid the rougher ground, but not too far from the creek. Return to sidle within 20m of the creek on the true right, often on shingle slopes. There is a huge boulder in the creek at E40 628 965, and it forms a bivvy rock by the stream. Although noisy and subject to flooding after any serious rain, it does offer good lunch shelter and a fine gravel floor.

At E40 627 961 pick up a small direct spur on the true left between small forks and climb the spur into an upper basin at E40 625 955. Where the spur is rocky, an easier line exists in a tussock gully beside it. Cross the stream in the upper basin to the true right and climb the tussock spur on the edge of it to the range at the Mt Aurum end of the saddle to avoid small bluffs on both sides of the range. Cross at E40 623 949 on shingle and descend the shingle basin below, sidling right to descend spurs down either side of the stream leading into the main upper basin of Stony Creek. There is a reasonable campsite by the stream at E40 601 934.

Times: Duncans Flat to saddle, 5 hrs; Saddle to Stony Creek campsite, 2 hrs.

FROM THE OLD SKIPPERS TOWNSHIP SITE

Skippers, an historic, popular and beautiful area, is in a recreation reserve managed by DoC. Branching off the Coronet Peak Skifield road, a rough, mostly one lane road leads up the Shotover Valley to it. Although 2WD cars regularly use the road, and a competent, careful driver in reasonable weather shouldn't have major problems, there are many places where clearance can be an issue and the state of the road varies from season to season. Some insurance companies don't cover vehicles using it. The road can become blocked by slips and storms in any season, but late summer and autumn are the more settled times to visit. Near Skippers, the road divides. The higher road finishes about 15km upvalley at Branches Station. The lower one descends to cross the vehicular swingbridge over the Shotover, and finishes at Skippers, about 1km further on, where there is a pleasant DoC campsite with track information about a range of excellent day and part day walks. There is cellphone coverage outside the old schoolhouse here (2003). Allow almost an hour to drive in.

SAWYERS CREEK CRYSTAL MINE AND MT SILVERHORN

From Burkes Terrace above the Skippers Cemetery, a signposted track leads up the true right of Sawyers Creek to the stamper and hut (private) at the Crystal Mine. From the stamper, the remains of a wire ropeway are followed north to the site of the mine tunnel, about 200m above the creek. Continue up past the mine to gain the main ridge line, just east of trig H. This ridge is followed all the way west to Mt Silverhorn. Several steps in the ridge, at trig H and above, are bypassed on the northern side. A direct descent can also be made from here into Upper Stony Creek, e.g. down the spur to the west of pt 1512m, reaching the river at flats, E41 612 867.

Time: Skippers to Crystal Mine, 2 hrs return; Skippers to Mt Silverhorn , 5 hrs.

SKIPPERS CREEK AND MT AURUM

A pleasant weekend trip up the Left Branch of Skippers Creek, onto Mt Aurum and down the Right Branch is described. (Note that these names of Left and Right Branch were named in early times when explorers named rivers and creeks as they went (looked) up them, before the current convention of true left and right evolved). This trip involves multiple crossings of Skippers Creek, which can quickly become impassable with heavy rain. From the old Skippers Cemetery a 4WD road is followed down into Sawyers Creek and around to Skippers Creek. Several crossings later, an old 1930s powerhouse will be found on the true right. Cross here, on a ford that can be tricky if the creek is high and follow a rough trail on the true left through scrub to the crest of a 10m high concrete dam. The dam is completely full of debris. From here the route follows up the gravelly bed of Skippers Creek, crossing innumerable times.

A trail starts on the true left of the **LEFT BRANCH,** but many crossings follow. After about 1 hr the track leaves the stream and traverses on an old bridle path on the true right to the site of New Zealand's first hydro electric power site on a high terrace above the stream. The plant, built in 1886 to supply power to the Bullendale Mine has been partly restored. A large hut nearby, Dynamo Hut, (sleeps 10) has been refurbished. From the power site easy open travel on tussock flats on the true right leads to the Aurum Basin. There is another hut in a patch of bush on the true left, 30 mins beyond the power site. There is an old hut, made of flattened water pipes, and a stamper battery in the middle of Aurum Basin. This was built by Archie McNichol, a previous runholder of the old Mt Aurum Station, in the 1940s to mine gold from the Copper Creek reefs.

To climb **MT AURUM,** traverse to the end of the basin and climb up an obvious gully under the huge rocky SE face of Mt Aurum to reach a notch in the ridge ahead, at E40 641 952. From the notch, the east ridge of Mt Aurum is a steep, but straightforward scramble in summer.

From E40 652 938 snowgrass slopes lead directly east down into the upper reaches of the **RIGHT BRANCH.** Follow directly down the rough stream bed to reach Caspers Flat and a little further on the site of the Bullendale Mine at the junction with Murdochs Creek. Do not drink the water in Murdochs Creek, due to heavy metal pollution from the mining. Machinery is strewn

■ The upper Flood Burn from Ox Burn Saddle (pt 1734m).

around everywhere. On the opposite (true right) bank, high in the scrub several huts still remain from a township that once housed 200 people. A bridle path through the bush on the true left of Murdochs Creek leads to a secluded little flat above the river with more house sites, including a bakery and several poplar trees. Several hundred metres downstream of the mine on the true right is the site of the old pub, a good campsite. About 100m higher and 200m downstream an old house is hidden among briar, matagouri, and wild fruit trees.

When Old Man Creek joins Skippers Creek a bridle path (Bullendale Track) will be picked up on the true left. The path sidles high above a small gorge to rejoin Skippers Creek about 300m downstream of the Left Branch Junction. When coming the other way, the entrance to this bridle track is found near a clump of poplars on the true left. In midsummer, when the creek is low, it is possible to traverse straight down the gorge. A deep slot, just upstream of the Left Branch junction, is traversed by a cut and blasted ledge on the true right.

Times: Skippers to Dynamo Hut, 2.5 hrs; Hut to Aurum Basin, 1.5 hrs; Aurum Basin to Mt Aurum, 3 to 4 hrs; Aurum Basin to Bullendale, about 3 hrs; Bullendale to Skippers, 3 to 4 hrs. At least 2 or 3 hrs should be set aside for exploring the Bullendale area.

FLOOD BURN

Below Duncans Flat, the Flood Burn is very rugged. The usual route into Duncans Flat leads from Sixteen Mile Hut over into the Flood Burn from the north instead. This is much easier than the gorge. From Duncans Flat, a crossing via Ox Burn Saddle can be made to Cashs Flat and the Rees Valley. Allow 3 days from the Shotover to the Rees. Snow can be expected on the saddle until January. See Rees Valley notes for the latter part of this route.

SHOTOVER AT SIXTEEN MILE HUT TO DUNCANS FLAT

From Sixteen Mile Hut, the route to Duncans Flat crosses the first creek to the west and climbs the first prominent ridge at E40 651 055 to pt 1704m on the Mt Bowyang-Mt Campbell ridge. To reach Duncans Flat, descend and cross the creek draining Mt Campbell to the true left at about the 1500m contour. Beyond some winter avalanche debris, a poorly defined old animal trail may be found by keeping high on the true left, until a descent to Duncans Flat can be made. However, scrub is getting thicker on this route. Alternatively, follow the creek bed to the flat.

In the opposite direction, follow the true left of the Savage Burn and then the tributary draining Mt Campbell to the high saddle at pt 1704m. On the Sixteen Mile Creek side of the saddle, head for the rocky ridge a little to the east of the lowest point on the saddle. It widens into a spur which leads down to near Sixteen Mile Hut.

At Duncans Flat on the true right of the Flood Burn, in the position marked on E40 Ed. 1, there is a tidy little Station hut (2 bunk, open fire). Between the hut and the river there is also a poor rock bivvy for 2. About 50m below the Savage Burn Junction, on the true left, there is an overhang that would also offer reasonable shelter for 2 or 3, about 5 to 10m above the Flood Burn as it enters the gorge. A tent could also be pitched here, but in fine weather there are plenty of better campsites on the flats.

Times: Sixteen Mile Hut to Campbell Bowyang Saddle, 5 hrs; Saddle to Duncans Flat, 4 hrs.

LOWER FLOOD BURN GORGE Hazeels Terrace to Duncans Flat

This difficult route involves extended sidling along steep, bluffy cliffs high above the river on the true right. It is very seldom used, and is not recommended for those carrying packs through to the Rees.

Such people will find the route from Sixteen Mile Hut, described above, preferable. Cross the Shotover at Branches Flat and climb onto Hazeels Terrace at the Flood Burn confluence, where there is a hut. Head through trees at the back of the flat to an old water race and follow it around the hillside to Dwans Creek. Descend slightly, then continue around the hillside, keeping high at about the 700m contour, until a sheep and goat trail leads through bluffs to the crossing at Shingly Creek. Don't try to travel up the bed of the Flood Burn to Shingly Creek as it is very badly gorged with waterfalls.

From Shingly Creek, climb the spur on the west bank to a high terrace at about the 700m contour and from here follow another water race as far as possible. Sidle at the same height then at about the 800m contour up to Ballarat Hut (sleeps 3), originally owned by Mt Aurum Station, on a terrace just below where the creek divides in three, and correctly shown on E40 Ed.1. From Ballarat Hut, sidle around the hillside at about the same height until Duncans Flat can be seen, then descend to it. There are many bluffs here, and finding a route through may well be very difficult. The best option is to climb high if necessary.

A variation on this route exists for strong, confident parties when the Flood Burn is low. Follow the above route upvalley until overlooking Ballarat Creek. Descend to the Ballarat/Flood Burn forks (difficult) and follow the river bed upvalley to Duncans Flat. This will involve very deep wades and crossings.

Times: Allow a full day from the Shotover to Duncans Flat via the gorge.

DUNCANS FLAT TO PRINCE OF WALES FLAT

From Duncans Flat, Prince of Wales Flat is reached by following up the bouldery Flood Burn, crossing as necessary. This is normally fairly easy, but can become more difficult if the river is high. If crossing the river is difficult, then the true right is the preferred side to sidle on. At Prince of Wales Flat, a detour on the true right SE of two small tussock knolls is slightly quicker than following the river. To approach Ox Burn Saddle (pt 1734m) from Prince of Wales Flat, continue by the river, sometimes following goat trails on the true right towards the head of the valley. Travel is easy. See Twelve Mile Creek (Ox Burn) notes in the Rees Valley for further information.

Time: Duncans Flat to Prince of Wales Flat, 3.5 hrs.

Alexander McKay Falls in Sixteen Mile Creek, showing the route around them.
Bob Entwistle

SIXTEEN MILE CREEK Shotover Junction to head

This valley contains the impressive Alexander McKay Falls, pleasant flats below them, and gives access to all the Centaur Peaks. A lightly marked route leads up to the Robertson Creek forks from the bush edge, with route entrances and exits to each patch of bush marked with QE2 Conservation Covenant signs. From the Shotover terraces overlooking Sixteen Mile Creek parties can either sidle tussock slopes on the south bank, descend and wade up the gorge, or a mixture of both until past the sizeable creek from the south at E40 632 059.

Once across this creek, climb 30m onto a tussock terrace on the true right of Sixteen Mile Creek and sidle across to the bush edge, looking for a large white plastic paint lid on a large beech trunk, partially hidden by branches at the 760m contour, E40 628 056. From the lid, the marked route (white permolat) sidles across to a smaller creek up valley.

Follow this open creek up for 70m distance to another paint lid, which indicates the beginning of an old cut marked route through the scrub. This marked route sidles out of the creek and leads up valley over a prominent shoulder across to a clump of beech forest at the 800m contour, E40 625 055. Continuing with intermittent cairns and permolat, the marked route sidles at this contour to gravel slopes 10 to 20m above the river then keeps in this slip zone, sidling up to the forks and finishing in a patch of beech forest close to the river. There are good campsites between the forks of Robinson and Sixteen Mile streams.

From the junction, the bed of the Sixteen Mile can be followed a short way, then the true right gives reasonable going until a crossing is made on the corner at the beech forest edge, E40 619 060. Once on the true left, minor goat trails close to the river in shingle and scrub lead up valley to extensive flats in about 1.5 hrs. To the north, Lima Creek enters from a spectacular gorge, while straight ahead are the Alexander McKay Falls, descending bluffs which appear to block the valley.

From the head of the flats, minor goat trails lead in 10 mins to the start of the gorge in front of the falls. This small gorge is turned by a climb of 30 to 50m on the true left bank and a descending sidle over unpleasant shingle slopes to a ford in the gorge (care needed with packs). Alternatively, it is also possible to bypass this piece of gorge on the true right, crossing a low spur at about the 1160m contour, but this involves a very steep scrub bash on the down valley side of the spur where the goat trails are mostly overgrown.

Up valley from the ford or spur, on the true right at E40 595 078, follow up an easy tussock tongue with a shingle patch at the top of it at the base of the main bluffs, about 200m south of, and across from, the main falls. From the shingle patch, to negotiate these bluffs, sidle left (looking up) up a sloping tussock shelf and at a distance of about 350m from the river climb fairly easily up past these bluffs. Sidle to the right on another tussock shelf at about the 1420m contour to a shoulder at the same height overlooking the falls and the valley above. Old remains of heavy goat trails are followable through much of the bluffs.

Travel up valley is straightforward except for the 50m fall marked at the 1700m contour, which can be bypassed on the true left up a spur beside the falls, although it doesnt look promising. Centaur Peaks are all easily approached from this basin above the falls, up an undulating glacier, but the high summits involve exposed climbing on loose rock.

Descending. Pick up the spur on the true left at the 1700m contour to bypass the first waterfall; sidle onto the tussock knoll at the 1420m contour on the true right, just above Alexander McKay Falls; stay low from the flats down to the Robertson junction and pick up permolat on beech trees, close to the river on the true right below the junction.

Times: Sixteen Mile Hut to Robertson forks, 1.5 to 2 hrs; Forks to Lima flats, 1.5 hrs; Flats to basin above McKay falls, 2.5 hrs; Basin to above 50m falls, 1.5 hrs.

Lima Peak is accessible by following grassy leads through the scrub a short distance up the Sixteen Mile from Lima Creek. The bluffs look spectacular, but are bypassed without difficulty.

LOCHNAGAR

This lake (Goats Lake), formed an estimated 500 to 1000 years ago by a tremendous slip from the north side of the valley, is well worth a visit. A hut built in 1982 by the lake was burnt down in 1988 along with a considerable amount of ground cover. However, the ground cover is growing back, and the hut was replaced by the Borrells who ran Branches Station at that time and their friends as a 150th Anniversary of N.Z. project in 1990. Their wonderful little hut is full of character (sleeps approx 4, and has a small open fire; (take extreme care!).

SHOTOVER VALLEY TO LOCHNAGAR

The route to Lochnagar from the Shotover 4WD track begins by a small pyramid of metal stakes and a wooden sign lying in the grass at E40 649 116. Initially a 4WD track leads up the true left of Lake Creek, sidling a small gorge opposite the Glencairn junction and descending into the Lake Creek basin above. This track crosses to the true right on a reasonable ford. A cable with a bucket pulley slung under it also crosses the creek here but is not operational. The 4WD track continues up valley now on the true right and generally not far from the creek (ignore the higher track marked on E40 Ed 1) to a QE 2 Protected Places sign and track sign to the left (looking upvalley).

The marked route leaves the bulldozed line and follows a stock track up through the scrub and grass clearings. It is only occasionally marked with red or white permolat, but with care the ground trail provides a reasonable lead through speargrass and scrub up to the Goatel. This is a large rock bivvy at E40 628 129 with a floor of compacted dry goat droppings near the lip of the slip, but with no close water supply. Climb up to the top of the Goatel Rock, where this name is painted in white and visible from above, and follow cairns and white paint lines across open ground to Lochnagar Hut (correctly marked on the map), close to the lake outlet.

Descending. It is important to locate the Goatel sign, painted in white on the bivvy rock at E40 628 129, from above.

Times: Shotover to Lochnagar Hut, 2.5 to 3 hrs up; returning, 1.5 to 2 hrs.

LOCHNAGAR TO SNOWY CREEK

This is a high route requiring reasonable experience, that crosses snow (ice axe necessary) above steep slopes until late summer. Cross the Lochnagar outlet and head up a reasonably open spur to the north, surrounded by *Dracophyllum* scrub. Once above the scrub, sidle further north into a basin and then easy slopes lead to the saddle between pt 1896m and pt 1865m. Head 250m north along the ridge to E40 631 160 before descending steeply to snowgrass benches above Pine Creek. Sidle along these benches, following the odd animal trail to reach the broad basin at the head of Pine Creek. Cross the wide flat pass between Pine Creek and Snowy Creek. About 300m over the pass at E40 625 186 a prominent spur between two deep creeks leads straight down to Snowy Creek. A rock band at the top of this spur is bypassed on the left. Be sure to climb out onto Rees Saddle and the track from the bottom of flats in Snowy Creek to avoid an impassable gorge below. Pine Creek itself is very steep and slippery and is not recommended. Glencairn Creek is badly gorged and is not recommended for tramping parties either.

Time: Lochnagar to Dart Hut, about 10 hrs.

THE UPPER SHOTOVER RIVER

The road from Skippers to Branches Flat is not always passable by cars. Huts around and beyond Branches Flat are the property of Branches Station (Manager ph 03 441 8421). To travel beyond Branches Flat permission should be sought from the manager. Wheeled access is discouraged, but foot access is usually granted. A stock bridge has been built across the Shotover opposite Campbells Saddle, 3 km downstream from The Branches at F40 723 957. There is also an open cableway in working condition (1998) at McLeods Bluff, F40 728 914.

From Branches Flat follow the Shotover riverbed upvalley between the Polnoon and the Shiel Burn, sidling where necessary on good stock trails. The Polnoon is bridged but carries almost no water here, as it pours into the Shiel Burn through the Polnoon Tunnel. A 4WD road now returns to the riverbed and continues up valley, fording the Shiel Burn (on a stock bridge at F40 703 043), the Shotover below Sixteen Mile Creek, Sixteen Mile Creek itself, and a further three Shotover crossings before Hundred Mile Hut is reached. In a washed-out state the 4WD track continues as far as Pine Creek Flat. A side road follows the true left of Lake Creek to a ford then the true right bank to about the 770m contour close to Lake Creek. Another 4WD track leads from Lindsays Tarn to the Polnoon Tunnel.

The ford in Sixteen Mile gorge can be avoided by following a track over the shoulder on the true left, or by a stock bridge across the gorge where the Shotover cuts through the tip of Greenland Spur, as marked on E40. The Sixteen Mile Hut (6 bunk, open fire; Care!) sits on a high terrace to the south, well back from the river, as marked on E 40, and near a clump of willows. A 4WD track leads up to it, also as marked on E40. The second hut marked on the map is really only a 3 sided shelter. About 5km further on, Lake Creek joins from the west, and Hundred Mile Hut (3 bunk, open fire, Branches Station) is about 2km above this junction on the true left bank of the Shotover as marked on E 40 (but wrongly marked on older inch to mile series maps).

When the 4WD track finishes at Pine Creek Flat, a stock track, occasionally marked with cairns, continues on the true left 10 to 70m vertically above the bouldery river through otherwise scrubby slopes to Junction flat. Tummel Burn Hut (Branches Station, 3 bunk, open fire) at Junction Flat is on the true right of Tyndall Stream, at the top of the flat, E40 662 177, not the position marked on E40, Ed 1.

Times: Skippers to Branches Flat, 4 to 5 hrs; Branches Flat to Sixteen Mile Hut, 4 to 5 hrs; Sixteen Mile Hut to Hundred Mile Hut, about 2.5 hrs; Hundred Mile Hut to Junction Flat, about 1.5 hrs.

SHOTOVER SADDLE Shotover River to Matukituki River

Reasonably experienced tramping parties should have no problem with this subalpine tussock crossing provided the weather is okay. The views are great, and the head basins of the Shotover and Shotover Saddle offer tops campsites with water in summer and early autumn. This route is described in reverse in the West Matukituki notes.

SHOTOVER SIDE The logbook at Tummel Burn Hut, however, has a number of unhappy accounts of scrub bashing and slow gorge travel. The most direct route avoids all that and is probably best and fastest. Cross Tyndall Stream opposite the hut to a white permolat marker post on the true left, E40 662 178. An overgrowing but followable old permolat marked route leads up to the NW, and 20 mins from the flat reaches an open creekbed with a shallow gravel gully leading up above it. Follow up this gully to the NE for a further 20 mins, helped by intermittent cairns. Further up the terrain is less steep and tussock begins. Close to here, dead celery pine trunks on the end of the ridge indicate the remains of a 1970s fire. (1020m contour approx, and E40 663 182).

Between the 1100m and the 1200m contours, head due north on tussock, crossing a dry stream (where there are usually tarns in basins) at the 1260m contour. Sidle over a shoulder at the 1300m contour and descend into the upper basin of Tyndall Stream, also at the 1260m contour. Easy short grass slopes on the true right lead up to the saddle. There is no need for scrub bashing and there is not much speargrass (*Aciphylla* spp) on this route.

The Tummel Burn and Tyndall Stream have also been used as routes to Shotover Saddle. Of the two valleys, the Tummel Burn has less scrub (but plenty of speargrass) and easier travelling than Tyndall Stream. Sidle above the bluffs on the true left of the Tummel Burn then descend to and travel up the Tummel Burn. Tyndall Stream has a gorge to bypass on the true left near the junction, then flats give reasonable travel for 1.5km. Above that, travel is slow with boulders in the stream and thick scrub at the edges. The stream is negotiable at low flows.

MATUKITUKI SIDE The descent to the Matukituki Valley is steep but not difficult. However, there are many small bluffs below and downstream from the saddle, making a sidle up valley the best option. From Shotover Saddle, descend into the basins of Brides Veil Stream, sidling left at about the 1000m contour across to roughly E39 667 242. From here, continue down easy tussock slopes and grass spurs to the valley track, passing about 350m to the true left of Brides Veil Fall. Because of many small bluffs below Tummel Burn saddle, it is adviseable to sidle across and follow this same route down.

Times: Tummel Burn Hut to Shotover Saddle via spur, 4.5 hrs; Shotover Saddle to Matukituki Valley, about 2.5 hrs.

EASTERN SHOTOVER TRIBUTARIES

Much of this country is in Branches Station (Manager, Ph 03 441 8421), and permission should be sought from the manager before entering it. Access on foot is usually granted.

CHURCH HILL AND CREEK

Climbing Church Hill is one of a number of trips in the Branches Station area. It gives an excellent view of the upper Shotover and its tributaries. Allow a day for the return journey. The forks of Church Hill Creek provide a pleasant camping area and further up the north branch is a swampy area of interest to naturalists. From Branches Station, cross Carmichaels Creek to the Amphitheatre, but instead of descending to the Polnoon, work east around the lip of the basin to meet Church Hill Creek. A trail leads up the true left bank to the forks. The Polnoon Burn may be reached from here by heading north through the swamp until overlooking the Polnoon Gorge, then descending the hillside. The ford to reach the stock trail on the true right of the Polnoon is not good, however.

POLNOON TUNNEL

Follow the 4WD track from Branches Station to where it peters out at The Neck, a little beyond the gate in a recent fence. This fence straddles the Neck roughly above where the Polnoon Tunnel is. The tunnel was driven in 1930-32 as part of a mining scheme. It is 270m long and carries practically the whole flow of the Polnoon Burn, which pours out of the tunnel on the Shiel Burn side in a powerful waterfall.

SHIEL BURN

The Shiel Burn Hut (5 bunks, open fire, and looking a bit worn) is 1km NNE of the tunnel, high above the river as marked. A single dark tree looking like a solitary beech from a distance, but in fact is a lawson cypress, indicates the huts position. From the hut, the few parties who continue up the

Shiel Burn do so by sidling down to the riverbed upvalley. Here, the Shiel Burn flattens off, with good going on fine gravel up the riverbed to begin with. More varied river travel with some scrambling follows. There is a small upright hut, Top Shiel Burn Bivvy (2 bunk, Branches Station) in the headwaters, as marked on E40.

POLNOON BURN

From The Neck, sidle the true right of the Polnoon to a crossing at Cabin Creek, then follow the true left upvalley to the flats. From the end of the 4WD track at The Neck, a stock trail continues on a climbing sidle to the 780m contour at F40 723 047. It then keeps this height and is easily followed to the ridge before Duries Creek. Descend 80m (height) down the spur to cross Duries Creek 100m (distance) from the Polnoon, and 30 mins from the 4WD track. A clear path exists through the scrub. At Duries Creek do not follow a tempting low level trail. It leads to dense scrub, and then back to the river. Climb 180m up the spur on the true left of Duries Creek to about the 880m contour, (do not follow the spur too far) then sidle, still on a good stock trail, keeping this height. When the 880m contour at F40 748 044 is reached, a descending sidle leads to the Polnoon just before Cabin Creek, about 1 hr from Duries Creek. Cross the river at a shingle ford.

At **Cabin Creek** there is a station hut, Cabin Creek Hut, (open fire, floor room for 5) as marked. A stock trail, now on the true left of the Polnoon, leaves Cabin Creek Hut but becomes indistinct in slips and scrub. Keep your height, gradually climbing and sidling about 100m above the river and pick up the trail again when the slopes are more stable. The trail now quickly leads to Blue Creek, about an hour from Cabin Creek. Blue Creek is interesting in that it previously flowed into the Motutapu. A moraine dam has forced it to flow into the Polnoon over a low rock ridge, into which it has cut a deep narrow gorge.

Above **Blue Creek,** both sides of the Polnoon Burn are negotiable and the best route will involve several fords. After an hour a large flat and Polnoon Hut (3 bunk, small stove, Branches Station) are reached on the true left. A further 2 hrs easy travel leads to a large 'shelter rock' on the true right, about 150m from the river at F40 752 139. This rock, however, offers no real protection from rain.

Trails upvalley are now somewhat indistinct and speargrass a major problem in places. A reasonably straightforward route to Sharks Tooth Hut follows. Where the river becomes gorged, continue up the riverbed to F40 755 147. Climb out here on the true left, following a light stock trail upvalley onto a tussock terrace about 50m above the river. Follow this terrace and descend to cross the stream draining Black Peak near its confluence with the river. At F40 752 154 climb onto another terrace on the true left and cross it at about the 900m contour until a stream is reached at F40 752 159, a little over 1 hr from the 'shelter rock'.

Upvalley from this stream is a large mass of partly scrub covered ground known as The Rockfall. An old stock trail, now indistinct, started about 100m upriver from the stream and led right, climbing steeply through scrub to the open tussock before dropping 100m to the top flats. An alternative is to follow the streambed up east around the Rockfall and descend from the saddle to the flats upvalley. There is speargrass to negotiate either way.

Sharks Tooth Hut (6 bunk, open fire, Branches Station/DoC), correctly located on F40 Ed. 1, has a checkered history, having once been almost buried in gravel (since dug out). A cracked roof ridge due to snow has also been fixed. Sharks Tooth is now quite close and is accessible for climbing parties. Craigroyston appears more difficult. The west branch of the Polnoon issues from a formidable looking gorge, a poor approach to Mt Repulse.

A crossing to the Matukituki may be made via the saddle between Sharks Tooth and Craigroyston by climbing parties, passing the first waterfall on the true left into the couloir above the falls. Alternatively, a much easier crossing can be made to the Matukituki via the Leaping Burn. See notes below.

Times: Allow 2 long days for the return journey from Branches Flat to the head of the Polnoon, or 3 for a more enjoyable visit.

POLNOON - LEAPING BURN - PHOEBE CREEK

This tussock crossing is not marked, and descends steep slopes between bluffs into the upper Leaping Burn. Travel up the east branch of the Polnoon is relatively straightforward, keeping in or close to the stream, and sidling when necessary in tussock or on gravel, mainly on the true right. There are good campsites under the saddle on gravel and drier ground near the stream. If you get it right, animal trails ease the way through tussock up to the saddle at pt 1449m. From the saddle, head to F39 782 206, a small knoll at the 1400m contour. Descend diagonally down towards F39 786 206, just above the 1200m contour, then head for the valley floor. This route remains in tussock and is not difficult in good weather, but it looks a bit mean from below.

To continue out to the Matukituki Road, follow the Leaping Burn and trails on the true right as necessary to the beech forest edge by the river. The Leaping Burn descends into a massive gorge below here, and it is important to sidle out correctly. About 300m downvalley from the first beech forest, sidle across a slip on the true right and gain height up to a shoulder of pasture with a fence on it at F39 820 202. From this shoulder, sidle without losing height under bluffs across to the bush edge at F40 822 194 before descending a gravelly stock trail to where Phoebe Creek opens onto the Matukituki flats.

It is important that any stock in the Leaping Burn or on the pasture shoulder remain undisturbed and are not driven up or downvalley. Parties planning to use this route should call the manager of Matukituki Station (Ph 03 443 4342) for access permission.

Times: Sharks tooth Hut to Saddle, 2.5 hrs; Saddle to Leaping Burn, about 1 hr; Leaping Burn to Matukituki Road, 2 hrs.

TREBLE CONE SKIFIELD - MOTUTAPU - POLNOON

Treble Cone Skifield road and the main quad chairlift are now open during summer on a limited basis. By following the road to the saddle (where there is a locked hut that is part of the skilift operation), the head of the Motutapu can be accessed. From the saddle, follow down tussock on the true left of the stream to flats at the 1350m contour. Sidle out on the true right at about the 1380m contour and keep this height until well down the spur. Descend to the Motutapu tributary draining the low saddle with Blue Creek. Easy travel back up this tributary along the bank leads past the collapsed remains of the hut marked on F40 Ed.1 at F40 805 053. Continued easy tussock travel leads to a swampy area and saddle at F40 772 043, overlooking the Polnoon. Descents can be made either downvalley directly to Cabin Creek, or from about pt 1278m upvalley to F40 763 054 down long tussock slopes.

Times: Treble Cone Skifield to Cabin Creek Hut, 6 hrs.

THE REMARKABLES

An unsealed road marked with DoC signage turns off SH6 2km south of Frankton and winds up to the Remarkables skifield in the head of the Rastus Burn. This provides open and free access to alpine basins in the Remarkables all year. Although the skifield has destroyed some of the former isolation of the Lake Alta Basin, it has also opened up a beautiful alpine region to many more people who would otherwise be unlikely to experience it. There is a log book to record intentions in at the shelter building at the road end. The shelter is also equipped with toilets.

DoC has marked walking tracks to Lake Alta and the Shadow Basin lookout at F41 794 639. Although there is no marked route, these can be connected to form a round trip of about 4 hrs, by crossing a shoulder at the 1940m contour between the two.

QUEENS DRIVE

Queens Drive is a ledge that traverses around the western face of the Remarkables about 300m below the jagged summit ridge. It is often picked out from the Queenstown/Frankton area by snow against the black rocky ramparts of the front face. Although sheep have been driven along it in times gone by, this route does traverse across a steep face. With ice or snow on the route it would be impractical for all but equipped climbing parties. However, in mid to late summer on a fine day it can be practical for strong tramping parties, offering a great daytrip, but it does require moderate route finding ability and confidence on steep ground to negotiate safely. Be aware that exposure conditions can develop very quickly up here and shelter is not readily available.

To gain the drive, follow the walking track from the top of the Shadow Basin Skilift to a prominent notch in the summit ridge just south of the viewing point. From this notch at F41 793 637, follow a rising rock shelf 200m SW out onto the front face to gain the shingle shelf of the Queens Drive. This undulating shelf is followed directly below great cliffs to the boulder field below the SW face of Single Cone, 1 hr from the notch. At this end, a large cairn marks the start of the Queens Drive from this boulder field.

Traverse this boulder field around under the south face of Single Cone until F41 808 618 is reached at the top of a bluff above a large tarn. The tarn is at the 1700m contour, in the upper Wye Creek basin below. Scramble NW up rocky slopes to reach the boulder shelf east of Single Cone, and so Lake Alta. Alternatively, from F41 808 618 follow down above the bluff to the outlet of the tarn at the 1700m contour then climb up the main Wye Creek Basin to either of two saddles with the Rastus Burn and the Skifield.

SINGLE AND DOUBLE CONE

From the Skifield follow the track up to Lake Alta. There is a bivvy rock (sleeps 4 to 6) just north of the stream a short distance below the lake outlet at F41 805 635. Another bivvy rock exists 200m to the north of this bivvy at about the 1840m contour. These peaks are climbs and climbing skill and knowledge is required to safely negotiate them.

SINGLE CONE 2319m. From Lake Alta, climb to the saddle at F41 806 628 and head SSW towards the SE ridge of pt 2319m. Just short of the ridge follow a ledge around to the right to a couloir leading to the summit. Steep hard snow often sits in the couloir until late summer. It can be bypassed on the right (looking up) by a series of cairned ledges beside the gut.

DOUBLE CONE 2307m. A rope and rock climbing skills are needed to climb the peaks of Double Cone. From Lake Alta, the best route is up the couloir between the main peaks. Near the top it forks and either branch can be climbed to its saddle. The easiest route to each peak is from its southern side.

Time: Roadend to Lake Alta, 1 hr; Lake Alta to the summit, about 3 hrs.

REMARKABLES SKIFIELD TO WYE CREEK

From the ski field, two easy saddles give access to the tarns and high alpine basins of the upper Wye Creek basin. Once in the basin, follow it down to the cirque wall below the last of the tarns where Wye Creek tumbles over a spectacular cascade between the 1650m and 1500m contours. The route down is on steep snowgrass slopes 100m to the true left of Wye Creek. The middle reaches of Wye Creek are easy going over rough tussock flats.

The lower gorge is very impressive where Wye Creek tumbles 300m over huge boulders. An initially lightly marked track will be picked up on the scrubline on the true right, immediately beside the stream at the end of the middle flats. This leads above then through open beech forest to the site of a small hydro electric scheme. From the intakes, a bridle path, then a 4WD track leads to State highway 6, about 300m north of the highway bridge over Wye Creek. Please leave gates as you find them.

To approach Wye Creek from SH6. From the carpark on the Queenstown side of Wye Creek, follow a 4WD track as it zig zags up the hill near the pipeline. Be careful to pick up the foot track where it leaves the bulldozed line to continue up Wye Creek. The track stays on the true right to the tussock flats in Wye Creek. As part of this route crosses private land, please leave gates as you find them.

Time: Skifield to Wye Creek Bridge on SH6, 7 hrs.

THE HECTOR (NEVIS) MOUNTAINS

Between the Remarkables and the Nevis Road, lies the Hector Mountains, the northern extension of which is known as the Nevis Mountains. The highest peak, pt 2307m at F42 835 549, is unnamed, though widely visible as a twin peak from the Cromwell area. The other peak of the twin is pt 2252m, also unnamed. With many peaks over 2000m, this country is clearly alpine in nature, and much more bluffy than the map suggests. A special feature of the area is the wonderful series of cirque lakes and fell fields of huge boulders. The rock and snow conditions are similar to the Remarkables. There are occasional bivvy rocks scattered throughout. Lack of bush means that a primus is necessary for cooking on. Good skills and equipment are required along with good weather to navigate this country, which can be savagely desolate at times.

ACCESS FROM THE NORTH AND WEST

From the north, via the Remarkables Skifield. In mid to late summer, it is possible to traverse south along the range over 2 or 3 days as follows. Cross into the head of Wye Creek by one of the saddles from the ski field. Head south through the basin to the spur at F41 816 604 then swing east over pt 2020m. Continue SE to a small tarn and cross south over a ridge between pt 2115m and pt 1967m, descending to the 1800m contour and passing three tarns in the head of Doolans Creek Left Branch. Sidle just below this height then climb up to a tarn at F42 827 570. Continue south to another tarn then follow up the gully beyond SW to another tarn just under pt 2087m. There is a good bivvy rock here (sleeps 4) at F42 821 561 near the tarn. Cross the ridge NW of pt 2087m and descend to Lake Hope. Lake Hope can also be accessed from main Wye Creek through bluffs at F42 798 557 and over a saddle at F42 810 552, (Hawkes Pass).

A side trip can be made to the highest summit in the area, **PT 2307M.** After traversing the saddle to the east of Lake Hope, access is gained to the northern slopes or west ridge of pt 2307m. Below the Lake Hope outlet in the head of Wye Creek South Branch, there is a bivvy rock (sleeps 3) at F42 814 547 on the true right at the 1680m contour. There is a better bivvy rock further down on the true left at F42 821 532 in the upstream forks of two creeks that join Wye Creek South Branch on a corner. From this bivvy rock, **BEN NEVIS** can be climbed. A high saddle (1880m) to the east of the bivvy rock gives access to a huge rocky shelf leading SE to Ben Nevis. Ben Nevis, recognised from Kingston by its long sweeping southern ridge, is often confused with pt 2307m.

SH6 access to Lake Hope via main Wye Creek and Hawkes Pass: This is the shortest and most direct route to Lake Hope. Ascend the Wye Creek Track to the hydro scheme intake. Cross the North Branch on the intake structure, follow along the pipeline that crosses to the South Branch (not shown on F42) and about halfway along leave it and ascend a slip that avoids most of the scrub to about F42 785 544. Then sidle/ascend ENE across huge tussock and shingle slopes to Hawkes Pass at F42 810 552, just south of pt 2090m. A short bouldery descent leads to Lake Hope.

SH6 access to Lake Hope via Skingut Pass and Wye Creek South Branch: About 200m south of the highway bridge over Wye Creek a 4WD track zig zags its way SE 3km across a tussock face to an altitude of about 1120m, ending at a fence. From the end of the track, sidle SE up and into 2 Mile (Neutral) Creek where an old stone musterers hut (sleeps 3) will be found F42 801 508 at the start of the upper basin. From the hut head NE to pt 1659m (Skingut Pass), and continue NE, dropping only slightly to meet Wye Creek South Branch on a corner where there is a good bivvy rock at about the 1500m contour (F42 821 532). Open travel leads to Lake Hope. Either follow the Creek all the way, or take a shortcut and head up a rock and tussock gully just under 1km before the lake.

Descending: From Wye Creek South Branch, sidle up to pt 1659m (Skingut Pass) and descend south into 2 Mile Creek below, and a small hut on the true left at F42 801 508. From the hut sidle down to meet the 4WD track on the true right and continue down it to SH6 beside Lake Wakatipu.

Times: SH6 to Lake Hope via Hawkes Pass; 8-9 hrs return with daypacks, (allow a day one way with full packs); Via Skingut Pass; SH6 to 2 Mile Hut, 3 hrs; Hut to Lake Hope, 2.5 hrs.

ACCESS FROM THE EAST

The Nevis Road from Bannockburn has been upgraded to a basic gravelled standard and is negotiable by a 2WD car as far as Commissioner Creek for 6 to 8 months of the year, depending on the severity of the winter. This road gives access to Nevis, Schoolhouse, Commissioner and Sproules Creeks, all of which provide good routes to Nevis Peaks. Scrub in the lower reaches of all these creeks is best avoided by cutting into the middle reaches on water races at about the 900m contour. Alternatively, each of the major spurs between these creeks have rough 4WD tracks which climb to about the 1700m contour.

BEN NEVIS

Ben Nevis may also be approached from Schoolhouse Creek via the lake outlet at F42 845 508, tarns above and a scramble up the east ridge from F42 845 518. Leave Schoolhouse Creek several hundred metres downstream from the lake outlet stream junction. It is also possible to climb Ben Nevis from the head of the Nevis Burn. From about F41 835 530 head directly up the huge slab boulderfield to the summit.

HIGH PEAK (PT 2307M) HECTOR MOUNTAINS

In summer this is a scramble. An approach from Lake Hope has already been described. Alternatively there is a good approach up the huge spur between the Nevis Burn and the Doolans Creek Left Branch. A rough 4WD track which branches off the Nevis Gibbston 4WD Road should be followed to its end at approx the 1700m contour. From here, follow westward along the ridge crest until the going gets steep and sidle on the northern slopes. Drop off a spur at F42 856 547 to gain a small lower lake which drains into Doolans Creek Left Branch. Climb up to the middle lake.

There are several good bivvy rocks by the middle lake here among a field of giant boulders at F42 849 549. Ascend the cirque wall behind this lake to gain another larger lake (often frozen over until November). Follow around the north side of this lake and up a gully of permanent snow to gain a col at F42 838 552 on the east ridge of pt 2307m. There is an easy scramble on good rock to the summit up the east ridge from the col.

Times: Nevis Bridge to the end of the 4WD track, 4 to 5 hrs; End of the track to the top, 2.5 to 3 hrs.

JAMES PEAK (2072M)

James Peak was named after James Hector, the Otago Provincial Geologist. From the Nevis Road ford of Sproules Creek head up the spur SW to pt 1012m then follow the disused water race to the main forks. Continue up the spur past pt 1796m to the saddle at F42 845 429 just north of a small tarn. From this saddle sidle north under large rock slabs until animal tracks show the way up steep grass ramps to gain the NE face below James Peak. Traverse diagonally across the face keeping to animal tracks which seek out the easiest route to gain the main Hector Range at F42 835 435 and the 1900m contour. Scramble along the main ridge over point 2019m to gain the summit.

James Peak can also be approached from Staircase Creek. Follow 4WD tracks well above Staircase Creek on the true left, then sidle on up valley on the true left and head for the peak.

Time: The climb can be done in a very long hard day from either the Nevis Road or SH6.

'You are what your deep driving desire is. As your desire is, so is your will. As your will is, so is your deed. As your deed is, so is your destiny.'

—Bridadaranyaka Upanishad IV 4.5.

AROUND WANAKA

DoC's Mt Aspiring National Park Visitor Centre (Ph 03 443 7660) by the main road into Wanaka offers a wealth of information about local short walks. Seek their advice. Useful contacts include the Wanaka Visitor Information Centre (Ph 03 443 1233), Edgewater Adventures (Ph 03 443 8422) and Goodsports (Ph 03 443 7966). Short trips around Wanaka include a climb to the top of Mt Iron (549m), and the walk north to Beacon Point. By far the best viewpoints, however, are Mt Grandview (1398m), east of Hawea, and Roys Peak (1578m). Mt Grandview is the point from which John Turnbull Thomson named Mt Aspiring, and is approached from the Hawea Back Road.

The track to Roys Peak commences at a signpost 6km west of the town on the Glendhu Bay road and is very popular. It is normally open to the public, although it crosses private land on Alpha Burn Station and is closed from October 1st to November 10th for lambing. An honesty box at the start suggests a $2 track maintanence fee for the use of the track.

MATUKITUKI VALLEY

From delightful flats and forests on the valley floors, there are wonderful views of dramatic, fully glaciated peaks in both branches of the Matukituki. All huts in the West Matukituki Catchment from Aspiring Hut up valley were originally built by the NZAC. They are now mostly managed by Mt Aspiring National Park who maintain them and collect hut fees. A slightly different fee structure applies from other huts on DoC land, and NZAC members receive a discount.

The 50km road to Raspberry Flat in the West Matukituki from Wanaka is sealed as far as the Treble Cone turnoff. The rest is gravel. Public transport to the roadend is offered by Mt Aspiring Express (Ph 03 443 8422) and Alpine Shuttles who both run daily schedules between November and the end of March.

Cameron Flat is named after Ewen Cameron who had Glenfinnan Station in the West Matukituki and Polnoon country from 1867 until about 1882, when losses of sheep to snow and keas caused him to abandon the property. The East Matukituki is approached from here across farmed flats that are part of Mt Aspiring Station. Please don't disturb stock or farming equipment. A good viewpoint is Glenfinnan Peak, a prominent point (1860m) on the ridge at the head of Glenfinnan Stream. It is easily reached up sheep tracks between Niger and Glenfinnan Streams (4 to 5 hrs from the road). Fog Peak (2225m) can also be approached from here.

See the Polnoon (Shotover) notes for access to the Polnoon via the Leaping Burn from the Matukituki Valley. Mt Oestre also makes a challenging day trip from the Matukituki Valley if river levels permit. This route is not marked. From the East/West Branch Forks, climb the open red beech spur opposite Cameron Flat to the tops. There is some scrub at the bushline, but it is not bad. The ridge above is straightforward with easy basins to the east. The views from the top are excellent. This trip will take about 5.5 hrs up and about 4 hrs back.

WEST MATUKITUKI VALLEY

RASPBERRY FLAT TO ASPIRING HUT

The West Matukituki is approached on foot from the carpark at Raspberry Flat, by Big Creek. There are toilets here and the surroundings are farmland. The track up the West Matukituki is all on the true right to bushline. Big Creek is bridged and a track marked with orange poles leads beyond it to a stile over a fence. Follow the poles to rejoin the 4WD track as it winds across bouldery gullies of a gravel fan, heading upstream. A DoC sign indicates the Rob Roy Stream turnoff leading to an access bridge across the West Matukituki.

Continuing up valley, the ground track is obvious and marked with orange poles whenever it deviates from the farm track. It stays near or on the flats to Wilsons Bluff. Here, the the 4WD farm track zig zags up 60m then descends gently to flats upstream again. At the high point on the farm track as it crosses the bluff, is a stream. Generally there are less sandflies here than below on the valley flats. Cascade Hut is a private NZAC hut.

Aspiring Hut is 20 mins beyond Cascade Hut, on the true right of Cascade Creek. Aspiring Hut (40 bunks and flush loos) was originally built by NZAC members after the 2nd World War, and A. P. Harper, one of the first presidents, laid the foundation stone for it. It is now administered by Mt Aspiring National Park staff. A warden is in residence from November to April inclusive. Gas stoves are provided for cooking during summer. The hut fee is currently $20 per person per night. In winter the fee is $10. A fee of $5 is charged for camping beside the hut in summer and a small camping shelter is provided. The view from the front windows up valley is impressive. Liverpool Bivvy and the lower portion of French Ridge are visible, Bevan and Joffre dominate the head of the valley, while Mt Aspiring is visible above the Breakaway.

Time: Carpark to Aspiring Hut, 2 hrs.

ASPIRING HUT TO PEARL FLAT

Shovel and Pearl Flats are wonderful places. From Aspiring Hut, follow the track through the bush near the edge of the terrace to the bridge across Cascade Creek, then back along the true left to grass flats. Follow poles and a ground track up the flat into forest and down to the swingbridge over Rough

■ West Matukituki Valley from the Cascade Saddle track. Skyline from left to right is: Mt Barff, Hector Col and Mt Aspiring.

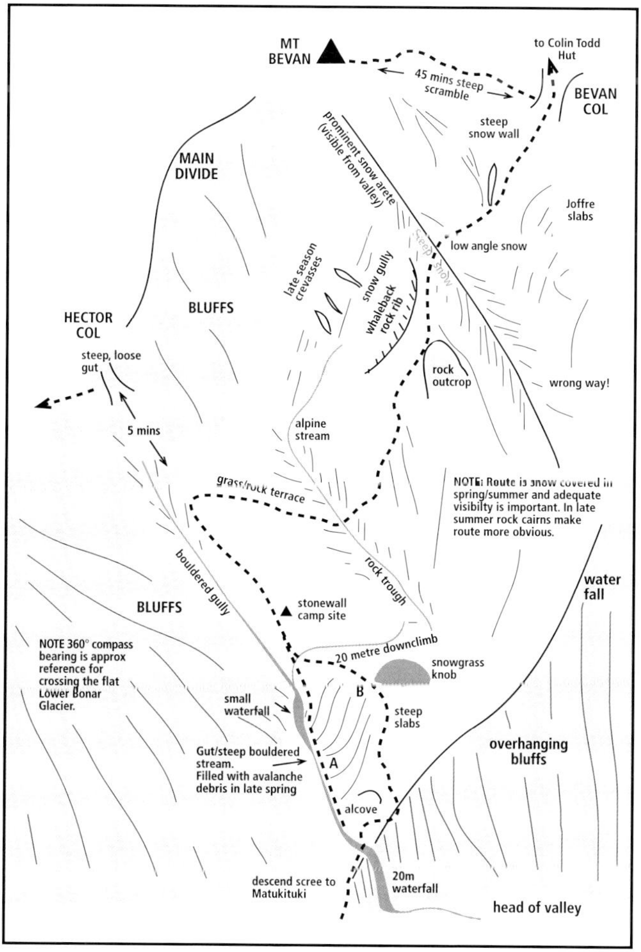

Access to Bevan Col from the upper Matukituki Valley.
Not to scale.
This diagram is based on pencil sketches of the route kindly supplied by Geoff Wayatt. (Mtn Recreation, Ph (03) 443 7330, Wanaka).

About trip leaders.

Of all the positions of honour held by the Great in the history of man … One unassailed bastion remains … The universally coveted status of [trip] Leader. Speak it aloud! Savour the tingling of the spine, the coursing blood, and the visions that shimmer on the dark waters of the imagination; visions of cloud-hung mountains, rainswept forest, trackless wilderness where [trip] Leader is at home, guiding the weak and helpless, the Pleb, into the iron currents of swollen streams, through valleys haunted by swarms of giant blood-sucking insects, beneath the brooding menace of the Black Lord Huey, guarding against the spine-bending pog and the eating of prunes in a zipped tent.

Yea, few there are who may give the special handclasp and look deep into the eyes of an equal with that moment of silent communion, speaking those words to which so few are entitiled: 'I bring them back alive' …

—Rex McDonald, *Antics 1971*, annual publication of Otago University Tramping Club.

Creek. Leading on through beech forest, the track enters the south end of Shovel Flat about 400m distance from the river. Poles and a ground track lead to the top end where the track re-enters the bush by the river and continues close to it to Pearl Flat. There are excellent campsites on Pearl Flat, and a moderate bivvy rock on the true left of the West Branch by the bush, 100m downstream from the start of the track to French Ridge Hut.

Time: Aspiring Hut to Pearl Flat, 1.5 hrs.

BEVAN COL Pearl Flat to Colin Todd Hut

Cross the Liverpool Stream bridge 50m above the West Branch confluence and follow the bank back to Pearl Flat. Follow the foot track and markers back into the bush at the top of the flat close to the river. They lead up over a small bluff and back to river level before re-entering the bush upstream. The track leads up past a swingbridge turnoff (wet weather access to French Ridge).

The stream with 45m and 91m waterfalls in it is a regular winter avalanche path, and is consequently swept bare of trees. The track, recently cut through the scrub at the down valley fringe of the avalanche path, sidles to 10m above river level and crosses gravel by the river to the next creek forks marked, 100m upstream at E39 659 335. Ascend this creek until about 80m (height) above the West Matukituki is gained. Here the track entrance into the bush is not always obvious. Climb a further 30m through fern on a ground trail to markers at the bush edge overlooking the creek at the 740m contour. A good track now sidles through forest then descends slightly through *Hoheria* and prickly shield fern (*Polystichum* sp) to a new wire crossing put in by DoC over the West Matukituki, about 100m below the bluff and old ford at E39 660 340.

A good bivvy rock can be approached from the old ford site. Across on the true left of the Matukituki, 3 large boulders are visible. The back one is cairned on top and is the bivvy. Head up a side stream, gaining 50m height to cairns on the true left. Follow these back down on a small dry watercourse until a track heads left. This leads to a clearing where the track peters out. Climb up 30m to the bivvy, at approx E39 663 338 (sleeps 5).

From the wire crossing, continue along the marked route upvalley on the true left, following a ground trail and cairns. Further up, these cross two streams at a distance of 60m from the river, then continue through open scrub another 100m to Scotts Bivvy Rock, marked with a cairn on top. **Scotts Bivvy** is at the 840m contour, about 80m distant from the river and 30m in height above it. This overhanging rock sleeps 2 in moderate comfort but has a resident stream in wet weather. A ground trail and cairns (not obvious) continues through scrub up past the French Ridge side of the bivvy then sidles left across to rocks, below two lone beech trees. This trail finishes 250m from the bivvy at the edge of the stream draining the Breakaway, 10m above the Matukituki and 30m from it. Cairns mark this point, which is the start of the continuous tussock upvalley.

All routes beyond here require alpine skills and gear. (See the route diagram. The boulder gully above the falls is usually filled with snow avalanche debris in spring/early summer). Cross the river to the true right and climb scree slopes until level with the top of the waterfall issuing from the narrow gut in the head of the valley. A trail leads around into the gut, crossing the stream immediately above the waterfall to the true left. There are now 2 main options. Follow the east side up rock slabs and tussock until a broad ledge is reached about 20m above the stream. Continue up the exposed slabs along a series of ledges about 10 to 15m above the stream (A). This is the waterfall route. An alternative slab route, (B), also cairned, but even more exposed, climbs higher and follows the line shown in the diagram. A third, unmarked, but also quite good option exists, staying in the stream more, and climbing around 3 small falls (9m max), generally on the true left using the slabs. Bolts at the top of the upper falls exist, but can be hard to find.

In the upper basin above the gut there is a rockwalled campsite (and others). From the top basin above the gut, Hector Col is easily reached. The Waipara side is a steep, loose gut with frequent rock-fall and is not a route. At the 1400m contour, sidle out of the basin 5 mins below Hector Col and climb up rock on the slopes of Mt Bevan. Traverse up and over a prominent snow arete (very distinctive from down valley) on Mt Bevan and follow up the snow gully beyond to Bevan Col. Colin Todd Hut (sleeps 12, NZAC, $20 per person per night) is approximately true north (360 degrees) from the Col across the Bonar Glacier. The route requires knowledge and gear for glacier travel.

Times: Pearl Flat to Scotts Bivvy, 2 hrs; Scotts Bivvy to Colin Todd Hut, 4 hrs.

MATUKITUKI SADDLE provides a feasible crossing to the Waipara valley for capable and experienced parties. From the basin above the slabs, pick a route up towards pt 1602m then follow near the ridge to the saddle. The descent on the Waipara side is steeper, down a stone gully initially, then further down, there are annoying bluffs to routefind through. The spur at E39 647 375 is suggested as one of the better options through the scrub down to the lake.

MATUKITUKI – ARAWHATA CROSSING. A good alternative to Arawhata Saddle exists for capable transalpine parties, especially later in the season. Head up to Matukituki Saddle as above. Cross the basin to the south, climb the tussock ridge on the other side until bluffs are reached on the spur, then sidle across a bench under pt 1785m to the Divide at the 1700m contour, E39 648 362. Other routes may be preferable leading up to this point, depending on the season. Descend scree and boulders on the Waipara side a short way and traverse across under bluffs to ascend back up a steep shingle gully at E39 646 360 (watch for stones) to the shoulder above at the 1800m contour. Follow gravel slopes west, then the ridge down to Waipara Saddle. (See p151). Allow a full day from Pearl Flat to the upper Arawhata.

PEARL FLAT TO FRENCH RIDGE HUT

There are 2 approaches to the French Ridge track at Pearl Flat. Either cross the river, (obviously faster), or follow up the valley track for 400m to a signposted turnoff, cross the swingbridge to the true left, then carefully follow a track down to Pearl Flat. This is the emergency flood route, taking about 15 mins more. Markers about opposite Liverpool Stream on the true left of the Matukituki now lead into the bush and the track climbs almost straight up the spur through bush and scrub and emerges on easy tussock slopes. This route is exposed to the weather above bushline. French Ridge Hut (20 bunks, NZAC, $20/night) is managed by DoC. For climbing info above here, see *The Mt Aspiring Region* written by Uren and Watson and published by the NZAC.

Time: Pearl Flat to French Ridge Hut, 2 to 3 hrs.

PEARL FLAT TO LIVERPOOL BIVVY

Cross Liverpool Stream swingbridge to the true left. From the bridge, follow the main track for 25m down towards the West Matukituki River. Here, on the true left of Liverpool Stream, the track to Liverpool Bivvy branches off. It is marked by a cairn, sign and good ground track. The track climbs steeply through bush, staying close to the crest of the spur then moves left and climbs across an old slip. At the top of the slip the track crosses a tongue of bush on the left and follows a dry creekbed till clear of the bush. From here, the route is marked with orange poles. It leads up through scrub and then steep, exposed shingle and tussock, which is dangerous if wet or snow covered. Once easy slopes are reached, bear left to reach a knoll overlooking the hut. A short descent upstream leads to a small stream crossing and then to the hut. On no account try sidling across below the knoll when the hut is first sighted. Liverpool Bivvy (DoC cat 3, sleeps 8). The route beyond to Arawhata Saddle is described in the Arawhata Valley notes, p149.

Time: Pearl Flat to Liverpool Bivvy, 2 to 2.5 hrs.

CASCADE SADDLE Aspiring Hut to Dart Hut

This marked route climbs steep snowgrass and rock bluffs from bushline to the pylon ridge, then traverses the Cascade Basin past Cascade Saddle to the Dart Glacier. The trip to the bushline on pylon ridge from Aspiring Hut is an easy day trip, with an excellent view of the West Matukituki Valley and Mt Aspiring. The crossing itself, however, is one of the more difficult marked routes in the area and parties should consider their experience and ability before attempting it. Ascending the steep Matukituki side is easier than descending it. The crossing should be avoided in wet or windy conditions and especially when any fresh snow is on the route. In addition to the steep Matukituki face, the traverse from the ridge to the Dart Glacier is above the 1500m contour and exposed to the weather. This is not an all weather route.

A signposted track enters the bush 100m south of Aspiring Hut and angles up through the bush more steeply than shown on E39 Ed.1. After 1.5 hrs it crosses a small creek, then 10 mins later crosses the main creek marked on the map close to the 900m contour. There is a small campsite near this larger creek on the Cascade Saddle side, about 10 mins below bushline. The track then continues south onto a spur and follows it up to the bushline at E39 642 262.

From bushline to Cascade Saddle, the route is marked with orange poles, though these may not always be standing. It climbs some rocky and grassy ledges, then zig zags up through short snowgrass. Three short rock steps and some steep snowgrass patches in the middle section require special care. The route is never more than 100m south of the true crest of the spur until, not far short of the summit, it swings left over easy slopes. The poled route then works right again to reach the skyline ridge of Mt Tyndall near its junction with the spur, and just below the marker pylon on the ridge.

Follow the marker poles and foot trail slightly uphill then across the slopes before descending into the Cascade Creek Basin. Cross Cascade Creek. The poles continue through small basins then lead down to a small shingle flat held back by moraine at about the 1400m contour, overlooking the Dart Glacier. This is a great place to camp. Follow along the trough until the poles finish and then cairns lead down to the ablation valley beside the glacier at the 1080m contour. The section on the marked route from this moraine trough to the valley is continually slumping, and a new line is usually cairned across it each year by park staff.

Gravel, then tussock flats with a foot trail and occasional cairn, lead down the valley to where the river now runs against a small bluff, about 700m before the Snowy confluence. Here a cut and marked track climbs about 30m and sidles across a tussock plateau to the Snowy Creek bridge and Dart Hut. See Dart Valley for more notes, including an account of this route in reverse.

MT TYNDALL is easily approached from the pylon ridge for those with the necessary snow skills, and provides wonderful views of the Dart, Shotover and Matukituki country.

Times: Aspiring Hut to Cascade pylon, 5.5 hrs; Pylon to Dart Hut, 5.5 hrs.

SHOTOVER SADDLE West Matukituki to the Shotover Valley

The saddle is a stiff climb but great daytrip from the West Matukituki, offering wide views, while Red Rock and pt 1853m offer even better views. Follow the main West Matukituki Valley farm track up river about 200m beyond Brides Veil Stream, to the next marked stream to the west. Cross this stream and follow sheep tracks up the spur on the true left of it to about the 900m contour. Take care not to disturb any stock. Tussock benches and basins lead up and across to the SE until under the saddle. Then follow the upper basin of Brides Veil Stream up to the saddle. There is water on both sides of the saddle in tarns, but the water on the Shotover side is clearer. There are great campsites here in reasonable weather.

To descend to the Shotover, drop down on the true right of Tyndall Stream to the basin at the 1260m contour and cross Tyndall Stream to the true left. Climb out from this basin to E39 661 210 at the 1300m contour on the ridge between Tyndall Stream and the Tummel Burn. Sidle along the side of this ridge at about this height in tussock above Tyndall Stream to meet the ridge crest overlooking the Tummel Burn at about the 1200m contour. Follow down the ridge towards a scrubby burnt area of dead celery pines (*Phyllocladus* sp) and pick up cairns in the gravel gully to the right (looking down) at about the 1000m contour, E40 662 181. This small gully almost splits the ridge but drains to the Tyndall Stream side just above the forks. Descend the gravel gully (more cairns) and pick up the permolat of an overgrowing Forest Service track partway down to Tyndall Stream at about the 850m contour. Follow this marked route to the left (looking down) from the gravel gully. The marked route sidles across then down through scrubby bush under bluffs to Junction Flat at the forks, about 15 mins from the gravel gully. Upper Shotover notes include a description of this route in reverse.

Times: Valley farm track to Shotover Saddle, 3.5 hrs; Saddle to Tummel Burn Hut, 5 hrs.

ROB ROY VALLEY

This stream drains the spectacular southern ice faces of Rob Roy Peak and is a pleasant place to visit for a day walk. A swing bridge crosses the West Matukituki River about 15 mins up valley from the Raspberry Flat Carpark. A good track then leads up the true left of the West Matukituki and swings up Rob Roy Valley, also on the true left, climbing to the bush edge and an interpretation sign.

Time: Carpark to Bushline, 2 hrs.

EAST MATUKITUKI VALLEY

The East Matukituki is relatively less populated and developed than the West Branch. The character of its scenery is different too, with more bush on the valley floor and a spectacular gorge.

CAMERON FLAT TO JUNCTION FLAT

The East Matukituki is approached from Cameron Flat, down a fenced off side road marked by a large DoC sign at a gate. From here, cross the West Matukituki to the true left and follow the old homestead road, branching off before the homestead and continuing up grass flats in the East Branch. If the West Matukituki is high, cross the footbridge 2.5km up the road from Cameron Flat and follow the riverbank back down the other side to the flats in the East Branch. Flats continue to the Glacier Burn, where a short track leads to a wire bridge crossing at the mouth of the gorge, just back in the bush. Beyond here, a well marked track leads through the bush to Junction Flat. At Junction Flat there are two recently built DoC 3 wire bridges, one across the Kitchener River (Holloway Memorial crossing) and the other over the East Matukituki itself, eliminating what have been, at times, deadly river crossings. South Albert Burn Saddle can be crossed from here to the Albert Burn. See the Albert Burn for crossing notes.

Times: Cameron Flat to the Glacier Burn, a little over 1 hr; Glacier Burn to Junction Flat, 1.5 hrs.

Access to the GLACIER BURN. A well marked track enters the bush 100m south of the Burn. It zig zags up over a spur on the true right before dropping back to the stream bed above, taking

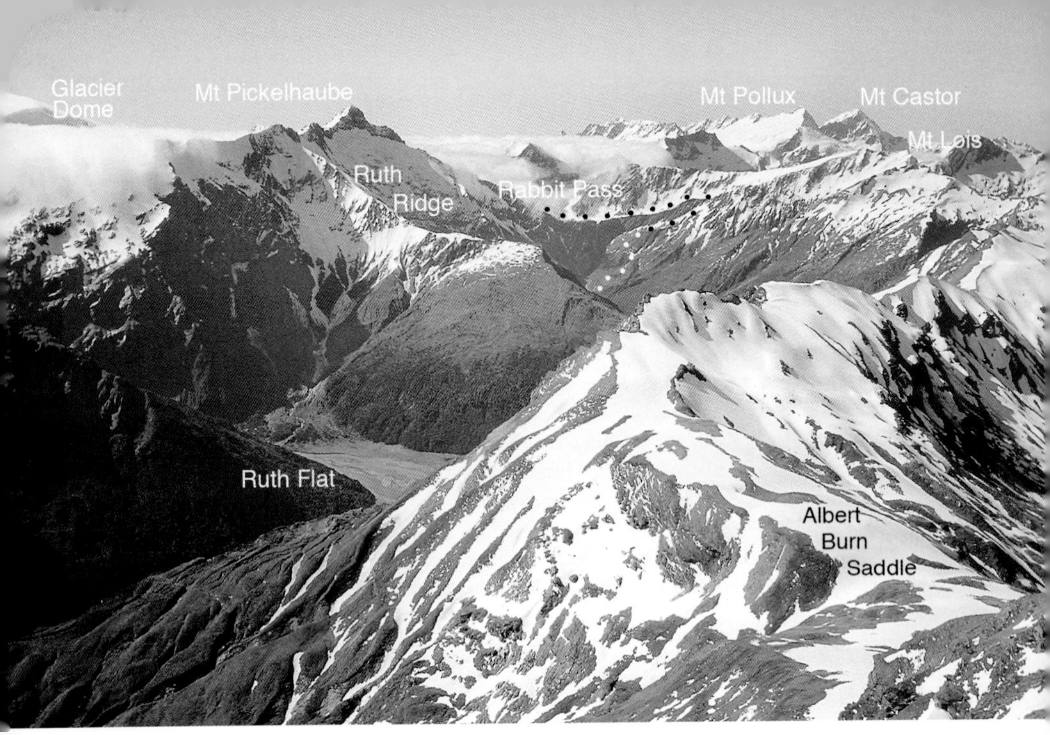

■ Looking up the East Matukituki Valley to Rabbit Pass from Dragonfly Pk.

1 hr. The marked track finishes here. Continue up the Glacier Burn on the true right to the head of the valley.

JUNCTION FLAT TO RUTH FLAT

For most people this will involve a traverse of the Bledisloe (Bloody Slow) Gorge, though fortunately this is no longer the daunting prospect it once was. Parties may like to reflect that in 1932 a stretcher was carried down the gorge. A well marked high level track climbs to bushline on the true left then descends through the gorge to Ruth Flat. Cross the DoC 3 wire over the East Matukituki just up from Hester Pinney Creek and follow a marked track up through the bush. From the bushline, orange standards mark the track as it climbs a further 200m, sidling up valley to a scrubby ledge from which Ruth Flat may be seen. Descend sharply back into the bush along a narrow and steep track then continue to sidle upvalley, before descending steeply to an open shingle creekbed 50m above the the river, F39 793 382, where the track is lower down than marked on the map. The track then follows above the river bank to the flats.

In the reverse direction, descending from Ruth Flat, pick up cairns, orange standards, and a cut line as they lead through two grass and scrubby fans. The gorge track enters the bush at a track sign and orange standards on the true left as indicated on F39 Ed.1, about 45 mins below pt 711m.

An unmarked low level route also exists. However, this low level route is difficult and it is stressed that it is for experienced parties only. It should only to be attempted when the river is very low and is described for coming down valley. Use the track to bypass a slow bouldery section and enter the river at the shingle creek F39 792 381. Then follow the riverbed, initially staying on the true left, then crossing as many times as necessary. When the river drops in boulders and a waterfall at about F39

782 363 (where crossing would be dangerous), back off upvalley 100 or 200m and find a way to climb out. Then sidle up on the true left to meet the sidle track at about the 600m contour above Hester Pinney Ck. Waterfalls make staying in the riverbed impractical in the last kilometre.

A third alternative, unmarked and much the longest route but with the best view, is to traverse via Wilmot Saddle or Sisyphus Peak. See Kitchener and Rainbow valleys for access to the Wilmot Saddle. From the saddle, traverse east, (right) or follow the ridge up to Sisyphus, then descend the tussock spur running ENE off it, swinging north down a tussock rib from the 1600m contour. At F39 786 401 on this rib, there is a rock outcrop; either sidle, or else descend steep tussock patches through scrub to an open tussock grass basin at F39 788 403. A thin gravel slip begins here. It follows the creekbed shown on F39, cutting down through thick scrub then beech forest to F39 788 411 where it joins a much larger stream draining Wilmot Saddle. (One small sidle (true right) required around big boulders in the creek). Coming up from Ruth Flat, keep taking the true right hand creek; as the terrain steepens, a slip enters from the true left. Avoid it, continuing up the more stable true right creek, which has a small fall over a flat topped rock in it. Avoid the slopes below Wilmot Saddle and to the north, due to steepness and rockfall. Fine weather is essential for this crossing.

Times: Junction Flat to Ruth Flat, via high level track, 4 to 6 hrs; Via the river low level route, 4 to 5 hrs; Via Wilmot Saddle, 7 to 9 hrs.

AT RUTH FLAT

There are two poor bivvy rocks, cramped and holding only 1 or 2 people each, at the back of Ruth Flat at F39 792 415. One is under the biggest boulder visible in the scrub. Approach it from tussock leads above. The other bivvy is within 100m of the first one. These bivvies are sometimes used by climbing parties approaching the Volta via Ruth Ridge. Further up the East Matukituki flats there is a much better rock bivvy at F39 809 439 which would sleep 3 or 4, beside the creek draining pt 1828m. It is 3m above the creekbed on the true right at the edge of the flat. It is dry and practical to use, though open to the south. Another rock bivvy exists at F39 808 441, close to the river on the true left, surrounded by scrub.

RUTH RIDGE is very steep and exposed near the top, with loose rock in the upper section. Steep snowfields lead up towards the Volta Glacier, and the Main Divide is frequently corniced here early in summer. Although it is a feasible transalpine route, many parties will find the steepness quite wild and time consuming in this upper section. It is not a tramping route, and alpine skills and gear are required. However, pt 1521m can be visited on a daytrip up snowgrass slopes from Ruth Flat in summer for the view. Head up from the south, bypassing scrubby lower slopes by following open streambeds close under the Main Divide. Sidle to the east onto easier tussock slopes at about the 900 to 1000m contour and head up to the ridge. The lower part of this route is swept by snow avalanches in winter and spring and is better avoided at that time.

RABBIT PASS Ruth Flat to the Wilkin

This difficult route is best approched from the Wilkin, but for those parties who must approach from the East Matukituki it needs to be accepted that the descent of the Wilkin Waterfall Face is a climbing proposition. It should only be attempted by experienced and capable parties. The route from the East Matukituki to Rabbit Pass is incorrectly marked on F39 Ed.1. See comments in the Wilkin Valley notes. Tussock and scrubby flats continue to give easy travel to the head of the East Matukituki. Orange standards will be found again in the streambed (true right branch) at F39 796 459. These lead up to F39 797 461, just above the scrubline, and generally continue all the way to Rabbit Pass.

Across the East Matukituki to the Kitchener cirque and Mt Aspiring from Dragonfly Pk.

Follow these orange standards up tussock then shingle slopes under a prominent shelf, climbing right (east) to gain the shelf at the 1600m contour, where a moderately steep, slabby rock ramp leads out through the bluffs at F39 804 469. Beware of loose rock. This point is 1km east of the big waterfall under Rabbit Pass, and 200m vertically above it. Along the shelf under Mt Lois, one or two standards may be replaced by cairns.

After an easy descent along the shelf to the west, swing north through Rabbit Pass and into the pleasant basins of the upper South Wilkin. Pearson Saddle appears to the west, and the basins terminate at the top of the Wilkin Waterfall, leaving a very steep and difficult descent to Waterfall Flat below. The descent route begins at the 1420m contour, where there is an orange standard, well to the NW and some 130m vertically above the waterfall TOP. The route initially descends out to the north for 150m across very exposed, extremely steep rock, hard earth and short grass, then leads more steeply down ledges until a descent to the right (looking down) can be made to the head of a snowgrass fan. The route down the waterfall including the tussock fan at the bottom is sparsely marked (1997) with orange standards. See Wilkin Valley notes and photo.

Caution; the descent of the Wilkin Waterfall Face is difficult, and is extremely dangerous in all but ideal conditions.

Times: Ruth Flat to valley head, 2 hrs; Valley head to Rabbit Pass, about 3 hrs; Rabbit Pass to Waterfall Flat, 2 hrs.

KITCHENER AND RAINBOW VALLEYS

From Junction Flat, a good track leads up the true right of the Kitchener to Aspiring Flats. Here either follow trails around a swampy area keeping close to the hill, or gain the gravel beaches and stay close to the stream, depending on the amount of water about. Near the top of the flats and upstream from the Rainbow confluence, just before the bush closes in again, cairns mark the start of a short track to the Rock of Ages bivvy, about 100m west of its marked position on F39 Ed1, and 10m above the river on the true right. This enormous rock will shelter up to 4 people in most weather. A short traverse west leads to the water supply, while to the other side a track leads to the top of the rock, a pleasant viewpoint. Campsites exist on the flat in front. The further hour or so tramp to the Turnbull Thomson Falls is time well spent.

Possibly the best view in the East Matukituki is from Sisyphus Peak, readily accessible via the Rainbow and Wilmot Saddle, and a days outing from Rock of Ages. Follow gravel up the Rainbow, crossing as necessary, to forks at F39 756 380. Continue up the true right branch a further 1km. Pick up the rib on the true left of this branch (about F39 757 391), follow it up to the top of the tussock and then sidle across boulder fields and scree under bluffs to Wilmot Saddle. Easy slopes lead to Sisyphus, with its superb view of Aspiring and the rest of the East Matukituki. On the return, avoid the temptation to follow creek beds down through the scrub. In dry conditions there is a small spring in a minor gully 300m due south of, and slightly lower than Wilmot Saddle. The main gully can be dry for some distance.

In spring, the Rainbow is subject to avalanche danger. A safe but longer alternative route is to climb through the bush on the ridge east of the Rainbow. Numerous windfalls near the bushline impede progress and it seems desirable to keep well to the left, away from the crest of the ridge. Above the scrub, snowgrass gives easy and pleasant travel. For crossing to Ruth Flat see p84.

Times: Junction Flat to Rock of Ages bivvy, 1hr; Rock of Ages bivvy to Sisyphus Peak, via the Rainbow, 5.5 hrs up and 4 hrs back; via the ridge, 7 to 8 hrs up.

A hut gives security, but the open tussock on a peerless night gives a sense of deep freedom that is one of the unforgettable bounties of mountain life. You can lie where you will and listen till long after sunset to the small voices of the Alps whispering in unison... the faintest stirring of the tussock, the solitary rock clunking down a couloir, the treble of small streams, and the deeper note of the main Matukituki far below. There was a sparkle of frost on my japara cover when I awoke at first light, and a rime of ice on the billies...

—Paul Powell.

ALBERT BURN

Clear water, pleasantly forested mid and upper reaches, lower rainfall and few visitors make this an attractive valley to visit. The lower valley has, for many years, been used to graze cattle, and past fires have removed some of the forest. Crossings can be made to the East Matukituki Valley and the Wilkin, though some tramping background will be required as these routes involve untracked travel. Some routes marked in the past are now substantially overgrown.

MAKARORA TO ALBERT BURN HUT

Most parties approach the lower Albert Burn by plane or jetboat from Makarora. The jetboat to near the mouth of the Albert Burn and the plane to a strip on the true right, about 6.5km up valley at F39 955 437, an easy 30 mins walk below Albert Burn Hut.

The approach on foot from Makarora depends on being able to cross the Makarora and Wilkin rivers, individually or combined, both of which can be deceptively swift and deep, even when clear, and require caution. From the Craigie Burn mouth down to the Albert Burn is a good hour's walk, utilising a major stock track. Cross the Albert Burn to the true right and follow a mixture of the old stock track marked on F39 and boulders along the riverbank (sections of the track were washed out in the 94 floods) to the beginning of extensive grazed flats.

The mid valley station hut on the true right, built in 1939, and an ex-NZFS hut at F39 936 442 built in 1984 on the true left were destroyed in 1994 floods, as was the airstrip marked on the true left. However, in 1995 DoC built a new Albert Burn Hut (2 by 4 bunk sleeping platforms and woodstove) on the true left, 300m downstream from the ex-NZFS hut position, in grassy mounds about 200m back from the river and about 50m from the bush edge. This newer hut at F39 939 442 could easily be missed.

Times: Makarora road to Albert Burn mouth, 6 hrs; Mouth to Albert Burn Hut, 3 hrs.

ALBERT BURN HUT TO JUNCTION FLAT

The track up valley begins 700m beyond the hut at the bush edge, as indicated on F39, Ed.1, where there is a DoC sign close to the river on the true left. Generally the track follows the mapped line and is well marked with red and white permolat and occasional orange triangles. However, it is a little indistinct where it drops onto the downstream end of meat-safe flat. There is still a derelict meat-safe here at F39 915 447. When leaving the top end of this flat, the track climbs and sidles a couple of contour lines higher than marked on the map for about 1km.

Where a tributary joins the river from the true left at F39 883 442, a deep pool butts into a bluff, a high sidle or two river crossings will normally be necessary to continue. The crossings are deep and poor. This is at the beginning of the spur to Junction Flats. The track finishes as indicated at a sign *Albert Burn Hut 3 hrs*, 100m below the actual forks on Junction Flat, still on the true left. Junction Flat is at pt 588m. There are good campsites at these flats, the main ones being in the SW corner.

Time: Albert Burn Hut to Junction Flats, 3 hrs.

Three major tributaries join the Albert Burn on the true left between Albert Burn Hut and Junction Flat, one at F39 883 442, and two others at meat-safe flat, F39 915 447. Routes in them are as follows.

First stream below the forks, F39 883 442. Use the true left bank and allow 2.5 hrs to the head of the valley.

Downstream tributary at meat-safe flat. Use the true right bank, along which there is an old permolat line and allow 1.5 hrs to the flats. A crossing can be made to the Craigie Burn from the top flats in this tributary.

Upstream tributary at meat-safe flat. Use the true left bank and allow 2hrs to the flats. For crossing from here to Jumboland in the Wilkin, see below.

MID ALBERT BURN TO WILKIN (JUMBOLAND) CROSSING

This crossing is unmarked and some off track route finding skills are necessary. However, it is a reasonable route that would make a good Albert Burn to Wilkin trip. It can also be used as part of an alternative route, along with South Albert Burn Saddle, to connect the East Matukituki with the Wilkin, bypassing the Wilkin Waterfall face. Ice axes are not normally necessary in mid to late summer.

Two major streams join the Albert Burn on the true left at meat-safe flat, F39 915 447. Immediately on the true left of the **upstream** tributary, an unmarked route leads up a spur through open bush. At the 740m contour deer trails sidle into the upper valley emerging at the bushline at F39 903 460. Easy travel along pleasant open flats ends at F39 896 480. The upper cirque basin is best reached by staying close to or in the streambed of the cascade to avoid heavy scrub. From F39 894 490 climb a slip NE to about the 1540m contour where broad shattered rock ledges give access to easy grass slopes below Mt Jumbo.

The Wilkin/Albert Burn divide is crossed at F39 894 500 at 1570m. From here descend tussock slopes north to a slip basin 1km directly west of Mt Jumbo. This basin is drained by two streams that were severely guttered out by 1990's storms. Follow the ridge at F38 890 506, which has the shortest subalpine scrub belt on it, down. Lower down, swing left into the open gravel streambed at F38 880 510, which offers easier travel in the lower reaches down to the Wilkin.

Times: Meat-safe flat to the top flats in the upstream tributary, 2 hrs; Top flats to the upper cirque basin, 2 hrs; Upper cirque basin to Jumboland Flat, 4 hrs.

SOUTH BRANCH Junction Flats to the upper flats

From Junction Flat, an old, unmaintained marked route leads up the gorge towards the bushline. Easily missed red permolat markers begin at the bush edge, 70m from the river on the true left at F39 872 432. They lead up beside the river, then climb in bush at the edge of a scrubby slip beside a cataract. At the 720m contour these markers cease at the slip edge and recommence in a tongue of bush over beside the river at the 740m contour. Between there is thick, unmarked scrub to negotiate.

In the bush again, red permolat initially marks the route, then the marking becomes less obvious, disappearing altogether while crossing a scrubby slip 30m above the river. Continue to sidle 10 to 20m above the river and pick up the marked route again in bush beyond the slip for the last few 100m till the markers finish beside the river, several on a tree facing up valley at F39 866 416, on the true left.

Scrub regrowth has made travel upvalley from here for the next 750m probably best near or at river level.

At a grass fan on the true left at F39 864 409 (marked as scrub on the map) leave the river as it closes in to form a small gorge with scrubby bluffs. Follow these grass clearings up to and across the slopes at about the 980m contour, well back from the river. Climb and sidle up valley, taking care to follow open leads and the remains of old deer trails at about the 1080m contour. No scrub bashing should be required. Still on the true left, keep sidling across tussock slopes, with another 100m climb to the 1180m contour necessary to pass the next little gorge at F39 854 399, before descending to a tussock flat at forks, F39 851 398.

Above here, an 'S' bend cataract in the river is passed on the true left, threading through spaniards between the cataract and bluffs, about 50m from the river, finishing up on knob pt 1269m. This is the beginning of continuous tussock flats up valley, giving good access via saddles to Minaret Saddle (see the Minaret Burn) and East Matukituki via South Albert Burn Saddle. See below.

When descending, keep towards the river while dropping from pt 1269m. Lower down, note the sidle, river travel, then the start of the marked route at river level on the true left from F39 866 416.

Times: Junction Flat to pt 1269m (start of the upper flats), 5 hrs; Then 1 hr to the top of the flats.

SOUTH ALBERT BURN SADDLE South Albert Burn to the East Matukituki Valley

This is a pleasant crossing with great views. Follow up the South Albert Burn flats to the base of the stream draining the saddle. Here, two streams join at F39 828 383 just below a waterfall, the first of two falls to bypass above. Pick a line up the spur/slope between them, on the true left of the saddle stream to a basin above this first waterfall. Follow easy slopes in the basin, cross the main (or saddle) stream and climb easy slopes to the saddle on the true right of the upper, 25m waterfall. Dragonfly Peak is a fairly easy climb to the south and provides wonderful views across the East Matukituki. On the Albert Burn side of the pass at roughly F39 824 375 there is a new private hut (Mt Aspiring Station). It is locked and not on Conservation land.

To reach the East Matukituki Valley from the saddle, descend to about the 1580m contour on the true right of Hester Pinney Creek then sidle across to pt 1534m on the ridge, sometimes on good, but old, deer tracks. Descend past the tarns and pick up the orange gorge track poles at the scrub edge, where there are reasonable campsites. The track gives access up or down valley.

In reverse. Cross to the true left bank of the East Matukituki and follow the track for the high level Bledisloe Gorge route to bushline. Reasonable campsites can be found here with streams providing water. Above the bush, follow the long, easy tussock slopes up to pt 1534m, sidle across to the head of Hester Pinney Creek and follow it up to the saddle. Descending to the Albert Burn, bypass the upper falls (F39 821 376) on the true right of the stream and the main falls (F39 825 383) to the South Albert Burn flats on a tussock spur on the true left.

Times: South Albert Burn Flats to Albert Burn Saddle, 1.5 hrs; Saddle to East Matukituki track, 1.5 hrs; East Matukituki at Junction Flat to the upper South Albert Burn flats, about 7 hrs.

NORTH BRANCH Albert Burn Junction Flats to the upper flats

Considerable care will be required to follow this old marked route, but generally it is still a good line. At the Junction Flat bush edge by the Albert Burn North Branch stream, look for red permolat on the true left just before the stream begins to climb. Follow red permolat up for 70 to 100m and sidle, mostly keeping this height above the river. Halfway up this section there is an open slip. Cross it, climbing only slightly. The permolat is intermittent but can be followed (1997) to the bush edge overlooking the flats and 70m above the river. The once-open scrub and deer leads here have been replaced by heavy scrub. There is an easy line through it, initially with markers, that sidles across prickly shield fern leads to small open grassy clearings on slopes below. Travel down through these clearings. A short last bank of scrub obscures them from the streambed.

Descending. At F39 857 437 climb 10m up the bank and locate small sloping grass clearings. Follow up to the top of these and climb a further 10m through prickly shield fern (*Polystichum vestitum*) before sidling on obscure leads through to the bush edge, 70m height above the stream. Markers are unlikely to be found until the bush edge.

Times: Junction Flat to upper flats, 1.3 hrs; The valley head is 2 hrs up the flats.

MINARET BURN

Although this valley is mostly open, there are scrubby sections in places. It is grazed in part, and permission will be required from the runholder to visit it. The river itself is the boundary between West Wanaka Station, (Mr Cochrane, ph 03 443 7144) to the south and in tenure review, and Minaret Station (ph 03 443 6001) to the north. Tenure review may ultimately bring public access to and up the Minaret Burn from the south, but until then, Station permission is required.

The normal 4WD track access approaches from the south and is easily followed up into the valley. (The 4WD track shown on F39 from the mouth of the Minaret Burn connecting up with this main track is completely overgrown with scrub and bracken and is impractical to use). The hut marked on F39 Ed.1 at the mouth of the Minaret Burn is small and in very poor condition. The lower Minaret Burn is badly gorged. From the end of the 4WD track at about F39 965 258, a stock track can be followed to beyond the first hut. There are two huts in the valley, both private. The lower one, by Slip Creek, sleeps about 6 and is a pleasant station hut. The upper one, at Boil the Billy Creek, is an 'A' frame. Shingle from the creek has flooded through it, leaving it in poor condition, and a dubious place to stay in rain. Beyond the top hut, a rough stock track leads through scrubby country on the true right to flats again at the 800m contour. Open travel continues to the top forks, at F39 864 348, beyond which there are saddles to the South Albert Burn and the Estuary Burn. Bush on the slopes around the top forks is composed of shrubs like *Phyllocladus, Totara, Dracophyllum*, *Hoheria* etc.

When descending, it is important to get onto the 4WD track in the lower Minaret Burn at about F39 965 258.

Time: From the bottom of the Minaret Burn to the top forks, 8 hrs; In the reverse direction, 7 hrs.

MINARET SADDLE (F39 845 377) Minaret Burn to the South Albert Burn

Minaret Saddle offers a reasonable crossing to the South Albert Burn. However, a line of bluffs cut across under the saddle on the Albert Burn side, and care needs to be taken to choose the right line through them. From the top forks in the Minaret Burn, sidle up the true right branch on the true left, using slips close to the stream, then climbing up to 50m above it in scrub that leads to the tussock. Above the 1150m contour, cross as necessary, following the stream on up to the broad easy tussock slopes of the saddle. On the South Albert Burn side, an imposing schist canyon draining from pt 1889m is marked on F39. About 100m to the SW of it at F39 844 381 there is another smaller, unmarked more stable creek. This smaller creek and the short scrub/tussock spur on the true left of it offer a steep but fairly easy route past bluffs down to the South Albert Burn valley flats.

In reverse. Pick up the smaller stable creek and spur at F39 844 381 that leads through bluffs to easier slopes over the saddle. Follow the stream down into the Minaret Burn, crossing as necessary. Down at about the 1020m contour, sidle on the true left in open scrub initially, before dropping down to gravel slips by the creek. Scrub marked on the map is thick in places. The stream at F39 860 353 also offers steep but open gravel from the tussock down to near the forks.

Times: Top Minaret Forks to South Albert Burn Flats, 5.5 hrs; in reverse, 4 hrs.

ESTUARY BURN

The pleasant little hut (2 bunks) 1km below the yards at the top forks belongs to Minaret Bay Station and is in reasonable condition. There are some patches of beech forest around these forks. The hut lower down at F39 943 350 also belongs to Minaret Station but is old and in very poor condition. A stock track on the true right below the old hut leads down to the next flat. From here, a scrubby stock track leads out on the true left to Minaret Bay. Alternatively, a good stock track sidles the lower gorge on the true right, leading to the Estuary Burn mouth. Permission should be sought from Minaret Station (ph 03 443 6001) before visiting.

PT 1546M SADDLE Estuary Burn to Minaret Burn

A saddle at pt 1546m can be crossed from the true right branch of the Estuary Burn to the true left branch of the Minaret Burn. Follow up the Estuary true right branch, initially on the true left past a canyon, then near the stream to a spur at F39 884 372. Climb up it to the pass. Follow the range about 250m SE before descending to the Minaret Burn. Follow the Minaret Burn down and sidle out over a shoulder at 1300m and continue west above the scrub, to descend the gravel creek at F39 860 353.

Times: Estuary Forks to saddle, 2.5 hrs; saddle to Minaret Forks, 3.5 hrs.

'Several miles futher up the Wilkin valley, a large opening in the bush brings to view the hut in Jumboland. The name Jumbo ... seems to suit the locality. Everything is on a large scale except the hut. Jumbo was a horse who once tenanted these pastures, and if he had an eye for anything above clover must truely have been in paradise.'

—Eric Millar, *NZAJ 1929.*

WESTERN MAKARORA TRIBUTARIES

In **MAKARORA WEST TOWNSHIP** the Makarora Shop (Ph 03 443 8372) is the centre of commercial life, and can help with accomodation. DoC also have a useful Visitor Centre here (Ph 03 443 8365). Virtually all the Makarora Catchment is silver beech forest, though there is a tiny patch of mountain beech in the Blue Valley and a remnant of podocarp forest in the Makarora Nature Walk area.

The farmland on the true right of the Makarora is in Mt Albert Station, (Manager Ph 03 443 4427). Wilkin River Jets (Ph 0800 538 945, www.wilkinriverjets.co.nz) run a jetboat service from Makarora up the Wilkin to Kerin Forks ($55 per person) on a daily basis in summer, the Young Valley ($25 per person), and the Albert Burn, Craigie Burn, on demand. Most parties going into the Wilkin make use of this. The same company includes Back Country Helicopters, who fly to these and other places eg Albert Burn near the hut, $220 per person.

Alternatively, Southern Alps Air (Paul Cooper, Ph 0800 345 666, www.southernalpsair.co.nz) based at the Makarora Airstrip beside the town, fly parties to many backcoutry sites. Eg, Wilkin (Top and Kerin Forks), Siberia, Albert Burn ($255 per planeload of 3 passengers), Hunter (Ferguson, Forbes Windpudding), upper Makarora ($255 per plane), the Landsborough (Toe Toe, Creswick and Harpers Flat $510 per plane) and as far away as Big Bay.

WILKIN VALLEY

The upper Wilkin and its side tributaries remains one of the finest valleys in Otago, despite major floods in 1994 that brought considerable amounts of gravel off the hillsides. The Wilkin combines beautiful mountain scenery with easy tramping country and provides a range of tramping trips. More experienced parties may make crossings to a number of surrounding valleys. However, access to the valley is complicated by the need to cross the Makarora and Wilkin rivers. See transport options above.

Those on foot should enquire at the Makarora DoC Visitor Centre for current river crossing information. Usually there are reasonable fords across the Makarora between the town and Wilkin Forks, but the Makarora can only be crossed on foot when the river is fairly low. Similarly, the Wilkin is often unfordable, and should never be under-estimated. Both rivers can be high but quite clear, and watch for soft quicksand after floods.

MAKARORA TO KERIN FORKS

Once across the Makarora, sheep tracks lead through grass and scrub to the Wilkin. Both sides of the Wilkin can be travelled to Kerin Forks, mostly along open farmed flats. The true left leads to the track into Siberia Valley without any need for Wilkin River crossings. A rough but well marked track beginning 2km up valley from the Makarora confluence leads through bush sections.

To visit Kerin Forks Hut and the track on up the Wilkin however, the Wilkin will need to be crossed. There is normally a good ford near the foot of Dans Flat. If the river is low, further crossings to stay on the flats will speed things up. There is a small old private hut (Mt Albert Station) on the true right bank about 1km below the Forks and Kerin Forks Hut (10 bunk, coal stove, DoC cat 2) is at the bush edge, also on the true right, as marked on F38 Ed 1.

Time: Makarora confluence to Kerin Forks, 5 or 6 hrs.

KERIN FORKS TO TOP FORKS

From Kerin Forks, a marked track leads up the true right bank. This sometimes reaches 100m above the river before Jumboland Flats are reached opposite Wonderland Stream. Mt. Jumbo (1945m) is accessible from Jumboland, and a crossing to the Albert Burn begins here. See Albert Burn notes.

Continuing up valley, the track leads through bush for half an hour, then is unmarked across open grassy flats for 2 hrs (still on the true right), to Top Forks Hut, (10 bunks, coal stove, DoC cat 2) as marked on F38 Ed 1. A second older hut here is used as a warden's quarters, but is otherwise also open to the public (6 bunks, DoC, open fire). Between Top Forks and Kerin Forks, the Wilkin River bed tends to be more confined since the floods, even at flats such as Jumboland, making crossings difficult.

Times: Kerin Forks to Jumboland Flats, 3 to 4 hrs; Flats to Top Forks, 2 to 3 hrs.

SOUTH BRANCH WILKIN RIVER Top Forks to Waterfall Flat

A marked track leads to Waterfall Flat. Between the loo and Top Forks Hut, this track enters the bush on the true right of the South Branch and climbs high before sidling to bushline, where the track is not far from the river again. The track continues through scrub, climbing 150m up a watercourse on the corner from a small lone beech tree. The track deteriorates as the ground is less stable in this upper section, though it remains well marked, mainly with orange standards and cairns. These finish where the tussock begins, 30m above the river (still on the true right) at F39 807 495, on the corner at the very beginning of Waterfall Flat. There is a poor bivvy rock at the bottom of the top flat on the true

■ Top Forks in the Wilkin Valley. Mts Pollux and Castor to the right overlook the North Branch. *Lloyd Homer*

left at F39 798 488. There is a better one which sleeps 3 or 4 at F39 807 490, on the true right at about the 1120m contour in the valley.

Time: Top Forks to Waterfall Flat, 4 to 5 hrs.

RABBIT PASS Wilkin Waterfall Flat to the East Matukituki Valley

The difficulty on this crossing is to bypass two waterfalls, one on the Wilkin side and one on the East Matukituki side of Rabbit Pass. The Wilkin Waterfall is the most difficult. A word of caution. It cannot be overemphasised that the route up the Wilkin Waterfall Face is extremely steep and exposed. Look for toeholds kicked into the hard earth. The route should not be taken lightly by parties at any time and be avoided altogether when wet or windy. Less experienced parties should carefully assess their ability before attempting the route, even with perfect conditions. It is more difficult to descend. See the photo on page 95.

Also note that F39 Ed.1 does not show the correct location of the poled route from Rabbit Pass to the East Matukituki. Follow the route described in this text instead. Orange standards begin again in the Wilkin South Branch near the base of the Wilkin Waterfall and lead up a snowgrass fan well to the right (west) of the falls. From the top of the fan, ledges lead up and further right. (See the photo). Then another sloping ledge higher up leads back to the left to the lip of the cirque, some 130m vertically above the TOP of the waterfall. Orange standards cease again here. An easy valley, often snow filled, now leads up past Pearson Saddle (see the Waiatoto Valley for crossing notes) to Rabbit Pass beyond. Good campsites, but the retreat routes are easily cut off in bad weather.

The route around the Wilkin Waterfall is shown.

At Rabbit Pass, orange standards and cairns recommence and continue to the East Matukituki. The route swings 1.5 km to the east (left), gaining 200m altitude to the 1600m contour along a shelf under Mt Lois. Here, a breach in the bluffs at F39 804 469, marked by a standard and a cairn, allows a descent. Although short, about 50m, this rocky descent is also steep, particularly near the bottom, on loose schist that some find quite awkward. Watch for falling stones and expect it to be quite difficult if icy. Orange poles lead through this bluff, then down scree and tussock slopes to a terrace above forks in the East Matukituki at F39 797 461. From here they descend to the infant East Matukituki at F39 796 459. See the East Matukituki section for notes on the reverse direction, P 85.

Times: Waterfall Flat to Rabbit Pass, about 2 hrs; Rabbit Pass to flats in the East Matukituki, 2.5 hrs.

NORTH BRANCH WILKIN RIVER

The Wilkin North Branch is one of the gems of the Wilkin. Ice avalanches cascade from high peaks and extensive glaciers while the valley itself nestles right up under these bluffs. A marked track leads up through bush into delightful alpine meadows past Lake Diana to Lake Lucidus and on to Lake Castalia. However, the route is dependent on being able to cross at least two snowfed rivers.

From the sign by Top Forks Hut, orange standards lead over the flat to the South Branch. Cross and continue over the grass terrace between the forks to the gravel beside the North Branch. Markers and cairns lead up valley, sidling through bush before descending and crossing a major stream draining the Ragan-Pollux cirque. The track climbs steeply up to a terrace through beech forest from these forks. The track then leads through wonderful open beech forest along the terrace edge past Disappearing Tarn. Clear but dark Lake Diana, visible from the track, is set between bush and scrub covered moraine. Beyond the moraine, swamp and tussock meadows are crossed, sometimes on boardwalk, to the Lake Castalia junction sign. Orange standards continue up to the Lake Lucidus outlet on the true right. There is a good bivvy rock (3 person) on the downstream edge of the moraine leading to Lake Lucidus, close to the track and no more than 100m from the lake.

From the track junction, orange standards lead across both streams draining Lucidus and Castalia to the true left of the North Branch. They then sidle up valley through grass, ferns and scrub to cross back to the true right at F39 833 556. The track, less obvious in places now, continues with intermittent orange standards and cairns across open tussock slopes. It crosses back again to the true left at F39 838 565 and cairns lead up stony slopes to the Castalia outlet. The head of the lake can easily be gained on the eastern side. See the Waiatoto Valley for crossing notes to the Te Naihi.

Times: Top Forks Hut to Lake Diana, 1 hr; Lake Diana to Lake Lucidus, 15 mins; Lake Diana to Lake Castalia, 2 hrs.

WONDERLAND VALLEY

Since the 1994 floods, access to this valley, like the Newland, has become more difficult because the Wilkin River is now more confined and bouldery, making crossing more difficult. However, in low flows, cross the Wilkin (and probably the Wonderland) to access the true left bank of Wonderland Stream. There is no marked route. Sidle through forest up valley, where occasional sections of the old cattle trail, 30 to 50m above the stream may be followable. Beyond the bushline, the valley opens out into beautiful alpine herbfields. The true right bank can also be followed up to the flats.

Times: Wilkin to the flats, 2 hrs; and another 2 hrs to the head.

NEWLAND VALLEY

The same access problems apply across the Wilkin as above, and it may be best to approach the valley on the true left of the Wilkin from Kerin Forks. There is no marked route up the Newland. From Newland Forks, bypass falls in the stream on the true right (west) bank by sidling onto a knoll at the 500m contour. Continue across an open creek sidling up valley, keeping about 30 to 80m above the stream. Rough bush, with boulders and prickly shield fern, makes travel slow until a small flat is reached at a creek about 2.5 hrs from the Wilkin forks. A further 30 mins in bush beyond here, (still on the true right, near the stream and sometimes up on a terrace), leads to the flats. The valley is open the rest of the way, and a further 3 hrs to the head. Do not attempt to enter this valley on the true left bank.

Note. On metric map F38 Ed.1, about 1.5km up the Newland Valley, the contour label 800m is wrong. It is the 700m contour.

NEWLAND PASS Newland Stream to the Te Naihi River

For parties crossing to the lower Waiatoto Valley via the Te Naihi, Newland Pass provides an alternative to Pearson Saddle, although Newland Pass is much the more difficult of the two. The difficulties are on the Newland Valley side on the higher slopes of the pass, where there are rockslabs and snowslopes to cross, and steeper loose rock up near the saddle itself. It is best to ascend this side rather than descend it.

From the pass, sidle across the Axius Glacier to the ridge NE of Lake Axius and across the outlet to pt 1581m. This connects with other transalpine routes to the upper and lower Te Naihi, Mueller, and Drake valleys. For further information, see those valleys. Parties need to be experienced and well equipped to travel on these western routes.

Time: Newland Stream to the pass, allow 4 hrs.

SIBERIA VALLEY Kerin Forks to Siberia Forks

Southern Alps Air based in Makarora flies into the airstrip in Siberia on a regular basis in summer, sometimes many times per day. This will detract from the valley's charm for some, but it is also a service that can be used to advantage.

From the Makarora Jetboat pickup and setdown point, about 1.5km below Kerin Forks, a good track leads up the true left of the Wilkin, and a short distance upstream from Kerin forks zig zags through the bush, gaining height quickly. After climbing 450m, the track sidles left around the shoulder and descends to Siberia Flats. The track continues, marked with orange standards and benched in places, to Siberia Hut (20 bunk, pot belly stove, DoC cat 2).

Beyond the hut, the track continues to a signposted junction, where the Gillespie Pass track separates from the track to Lake Crucible. Grass flats continue on up valley, past the tiny old meat-shooters hut at F38 929 635 which is locked. These open flats provide easy travel right to Siberia Forks. The flat marked as scrub on F38 between the Siberia Forks is actually all grass.

Times: Kerin Forks to Siberia Hut, 3.5 hrs up and 2.5 hrs down.

SOUTH BRANCH SIBERIA (True Right) Forks to the valley head

The scrub belt in the South Branch has thickened considerably since the last edition. However, a scrubby but reasonable line still exists with care. Follow open beech forest up valley on the true left and when it finishes, head uphill through scrub towards the first creek marked on the map (F38 916 650), which is open and grassy. Follow it up. Sidle out up valley at the 760m contour through scrub across to another clump of beech trees. Follow up under them to the second stream at F38 914 650. This stream is open and scoured. Climb up it to the 900m contour. Sidle across through thick scrub and prickly shield fern at this height, above three larger totaras, to clearings which become visible at the same altitude. These grassy clearings begin at about F38 910 650, and travel quickly improves. Travel beyond to the head is open and easy. The large patch of scrub further up valley indicated on F38 Ed.1 is actually mostly tussock. There are some large boulders in this basin.

Times. Forks to tussock, 2 hrs; In the reverse direction, 1.5 hrs.

STEWART PASS. This is not a practical crossing to anywhere. Although the pass is quite approachable from Lake Dispute in the head of the Mueller valley, mostly on gravel, the Siberia side is all rock and impractical to descend with packs due to steep, exposed, sweeping schist slabs. Lower down a steep confined gully surrounded by rocky bluffs into which rockfall is channelled exacerbates the dangers. It has been roped down, but don't even think about it.

NORTH BRANCH SIBERIA (True Left) Forks to head

From the forks, follow the riverbed up to the 820m contour. Beyond here, travel in the river is difficult. Follow the stream on the true left of the river at F38 929 666 up to the 920m contour and sidle across to the upper basin through open scrub. Travel up valley beyond here is straightforward. It is better to resist the temptation to sidle up towards Siberia Saddle too early.

Time: Forks to head, 3 hrs; or Head to Siberia Hut, 4 hrs.

SIBERIA SADDLE Siberia to the Ngatau Valley

From the cirque at the head of the North Branch of Siberia, climb up steep tussock spurs and gain a flattish area at about the 1460m contour under and west (upvalley) of the saddle. This flattish area is probably best described as a ledge covered in shattered rock, and it angles up towards Mt Doris. Depending on the time of year, there is usually a snow slope under the saddle here too, but the direct ascent to the saddle is very steep. The easiest option is to ascend loose, shattered rock up a steep gully trending right on the Mt Doris side of the saddle. About 20m from the top of the gully, ledges lead left a few metres to come out about 200m east of and 50m higher than, the low point of the saddle. In spring and early summer an ice axe may be necessary here. Beware of loose rock.

To descend to the Ngatau, follow down the true right of the stream draining the saddle, cross this before the 1200m contour to the left and sidle further left across other basins towards the prominent spur jutting out into the Ngatau. To gain this prominent spur, cross a deep gulch just above the bluff and scrub zone. On the true left of this gulch is a tussock ramp leading back east into the alpine scrub below the bluffs.

There are two routes that have been used to the valley floor from here:

1. The more popular one leaves the prominent spur at about the 1000m contour and sidles right (east) through this alpine scrub zone below the bluffs to a small open knob (820m) at F38 922 703. Descend into the bush. Initially it is very steep, but there is plenty to hold onto. Don't cross the stream that flows parallel down through here, but remain on the true left of it. The angle eases out after approx 10 mins with larger trees. Continue a steady descent to the Ngatau River bank at stream junction F38 924 706. The bush is not dense, and is easily travelled.
2. An alternative route is reported to descend the prominent spur to the valley floor near Hailstorm Gully. In the scrub and bush, trend left to avoid hidden 200m high bluffs. A large cairn may still mark the start of the ascent from the Ngatau coming the other way.

Times: Siberia basin to Saddle, 3 hrs up (or 2 down); Saddle to Ngatau River, 3 hrs down (3.5 hrs up).

CRUCIBLE STREAM AND LAKE

This is a superb side trip from the Siberia Valley. From the Gillespie/Crucible track junction sign on the flats, orange marker standards lead across Gillespie and Siberia Streams to the bush edge on the true left of Crucible Stream. Track markers lead up the spur beside the cataract to approx the 900m contour before sidling into the upper basin. Cross the stream to the true right. Mostly open travel now leads up through grass, prickly shield fern and clumps of *Hoheria*. A reasonable ground trail, marked with cairns, climbs to the lip of Lake Crucible.

Times: Siberia Hut to Flats bush edge, 1 hr; Bush edge to stream crossing in the upper basin, 45 mins; Stream crossing to the lip of Lake Crucible, 1 hr.

GILLESPIE PASS Siberia Flats to the South Young

Note that map F38 Ed.1 is incorrect in this area on several points. The flats centred on F38 950 630 are largely open and grassy, not the extensive scrub as marked. The contour marking 1400m on the Young side just north of here is actually the 1300m contour. The contour at F38 948 615 marked as 1000m is actually the 900m one. Pt 1514m on the range should read pt 1574m. The route marked over Gillespie Pass is also incorrectly shown from the 1320m contour on the Gillespie Stream side through to the Young Basin.

From the Crucible-Gillespie sign on the Siberia flats, standards lead to the bush edge on the true left of Gillespie Stream, where there is a reasonable campsite. A marked benched track now zig zags up approx 200m to the 900m contour where the benching finishes. The track sidles on up into the basin. There are excellent flats in the basin near the bush edge for camping on. Track markers lead on up through a tongue of bush into *Dracophyllum* scrub and orange marker poles are continuously followable from there across Gillespie Pass to Young Hut.

From the 1320m contour on the Gillespie side, the marker poles arc around through tussock then rocks to about 100m west of pt 1629m. They then follow the ridge north to pt 1514m (actually 1574m) where there is usually water in small tarns. The markers then follow a shallow gully and descend the moderately steep spur off pt 1514 m (actually pt 1574 m) swinging left near the bottom to finish just south of the stream draining the lowest point of the pass (1501m, which the track does not go to). The true right of the Young can now be followed down to Young Hut. Most parties prefer to traverse this route from the Young to Siberia and the route is described in that direction in the Young Valley notes over the page.

Times: Siberia Hut to Gillespie Pass, 4 to 6 hrs; Siberia Hut to Young Hut, 6 to 8 hrs.

TIEL (TEAL) CREEK Makarora to headwater forks

This is an attractive little valley opposite Makarora township. It offers moderately capable parties an interesting route to Siberia Flats that can be completed back out to Makarora township via Gillespie Pass in about 3 days. An overgrowing permolat route leads up the true left of Tiel Creek.

Use the short access road at the southern end of the town to approach the Makarora River. It turns off just south of White Creek, leads past the local tip to a ford, and is the Mt. Albert Station (manager Ph 03 443 4427) access. The jetboats based nearby offer a crossing option if the river is up. Cross carefully and follow along the true right bank of the Makarora, where either:

1. About 300m upstream from the Tiel/Makarora junction, an old sign indicates an overgrown route through scrub and bracken up onto a low ridge overlooking Tiel Creek.
2. Alternatively, take a shortcut route beginning about 600m upstream from the Tiel/Makarora junction, where a drainage ditch and fenceline lead across paddocks to the foot of the hill. Follow the south edge of open beech up to the bracken then bear slightly left on minor stock trails to the north end of the same long narrow flat spur overlooking Tiel Creek at about the 380m contour where these two options rejoin.

On the spur here, red and white markers following an old blaze line will be found where bracken returns to bush again at F38 068 567. Markers lead on up the spur, sidling across at about the 580m contour above bluffs and descending slightly to F38 060 568, where the markers are within 30m of Tiel Creek. This old marked route is not maintained and is not easy to follow through some windfall areas. The position of markers facing the opposite direction is often the only indication as to where the route travels next. From the top end of a forest flat overrun with river gravel at F38 053 569 the permolat markers climb to about 60m above the river and are easily followed as they sidle up valley, but become indistinct again near the bush edge in an area of slips. Keep 20 to 30m above the river through this band. Markers should be picked up again just before the grass flats, where they finish about 10m vertically above the river on the higher of two terraces at the bush edge by a tracksign, F38 041 568. There are excellent campsites here.

Open grass and gravel flats lead from here up to the forks and travel is easy, apart from a 15 min sidle through bush on the true right where the 700m contour crosses the valley. The bivvy rock halfway up the flats mentioned in the last edition now sits on an island flooded with gravel. Better dry bivvy rocks can be found on the true left in a tongue of beech forest at a height of 20m above the stream, F38 017 584, among huge boulders, but water may not be so handy. At the forks there is also an excellent campsite on the true right of the south (true right) branch.

Times: Makarora River to the start of the flats, 3 hrs; Start of the flats to the forks, 2 hrs.

SOUTH BRANCH: Forks over to Siberia Flats.

From the forks, sidle through beech forest on the true left of the South Branch, then along slipping shingle slopes until scrub forces travel into the streambed. Follow the streambed up into the tussock and continue following it to the 1300m contour. Sidle out WSW on old deertrails using a small spurlet to cross into a small tussock stream basin above waterfalls at the 1500m contour. This stream is now easily followed to its source at pt 1714m on the dividing range with Siberia. Sidle west from pt 1714m on old major deer trails to the tussock spur leading directly down towards Siberia Hut. However, to avoid the worst bluffs in the bush, do not continue right down this spur to the hut. Just above bushline, this spur splits into two and a small creek develops beween them, marked on F38. Take the southern spur, but as you approach Siberia Flats, sidle back towards this creek to avoid most of the bluffs, finishing on Siberia Flats still on the true left of this creek.

Times: Forks to tussock, 1.5 hrs; Another 2 hrs to the saddle, and 2 more hrs down to Siberia Flats.

NORTH BRANCH: No recent information is available. From the Forks, sidle up valley through beech forest on the true right. Straightforward tussock slopes lead to the dividing ridge and saddle with the South Young, but very steep bluffed tops and bush slopes on the Young side make this a difficult and impractical route for all but the very experienced. Forks to head, at least 1 hr.

YOUNG VALLEY Makarora to Young Forks

This pleasant, bushclad valley joins the Makarora River 4km north of Makarora township. It is part of the Gillespie Pass circuit, a popular tramping route with DoC facilities. Currently, foot access begins at a large orange triangle 2km north of the Makarora Visitors Centre beside SH6. However, both the Makarora and Young Rivers need to be crossed, and both can be deceptively deep and swift, requiring great care. Many avoid the crossings by taking the jetboat instead. DoC plans a new access from the Makarora Blue Pools bridge down to the Young, but the Blue also needs bridging first. Check with DoC.

A good marked track starts at the Makarora confluence on the true left (north) bank of the Young at the bush edge. Here, DoC has installed a two way radio link to the Makarora Visitors Centre, for ordering jetboats (check with DoC whether this is currently operational before relying on it). The track generally stays near the river, and gives easy tramping to the Young Forks. A bivvy rock with fern and *Hoheria* by it at F38 030 621 on the flats at the foot of bluffs sleeps two. A major swingbridge across the North Branch 1km above the Forks, gives access to the South Young track and the pleasant grass flats between the North and South Branches. Across this bridge a signpost also indicates a short (2 min) track up to a levelled DoC campsite where there is a tiny shelter and toilet.

Times: SH6 to Young confluence, 30 mins; Confluence to Young Forks, 2.5 to 3 hrs.

SOUTH YOUNG VALLEY Forks to Young Hut

The South Young emerges from a hidden valley, enclosed by bushclad slopes and guarded by a gorge.

From the bridge, follow the marked track across the flats into the South Branch. The track climbs high over a shoulder, through an area of slips then descends to follow the river. At the first clearing there is a good bivvy rock across the river on the true right, a little over an hour from the Forks. This sleeps 2 or 3 people and is 10m above river level at F38 000 621. The track continues on the true left through bush and small clearings, crossing a bridge over Stag Creek on the way. It then climbs up to the lip of the tussock basin and continues up the true left, past the hut which is seen across the river, to the bridge which is 150m upvalley from the hut. The track is marked with orange poles in the tussock. The hut has a brilliant view from its window, but in winter and spring there is a possibility of snow avalanche danger. Young Hut (10 bunk, stove, coal supplied, DoC cat 2).

Times: Young Forks to Young Hut, 3.5 hrs.

GILLESPIE PASS South Young to Siberia Valley

Note that the poled route over Gillespie Pass shown on F38 Ed.1 is incorrect, as are other map features in this area. See Siberia Valley/Gillespie Pass notes in the Wilkin Catchment, P 98. From the hut in the South Branch of the Young, continue up valley about 1.3km (20 mins) on the true right to orange poles and a sign indicating where the route begins to climb at F38 966 652. This is just down valley of the stream draining the marked Gillespie Pass. The poled track leads up through thick but low *Dracophyllum* scrub, climbing onto the spur from the north. Leading up the spur, the track emerges on the range at pt 1514m (actually 1574m), about 500m SE of the marked Gillespie Pass. There is often, but not always, water in small tarns here.

The poles continue SE along the range, climbing to about the 1600m contour before sidling down through rocky slopes and slumps, curving slowly in lengthening tussock towards the bushline and a little lower, excellent campsites on grass flats by Gillespie Stream at about the 950m contour. The track sidles on down through beech forest on the true left of Gillespie Stream, then rises onto a spur overlooking Siberia. It then descends from about the 850m contour on a benched zig zag track to the Siberia Flats and down them to the hut.

Times: Young Hut to Gillespie Pass, 2 to 3 hrs; Young Hut to Siberia Hut, 6 to 7 hrs.

NORTH YOUNG VALLEY Forks to Headwaters

There is no track up the North Young. In sometimes very thick scrub and boulders, follow the true right to the clearing 3km up valley, then the true left to Waterfall flat and beyond. River crossings require a normal to low river flow. From the DoC campsite upstream from the bridge, follow the river edge on the true right until a pool makes this impractical. Sidle through huge boulders under forest not far from the river, utilising light deer trails and the remains of an old blaze line where possible. At a washout gully, and beyond, keep on the terrace lip overlooking the river; slopes further back are very densely covered in vines, wineberry and tall prickly shield fern. They are very slow going. About 100m beyond two very close, minor creeks marked on F38, the riverbed boulders can be followed again and these turn to shingle as the flats marked on the map are approached. Misty Peak is the main peak up valley, but Young Peak is just visible to the left.

Cross to the true left along these flats (the best options are at the top end). There is an excellent mossy campsite on the true left at F38 008 660, near windfall and 6m above the river. If the river is high it is possible to reach the headwaters on the true left without recrossing. If the river is normal it is far easier to keep to the riverbed as much as possible, climbing into the bush only to bypass a cascade at F38 000 671. At the bottom of the next flat, which is more open and grassy than the map indicates, cross to the true right. Recross to the true left again at the top of this flat, opposite Waterfall Creek and stay on this bank to the head. From this junction, head up through the bush to the 620m contour then sidle on reasonable going to the next flat at a stream draining Foggy Top. Cross this Foggy Top stream and enter the bush a few hundred metres further on. Very rough head high fern, *Hoheria* and *Olearia* scrub now leads up valley for 1.5 hrs and finally ends on open swampy ground.

Alternatively it is also possible to cross the river at Foggy Top stream flat and climb over a steep bushclad ridge on the true right (south) side, to the riverbank below the top meadows. Continue over meadows on the true left and climb through more fern and ribbonwood to the last patch of bush. At the end of this patch, looking out on the upper basin and about 100m away from the river, is a good bivvy rock. This sleeps about 5 in dry comfort and is at F38 957 686. The upper basin of the Young is snowgrass, not scrub as indicated on F38 Ed.1.

Times: Bridge to first flat, 1.5 hrs; First flat to Waterfall Ck, 1.5 hrs; Waterfall Ck to bivvy rock, 4 hrs.

GOVERNORS PASS North Young to the Ngatau

From the North Young, a prominent snowgrass ridge leads up to loose rock above waterfalls. Climb until level with the pass before sidling to the left. From the cairn on the pass move left for 400m above bluffs, then sidle NE into the Ngatau tributary draining Governors Pass, or else descend steep tussock and rocks into the same basin, south of pt 1181m. Sidle west between the 1100m and 1000m contours under bluffs and continue to sidle down across three or four gullys to the true left of Flicker Creek at F38 938 706, and follow the bushed spur here to the Ngatau River. The route described in the previous edition, down an extremely steep face 200m west of the tarn at the 840m contour, is not recommended. Note that on the old S98 map Shelter Ravine and Flicker Creek were named in different places compared to today's F38 map. Moir's takes F38 to be correct. This is a difficult route, for experienced parties only.

Times: Young headwaters to the Ngatau Valley, 9 hrs plus; In the reverse direction, add 1.5 hrs.

LEVEN STREAM

Like the Ore and Teal Creek, this delightful little valley has scenery archtypical of Aspiring Country but on a smaller scale. The Leven and Ore valleys can be combined to make a challenging, but reasonably comfortable long summer day trip. Or a 2 day trip, as the upper basins offer wonderful campsites. The permolat marked route up the Leven starts on the true right bank at G38 102 619 and remains quite followable until the first flats are reached at F38 093 625 (2000). From there, travel is generally easy to the valley head, sometimes in the riverbed, sometimes sidling. The largest sidle avoids rough stream travel. Just across a creek at F38 075 627, on the true right of the Leven, climb about 150m up a spur (light deer trail, open bush) and sidle before descending 40m to the start of midflats, at F38 067 634, a little over 1 hr below the top flats. Several bivvy rocks exist in the valley.

Time: Makarora Valley to the first little flat F38/ 093 625, 1.5 hrs; First flat to top flats, about 3 hrs.

CROSSING TO THE ORE takes 2 to 3 hrs. From upper Leven flats at F38 055 646, a little beyond the beech forest, head ENE up an open Hebe covered fan, carefully picking a line within 20 to 30m of the bluffs above. Continue up scree above the scrub, and swing slightly left, exiting out up a steep little gut just to the west of pt 1370m. A small tarn sits on the ridge here. Head down NE to the grassy Ore flats through open, easy travelling silver beech forest.

ORE STREAM

Flats above the 800m contour in the Ore are open grass, not the scrub marked on F38 Ed.1. To travel down the Ore, generally keep to the true right (essential lower down). There is no marked route initially. Some small flats are passed, but much of the route is bush sidling, generally not far from the river. After a while, an obvious bluffline at the end of a spur (F38 092 634) will be seen down valley. Continue down under it, and on bush slopes 100-300m beyond, old blazes should be picked up at about F38 096 635. (There is one white permolat marker here too, on a corner about 40m above the stream). Follow this unmaintained blazed route, which at once leads out away from the lower Ore gorge following the 650m contour and then climbing gently above bluffs to a flat bushed ridge at about F38 098 631. It is very important to pick up this blazed route and follow it out above the main gorge. It is currently overgrowing but followable (2000). The marked route then heads SE down the obvious ridge high above the true left of Leven Stream. It is marked with permolat down much of this spur, but the spur is open, offering easy travel.

If **going up the Ore,** simply head up the spur on the true left of the LEVEN, beginning close to Leven Stream. Permolat markers at the start are not worth chasing. The spur provides open easy travel and intermittent markers will be picked up once on the spur. Further up, try to stick with them. They lead up the spur to the 650m contour then sidle right, turning into an old blazeline that leads across above bluffs to the Ore Valley before petering out. Continue up the true right.

Time: Makarora Valley to the upper Ore flats, about 5 hrs up; 4 hrs down.

BLUE RIVER Haast Pass Highway to the top flats

The Blue is a classic tramping valley, with Maori Saddle leading from the head across the Main Divide to the more difficult Okuru River. There are extensive flats in the head of the Blue. From the Blue Pools carpark by the Haast Pass Highway, a good walking track leads to the swingbridge over the Makarora River, just above the Blue junction. Immediately across the bridge, a signed and well marked tramping track climbs steadily over a shoulder high above the Blue and dips to cross a basin of very open mature silver beech forest, crossing a couple of streams in the process. Kaka are frequently heard here. The track then climbs again, continuing to sidle up the gorge, before descending to a grassy river flat where the river is lightly screened off by beech regrowth and a neck of bush. This is Camp Flat, G38 111 668, a pleasant picnic and camping spot.

It is great to see that the old permolat route upvalley from here has just been remarked and recut this year (2005). This has been done through DoC as a community project by the Wanaka Tramping Club. Above the main Blue crossing at the North Branch this marked route is all on the true right and links the flats in the valley together, avoiding small gorges. There are extensive grassy flats in the upper valley.

From **Camp Flat**, a scrub and grass corridor between beech forests leads up-valley. This corridor curves back to the river 600m upstream on a light ground trail through open beech saplings. Follow this grassy lead and continue upvalley on the true left on riverstones past the base of a semi-active slip. There is an awkward rock to bypass at the river edge here. At the confluence of the river and a side creek, G38 110 679, markers lead on the true right of this side creek up to a point 50m from the creek at the base of the hill, crossing a patch of prickly shield fern on the way. The marked route then leads directly uphill, climbing 50m to bypass a bluff in the riverbed. At G38 109 682 it descends to about 10m above the riverbed again then follows the riverbank up towards the North Branch. Alternatively, if the river is low, the river can be followed from Camp Flat up to here.

About 50m below the North Branch confluence, there is a very good, wide gravel crossing of the main Blue River, currently the best for several kilometres in either direction. Cross the main Blue River to the true right and remain on the true right to the extensive upper flats. Once across, follow the river edge upvalley to a grassy river channel at G38 104 685. At a cairn on a boulder, 100m up this channel, the marked route climbs onto a grassy terrace, part of an old slip, where there are reasonable campsites. Behind this terrace, 40m distance from the river and obscured by scrub, is a bivvy rock (sleeps 3) at G38 103 686. The route continues along the grassy riverbank through saplings and windfall without climbing and returns to the riverbed upstream. The riverbed, then markers close by, can now be followed to a creek at F38 100 688.

This creekbed has burst its banks, spreading fresh gravel under the trees. A tracksign will be found on a tree on the true left of this creek not far from the river edge. Follow the marked route up on the true left of this creek, away from the river through ferns under the trees for 150m distance. Here, the streambed butts into the hillside. The marked route climbs onto the hillside and sidles up-valley about 50m or more (height) above the river, avoiding a cataract, before descending to a bush terrace close to the river again. Markers now provides good travel along this terrace to a stream junction at F38

093 690. A huge bivvy boulder at F38 094 689, by the track may sleep 2 or 3.

From the stream junction, follow a mix of the riverbed and the marked route 5 to 10m above, still on the true right, to an open gravel washout creek at F38 091 692. About 100m further, at the Blue River edge, markers indicate the start of another sidle up-valley to avoid a small gorge. This sidle climbs to about 60m height above the river before descending again to the river edge at F38 084 693. Follow the riverbed up for 20 mins to the start of major grass flats. These extend upvalley from F38 078 694 to F38 063 692. Scrub marked through here on F38 Ed.1 is incorrect. On the south side of the flat, at F38 075 691, there is a good bivvy rock built by cullers in the 1960s. Look for two large rocks where a large tussocky fan comes out from an extensive area of ribbonwood. From the eastern rock, which looks a bit like an elephant (large and grey) go to the back of the tussock just to the west and head directly uphill for 50m. The biv is above some other large boulders, and sleeps 2 or 3 on a raised wooden platform. Water is available just to the north.

At the top of the flats, just beyond a very scrubby side creek delta, the river gorges and another sidle is necessary. Follow the marked route which, upvalley from the side creek, is 200m from the river on a terrace. The marked route sidles along this terrace and then about halfway to the upper flats climbs to sidle about 70m height above the river. As the upper flats are approached, the markers sidle down slightly to the same height as the grass terraces and continue at approximately that height for the last 10 mins to the flats which begin at F38 054 691. Easy travel on grass now leads to F38 022 698. Scrub marked on F38 Ed.1 is incorrect. There is a good campsite at F38 023 697 and others along the flats. See Maori Saddle notes on facing page.

Descending. At the downstream end of the upper flats on the true right, F38 054 691, cross a small creek and find markers at the bushedge, at the same height as the last grass terrace. Follow the markers and ground trail, sidling at this height for about 10 mins. The marked route then sidles gently up, keeping about 50 to 70m height above the river, descends to cross a terrace, then returns to the river edge. The lower flats begin just after a scrubby creekbed at F38 062 692 and last for about 45 mins.

From the end of the flats, follow the river edge on the true right for 20 mins to F38 083 693. Here, the river becomes gorged and across the valley there is a waterfall. At a cairn on a boulder, climb up the bank and locate the markers about 30m above the river. Follow this marked route until it finishes by the river just upstream of a gravel washout. Mixed travel both in the riverbed and 5 to 10m above on the marked route leads in about 20 mins to a side creek at F38 093 690. Beginning right at the forks, the marked route offers good travel downstream on a beech terrace near the river for about 10 mins. Be careful at F38 097 688, where the marked route swings abruptly uphill near the end of a terrace, and is easy to miss. Follow markers up and sidle about 50m above the river then descend by a gravelly stream under the trees to the riverbed again at F38 100 688.

The riverbed or closeby are now followed to the North Branch confluence crossing of the main Blue River. If the Blue is too high to cross, there is a reasonable rock bivvy to wait at, G38 103 686. See P103 (lower) for more details. Once across on the true left, follow the riverbank for about 300m, picking up markers again. After a short sidle and 50m climb the markers lead back to the river at a streambed. Follow the riverbank from here to the downstream end of a slip. Continue for 100m beyond the slip to where a ground trail and a cairn on the riverbank can be found, leading away from the river and along an old flood channel of light scrub and grass down to Camp Flat. A big cairn marks the track entrance from the bottom of Camp Flat out to the road.

Times: Haast Pass Highway to Camp Flat, 1.5 hrs; Camp Flat to main upper flats, 6.5 hrs.

MAORI SADDLE Blue River to the Okuru River

Enter the beech forest at the top of the main flats on the true right, F38 022 698. Sidle on up the Blue through open scrub and clearings, keeping about 5 to 15m from the river to a boggy grassy flat at F38 018 702. There is a very good fine shingle crossing of the Blue River here. Cross to the true left and continue to the top end of the flats where there are campsites in alcoves just before entering the beech forest. A more awkward section follows through fern, *Hoheria* and beech. Sidle on the true left close enough to the river to boulder hop where feasible.

From the bushline on the true left, continue 100m to the top end of a massive boulder in the river. From here, F38 016 706, follow a gravel creekbed on the true left of the river to the 900m contour. Travel is easy. Now sidle across short scrub and clearings to a second gravel stream and continue to sidle from the 920m contour up to F38 016 714 at the 980m contour, where continuous tussock begins. Scrub and fern are mixed with tussock clearings across this sidle. If care is taken, travel involves little scrub bashing. There is a campsite by the river on the true right at F38 014 717.

Do not cross Maori Saddle itself. Instead, cross the Main Divide at F38 018 723, 100m further south along the Main Divide from the saddle. The route is partly obscured from the Blue, and this has caused some confusion. From the Blue basin, follow up tussock slopes to the base of very steep ground 100m below Maori Saddle at the south end. Then a look up to the right without packs should reveal a straight forward and obvious route. It does not go up any bluffs, but sidles across under them. Sidle up a tussock gully to the right (looking up) to the crossing point, only about 20m height above the saddle. Take care, but travel is not difficult or exposed. On the Okuru side, descend a tussock gully at the base of a slab and head across towards Atom Creek. Once at F38 019 725, across the gully draining Maori Saddle itself, descend the tussock spur to F38 024 725.

At F38 025 725 three huge boulders lean on each other. Between two of them, a tunnel with a dry roof and damp gravel floor offers limited shelter. There are good carpet grass campsites closeby. To descend to the flats in the Okuru, continue down the tributary draining the saddle to F38 025 722 at the 870m contour, where the river drops through big boulders in cataracts. Sidle south for 100m across scrub and fern to a stream visible on the true right. This stream provides reasonable travel down to the 780m contour, where it joins the river. Follow the river down to the grassy flats, sidling close to the river on the true right once in the beech forest. F38 shows the upper Okuru basin as scrub, but an extensive grassy flat extends from F38 032 720 to F38 042 719.

In reverse: Okuru to the Blue. From the upper Okuru flats, enter the bush by the river on the true right. Beyond the bushline follow the riverbed up to the 780m contour, where the river appears to fork, with a major flow entering from a confined channel on the true right. Follow up this channel for about 40m to where an unpromising creek enters, again from the true right, with occasional branches draped across it.

This creek offers fairly good travel up to a prominent corner at F38 025 721 where the creek abruptly swings away from the river and steepens. From this corner, sidle up and across 100m distance of scrub to the main river again, which now flattens off into gravel. From the basin at the 900m contour, follow the rib of tussock up on the true left of the stream draining Maori Saddle to the 1180m contour. Cross to the true right and continue up diagonally to the south on tussock at the base of slabs to the crossing point at F38 018 722, 100m south of the saddle. From here, a diagonal tussock gully leading towards the head of the Blue provides a good route down. The saddle itself is not crossed due to bluffs on the Blue side.

From the head of the Blue, sidle out on the true left at the 970m contour, (F38 016 714) when the river begins to drop near the scrub edge. Open scrub and clearings offer fair travel across to a first gravel creekbed, reached at the 920 m contour, then a second gravel creek, immediately before the beech forest. Easy open travel leads down this creekbed to opposite a massive boulder in the Blue River. About 50m before the river, a ferny valley to the left leads 150m downstream on an old deer trail, cutting out an awkward section of river boulders. Alternatively, the river boulders can also be descended. Continue down the river edge and bush as necessary on the true left to a small swampy flat at F38 018 702. Cross on a good gravel crossing to the true right. Sidle in open scrub and clearings on the true right, 5 to 15m from the river, to the beech forest. Continue to the flats.

There is an alternative Divide crossing 200m south of pt 1383m at F38 019 719, although it climbs 100m higher than Maori Saddle. Easy tussock slopes lead up to it from the Blue, while on the Okuru side, a tussock gully leads NE down to easier slopes in the upper basin at F38 025 725.

In the head of the Blue River, there is also a route below the tremendous east face of Mt Eyetooth. It leads up a rocky ramp and gives moderate access to a saddle on the Main Divide overlooking the Ngatau. Snow lies on parts of this route until late summer and an ice axe at least will be required.

Times: Upper Blue to the upper Okuru Flats (pt 744m) will usually take about 6 hrs in either direction.

SOUTH BRANCH OF THE BLUE. This route is seldom used. From the true right of the Makarora River, below the Blue confluence, climb straight up the slope without sidling to the dwarf beech trees near the bushline at about the 860m contour. Then sidle into the hanging valley, picking a line between bluffs. Alternatively, cross the main Blue at Camp Flat and sidle above bluffs into the true left of the South Branch. Descend to the valley floor above the gorge.

Times: South Branch; Makarora River to head, about 4 or 5 hrs up.

NORTH BRANCH OF THE BLUE. This route is seldom used. From a good crossing of the main Blue River just below the North Branch confluence, climb the spur on the true left of the North Branch. A knob in the bush at the 900 to 1000m contour (G38 113 687) is a good point to aim for when going both up and down valley. Resist the urge to sidle until the floor of the hanging valley can be seen over the lip at the lowest point. Sidle up valley at approx the 1000m contour and descend to the flats at G38 118 698. Travel is thick and rough. It is easier as a descent line.

Times: North Branch; Head flats to the main Blue River, about 4 hrs down.

CROSSING FROM THE BLUE TO THE NORTH YOUNG

Starting at the lower end of the upper flats in the Blue at F38 035 695, ascend the bushed spur between two prominent gulches. At about the 1320m contour sidle west into a tussock basin below pt 1830m. Climb onto the ridge immediately east of pt 1830m via a snowgrass rib at the head of the basin. A short section here is steep and exposed. From pt 1830m, head north directly along Haunted Spur towards Mt Eyetooth over pt 1583m until about 200m south of pt 1562m. From here, descend tussock slopes just to the north of the gulch draining west from pt 1583m to flats in Waterfall Creek at F38 998 692, staying close to the stream to avoid bluffs in the bush. Descend Waterfall Creek through bush on the true right to the Young North Branch. This crossing requires good visibility and good conditions.

Times: Blue to Waterfall Creek, allow a full day, and a further 2 hrs to the North Young.

FISH RIVER

This valley is untracked, but the forks are accessible from the Main Divide above Haast Pass. There are wonderful views on the way in on a fine day. The route is best avoided in the mist. Leave the Haast Pass road at the summit and head up to the west through mossy bush with a few small bluffs (these are easily turned to the south). Within 30 mins open rocky slopes mark the lower edge of an old burn which provides clearer going, minor bluffs to scramble up etc. Aim for a small knob at G38 174 716. From the saddle behind it, head up slightly to the right, aiming for the bushline at G38 169 718 , where there are small tarns. The bush becomes stunted, but tussock leads help.

Travel on the Divide is now superb, on short carpet grass past pt 1309m. Sidle over to, and descend the spur at G38 158 735 leading west directly to the main forks in the Fish. Enter the bush about 20m to the right of the bluffs on the south edge of the spur at a many branched beech tree. 100m below the bushline, there is a short scramble (10m) down a steep section with *Dracophyllum* scrub but otherwise it is open beech forest to the forks. There is a poor bivvy rock (sleeps 2, uncomfortably) on the upstream edge of the bush flat right at the forks, on the true left.

The **North (true left) Branch** has tussock and boulder travel right to the head. Enter the **South Branch** on its true left. Climb a small sharp spur for 100m directly opposite the rock bivvy (not at the gorge) and pick up an old but well worn deertrail. Follow this past large boulders onto flatter going, then on a climbing sidle on a sloping terrrace into a small gully. The deertrail climbs out of this gully and splits; take the fork heading slightly uphill. With care, the trail can be followed all the way into the South Branch, emerging onto a scrubby avalanche chute. Note this point for returning and follow the streambed on up to tussock flats. A reasonable tussock pass to the Howe exists a little south of pt 1620m, which competent tramping parties will have little trouble crossing. (The saddle north of pt 1620m is bluffed on the western side).

Times: Road to forks via the Divide, about 4.5 hrs; Forks to either head, 1.5 hrs.

'Our attempts to sleep were rudely frustrated by an intermittent soft whirring of wings as one or other of a covey of keas would descend from his perch on a high rock above us and investigate the camp, noisily upsetting cooking utensils, clambering over sleeping bags, and giving the occupants serious concern for the safety of their kidneys. When at last I had succeeded in dropping off to sleep, I had the nightmare experience of being suddenly awakened by a hideous vulture, which tugged the flap of my sleeping bag off my head and attempted to kiss me.'

—Eric Millar, *NZAJ 1934*. Camped near Lake Castalia in the Wilkin Valley.

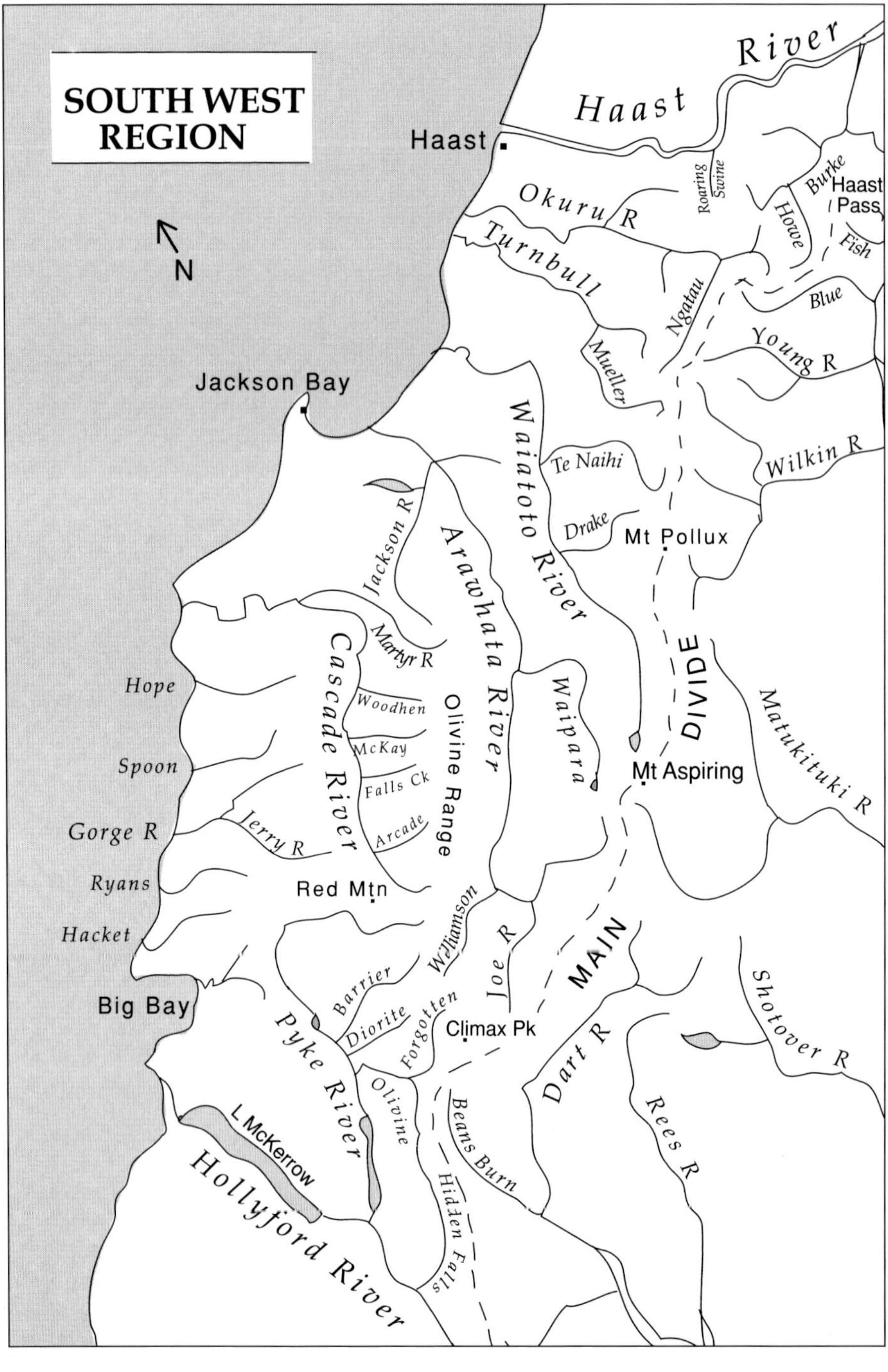
SOUTH WEST REGION
N
Haast
Haast River
Okuru R
Turnbull
Roaring Swine
Burke
Haast Pass
Howe
Fish
Ngatau
Blue
Young R
Mueller
Jackson Bay
Waiatoto River
Te Naihi
Wilkin R
Drake
Mt Pollux
Jackson R
Arawhata River
Martyr R
Cascade River
DIVIDE
Hope
Woodhen
Olivine Range
Waipara
Matukituki R
McKay
Spoon
Falls Ck
Mt Aspiring
Gorge R
Jerry R
Arcade
Ryans
Red Mtn
Williamson
Hacket
Joe R
MAIN
Barrier
Big Bay
Diorite
Forgotten
Climax Pk
Shotover R
Pyke River
Dart R
Olivine
L McKerrow
Beans Burn
Rees R
Hollyford River
Hidden Falls

PART 2: THE SOUTH WEST REGION

The Pyke, Coast, Olivines and Arawhata up to the Haast

INTRODUCTION

Routes in each catchment begin with a description up the main valley and over the pass at the head, followed by the major tributaries and side routes.

This is a remote, wild and rugged area, generally untracked and covered in thick, dripping, scrub laden forest. Massive rivers like the Arawhata, which drains the Olivine Ice Plateau, characterise the country. The Olivine Ice Plateau is a gazetted wilderness area. DoC facilities in the region for trampers are very limited beyond the excellent Visitor Centre at the Haast turnoff from SH6 to Jackson Bay. There is also a Visitor Centre at Makarora.

Even small amounts of rain can make stream and river crossings in this terrain difficult, and the region is not known for its small amounts of rain. Metres of rain fall on a regular basis. The best time of year for transalpine trips is January to March, while winter, which can be cold but settled and drier, suits trips along the coast. October and November can be diabolically wet and unsettled, but great, unpredictable changes occur all year.

Throughout the region, the bedrock is mainly schist. The main exception is the Red Hills ultramafic rock, where high concentrations of some minerals and low concentrations of others has produced a stunted and depleted flora. Forests are predominently beech, with extensive podocarp in places on the flats. Subalpine scrub is dominated by such delicacies as leatherwood, and is extensive in places. Kakas, keas and blue ducks enjoy the mountain strongholds, while fernbirds inhabit the scrub along the coast. And remember that this is the centre of the universe for sandflies and mosquitoes. For a history of the Northern Olivines, see the *NZAJ 1971*, p 140.

Trips in this region are generally restricted to those who are fit and experienced. It is not an area for those new to tramping or for those on their own. Only the trip to Stafford Bay could be called relatively easy. The easier of the hard trips include the trip down the coast to Martins Bay. Most other trips are strenuous and require good bush and often alpine skills. These include:

- Siberia/Ngatau/Okuru/Blue, 6 days.
- Turnbull/Okuru, 5 days.
- Cascade/Red Hills/Pyke to the Hollyford, 7 days.
- The easiest route to the Olivine Ice Plateau is via the Beans Burn and Forgotten River Col. The return can be varied by descending the Rock Burn, or the Olivine Gorge. Allow 9 days.
- A long journey can also be undertaken from Fohn Saddle through a series of passes to Stag Pass and the upper Pyke, 2 weeks.
- Matukituki Valley, Arawhata Saddle and Valley, 7 days.

COASTAL ROUTES From Jackson Bay to Martins Bay

The wonderfully wild isolated coast south of Haast offers some great low level trips. This includes during winter, when fewer sandflies, long fine frosty spells of weather, and great coastal and bush scenery help offset the shorter daylight hours. Add 1 hr to Westport tide times. Travelling at low tide will help in many places.

JACKSON BAY TO SMOOTHWATER AND STAFFORD BAYS

This is a reasonably short 2 day trip suitable for groups with less tramping experience, though some tramping skill is still required. It leads through low saddles and wonderful, mature podocarp and beech forest. A return along the coast to the Smoothwater makes a round trip, but both favourable tide and sea conditions are essential. Sections of the route follow a benched track constructed in 1876, built to service an attempted settlement at Smoothwater Bay. At Stafford Bay there is a hut, but there are no bridges across the Smoothwater or Stafford Rivers. Normally they are easily waded.

There is vehicle parking 600m before Jackson Bay, at the DoC sign indicating the start of the track. Initially the track climbs steeply towards the saddle above, but then it joins the old benched track. An excellent track now leads through magnificent lush forest as far as the Smoothwater riverbed. When returning, this track entrance from the riverbed is well marked with orange triangles. Follow the river up valley for 15 mins, crossing as required. Occasional markers and thin grass flats in places on the true left assist. When Kakapo Creek, marked by permolat and orange triangles, is reached, follow the creek for 200m; then the markers continue along the true left bank. Though mostly on the true left, both banks (and the creekbed for short distances), are used at times. The marked route leaves Kakapo Creek on the true left and heads for Stafford Saddle.

Beyond the saddle, the marked route follows the range north, sidles, then descends a spur into the headwaters of a creek draining to the Stafford. Markers cease at forks in the creek at the base of the spur, E38 550 797. The creek offers good travel, with small open flats 20 mins before the Stafford. The stream runs into the Stafford at E38 532 797, beside deer pen remains. Follow the river down valley, (usually 5 crossings) to pick up the short marked track on the true left leading to Stafford Hut (6 bunk, open fire, DoC cat 3). Stafford was relocated to the site by the NZFS in the 1980s.

If returning along the coast, remember that low tide and a calm sea are necessary, particularly at E38 565 833, a hundred metres west of the Smoothwater, where the sea butts a rockslab for 10m. Headlands on either side of Homminy Cove are best bypassed on roughly marked routes (some new markers here) across their necks. From Smoothwater Bay, follow up Smoothwater River for about 40 mins, either wading as required, or along a lightly marked route on the true right bank to the well marked start of the benched track out from the Smoothwater to the Jackson Bay Road.

Times: Jackson Bay Rd to Stafford Hut (inland marked route), 4 to 5 hrs; Stafford Hut to Smoothwater Bay via the coast, 3 hrs; Smoothwater Bay to Jackson Bay Rd along the riverbank and track, 2 hrs.

CROSSING THE TEER AND CASCADE PLATEAUS

The Cascade Plateau is a huge lateral moraine of ultramafic rock originating from the Red Hills which has produced a stunted, subalpine type of vegetation only 300m above sea level. Routes here are not marked, and good navigational skills are essential. Below the Martyr Homestead the Cascade River enters extensive swamps, and crossing the river is impractical without swimming. It is practical (low tide and sea permitting) to follow the coast from the Stafford west as far as Whiskey Creek and a little beyond, but definitely not around Cascade Point due to major bluffs. Open travelling on the

The South Westland coast near Teer Ck.

Cascade Plateau can be approached up Whiskey Creek. Work up boulder blocks in the creek to falls, and sidle them on the true right. Return to the stream, and about 200m beyond the falls a deer track leads out on the true left to the plateau and open travel.

STAFFORD BAY TO THE CASCADE VALLEY

To reach the Cascade Plateau from Stafford Bay head up the spur directly south of the hut. A map and compass is necessary to keep to the route. At about pt 290m you should stumble across the unmistakeable line of the old overgrow benched Jackson Bay-Cascade pack track. This is followable with care through ever more stunted bush at approximately the 300m contour until open scrub near the Teer Plateau is reached. Then it sidles down towards a stream and disappears by it at about E38 519 776. (In reverse, cross 100m downstream, and climb up to find/meet the track).

Keep heading in a SW direction, crossing the deep gulch of Teer Creek directly at about E38 514 755. (Going the other way, a cairn at E38 512 755 indicates a good descent line). Follow over the stunted manuka, shrub and fern, about knee high, to the head of the Cascade Plateau, pt 587m. There is a great view here out to sea and inland towards the Red Hills and Olivine country. There are good campsites on the bush edge, beside a small stream. Dry campsites can be hard to find on the plateau itself. From pt 587m, drop down the main spur on the true right of Laschelles Creek, keeping well above the creek, and traversing down and around some bluffs in the heavy bush to reach the open farmland of the Cascade Valley at E38 515 713. Travel down the open riverbed of the lower Laschelles Creek, fording the Martyr River to the road.

Times: Stafford Hut to Cascade Valley over the plateaus, allow 2 days.

CASCADE COAST TO THE HOLLYFORD

Tides are an important consideration on this route. Add about 1 hour to the tide times for Westport. In the early 1970s, mining companies bulldozed out to the coast, south to Big Bay and into the upper Pyke. This tramping route essentially follows the same line. Parts of the old bulldozed trail still exist, sometimes in the most unlikely places, such as the intertidal zone on this wild coast.The sea still hasn't rolled the boulders back. But at places like Sandrock Bluff, the vegetation has reclaimed the track with a vengeance. Along with others, Mauryne Cannell from 'Round About Haast' (ph 03 750 0890) offers road transport down to the Cascade and other local areas on demand at reasonable rates.

The route begins at the Martyr Homestead in the Cascade Valley, where normal car access along the gravelled Jackson River road finishes. If anyone is in residence, parties should seek permission, as the route crosses private land at the start. There is normally no problem. This farm in the Cascade has recently changed hands. Usually it takes a day on a bulldozed track to reach the coast, then at least another two full days of mainly boulder travel to Big Bay and a shorter day to Martins Bay. This assumes there are no problems crossing the Cascade and Gorge Rivers, both of which can hold parties up for days. Heading south gets these crossings over with in the first half of the trip. Along the route, fishing buoys hanging in trees are often used to identify the start of sidles inland around coastal obstacles.

CASCADE RIVER TO BARN BAY

From the gate at the roadend, follow a 4WD track out towards the Cascade River, almost looping upstream before heading down the river edge. Choose a crossing carefully, as the Cascade is a big river, then pick up the 4WD track again, this time on the true left. About 700m from the river the track forks. Take the left fork through a gate marked by fishing buoys and follow the track into the bush. (The right hand fork heads down to a shed). Continue through the next grass clearing, which is dotted with kahikateas and blackberry, parallel and close to the base of the hill on a less distinct trail which improves on re-entry to the bush again. This trail follows a more direct line closer to the hill than the loop marked on E38 across this open area.

At Dee Creek there is an open shinglebed to descend. Watch out for where the track heads left again, and the same applies at Limestone Creek, which is more forested. There are dead trees and open shingle at Robinson Creek but the route remains easy to follow to an unlocked private hut on a terrace above the Hope River. (Sleeps 5 or 6, and belongs to Ken Landaus of Haast; treat it with care and clean up well). The 4WD track finishes down a gravel bank just below the hut, where the river changes from greasy boulders to shingle flats. A couple of easy crossings and a short wade on the true left at mid to low tide leads to the coastal beach, passing river flat campsites en-route. The house by the airstrip on the true right at Barn Bay is private.

Times: Martyr Homestead to Dee Creek, 3.5 hrs; Dee Creek to Barn Bay, 2.5 hrs.

BARN BAY TO THE GORGE RIVER

Travel down the coast is now on rounded boulders of varying sizes. There is a small useable campsite in the rocky bay 1km down the coast from the Hope River mouth. Fresh water can be found in a small trickle 100m further south. Campsites are uncommon down to Sandrock Bluff, but there is another small tent site clearing at the back of the beach at E38 318 660. Fresh water is a problem here though.

At Sandrock, an overgrowing and poorly marked bulldozed line zig zags up and over the bluff. Fishing buoys mark the route entrance on the northern side, about 350m back from the Point at E38 317 654. Hookgrass, cutty grass, and fierce nettle line the route which gains 100m height to the ridge.

At Big Bay, looking north.

The track turns right, following the ridge before sidling down in more zig zags to Bluff Creek, about 250m upstream from the coast. Intermittent permolat and buoys mark the track and exit to the creek. Follow the creek down to the coast.

The coast is now fine gravel and sand beaches, with good campsites in the vicinity of Bluff Creek, Callery Creek, Spoon River, and both banks of the Gorge River. Beyond Browns Refuge, travel reverts to boulder bashing. At D38 271 591 there is a limestone bluff with a good bivvy rock (sleeps 4) under it on the southern side, 10m back from the coast. A red lettered sign 'Rock Bivvy', visible from the beach, indicates its position when approaching from the north. There is a small creek close by.

The Gorge River has a very high, steep bluff on the south bank that is better avoided. Although there is a deep pool extending well upstream from the sea, at low tide a gravel bar in the pool up near the bluff usually allows a waist deep crossing. Failing that, there should be an aluminium dinghy tied up on one side or the other near the bluff. Take care to tie it up securely again away from the floods. Sometimes the Long (Beansprout) family will be in residence and may be able to help if the dinghy is on the southern side. Give them a yell, the're closeby and normally hear. Gorge River Hut (sleeps 6, new stove 2002, DoC cat 3) is beside the airstrip, just south of the Long's home.

Times: Barn Bay to Sandrock Bluff track start, 2.5 hrs; over bluff, 30 mins; Bluff Creek to Gorge River Hut, 3.5 hrs.

GORGE RIVER TO BIG BAY

Taxi along the airstrip back to the beach stones. These lead to a small bluff 10 mins further down the coast. In calm conditions at low tide the bluff may be passed with care. Usually a 10 min sidle in tall scrub is required. It starts up a small creek (buoy markers), climbing about 15m vertically before sidling on shelves and descending a toitoi and scrub slope to the beach again, just south of the bluff. More boulders. In high seas and tides, the section just north of Longridge Point is also difficult as boulders butt into the gravel cliffs.

Where Ryans Creek and the Hacket River reach the coast there are fine gravel and sand bays, with good campsites. There are two further moderately good campsites at D39 156 497 on the true right of a stream and D39 164 486 with water in small creeks from flax swamps. Crayfish Rock is bypassed through a low saddle in scrubby bush on a ground trail from a small gravel beach on the west side and is marked with a buoy on the east side. Travel from Crayfish Rock to the beach at Big Bay is slow, hard work over endless greasy ultramafic boulders. At Big Bay, there are several campsites on the true right of the Awarua, near the mouth and better ones along the start of the Pyke Valley track.

From the beach by the Awarua River, there are two approaches to Big Bay Hut, depending on conditions. Much the easiest line, useable at low tide, is simply to cross the Awarua on the beach and follow the beach south, looking for the tall marker pole and a buoy on the first row of sandhills marking the track into the hut. Behind the sandhills along here is a confusion of tracks and private huts.

The second approach, necessary at high tide or if the Awarua is up, is to follow a marked track through the bush along the true right bank of the Awarua upstream for 30 mins until a swingbridge is reached. Cross and follow a good track for 10 mins through forest towards the coast again, swinging north to join the track from the beach. Big Bay Hut (9 bunk, wood stove, DoC cat 3) is about 100m beyond this track junction, at D39 205 450.

Times: Gorge River Hut to Longridge Point, 2 hrs 20 mins; Longridge to the Hacket River, 2.5 hrs; Hacket River to Awarua Point, 1.5 hrs; Awarua Point to Big Bay Hut, 4 hrs.

BIG BAY HUT TO MARTINS BAY

Fast travel on sand leads from Big Bay Hut to the McKenzie Creek bar, which is easily crossed. There is an old overgrown and wet bulldozed line a couple of metres back from the beach through scrub that leads to a private hunters hut right on the coast. The route mostly continues along the beach though. Orange markers indicate a muddy track through scrub to bypass Penguin Rock, as marked on the map.

Further on at Long Reef Point, the open ground marked on the map is actually all thick scrub. An old permolatted track cuts across the base of the point (where there is a seal colony), but it is hard to locate and very muddy. The alternative is to continue on the boulders round the Point to the shallow bay beyond. Pick up the well defined track at a DoC sign at the edge of the vegetation, D39 113 406. This track now leads to Martins Bay Hut at D39 116 405 (sleeps 12 on platform bunks, stove, DoC cat 2) beside the Hollyford River mouth. About 10 mins south of the hut along the track there is a short signposted side track to a boat landing beach by the river, used by the jet boats and others.

Time: Big Bay Hut to Martins Bay Hut, 5 hrs.

UP THE HOLLYFORD RIVER

The lower Hollyford is described in *Moir's Guide South*, edited by Robin McNeill, but here is a short route summary. From Martins Bay Hut, it is about 1 hr 20 mins to the Air Fiordland airstrip, the northern one marked on the map, and another 20 mins to the Hollyford Walks Ltd airstrip near their Martins Bay Lodge. Hollyford Walks also operate jetboats, open for public charter, from the Lodge as far up the Hollyford River as Rainbow Reach, just beyond Rainbow Creek. There is also a wilderness homestay at Jamestown, called Charlies Place, open from Nov to April. Cost; trampers about $25 per person night. B&B and homestay options are also offered at higher rates. Ph. 0274 893 570 for more info.

The track continues to Hokuri Hut, (sleeps 12 on platform bunks, stove, DoC cat 2), 5 hrs from Martins Bay. Then a slow sidle up and down along the McKerrow Lake shore leads to Demon Trail Hut (sleeps 12, stove, DoC cat 2), and 6 hrs from Hokuri. The Hollyford track continues to the Pyke swingbridge, crosses and continues along the true right bank of the Hollyford. The track is now of a high benched standard and continues this way to the roadend at Humboldt Creek, passing the marked sidetrack to the new Hidden Falls Hut (sleeps 12, stove, DoC cat 2) 8 hrs from Demon Trail Hut, and 2.5 hrs from the roadend.

Old Hidden Falls Hut has been removed. About 50m from the old hutsite a signposted sidetrack leads several hundred metres to the new hut, sited on the grassy pt 43m flat, closer to the river. At the roadend, the toilet provides better protection than the tiny Shelter, through which drizzle blows when it rains and sandflies have free reign, but at least there's something there. At the roadend a short track leads 15 mins in towards Humboldt Falls. The viewing point offers a wide panorama up valley to the Falls and is spectacular, particularly when Humboldt Creek is in flood. Gunns Camp, run by Murray Gunn, is about 8km from the roadend. It provides good cheap accommodation and has a shop and petrol, but no phone.

On the Road to Martins Bay.
(Tune: Road to Mandalay)

By the shores of Lake McKerrow
Looking westward to the sea
There's a swarm of sandflies waiting
And I know they wait for me …

—*The Southland Tramper 50th Jubilee Edition 1997,* Southland Tramping Club.

'Didn't enjoy the bugs, but they enjoyed me.'

—Quote from the Gorge River logbook.

THE PYKE VALLEY

The Pyke Valley is the northern half of the Hollyford Catchment. It drains the Red Hills Range and Olivine Range, and its main tributaries are used as access to these regions, despite them being gorged and untracked. The main valley itself is famous for its sandflies, mosquitoes, scrubby swamps, bad flooding and an overgrown track. Only a marked route leads up the valley from Lake Alabaster to the Big Bay track. The most common trip in the catchment is the Hollyford-Pyke, but this in itself is still demanding, despite its low altitude.

There are various transport options available in and around the Pyke area and DoC Te Anau should be able to offer up to date information about them. Hollyford Walks offers a jetboat service in much of the lower Hollyford from the sea to Rainbow Reach, and up the Pyke as far as Olivine Hut. Various companies fly to several strips in the Hollyford from near the Hollyford Roadend, to Martins Bay and some fly to Big Bay, landing on the beach at low tide. A new Pyke Lodge has been built to replace the old lodge that burnt down in 1997. This is a private facility.

LAKE ALABASTER TO BIG BAY

From the Pyke footbridge a good track leads to the new **Alabaster Hut** (sleeps 20 on platform bunks, DoC cat 2). In heavy rain the Pyke floods, the lakes fill and travel on the marked route up the Pyke beyond here will become impassable. Water levels may remain high for many days. This applies especially to the Lake Alabaster shore and flats beyond, river crossings and the Lake Wilmot area. Even in normal conditions, knee deep water can be expected, especially towards Alabaster Creek. Parties should always keep this in mind. Orange triangles on poles have been used by DoC to mark the route up valley to the Big Bay track through open and scrub areas. In the bush, markers on trees replace them, but this is not an easy route to negotiate. It is not intended to maintain it beyond a marked route standard.

Follow the shoreline right around the SE side of Lake Alabaster. The track marked on D38 Ed.1 is now overgrown and unfollowable. Cross the mouth of Alabaster Creek on a gravel bar by the lake. After rain, this can become a deep and dangerous crossing. Marker poles lead from here through grass and scrub, then markers continue through forest on the true left of the Pyke, as the map shows, to **Olivine Hut** (6 bunk, good condition, stove, DoC cat 3).

An airstrip hut (3 or 4 bunks, open fire, old) on the true right, midway between Lake Alabaster and the Olivine, is marked on D39, and is occasionally used by hunters. Opposite here, the marked route on the true left passes through an area known locally as the Black Swamp.

About 1.5km below Olivine Hut a large section of the marked route that had been washed out by floods was remarked by DoC staff. However, the section from the bush edge above Lake Alabaster to the Black Swamp is difficult to follow in places. If route marking is not obvious, the riverbank is preferable to the swamp. The cage across the Olivine is in good condition. Olivine Falls, a good 40 mins up the riverbed from the hut, is an interesting side trip.

Beyond Olivine Hut, the marked route to the Barrier River is correctly shown on D39 Ed.1. It follows the old stock route, but is overgrown and can still be hard to follow in places. Between the Diorite and the Barrier, which are both unbridged, the marked route passes through flax and tussock wetlands.

There are campsites on the true left of the **Barrier** near the crossing. There were once cattle yards here. From the far (true right) channel of the Barrier, the marked route heads through tall beech forest directly towards the base of the hill at the SE corner of Lake Wilmot, making a straight line to Larnachs Creek. (The route marked on D38 Ed.1 here is incorrect). The route around the lake is difficult, especially if the lake level is high. At the top end of **Lake Wilmot,** at D39 294 368 there is a bivvy rock (sleeps 3, open to the west), 20m above and about 50m back from the lake in the bush.

Beyond Lake Wilmot, marking with poled orange triangles continues to the Pyke Crossing, at Paulin Creek. There is an old airstrip at D39 288 428 on flats near the river, with higher ground in the middle of it. At the airstrip is an inhospitable tin freezer which could be used for shelter in an emergency. In normal conditions there is a reasonable crossing of the Pyke near Paulin Creek, but after rain the crossing becomes impassable. Good campsites exist on both sides of the Pyke here.

THE TRACK TO BIG BAY from the Pyke is as marked on D38 Ed. 1. This track is in much better condition than the marked route up the Pyke. It is well marked at the Pyke Crossing with big orange plastic markers and initially follows up Paulin Creek. Considerable care is required to pick up where the track leaves this creek. Then it cuts through the bush to the Dry Awarua and joins an old bulldozed line to the coast. The track finishes at Big Bay on the true right of the Awarua, where the track entrance is signposted. Cross the Awarua River on the beach if possible. Follow the beach south, keeping a close lookout for the orange buoy and tall cream pole in the sandhills, which indicates the short track to Big Bay Hut. Alternatively, at high tide or in flood conditions, a track on the true right of the Awarua leads for a further 20 mins to a bridge across the Awarua. Big Bay Hut (sleeps 9, DoC cat 3) is at D39 205 450.

Times: Lake Alabaster Hut to Olivine Hut, 7 to 10 hrs; Olivine Hut to Paulin Creek confluence, 6 to 9 hrs; Paulin Creek to Big Bay, about 4 hours.

PYKE GORGE Big Bay turnoff to Pyke Camp (Simonin Flat)

This gorge is essentially sidled on the true right. In low river conditions, the Pyke can be followed up to E39 330 444 (with some crossings required) where the first sidle is necessary, due to deep rapids entering a pool between rockwalls. Climb onto a terrace on the true right, sidle, and descend steep slopes to the river again at E39 336 442. Follow along a good dry river channel upstream (there are reasonable campsites at E39 338 440 on this side, and wonderful camping flats at E39 335 441 and E39 327 441 on the true left). Then sidle (true right) again, often on good deer trails near the terrace edge overlooking the river, in beech/kamahi forest, climbing about 100m over a shoulder before descending steeply directly to the Red Pyke/Main Pyke River confluence.

Cross (normally not hard) the bouldery Red Pyke River to a small campsite on the true left and climb out up to the 300m contour, sidling at that height under pt 429m to a bush terrace at E39 358 435. On the big corner under Red Mountain, travel becomes very scrubby and slow as one progresses towards Simonin flats and many parties have problems here. Stay high, where travel is very rocky but easier. Lower down especially, scrub is thick, deer trails overgrown, and some of the gullies deeply eroded. Sidle to an eroded open gully at E39 364 435. Ascend it to about the 500m contour, then sidle again through open scrub and ultramafic rockfields to the running stream at E39 369 427. Carefully head south through scrub and open leads to the start of Simonin (Pyke Camp) Flats. The true left of Pyke Gorge is best avoided.

In the reverse direction, from the flats it will help to find a route through scrub to rocky slopes above. An old deer trail begins on flats about 50m from the river, climbing steadily through scrub to the scrubline in a down river direction. If this can be found it will help. Two now-historic mining camp huts on Simonin Flat are all that is left of a prospecting flurry and conservation battle in the 1970's that led to the area being protected. The main one is quite spacious and useable but leaks in heavy rain. The smaller hut has rock core samples in it. Reasonable campsites also exist.

Times: Pyke/Durward fks to Red Pyke, about 5 or 6 hrs; Red Pyke to Simonin Flat, about 7 hrs.

PYKE CAMP TO SIMONIN PASS

In the hut clearing about 200m downstream from Pyke Hut, by a minor rivulet at E39 369 421, a cairned route climbs up through beech forest towards Red Mountain (2004). This is a bit hard to find, but easy to follow once on it. It goes straight up a rocky open part in the scrub then veers to the right. The cairns peter out once clear of the vegetation. Sidle on bare ground round to a shoulder at about the 750m level then descend slightly to Simonin Stream. Follow Simonin Stream up to the Pass. There is a campsite 20 mins before the pass, but the pass itself is dry and composed of big, orange boulders. There is also a bivvy rock downstream on the true right.

Time: Pyke Camp to Simonin Pass, 5.5 hrs.

PYKE/DURWARD CONFLUENCE TO THE RED HILLS RANGE

This route has been used as an approach to the Red Hills Range from Big Bay and can be combined with routes on into the Cascade Valley. There are various options:

1. Climb up a heavily bushed spur onto pt 1166m from near the Durwards/Chrome Creek junction.
2. Climb a bushed spur directly from further up the Pyke, if the river is low, onto the same tussocky pt 1166m. Good travel in pleasant grassy troughs along the ridge, surrounded by forest again, then leads to the Red Hills tops at pt 1208m. There are excellent bush campsites near the tarn between pt 1023m and pt 1086m.
3. Follow up Durwards Creek and climb onto Telescope Hill.

There are also good campsites at the bush edge on these ridges, and near the tops tarns of the Red Pyke River. In fine weather, the tops basins of Peridot Stream provide easy travel to Barrington Saddle at the head of Barrington Creek. Red Mountain (1705m) is accessible from here up a long bouldery gully that curves around from the north under pt 1611m. See notes on the Cascade approaches to the Red Hills, p 135.

Times: Pyke to the Red Hills tops, about 7 hrs; Red Hills tops to the Pyke, about 5.5 hrs.

BARRIER GORGE Pyke Valley to Barrier Flats

Follow the true left bank of the Barrier River, using dry channels initially, then sidling in bush towards the gorge. At about E39 316 338 climb steeply, then carefully pick a line back through bluffy bush to a major shoulder at the 320m contour.

Beyond the shoulder, sidle across to a large scree slide about 100m above the river. There should be cairns here and on subsequent screes to help indicate the route. This middle section of the route tends to be more open and scrubby than the first and last sections which are more heavily bushed. Other, narrower screes follow, then a rocky gut crossed at about the 420m contour, followed by more screes, keeping 60 to 100m height above the river. From the last side creek marked up valley, climb more sharply up to a bench at the 600m contour and sidle at that height through huge mossy boulders under beech forest to the flats, keeping to the hill side of the bench rather than the river edge.

Descending: Follow the true left, sidle at the 600m contour, then descend sharply to cross numerous screes and gain the shoulder at the 320m contour between bluffs. Sidle left through bluffs then descend quickly to the river.

Time: Variable, but about 8 to 10 hrs up, and 7 or 8 hrs down.

BARRIER FLAT TO OLIVINE ICE PLATEAU

Follow either bank of the river (the true right being easier) to the start of the north branch gorge. Here, a good deer trail climbs the scrubby spur overlooking the gorge on the true right and gains the undulating tussock bench at about the 1060m contour. This bench can also be accessed across from Saddle Stream at about the same height. Follow the bench to the head of the valley. From pt 1271m descend SE to two big boulders (1200m contour), then sidle upvalley to the river. Amongst moraine and by the flats there are good campsites at E39 387 354. The tarn at the head of the valley is gravelled up (1999). From E39 390 354 follow an unmarked creek then snow basins and moderate slopes up to the Pic d' Argent divide at E39 401 343. Traverse across the neve of the Gyrae Glacier and over Little Ark to the Plateau. Alpine skills and equipment will be required above the valley.

Times: Stag Pass sidle to valley head, 4hrs; Valley head to Pic d' Argent, about 3.5 hrs; Pic d' Argent to the Ice Plateau, about 2.5 hrs, depending on conditions.

Stag Pass and the Barrier Flats. *Lloyd Homer*

STAG PASS Barrier River to Upper Pyke River

To gain Stag Pass from the Barrier Flats, walk up Red Stream for a few hundred metres and Southern Cross Creek will be seen as a series of cataracts on the true left. About 100m beyond, climb a dry gully on the true right of Southern Cross Creek and having passed the cataract, cross to the true left at very roughly the 900m contour. Avoid climbing too far away from the creek as you sidle on up towards Stag Pass (2004). Alternatively, a route on the true left of Southern Cross Creek beginning at E39 347 360 has also been used, climbing an open boulder gully and sidling into Southern Cross Creek. Alternatively, (again!) follow the true right bank of the Barrier to Saddle Stream (10 to 15 mins), then follow the true right bank of the latter, keeping out of the stream. Sidle across red rocks to the tussock and continue past tarns to the pass. Little Red Hill is only 160m higher and worth the effort. There is a reasonable rock bivvy (sleeps 2-4) at the east end of the pass at the foot of the ridge to Mt Ellespie.

Various routes have been descended from here to the Pyke. The main one is described first. From the pass, descend to a wide red rock shingle shelf at 980m and follow it to overlook a deep gully at its northern end. Look up here and a waratah and cairn should be seen at E39 364 388. The goal is to gain the broad shingle ridge that divides Rata and Kea Creeks. The problem is a ring of low cliffs across this route. Ascend to this waratah and cairn on the skyline which marks the best place to descend some initially steep scree through the cliffs down to the ridge. The remains of a blazed deer trail down the ridge through the bush from pt 601m is overgrown but still quite useable; an alternative is to descend a scree gully on the right (east) of the ridge just before the continuous bush is reached, leading down to the Pyke at E39 371 402. Alternatively, from the end of the shingle shelf, the ridge between Rata and Kea Creeks can also be accessed by descending bush through bluffs into Rata Creek and sidling 100m across to the ridge.

If the Pyke River is not up, it is worth a couple of crossings to bypass the knob at E39 370 407, then as necessary, follow along the edge of the terrace above the Pyke River on the true right in taller forest. With low flows and dry stones travel right down the riverbed itself can be very pleasant, but some of the serpentine rocks get very slippery in the wet. The knob is okay to traverse if necessary though with open clearings on the south side; and keep overlooking the river when dropping off the knob to the north. Most of the open clearings shown along the tongue between the Pyke and Simonin Stream are swampy and scrubby however. At Simonin Flat (Pyke Camp) are two historic mining huts, (2004) all that is left of a prospecting flurry and conservation battle in the 1970's that led to the area being protected. The smaller hut has mining samples in it and both can be damp in heavy rain, but a roof over your head would still be welcome. Good camping is also available.

Times: Barrier Flat to Stag Pass, 2 to 3 hrs; Stag Pass to Pyke Camp, 4 hrs.

DIORITE GORGE Pyke Valley to Diorite Flats

The Diorite gorge can be approached by either sidling from the lower Barrier River, or the lower Olivine. Travel is slow through thick bush.

1. From the lower Barrier River, sidle through bush up near the base of the hill to the Diorite Stream and cross to the true left. A steep spur leads up to the 300m contour. Continue on up as described below in 2.
2. From the Olivine Hut, follow the Olivine River bed up towards its gorge, then sidle left through forest, keeping near the base of the hills. Sidle to within 500m of the Diorite, then climb diagonally up towards the spur overlooking the Diorite at the 400m contour before sidling up

valley through thick forest, about 100m above and 200m from the stream itself, to emerge on the flats on the true left.

Time: About 6 hrs from the Barrier or Olivine Rivers to the flats.

BERESFORD PASS Diorite Stream to the Barrier River

The route to Beresford Pass from the Diorite is straightforward, the best route being initially up the spur on the true right of the creek. From the pass, descend keeping right (east), a little away from the creek at the bush edge. The route lower down in the bush swings left and follows closer to the creek, still on the true right. Cross the creek at about the 840 m contour, sidle out on the true left to a prominent spur and then descend open bush to some glades beginning at E39 348 348. Follow these to the flats. Recent reports indicate that old blazes on this route are now very hard to locate descending, but are initially followable going up. Well away from the creek on the true right, deer trails can also be followed directly to the flats, too.

The Reardon Memorial, a pair of antlers set in a concrete base, is on a small terrace on the true right of the Barrier river set back amongst the tussock. There is a good campsite at the top of the flats on the true right.

Times: Diorite to Beresford Pass, 3 hrs; Pass to Barrier Flat, 2.5 hrs.

FOUR BROTHERS PASS Diorite Stream to Olivine/Forgotten Rivers

From the Diorite Flats follow an obvious scree gully somewhat to the west of the pass. Traverse left from the top of the gully over boulder scree to reach tussock slopes below the pass. Other routes may be found up narrow creek beds in the bush. When descending to the Diorite from the pass, go straight down initially before sidling left, to avoid slow travel on boulder fields higher up.

1. The Lower Olivine Flats are readily reached from Four Brothers Pass by descending the steep streambed.
2. The Forgotten River Flats are reached by a sidle above bushline. From the pass, descend 100m and sidle left around Angle Peak on tussock and rubble. Sidle steadily 200-300m above bushline until above the Forgotten River Flats, then drop gradually, reaching the head of the valley above the bush. A prominent lake may be seen about an hour after the pass, but it is not necessary to climb quite that high. Alternatively from Four Brothers Pass, climb to about the 1800m contour under Angle Peak then descend to the lake. Then angle down easy tussock slopes to the Forgotten Valley head above the bushline.

In the reverse direction, once past the lake, sidle down keeping as high as possible under the bluffs.This route may also be reached from the lower reaches of the Forgotten Flats via a prominent steep gut through the bush, or by old deer trails opposite the Blockade Stream confluence.

Times: Diorite Flats to Four Brothers Pass, 3 hrs (2 going down); pass to Olivine Flats, 2.5 hrs; Pass to Forgotten River head, 3.5 hrs.

OLIVINE GORGE Pyke Valley to Lower Olivine Flats

A very good blazed track was cut up this gorge on the true right in the late 1930s. Much of this is now unfollowable over the lower portion of the route and time is best spent making progress instead of searching for blazes. However, later on an attempt should be made to find the trail and stick with it where it leads from cairns on open rock knolls around a bluffy spur through thick bush and scrub to easier bush travel beyond the major difficulties in the gorge.

From Olivine Hut, if the river is low, proceed up the true left bank and cross a few hundred metres upstream. Follow the Olivine riverbed for 20 mins towards the base of the Olivine Falls. Travel is easy and mostly on gravel. Alternatively from the hut, cross to the true right via the wire cage and thrash upstream (a marked track will be found for a short distance). As the river bends back towards the falls, easy going will be found in a flood channel on the true right issuing from near the foot of the falls.

Leave the flood channel as it nears the hillside and climb straight up to gain the narrow ridge between the Olivine and the creek runnel to the NE, keeping towards the creek, rather than Olivine, side of the spur. Continue about 300m past pt 293m along the ridge. Further along this ridge, bluffs bar the way. To avoid them, sidle down into the creek runnel to the NE (the 'Gulch' in previous editions) and out up the other side. Progress is slow until easier going is reached at about E39 310 293. Continue climbing to reach patches of bare rock and hopefully a view with cairns.

At this stage try and find cairns and very old blazes at about the 600m contour… The trail climbs a little more and at approx. the 700 to 800m contour traverses level round a shoulder at about E39 314 288 through stunted bush about 200m above the Olivine. It is well worth sticking with the trail at this point and the first glimpse of the Olivine Flats will be seen during this traverse. The trail then descends through leatherwood and follows down a spur at E39 318 287 to a terrace in good bush above the still wild river where the old blaze line is usually lost. Stay on the sloping terrace at just under the 600m contour. Cross two small streams and descend to the river a few hundred metres downstream of the bluff at E39 325 273. In 1998 it was necessary to climb a little to negotiate this bluff. If the river is low the bluff can be bypassed by crossing.

Descending. Below the bluff at E39 325 273, cross the Olivine River to the true right before the river begins to seriously descend through rapids. Enter the bush and follow downstream for 10 mins until meeting a scree slope. Climb up this for 5 mins and then sidle, gradually gaining height until a small terrace is reached approx 100m above the river near the 600m contour.

At E39 318 286, where the terrace meets a prominent spur, bluffed on its eastern side, it is well worth while trying to locate the old blaze line. This would be difficult but very useful. The start of this blaze line is currently marked with a piece of orange tape. The old blazed line climbs and leads around the shoulder then follows along a bushed ledge rising up until the middle of the gorge (care should be taken not to follow false blazes directly up the bluffed spur). From the end of the ledge the trail descends slightly onto the open rock of a shoulder, where cairns will be found.

From here do not go down towards the river, but descend over the bare rock patches and through stunted bush in a direct line with Lake Wilmot. The old blazed line is largely unfollowable below here, but travel on this line is reasonable. Occasional blazes on stunted beech may be seen leading down into heavier bush on the right. From here, continue down through mossy boulders. Take care not to stray too close to the gorge on the left as rock formations, particularly along the edge, are deeply dissected and potentially quite dangerous. Note that sidling this gorge is slow, demanding and requires good bush skills. The true left contains major continuous bluffs and is not a practical route. It should be avoided.

Times: Olivine Hut to Olivine Flats, one very long day in good conditions.

FORGOTTEN GORGE Olivine River to Forgotten River Flats

The Forgotten leaves its gorge through a deep blue pool that is well worth a visit. There are good campsites nearby. From the lower Olivine Flats follow along the true right bank of the Forgotten River to the start of the gorge, then swing left (looking upvalley) through swampy bush at the foot of bluffs. A lightly blazed trail begins at E39 339 263, about 70m from Blue Pool. Follow this old blazed route

■ Forgotten River Col from Forgotten River Flats.

as it swings right (looking up) up a shelf, just before (and on the true left of) a creekbed, climbing up bedrock through gradually thinning bush. With care, the old blazes and remains of an old deer trail are still followable as they cross rocky knolls near bluffs plunging directly into the river.

However, a myriad of other old trails confuse the issue. Concentrate on the blazes and cairns. Towards the lip of the gorge, the route climbs and sidles at about the 840m contour through celery pine and beech before sidling down to a small rocky spur at the bush edge, about 40m above the river, where there is a cairn at E39 351 260. Follow the trail down through open prickly shield fern to the river gravel flats. About 1994 a large slip on the true left dammed the Forgotten River just below the bush edge, backing a deep blue channel up to the flats. The riverbed has since gravelled up (2000), and now provides good travel. Follow the riverbed (crossings necessary) or sidle in ferns the last 500m to the Forgotten River Flats. From these tussock flats to the head of the valley is open.

Descending, pick up the trail on the spur at the bush edge, about 40m above the river on the true right at E39 351 260. The trail sidles up and across for a time before descending.

Caution. The true left bank contains major bluffs and is not a practical route. It is best avoided.

Times: Olivine to Forgotten Flats, 2.5hrs (2 hrs descending); Forgotten Flats to valley head, 2.5 hrs.

FORGOTTEN FLATS TO THE OLIVINE ICE PLATEAU

An excellent bivvy rock (sleeps 8) visible from downstream in the upper Forgotten Valley is accurately marked at E39 390 301 a little before the cliffs at the valley head. Follow the riverbed until directly under it, then head up. It is beside a small stream and is the largest rock in the vicinity.

The route to the Plateau runs up the south side of the valley. Just beyond the continuous forest, sidle up snowgrass slopes between two small patches of beech until close under the huge bluffs of the

Climax Pk
Gable Pk
Memorial
Icefall
Olivine Ice Plateau
Futurity Rock
Andy
Icefall
Bench

Blockade ridge, E39 387 296. Continue to sidle uphill, under the bluffs. The route crosses a broad slab with a creek running down it and continues east, in general keeping within about 50m of the bluffs above. Where the creek/slab abuts the bluffs is a reasonable rock bivvy (sleeps 3) with another (for 2 or 3) about 400m down valley, also close under the bluffs.

At about the 1500m contour, a stream in a bedrock gut is crossed (not difficult) and beyond it there are shingle slopes at the base of the snow. Above here, several parties have been surprised in recent years by the difficulty getting up and down from the col. Without the snow, rock scrambles are involved. Climb up to the permanent ice at the 1750m contour and onto Forgotten River Col, where there are usually rockpools and reasonable, but exposed, campsites. More shelter can be gained to the south, tucked under the Blockade ridge or by snowcaving, depending on the snow. Traditionally, old snow caving shovels have been kept among rocks on the south side of the col.

Caution. For climbing parties only above the snowline.

Times: Forgotten River to snow, 4 hrs; Snow to Forgotten River Col, 30 mins to 1 hr.

FORGOTTEN FLATS TO BARRIER ICE STREAM. This route begins up a confined (watch for stones) gully (easier scree slopes higher up) and involves bypassing a couple of minor falls caused by big boulders. A 5m packhaul may be necessary. Ascend the gravel and boulder choked gully from E39 387 303 to E39 384 312 where there are campsites and tarns on Intervention Ridge. Continue up the ridge, descending snowslopes at E39 399 316 to the Barrier Ice Stream. Climbing parties only.

INTERVENTION SADDLE Forgotten to the South Barrier

This alpine route is seldom used. The saddle is correctly marked on E39. The couloir on the Forgotten side is steep, very confined and subject to ice and rockfalls. If the snow is not continuous (probably from late January onwards) the route may be very difficult. From the top of the couloir, traverse north a short distance, cross the saddle and descend the true right side of the conspicuous gut (very steep snowgrass near the top) to the South Barrier. Follow the true left bank to the junction with the North Barrier, then the true right.

In the reverse direction, follow the true left of the South Barrier until the bush is left behind and the river swings east, then gain the saddle via the true right of the conspicuous gut. Cross the saddle and sidle south a short distance before descending the couloir. Caution; for climbing parties only. Recent information (1997) states that travel up the South Barrier is extremely slow, along scrubby banks cut by incised gullies.

Time: Forgotten River to the Barrier Flats will take over 9 hrs.

UPPER BEANS BURN TO FORGOTTEN RIVER DIRECT

This route is dependent on continuous good snow in the couloir descending north towards Forgotten River from the Main Divide and the Merkyl Glacier at E39 361 238. Alpine parties only. From the upper Beans Burn, climb up to the Main Divide at about E39 352 223, NW of Brenda Peak. Traverse along the Main Divide to the Merkyl Glacier and ascend to E39 361 238, west of Irvine Peak overlooking Forgotten River Flats. Descend to bushline and these flats at E39 369 261.

Variations exist. From Forgotten Flats, ascend scrubby bush then sidle across tussock basins to E39 355 247. Head directly up the gully up to E39 358 239, east of Terminal Peak. Descend steep scree and a snowfield into a basin, (which may involve an abseil on the way) and sidle across scree to a steep tussock slope that leads up to join the previous route on the Divide at about E39 358 229.

The Olivine Ice Plateau and Andy Glacier from Mt Gyrae.

DART VALLEY-DERIVATION NÉVÉ ROUTES TO FORGOTTEN RIVER AND THE OLIVINE PLATEAU

A knot of complex alpine routes connect the Dart Valley with Forgotten River and the Olivine Ice Plateau. These routes vary with the season and year and require good transalpine skills and equipment in full-on ice country.

Times: For all the following routes; Daleys Flat to bushline, 3 to 4 hrs; the full crossing in either direction will take 12 to 16 hrs in good snow conditions and it is probably necessary to plan an intermediate camp.

MARGARET GLACIER ROUTE Dart Valley to Glacier Col (Derivation Névé)

Cross the Dart on the bridge at Daleys Flat, and climb directly to bushline on Mt Hedin. Climb another 300m keeping well to the NE (right) and then sidle and descend to the big bend of the Margaret Glacier, below the 1600m contour. Conditions on the upper Margaret Glacier vary considerably, and the route has been cut off by crevasses completely in some years. A feasible line through sometimes exists early in the season, though parties should still be prepared for badly crevassed névé slopes. Glacial recession has left the final snow slopes leading up to Glacier Col moderately steep. Descend to the Derivation Névé.

In the reverse direction, from Glacier Col, descend to the Margaret Glacier. Once around the end of the ridge off Hedin, climb and sidle downvalley, (with respect to the Dart) until clear of the collapsed slopes above the Margaret Burn, then descend to the Dart, aiming for the bridge at the north end of Daleys Flat.

Caution. If there is fresh snow around, the Margaret Glacier is subject to avalanche danger from surrounding mountains, particularly on the northern side. Also, this route is almost invariably cut off later in the season.

SEAL COL ROUTE Dart Valley to Glacier Col (Derivation Névé)

This route is less subject to being cut off by crevasses than the Margaret Glacier route, but may be awkward for parties with heavy packs in the vicinity of Desperation Pass. Cross the bridge over the Dart River at the top end of Daleys Flat to the true right. Follow along the riverbed (mostly) to the Margaret confluence. Cross the Margaret Burn on a natural rock bridge just upstream of the confluence and ascend the spur on the true left of the Margaret Burn to bushline. Travel is reasonable and the bushline largely free of scrub. Continue on up a broad tussock ridge which gives way to easy bedrock. There are tarns at about the 1540m contour. Water can sometimes be found in small creeks by sidling across the broad ridge at the bushedge too, but this shouldn't be relied on.

Ascend easy snowslopes from the 1700m contour, E39 428 234, arcing around to the north then west just under pt 2101m. Descend into Desperation Pass (slightly more difficult for the last 50m, either side of the ridge, depending on conditions). Continue out (slightly on the Margaret Glacier side) onto a steeper snow shoulder and reach the Main Divide again just west of Stefansson Peak. Travel is easy again from here. Continue along snow to Watkins, crossing onto the Joe side for a short while between rocky gendarmes. From Watkins, a long sidling snow descent leads to Glacier Col. Alternatively, a quicker route is to descend north off Watkins to reach the Derivation Névé at about E39 407 255.

POSSIBILITY COL Derivation Névé to Forgotten Flats

From Derivation Névé, follow the Gates ridge about 500m north from Possibility Col to about E39 391 258, where the ridge flattens out at the 2020m contour. Descend moderately steep snow or rocky slopes NW from here to about E39 388 262, then sidle right (upvalley) down rock ledges and steep snowgrass, keeping as close as practicable to the bluffs of Gates until it is possible to traverse right to the scree below these bluffs. It is important to note that the ridge is not crossed at Possibility Col. The direct descent from the col is possible, but much more difficult, and is not recommended.

In the reverse direction, from Forgotten River Flats at E39 372 267 work up the stream draining the face of Mt Gates until close under the main bluffs. Then, keeping as close to the bluffs as practicable, sidle right (downvalley) up steep snowgrass and then rock ledges to reach snowfields then the south ridge of Gates at E39 391 258. Descend to Possibility Col and the Derivation Névé.

THE GATES RIDGE Derivation Névé to the Plateau

The feasibility of the route from Mt Gates to Key Rock, which traverses the Thunderer Névé and snowslopes, varies considerably. Glacial recession is not helping. Gullies and schrunds NE of Mt Gates can often present real problems to cross and major schrunds can exist in several places across the Thunderer Glacier, cutting the route off completely. These make the route unpredictable, so it's very tenuous as a packing route. In good early summer conditions in the right year it may be fine. On the other hand, in some years it may be quite impractical. It should be thought of as a climbing option, for those suitably equipped and prepared. Alternatively, the Plateau can be accessed from the Derivation Névé via Possibility Col and Forgotten River Col.

ROUTES FROM COW SADDLE TO THE OLIVINE FLATS AT THE OLIVINE FORGOTTEN CONFLUENCE

For access to Cow Saddle, see Hidden Falls Creek (below) or the Rock Burn (Dart Valley notes).

1. VIA FIERY COL AND THE FULL OLIVINE LEDGE

This is normally the fastest and easiest option from Cow Saddle to Olivine Flats. From Cow Saddle, climb scree slopes (often easy snowslopes higher up) to Fiery Col. Descend to the Olivine Ledge, a broad grassy bench at about the 1100 to 1200m contour, and follow it down valley, crossing a large creek from Fohn Lake in a small gulch, and beyond it to a smaller creek draining the smaller Fohn Lake. Continuing north, the bench rises to a small bouldery moraine knoll at the 1120m contour, with the easiest travel in grass behind (east) of it. On the SE edge of the knoll is a rock bivvy that will shelter 4 people in most weather, marked with a cairn at E39 327 223.

From the end of the ledge, E39 329 227, the easiest option is to head due north down through scruffy bush and minor bluffs then sidle in relatively open forest below at about the 800m contour for a while before continuing the descent down the open spur to the Sunset/Olivine junction. Keep well above the Olivine until near the junction as slopes closer to the river become steep and thick again. Sunset Creek drains Sunset and Terminal Peaks and enters the Olivine as a small gorge. To cross Sunset, follow the rib down almost to the forks, where it is easier to drop to the Olivine riverbed. Follow up Sunset for 20m and locate a good but hidden trail that leads easily through cliffs on the true right to the terrace above. Alternatively, cross 200m up from the forks on a trail.
Alternatively from the Ledge, sidle into the bush, descending gradually. When a creek in a deeply eroded gully is reached, cross it and descend steeply to about the 750m contour, before veering off downstream to the Sunset/Olivine junction. Old deer trails may help.

Cross Sunset Creek and continue down the true right bank of the Olivine, initially about 20m above the river on a terrace through several swampy clearings on old deer trails. Then follows slower

Terminal Pk
Sunset Pk
Corinna Pk
Fohn
Saddle
Bivvy Rock
Olivine Ledge
Fiery Creek
Sunset Ck
Olivine River
Barrington Flats

going in an area of large boulders before picking up an old blaze line (not essential) to follow along the true right river bank to the flats. In low river conditions, much of the riverbed itself can be travelled more quickly and easily, from Sunset Creek down.

Ascending, follow the Olivine until the first large boulders appear in the riverbed (E39 332 256). Sidle on the true right in forest on a good trail past this bouldery area then either travel up the riverbed or sidle along a terrace on the true right, depending on conditions. A cairn about 100m up Sunset Creek on the true left marks the start of the track to a good rock bivvy (sleeps 6). This cairn is directly across the stream from a clearing that offers good camping. The track is reasonably easy to follow and in 45 mins leads straight to the rock biv, saving a bush bash and providing reliable shelter. Otherwise, strike into the bush, heading away from both rivers. A small creek is crossed soon after leaving Sunset Creek. As the valley floor is left, continue a climbing sidle up the Olivine to a second creek at about E39 331 233. When the Olivine/Sunset confluence can be seen (about 2 hrs from the junction), cross the creek and continue on a climbing sidle up the Olivine, until the upper edge of the scrub is reached, then the Olivine Ledge. The route along the ledge and over Fiery Col is straightforward.

Times. Cow Saddle to Olivine Ledge Bivvy Rock, 5 hrs; Ledge to Sunset/Olivine confluence, 2.5 hrs, (3.5 hrs in the reverse direction); Sunset to Lower Olivine Flats, 2 hrs.

A LOW LEVEL ALTERNATIVE ROUTE AVOIDING FIERY COL EXISTS from Cow Saddle to the Olivine Ledge, (avoids snow on Fiery Col), via the Olivine River. Bypass boulders at D40 291 188 (see photo p131), then at D40 293 196 sidle (true right) through tussock and patchy scrub to a shoulder at D40 295 200, about 40m above the river. Descend open slopes (winter avalanche path) through thick scrub back to the river and follow it to Barrington (Upper Olivine) Flats, E39 300 212. At the bottom of the flats, ascend an open lead on the true right to about the 900m contour and sidle down in mostly open tussock, bedrock, and short manuka to Fiery Creek. Alternatively, keep under beechforest then swing up to open ground. Cross Fiery Creek about 250m up from the Olivine junction (E39 311 216) and climb easy slopes on the true right of Fiery Stm to the Ledge.

Time: Cow Saddle to the Olivine Ledge via the Olivine River, about 5 hrs.

VIA FIERY COL, FOHN STREAM AND THE OLIVINE RIVER. From Cow Saddle, cross Fiery Col to the stream draining the larger Fohn Lake. Head straight down parallel and close to this stream on the true right as it develops into a deep gully. Keep on through steepening scrub and bush until the final short scramble down to the Olivine River. Travel is straightforward. In low river conditions, continue down valley, crossing and sidling as necessary to the Sunset Creek. If much sidling is required, travel will be slow and arduous. This route can become very difficult if the river is not low.

Times: Olivine Ledge to River, about 2 hrs; Fohn Jn to Sunset Creek, about 4 hrs in good conditions.

2. VIA THE FULL OLIVINE RIVER

Descending. This route is best avoided unless the river is low. It also has its fair share of scratchy scrub. From Cow Saddle, follow the Olivine River down to Barrington Flats (see above). Below the flats, sidle on the true right along a beech terrace. Descend to the riverbed at E39 307 216, and follow it down to about E39 309 218 (about 400m above Fiery Creek Junction). Climb out here on the true left and sidle along an open beech terrace as bluffs below increase, then ascend a creekbed at

■ The Olivine River and Bench from Alabaster Pass.

E39 313 219 to scree slopes that can now be followed well above the river at roughly the 8-900m contour down valley. Descend the creek leading down to where two creeks almost join (cairns here, E39 321 229) and cross to the down valley creek. Cairns then indicate a ground trail which offers scrubby travel down valley along a terrace at about the 740-720m contour, not that far from cliffs dropping into the Olivine itself. Carefully follow this vague trail (partly followable 1999), through scrub, clearings, rocky areas and across creeks (old blazes and cairns help) before descending to forks in the river at E39 329 237. Continue down the river. See P 127 notes.

Ascending. From the Forgotten River junction (Olivine Flats) travel up the bed of the Olivine or on deer trails on the true right as already described in the Olivine Ledge notes. Where the gorge begins at about E39 329 237 cross to the true left, and travel on ultramafic rock terraces at about the 720m contour. Look for the remains of a very old blazed trail. Occasional more recent cairns at stream crossings may help locate this trail. Where two streams almost join at E39 321 229, to avoid scrub, climb the upvalley stream to scree slopes above and sidle at about the 850m contour. Descend to the beech forest opposite Fiery Stream, sidle, and drop down to the riverbed at E39 309 218. The true right now offers better travel if the river can be crossed. Otherwise continue on the true left through a jumble of large mossy boulders to the flats under Alabaster Pass.

Time: Cow Saddle to the Forgotten River confluence, about 8 to 9 hrs in good conditions.

ALABASTER PASS Upper Olivine River to Lake Alabaster

Nice camping exists on Barrington Flat in the upper Olivine. A side trip to the pass and Bryneira Range is well worthwhile. Enter the bush at D39 299 213, right under the pass by a large rock near a muddy stagnant creek. If old blazes can be found then stick with them (vague but OK in 1999). Otherwise, the route is basically straight up to a narrow channel in the ridge that becomes the pass.

Cairns mark the pass and some of the route down the other side. From the pass, follow the route west and down towards the small hollow below. About 5 mins below the pass a small bluff is descended. Follow the ditch that drains north from the hollow until the route steepens and is eventually blocked by large boulders, about 20 mins from the pass. From here, traverse out to the true left onto a north facing broad rock shoulder.

This spur is initially scrub free and the route down is marked with large cairns visible from a distance. Follow the cairns north until the route is lost in steep bush. Descend through the bush until the creek is reached. Follow the creek down or take to the bush on the true right. Apart from the odd slip, progress is straightforward but slow. Keep within earshot of Alabaster Creek on the high terraces to keep navigation easy. Once overlooking the Lake, at about the 300m contour, head north and descend steepening banks right to the valley floor, about 1km north of Lake Alabaster.

This is not the good route it appears to be on the map, unfortunately. Thick rough bush makes travel slow and tiring. There are numerous little bluffs and little is left of old animal trails. Most parties take longer than they expect over it, but it is still used, mainly as a descent route.

Times: Olivine to Alabaster Pass, 40 mins up, 30 mins down; Pass to Lake Alabaster, about 7 to 8 hrs down.

PARK PASS TO COW SADDLE

Follow the good ground trail down off Park Pass to enter the bush near its highest point on the steep spur below and follow orange marker tape and old blazes down the right hand (north) edge of it.

■ Cow Saddle, with the Olivine River in the foreground and Hidden Falls Creek beyond.

Poseidon Pk
Mt Somnus
Park Pass
To Fiery Col
Cow Saddle
Olivine River

When the spur runs out into the valley floor, continue directly ahead to Hidden Falls Creek. The best route is then close to the river on the true left. Cross Hidden Falls Creek at D40 291 144 where the bush on the true right gives way to to scree slopes. The rest of the route to Cow Saddle is along the foot of these screes and then up easy tussock slopes.

In reverse, follow the true right of Hidden Falls Creek until the end of the scree slopes and then cross to the true left at D40 291 144 and follow a dry channel 200m downstream. Pick up a good trail (lightly blazed) relatively close to the river (true left) and follow it down valley to flats beginning at D40 291 137. Continue down to the stream entering on the true left at D40 291 126. About 5 mins below here, also on the true left of Hidden Falls Creek, there is a second, smaller stream. On the true left of this small creek, near forks with the river, there is a red/white permolat marker, and a cairn on the ground (1999). Markers and old blazes lead away from the river on a light ground trail across a bush terrace and a very steep ascent begins leading SE up a spur to Park Pass. Steady use of this route means that there is now (2004) quite a good ground trail up the spur, and orange plastic marker tape. Old blazes stay close to the left hand edge of the spur (going up) for most of the way.

There is a rock bivvy (sleeps 2) in moraine north of Cow Saddle at the foot of Fiery Peak. However, the bivvy and open flats on the saddle are subject to rapid and extensive flooding. There is a better bivvy rock (sleeps 4) in an open gully, 50m from the bush edge on the true left of Hidden Falls Creek, 200m from the river at the 900m contour at D40 297 154. It is cairned.

Times: Park Pass to Hidden Falls Creek, 1.5 hrs (2.5 hrs in the reverse direction); Hidden Falls Creek/Park Pass Creek confluence to Cow Saddle, 2.5 to 3 hrs.

HIDDEN FALLS GORGE Flats in Hidden Falls Creek to the Hollyford River

Although this route is rough, it does provide a quick route out to the Hollyford Roadend from the prime tramping terrain of the Olivine area for fit, competent parties. The lower section, however, has few views and includes some very slow bush travel. It would be a miserable way to start a trip.

Descending. In Hidden Falls Creek below Park Pass, follow deer trails on the true left. This middle section of Hidden Falls Creek is delightful, and consists mainly of open flats and beech forest travel, with good campsites. If the river is low, cross as required, cutting across the 'bend' on the true right then crossing to the true left at a small flat (campsite), D40 271 089. Otherwise, return to the true left before the bend is reached. A good bivvy rock (sleeps 2 or 3) exists 20m above the river on the true left at D40 274 089. Upvalley from the stable mossy creek entering at the bend, there is a tiny creek, and the bivvy rock is 60m upvalley from that. Continuing downvalley, deer trails are still a help (1999). Follow these trails, generally 10 to 80m inland on terraces, occasionally returning closer to the water. Stay on the true left. Trails lead in and out of numerous deer wallows near the river as it descends through the 380 to 360m contour region.

At approx. D40 257 087, there is a stable gravel gully that extends from bluffs above to within 30m of the river. Beyond it, slower going is encountered amongst large boulders and rotten tree covered scree slopes for about 1.5km. This has potential to really bog down progress and is the worst of the Gorge. In general, keep up, (it doesnt improve down at riverlevel), choose slopes of large tree ferns to sidle in, and beware of abundant stinging nettle. There are a couple of options, both hard work. Some suggest to sidle at roughly the 420m contour and hopefully reach a stable scree at D40 246 085 which offers a rest and wonderful view of the Darrans. From the scree, plunge into the bush again staying near the 400m height. Initially tree ferns provide easy going, however the next section, less than a km, is again fairly slow.

Alternatively from D40 257 087, go lower, but still keeping well above the river, contour around through diabolical greenery, aiming for D40 240 085, and the start of the bush flat (where travel improves) at the 320m contour north of pt 406m. Both options lead to this knob at pt 406m then descend in a SW direction (magnetic south initially), aiming for the junction (D40 232 074) of a stream to the south and a runnel parallel to the Hollyford and draining bluffs above the falls. These bluffs will be encountered if off route. If this happens, head further south. From the junction indicated, sidle on the true right of the stream to the valley floor where the stream disappears into swamp. Head straight out onto the Hollyford Track

Going up. About 1km south of Hidden Falls a Hollyford Track footbridge crosses a small sluggish creek marked on D40. A long, thin spur heads north on the true right of this creek. Cross over the lower end of the spur and also cross the small creek behind it near its forks, D40 232 074. The eastern side of this creek is badly bluffed further up. Head NE initially, swinging north to pt 406m. From pt 406m, hold your height till the river is reached. At about D40 260 087, travel improves.

Caution. The true right bank is best avoided although it has been used.

Times: Park Pass Junction to the 'bend', 2.5 hrs; 'bend' to pt 406m, 6 hrs; Pt 406m to Hollyford Tk, 3 hrs.

HIDDEN FALLS CREEK TO NORTH COL

About 700m downstream from the main bend in Hidden Falls Creek, an open stream bed can be followed until the stream forks. Climb up a steep spur on the true right of the creek through scrubby forest. A small steep slip at the bushline assists through thick scrub, but this is a moderately slow steep and difficult route.

Time: Hidden Falls Creek to North Col, about 4 hrs.

The spirit soared willingly up through the leafy wilderness, but the flesh felt dreadfully weak as it heaved itself, plus the heavy pack pulling on to the stems and branches and pushing through them at the same time; in fact the effort of making flesh and spirit meet was often excrutiating.

—Marie Byles, 1937.

CASCADE VALLEY

The Cascade Valley is approached along the Jackson River Road, which turns off the Jackson Bay road at the south end of the Arawhata road bridge. The big, clear Cascade River drains both the Red Hills and the Olivine Ranges, and can be used for access to both. Farm flats in the lower Cascade around the Martyr Homestead are private, so if someone is in residence, seek permission to cross them. This is normally given. For transport from Haast to the Cascade and other local areas, Mauryne Cannell of 'Round About Haast' (ph 03 750 0890) offers a reasonably priced, on demand service.

JACKSON RIVER ROAD TO FALLS CREEK

Look for the DoC interpretation sign by the road overlooking the Cascade River at Whisky Corner, 400m north of pt 172m, E38 530 672. Descend the bank behind the sign towards the Cascade River for 10m where a roughly maintained benched track originally built in the 1870s will be found in scrub. Follow this track for 15 mins down to The Bend by the Cascade River where the track formation disappears. There is a wonderfully deep clear green pool here. An easy bash up the true right leads to gravel flats.

From The Bend, the Cascade Valley is untracked and the route follows the true right all the way to the Cascade Gorge above Falls Creek. Keep close to the river the whole way, either on the boulder beaches or on terraces just above the river. The bush can be surprisingly rough going. For a couple of km below Woodhen Creek and between McKay and Falls Creeks, bouldery backwaters and rough toi toi flats away from the main channel give the easiest going. If the river is low, some strategic crossings on the flats will speed things up but take care. The Cascade is a large river and there are few safe crossings, unless the river is very low. Often the river can be running high and deceptively deep, but still appear clear.

Between Woodhen Creek and McKay Creek, the best route remains on the true right, close to the river. However, in one section it is necessary to sidle above a small gorge. To do this, climb up from about E38 470 601 and sidle upstream at about the 200m contour before descending to the bend in the river at E38 467 592.

There are 2 alternative routes, both poorer than that described above, between Woodhen Creek and McKay Creek that will be briefly mentioned:

1. On the true left of the Cascade, stay as close to the river as possible, utilising gravel flats. The bush is rough travel. Near Kappa Creek, where travel is slow on steeper forested banks, the old benched track up the Cascade, marked here with permolat in the 1970s, but now full of windfall and slips, may offer some sort of break. Travel is particularly difficult and slow at Spoon Slip. Beyond Saddle Creek there are more flats and riverstones leading up to McKay Creek.

2. On the true right, it is also possible to bypass the river altogether between Woodhen Creek and Elsie Creek. The difficulties are navigation and thick bush. Thick scrubby kamahi/podocarp forest on the foothills of the Olivines and more open beech on the lower slopes. Woodhen Creek provides fast travel to beyond the Woodhen Pond outlet indicated on E38 Ed 1. (Woodhen Pond actually drains into the Cascade down the creek to the west of pt 168m, not Woodhen Creek). Get out your map and compass. From the 220m contour, Elsie Creek is easy travel down to Theta Tarn. Sidle or wade the tarn on the northern side which is less scrubby. From the outlet to McKay Creek, travel is slow but okay, taking about 40 mins. This route is only worth considering if the river is high and you have good bush skills.

Times: Road to Woodhen Creek, 3.5 hrs; Woodhen Creek to McKay Creek, about 5.5 hrs; McKay Creek to Falls Creek, about 1.5 hrs.

THE UPPER CASCADE VALLEY

The Cascade Gorge can be sidled following an old fault scarp through thick bush on the true right, initially about 50 to 100m above the river from E38 433 518. The last section is sidled at about the 320m contour, before descending to the river bedrock at the top of the Durward Falls. The river bank on the true right can now, with care, be followed up to delightful flats.

From the flats, an old route up to the Red Hills Range via a creek and then the **WHITE SLIP** is still useable. However, the slip is steep, loose and still eroding near the top, making it a poor route.

The easiest route (usually) from the flats above Durward Falls to Simonin Pass leaves the Cascade River on the true left about 1km below Arcade Creek and sidles at about the 1100m contour past Barrington Creek to Simonin Pass. Although this is mainly on easy open rocky country, it is sustained and hard on the feet. River travel in the Cascade above Durward Falls varies from easy to challenging, but in dry conditions and low river flows also offers a practical route to Simonin Pass. Some bush sidles are necessary, particularly in the most demanding stretch, a huge boulderbed at E39 417 454. Riverside campsites exist on the true left at E39 418 428 and on tiny grass flats at E39 418 424, further upstream. From the latter, an easy sidle up ultramafic boulders leads to Simonin Pass. Keep on the barren side of the contact.

Times: Falls Ck to Durward Falls, 4.5 hrs; Falls to the flats, 20 mins; Flats to E39 418 424, 8 hrs.

RED HILLS RANGE ACCESS FROM THE CASCADE VALLEY

There are various routes up onto the Red Hills and opinions vary as to which option is best. The spur previously described starting on the true left of the Cascade at E38 435 519, and leading up to pt 1031m offers reasonable and direct travel, but this can be a long dry ascent on a hot day. There are several large cairns marking the entrance into the bush at pt 1031m and in this vicinity there are some

■ The Pyke Valley and Red Mountain from Mt Gyrae.

excellent campsites. Another, probably easier option, is to use the narrow spur, quite steep at the bottom, that begins at E38 443 539. This spur is used by the deer, travel is open and clear, and water is accessible higher up it. Then mostly open travel leads SW past tarns at pt 890m onto the range. At the base of this spur, there is a good crossing of the Cascade which is split into channels here. Other fords across the Cascade should also be possible above McKay Creek, and there are good crossings just above Falls Creek too.

It is also possible to climb to bushline on the Red Hills Range from E38 444 552, passing over pt 906m enroute to the tussock tops. In fine weather the tops then provides excellent travel to Barrington Saddle at the head of Barrington Creek. Roughly north of pt 1306m, the tops are covered in lush tussock and travel is easier along the range crest. Roughly south of pt 1306m, the ground is bare and rocky and the basins of Peridot Stream at the 1080m contour then provide fast and easy travel.

From Barrington Saddle, the Cascade can be approached again. Alternatively, a reasonable but dry sidle at about the 1000 to 1100m contour leads south on mostly bare sharp rocks, hard underfoot, to Simonin Pass.

RED MOUNTAIN is most easily approached on its northern side, beginning near pt 1121m. A prominent boulder gully starting at E39 385 450 leads all the way to the summit, keeping close under a huge line of bluffs that lead NW off pt 1611m.Travel up over the gigantic boulders is not difficult. The gully leads directly to a notch, a few metres to the NW of the high point at 1705m. The ridge here is an easy scramble. Snow will usually be encountered for the last few hundred metres in the gully.

Times: Cascade River to the Red Hills tops, allow about 5 hrs; Red Hills bushline to pt 1121m, about 4 to 5 hrs; It is possible in a long day to climb Red Mountain from pt 1031m and return.

OLIVINE RANGE ACCESS FROM THE CASCADE VALLEY

Much of the Northern Olivine Range is rockier than the map suggests, including Mts Dagon, Staircase and Tararua.

Mt Raddle, Mt Riddle, Martyr Spur and the bottom of Red Spur are all barren and scrubby ultramafic blocks, similar to the Red Hills, and quite distinct from the rest of the Olivines.

The easiest way onto **MARTYR HILL** from the Cascade is via a tributary of Woodhen Creek, the first creek on the true right, about 1km up from the river and beginning at E38 503 614. Follow the bouldery staircase of the creek itself all the way to Martyr Hill. This is a good route. Other creeks also offer reasonable routes to the tops near here. See other approaches to this area from the Jackson, in notes below.

In fine weather, **STAIRCASE MOUNTAIN** can be approached from Martyr Hill. From Martyr Hill, travel through a narrow belt of beech forest into the schist country beyond. There are idyllic campsites beside the tarns at E38 545 597. From here, follow your nose south along the ridge to a saddle between pt 1259m and pt 1368m. An obvious bench above a 72m waterfall leads to a gut just to the east of Staircase Mountain. Follow up this gut and gain ledges on the SE side of the peak that lead easily to the summit. There are spectacular views from this peak. The whole Collyer-Dagon-Staircase-Tararua Peak area is much more rugged than the map suggests. A return to the Jackson River can be made with care down Martyr Spur.

MT RADDLE can be approached from the Cascade by following up the first stream south of McKay Creek beginning at E38 455 558. Although this route is only fair, it leads up through scrub to the open country above. The ridge between this creek and McKay Creek also offers reasonable access at several points. Easy, if rocky, ridge travel leads to Bald Mountain. With some sidles on the Cascade side, the range from Bald Mountain to Staircase Mountain can be traversed by experienced and equipped parties. South of Bald Mountain the range becomes an exposed razorback where a rope is useful.

Lower **ARCADE CREEK** is gorged. Climbing into Arcade Creek from the Cascade is okay on the true right bank, but the bush has many giant goolies in it. Drop into the creek as soon as possible, about E39 430 462 and continue upstream. In 1990 there were reasonable deer trails on the true right with no need to cross Arcade Creek at all to the flats in the head. Arcade Saddle can be crossed directly into McTavish Creek down steep tussock or snowlopes depending on the season. From the Cascade flats above Durward Falls to E39 430 462 will take about 5 hrs.

The Olivine Range can also be approached from small flats in the Cascade just above **HOLLAND CREEK** at E39 418 424. Climb up through the bush (with lawyer) watching for small bluffs and rock crevasses near the bushline. Sidle into Holland Creek basin at about the 1000m contour. Scrub marked on E39 is mostly tussock and beech glades providing fair travel. Tops travel is then straight forward to the Range. There is a bivvy rock on the true right of the Cascade 100m vertically above the river, opposite the contact between beech forest and barren Red Mountain rock.

The upper **LIMBO VALLEY** can be approached from the ridge south of Simonin Pass by sidling from E39 406 410 at the 1120m contour then descending to a ridge of rock above the Limbo at E39 409 405. Sidle up around the corner, still on the true left, to the upper tussock flats. Note that the contour marked 900m in upper Simonin Stream is actually the 1000m one.

To reach **HURRICANE COL** from the Limbo, climb up steep scree or snow and boulders, angling left to the lowest point. Follow the ridge west for 200m and descend snowslopes to the Sealy.

Caution, for climbing parties only.

The Central Olivine Peaks in this block are a transalpine climbers dream. While routes exist through all of this country, and the Olivine tops have all been traversed (but not necessarily on the range crest) from Carl Creek to the Dart, the area is very demanding. Parties must be competent, fit, and experienced. Those looking for a challenge will find one here.

NORTHERN OLIVINES FROM THE JACKSON AND MARTYR RIVERS

For the more experienced, in fine weather, there is a great 5 or 6 day trip on the Thomson-Olivine tops. Up Carl Creek, along the Thomson Range, across the head of the Martyr River, and out down Martyr Spur.

CARL CREEK, draining from Lake Clarke to the Jackson River road gives good access to the Thomson Range tops, a northern extension of the Olivines. Cross the Jackson River (easily forded at E38 613 707 at normal flow) and follow up Carl Creek. Just before the 100m contour, shingle and flats narrow to a bouldery streambed; follow this, in and out of the creekbed, up to the forks with Moonlit Gully. Beyond here, sidle up the true right of Carl Creek in reasonably open bush, keeping out of the creek but swinging back towards it higher up, keeping just above the lip of the gorge, and climbing up a spur off Mt Jackson above the 800m contour towards the tops. Climb to about 1050m to avoid scrubby guts in the tussock towards the Lake Clarke outlet, sidle across above then descend to the outlet, where the bushline is relatively scrub free. Otherwise, north of Mt Jackson, thick scrub will be an issue. There is a good bushedge campsite with a mossy tarn for water at E38 638 676, but the best local campsites are on the rib between Sweetheart Creek and Lake Clarke. There are tiny, protected native shells (Sphaeriids) that look like miniscule pipis living in the sandy edges of this lake.

Time: From the road to Lake Clarke, about 6 hrs up.

LAKE CLARKE TO THE UPPER MARTYR FLATS. Follow the Sweetheart Creek trough (there is a trail on the true right) to Lake Leeb and follow around the east side to the southern end. Sidle across to the bush ridge leading to pt 1056m. Travel here is through scrubby Coprosma on boulders under beech forest, but it is reasonable. There is a good campsite at pt 1056m with water in a swampy tarn at the bush edge.

Climb lank tussock to the west, back onto the tops and follow the range south towards Mt Dagon. Travel becomes slower and some route finding through scoured and broken bedrock is required along to and past pt 1255m. Further south, a broad bouldery shelf leads to a rocky and snowy gully descending from the Northern Olivine Range between pt 1544m and pt 1478m. Things are pretty rugged here. However, the descent down into the Martyr River is straightforward. Continue on down the Martyr, sidling through the bush on the true right. South of pt 984m, sidle back east to the valley floor and the swampy flats at the 840m contour. Avoid the Martyr gorges below here.

Easiest access to **DAGON** is from the Martyr at E38 586 600, mostly up the main gully and a shelf on the true left. There is a bivvy rock (sleeps 3 or 4), on the true left of the Martyr Right Branch, about 75m from the stream on the top flat at about the 1060m contour, E38 585 601.

Times: Lake Clarke to pt 1056m, about 4 hrs; Pt 1056m to saddle at E38 594 607, about 5 hrs; Saddle to Martyr Flats, about 2.5 hrs.

THE UPPER MARTYR RIVER FLATS can also be approached from Martyr Hill. Just above Martyr Hill, sidle on the south side of the ridge to avoid bluffs in a patch of beech forest, then head east to two tarns at about the 1200m contour, E38 540 598. Climb to the ridge between pt 1449m and pt 1462m and descend the steep but okay gully between them to the Martyr. Sidle down on the true left opposite pt 1027m through beechforest to the flats. The lakes at the flats are very shallow and swampy and it is necessary to sidle 10 to 20m up into scrub to move from one branch to the other.

Time: Martyr Hill to the upper Martyr River flats, about 5 hrs.

MARTYR SPUR is scrubby and can be hot and dry. From Martyr Hill, travel down Martyr Spur is initially open and easy. There is water in a tarn in a basin at the 880m contour, 300m south of pt 933m. Further down, from pt 668m, follow open leads through scrub into a bare trough surrounded by scrub just short of pt 573m. At this point, find the start of an old but good deer trail, marked in the basin with a cairn. This trail should now be followable, with care, much of the way to pt 472m and heavier forest. Below here, water may be found in a pond at E38 539 653 (draining towards the Martyr River). From the knoll north of here at E38 540 654, either descend the spur to the Martyr River at Saddle Creek West and cross to the Jackson River road, or follow the ridge WNW through E38 536 659 using the least dense patches of forest then more open manuka growing on ultramafic rock down to the Jackson River Road at E38 536 667. Allow about 6 to 7 hrs for the descent.

See the Cascade River approach for an alternative route to Martyr Hill.

ARAWHATA VALLEY

This huge catchment is virtually trackless and the terrain very rugged. Branches of the Arawhata drain from the Olivines to Mt Aspiring and require parties to be self sufficient and self reliant. However, with initiative and flair, some great trips can be planned. The forest cover is generally beech forest, with lush undergrowth. In places, the subalpine scrub vies with the best in the country. Many of the crossings require good transalpine skills and equipment.

THE LOWER ARAWHATA

JACKSON BAY ROAD TO TEN HOUR GORGE

Jetboats are frequently used for access up the lower Arawhata as far as the bottom of Ten Hour Gorge. John Nolan at Okuru (Ph 03 750 0822), who runs cattle in the Arawhata and has freehold land at Callery Flat, can offer this service and Maurice Nolan (Ph 03 750 0824) may be able to as well as Waiatoto River Jet (Ph 03 750 0780). Alternatively, planes can be chartered locally or further afield to land at Grassy Flat strip or helicopters to other sites. Seek permission to use huts from John Nolan. An old disused track on the true right that led to Callery Flat is washed out and in poor condition. It is possible to go all the way to the Waipara Junction on this side if necessary though.

The main track is on the true left bank. From the Arawhata road bridge, follow the Jackson River road to E38 673 752 (600m) where a careful look should locate a track leading to a crossing of the Jackson (easier crossings 1.5km upstream if necessary). Follow the gravel bank up the Arawhata to a farm bike track entrance at E38 673 741. In general, this stays close to the river and is followed up to Callery flat. There is sometimes a moss picking team based here in the huts during summer. They are serviced by jetboat. The huts (J Nolan) are private and locked when not in use. Callery Flat is all grass; E38 incorrectly marks it as scrub.

Beyond Callery Flat a bulldozed track leads through bush to Jubilee Flat, and continues through more bush beyond to Thomson Creek. Thomson Hut (Private, Barry Horne) in the confluence here is locked. Lumber Flat can be followed to opposite the Waipara Junction. Just below McIntosh Creek, between E38 609 533 and E38 603 526 a slow, awkward bush sidle is necessary (1999).

In fine weather the Arawhata can usually be forded to Waipara Hut (4 bunks, locked, J Nolan) located at the edge of the bush on a flat about 1km up the Waipara on the true left at E39 630 528. This is normally the limit for jetboats in the Waipara too. Further travel on the true left of the Arawhata River leads to Grassy Flat Hut, (3 bunks, locked, J Nolan) just south of the airstrip between McArthur and Joe Creeks. Travel remains mostly easy on grass flats to Collins Creek Hut on the true left of Collins Creek. This hut (J Nolan) is open, has 1 bunk, an open fireplace, and a broken window. It keeps out most rain, but few sandflies (1999). Beyond the hut, it is necessary to bush bash for 1km to the base of a forested island, shown on the map. (At this point, in dry conditions, there is often a feasible ford of the main river). Continue up the main riverbank rather than the dry but bouldery channel, as it's faster and easier, to the top of the island and the start of the gorge.

Times: Road to Callery Flat, 3.5 hrs; Callery Flat to Jubilee Flat, 30 mins; Road to Waipara Hut, 10 hrs

FEZ CREEK TO TURKS HEAD TOPS. An old permolat route begins on Fez's true right where Fez Creek emerges from bush. After sidling at the back of flats under bluffs for several 100m it climbs a wide face to bushline. Originally well marked, it is now hard to follow, but most of the Fez Creek face is unbluffed and travellable. Aim for bushline below the spur at E39 559 405 to avoid evil scrub further south. A basin, or the spur directly, lead to good ridge travel above. Time from valley to tops, about 4 hrs.

NORTHERN OLIVINE RANGE ACCESS

MT DAGON can be approached up Shady Creek. (Also see Martyr and Jackson approaches).

ARCADE SADDLE can be approached from **MCTAVISH CREEK**. From below the McFarlanes junction, follow the true right of McTavish Creek up through red beech which naturally leads to a knobbly spur. Follow the main deertrail off this spur as it leads down under a large bluff to cross McTavish Creek at E39 539 458. Follow a terrace edge in swampy bush on the true left until steeper going at E39 535 454. Sidle back to McTavish Creek and cross to the true right again (30 mins from last crossing). Pick up a trail which soon leads to a good bivvy rock (1 of 2 here) at E39 532 454 (sleeps 4 or 5), 200m down from a side creek. Continue up on the true right. At E39 523 459, just past a narrow rocky gut, climb 1-200m on trails to scrub. Trend west at the base of bluffs to a creek. Sidle a fall in it on the true left to reach the SE end of the tussock basin behind pt 977m, a full day from the Arawhata. There is another bivvy rock here at E39 511 462 (sleeps 4 or 5). The hanging basin below Arcade Saddle can be approached up the true right. From there, travel up to the tussock saddle is fairly easy, although quite steep near the top. The descent to Arcade Stream is reasonably straightforward, enabling a crossing to the Cascade River. Travelling south, the Findlay Glacier can be reached by climbing parties from the Arcade Valley slopes via an average snow gully between the Remote Peaks.

COLLINS CREEK can also be used to approach the Olivine Range, but not by going straight up this creek. Instead, go about 500m up Collins Creek to a branch entering on the true left, E39 534 428. Follow up beside this side stream on the true left to the 600m contour. Then leave it and sidle around the spur keeping height to Collins Creek again at the 700m contour. Travel on this route is reasonable and good deer trails help, although some scrub will be encountered near the bush edge. Now continue up Collins Creek. There is a 2 person bivvy rock at E39 500 438 on the true left of Collins Creek, at about the 980 to 1000m contour. The cataract in the valley at about 1060m can be bypassed by sidling on the true right.

NORTHERN HAAST RANGE

The Northern Haast Range is part of the Haast Tokoeka (Brown) Kiwi sanctuary, and has a trapping network for stoats and other predators. Consequently, Thirsty Ridge, north of Tuning Fork Creek has a marked route up it. Let DoC know before entering the sanctuary. From Yards on the true right of the Arawhata at the bridge, cattle tracks and pink markers lead to Tuning Fork Creek. They continue up it on the true right fairly close to the stream. At a second track junction, about E38 696 740, markers head away from the creek and lead onto Thirsty Ridge. Follow markers up the ridge until the open tops are reached at F38 724 731. Head in a NE direction to skirt through a line of bluffs following markers and then travel south, descending from the 1120m contour to the outlet of Lake Minim Mere. Further markers finish at the outlet to Lake Greaney.

There are good campsites beside the lake and a locked DoC hut used by the Kiwi study team. From here, easy slopes SE of the lake lead to the Haast Range. The range offers exceptional views west over the Haast plain, south to Mt Aspiring and the head of the Waiatoto and east up the Te Naihi to the great wedge of Mt Alba. Travel along the Haast Range itself as far south as the bluffs of Mt Gerard is reasonably practical, although some minor sections need to be sidled. South from Gerard things get much more gnarly. See the Haast Range in the Waipara Valley notes.

Time: Arawhata Bridge to Lake Greaney, about 6 hrs.

TEN HOUR GORGE Flood channel to McArthur Flat

Boulder hopping along the true left (west) bank, keeping as close to the river as possible, offers the fastest route up the gorge. High sidles, although feasible, are often slow and arduous. A bivvy rock Arawata Bill once used sits right by the river less than 150m above the island on the true left. There are huge boulders by a long deep pool at the bottom of the gorge. Stay close to the river on small terraces until the long pool ends, then use mossy boulders alongside the river till the river steepens again. A very spectacular section of rapids follows to almost Halfway Creek, clambering up, down, round or over boulders that look grim, but usually with a way around them. In the steepest sections, huge boulders choke the riverbed. There are active slips and an especially scungy sidle before emerging onto shingle 200m below Halfway Creek junction where the river levels off. An open terrace just inside the bush here is fast and easy, and it is possible to camp. Many parties will take about 4 hours to here.

At first it is okay beyond Halfway Creek, then more bush sidles follow, some 60 to 70m above the river, while negotiating the next steeper, bouldery section, including a tough sidle amongst old avalanche debris. A house sized boulder bridges the river, which is very spectacular. At E39 505 395 the difficulties ease. Beyond Ridge Creek, flats lead upstream to a short bush sidle where the river swings hard against the true left bank. The flats continue upstream to near the Williamson River, which is almost 1 hr from Ridge Creek. The bivvy rock at McArthur Flat is almost as marked on E39, but it's barely a rise off the flats to reach it. It sleeps 2or 3, but beware of mossies! Good campsites nearby. The true right has been traversed, but it took 3 tough days and a climb to snowline.

Time: Up Ten Hour Gorge, allow 5 to 9 hrs in normal river conditions. If the river is up, more sidling will be required in the bush and times will increase substantially.

WILLIAMSON RIVER

MCARTHUR FLAT TO ANDY FLAT AND THE OLIVINE ICE PLATEAU

Normally the true right is followed. If the river cannot be crossed, the true left can and sometimes is used up to Tornado Creek, where there is a natural rock bridge over the Williamson. Given the problems the river can present, this isn't a bad option and is only a little slower. (5-6 hrs). See P 143.

From the Arawhata confluence, old blazes and a good quality deer trail (1998) on the true right of the Williamson River lead through open forest to small glades and flats about 1.5km up valley. Generally easy bush sidling on the trail continues until about 500m below Tornado Creek where there is a huge area of flattened bush, about 20 hectares in extent, alongside the river. From the upriver side of this, locate the deer trail and follow it, ascending slowly until an open and steep creek is reached. Go up and cross on the deer trail and follow through on the trail until you reach an open slip covered in small beech and moss (about 400m). Ascend this open slip to about the 750m contour (almost the top of it). Strike off up valley holding this height and sidle until above Andy Flat, then descend steeply just inside open beech forest, followed by scrub nearer the flat. Travel isn't flash, and along the route beech forest will change to big scrub. However, 100m vertically lower travel is worse.

The Bivvy rock at Andy Flat is 150m north of its position marked on E39. At the river outlet from the flats, follow the true right bank past 2 beech trees, then a track cut through scrub leads under a third beech 30m to the bivvy rock. It is a confined but well protected dry rock, sleeping up to 4.

To reach the Plateau from Andy Flat, climb to pt 991m, sidle at about the 1000m contour above Lake Williamson, and ascend a snow couloir to the Plateau, just south of Futurity Rock. The old route to pt 991m past pt 899m is still okay (1998) but be careful to go high initially. Some have scrub trouble here. A better approach follows up past pt 719m to the rocky ridge that holds back the lake. At a saddle by a beech tree (and campsite), E39 447 344, sidle SE to a stream and follow it up (2000). This stream directly east of pt 991m can also be ascended (with sidles) from the flats.

Climax Pk
Mt Tutoko
Intervention
Mt Ark
Mt Darkness
Mt Gyrae
Coulo r
Bench
Trinity Col
Andy Flat

Follow the ledge until it ends and gain the Plateau via the snow couloir between Gable and Futurity Rock. Filled with snow, the couloir is the best and easiest route. However, the couloir is difficult when the snow is not continuous. If the couloir can't be used, a few alternative routes exist. A route reported to be straight forward crosses the couloir at the ledge to the true left and follows up tussock slopes sidling above the couloir. As you approach the large bluffs above, there is a side gully where you can reaccess the couloir, but this still leaves one huge boulder to scale. It is better to stay high and sidle around the bluffs, leading straight onto the Plateau. A second option, this time on the true right of the couloir, leads up from the ledge itself and finishes beside the Couloir top. This involves short bluffs and guts (rope necessary) connecting shelves. For those wanting a third option, it is also possible to ascend a tussock gully leading up under pt 1560m to overlook the Andy Glacier, then, right at the ridge, climb up to ledges and traverse over Futurity Rock. However, this involves a full ropelength on steep and exposed rock and tussock and usually some pack hauling. For climbing parties only, beyond Andy Flat.

Times: McArthur Flat to Tornado Creek, 3.5 hrs either direction; Tornado Creek to Andy Flat, 5.5 hrs (4.5 hrs in the reverse direction); Andy Flat to the Olivine Ice Plateau, 7 hrs (5 hrs in the reverse direction).

CAMP OVEN DOME can be approached from Andy Flat and a crossing of the Five Fingers Range made to Williamson Flat. From Andy Flat, head up the shingle slip stream (not too far), then swing left (looking up) to gain the ridge on the true right of the stream where scrub turns to tussock. Beware of danger from loose stones and choose a route to minimise time and exposure to rockfall here. Higher up, easy knolls and basins provide good going to the range and Camp Oven Dome.

To continue to the Joe from Camp Oven Dome, follow the spur down towards pt 1284m, and sidle left into the stream draining Five Fingers. Follow this stream down until the bushline is reached, thus avoiding the scrub and huge boulders. When the stream becomes difficult at about the 900m contour, bale out on either side, though the true right is probably best and angle down reasonably steeply through the forest to the Joe river bed. The bush is sometimes thick and scrubby and full of big boulders, but it goes. An older route down a slip further east is now overgrown with bush lawyer. The Joe is a big dirty river here. Ford it with care. Allow a full day for the crossing from the Williamson to the Joe.

TRINITY COL AND PASS McArthur Flat to the upper Pyke

Follow the true right bank of the Williamson as in the McArthur Flat to Andy Flat description. Just above an extensive area of flattened forest, cross the Williamson. Easy riverside travel on the true left now leads in about 10 mins to the Tornado Creek junction. If necessary, about 20 mins further upstream (on the true right) from the Tornado confluence, (and over 1 hr with a bushbash on the true left) there is (1999) a good rockbridge over the Williamson. Alternatively from the Arawhata, the true left also offers reasonably good travel up to Tornado Creek, though a little slower (about 5-6 hrs).

Enter the bush on the true right side of the unnamed tributary south of Tornado Creek E39 464 364. On E39 this tributary is shown entering the Williamson independently, but in fact it enters Tornado Creek first. In open bush, sidle up and away from the Williamson, heading almost due west. Aim to come out of the bush by the creek draining between Trinity Col and Mt Temple. Good campsites here, E39 452 364. There are bluffs just above bushline on the true right of this creek. A fault will be seen in these up this creek at approx the 1000m contour, 150m above the bushline. Climb until opposite this fault, cross the stream and then the bluffs can be passed easily. Gain the prominent

■ The Olivine Range at the head of the Williamson River. The route to Trinity Col is visible on the right and the route to the Couloir, Futurity Rock and the Ice Plateau is visible on the left.

knob where the rock bivvy is marked (sleeps 4, but water can enter in rain), about 6 hrs from the Tornado/Williamson forks.

Alternatively from the bushline, cross the creek at the 900m contour to the true right below a steep face. Scramble up through a tongue of bush then steep rock and tussock directly onto the spur, which can then be followed up to the bivvy rock. If there is much snow still around, this bivvy rock can be hard to find.

There are tarns and campsites here too. From the bivvy rock, a sidling climb to the west offers easy travel up a snow basin to gain the ridge south of the col at E39 435 363. Access to the Trinity Glacier is gained towards Trinity Col, via a snow/gravel gully. Descend to the Trinity Glacier and follow it and the gravel basin across to Trinity Pass, E39 417 368, (not where shown). The gravel basin drains back under the ice into the Williamson. To continue to Trinity Stream, descend a little from Trinity Pass and swing right, over a rock spur, to the top of a scree filled chimney. Follow this to the bottom, where it joins up with the stream emerging from a cleft onto the flats. Packs may need to be hand lowered down a couple of minor steps. The tussock flats give good travel until the Trinity enters a gorge. Just before that, an old deer trail leads up to pt 1136m, where there is good camping by tarns, and on across a wide basin between Trinity and Sealy Streams.

ACCESS TO THE PYKE FROM PT 1136M

Gain the ridge beside the Sealy and follow it through scrub and fairly rough bush to the junction of the Sealy and Pyke. Bluffs at the foot of the ridge can be avoided by keeping slightly to the Trinity side. From this junction the route down the Pyke lies on the true right. Stay on the riparian strip close to the river in tall forest to the Pyke Camp Flats. Light trails help. See the Pyke Catchment for further notes.

Times: Mc Arthur Flat to Tornado Creek, 2.5 hrs; Tornado Creek to Trinity Col, 6 hrs; Trinity Col to Sealy Pyke junction, 8 hrs; Sealy Pyke Junction to Simonin Stream, 2 hrs.

ACCESS TO SIMONIN PASS FROM PT 1136M. The descent off the pt 1136m ridge to the Sealy is very steep, but has been used, descending a gully (open at the top) into scrub where the first tongue of beech meets the ridge. Take extreme care and be prepared to use a rope. A less steep option is to continue down the scrubby spur and sidle across under bluffs to the Sealy at the 800m contour and then follow the stream up. From Sealy Stream, climb steeply to pt 1309m and sidle across easy tussock on old deer highways to Simonin Pass.

OTHER ROUTES FROM TRINITY GLACIER

INVITATION COL can be crossed by climbing parties from the Trinity to Sealy Stream. On the Trinity side, follow up a snow ramp which varies in difficulty seasonally and may sometimes be cut off. On the Sealy side, sidle left under Trinity Pks and zig zag down ledges into the basin that begins at the 1600m contour, E39 430 377. See Cascade Valley notes for Hurricane Col.

Traversing south from **TRINITY GLACIER TO THE PLATEAU,** crossing the Gyrae ridge at the 1800m contour (E39 420 361), requires good alpine skills, equipment, and conditions, but is used as a transalpine route. Slots can be a problem at E39 416 354. Cross a glacier, ascend the ridge overlooking the Andy from the 1600m contour and traverse Little Ark to the Plateau. A nice line in a good season.

THE JOE VALLEY

JOE RIVER GORGE Joe Glacier to Williamson Flat

Above Victor Creek, use the true left. Below Victor Creek, use the true right. Cross on a good natural rockbridge (1991) over the Joe, 200m below the Victor Creek confluence. Alternative crossing places are very sparse all the way down. Another more difficult natural rockbridge (2000) exists across the Joe under the prow at E39 453 260. A rockbridge is also reported within 100m of a creek on the true left at E39 464 274 (1997). There is a good campsite on the true left at E39 450 259 and more on small flats 700m downstream at the bushline on both sides of the river. The true right can also be followed from the glacier flats above the prow to Victor Creek, but the scrub zone is traumatic for the last 500m to the Creek. However, this bank is useful if heading to O'Leary Pass.

From the natural rockbridge over the Joe below Victor Creek, climb directly up on the true right through bush to the terrace and cross it to reach the rock bivvy clearing. The Victor Creek rock bivvy (sleeps 4) is approx 150m NE of the marked position on E39. It is hidden behind ribbonwoods at the foot of the hill, about 50m in from the SE corner at the top of the clearing and about 150m from Victor Creek. This large overhanging rock drips in heavy rain. A tent can be pitched under it.

From the bivvy rock, follow swampy *Hoheria* clearings and bands of beech forest down valley and enter the bush at the lower end at about E39 465 270. Skirt through more swampy clearings then follow a terrace in the bush at about the 740m contour. There are various route options on down to the minor grass flats at E39 468 295, and some follow closer to the river than the route described below.

The route crosses a wide scrubby creekbed draining Mt Victoria about halfway between the river and the scrubline, also at approx the 740m contour. Continue through more bush to the next creekbed at E39 468 282 and climb it until it runs out into the larger bed of Victoria Creek at 780m E39 469 284. Cross Victoria Creek diagonally downstream and old deer trails may be found entering the bush opposite a large boulder. From here, follow down to and along the open bush terrace sweeping north, reaching the river at forks, E39 468 294 where there are pleasant *Hoheria* glades and a small flat. Follow generally along the riverbed to another small grassed clearing.

Travel now becomes rough and slow with most parties staying close to the river, and (where possible) on the boulders. The bush slopes are exasperating, though an old deer trail once sidled up and down through guts and slips near the river. Don't go high. Eventually another grass flat is reached at E39 485 312. To bypass the gorge downstream, the route from this flat zig zags straight up through bluffs in the bush (old blazes), onto and along the lip of a bush terrace at the 560m contour (which could be seen before leaving the last flat). The route sidles then descends steeply into a small chasm, climbs straight out the other side to the 540m contour, then gradually descends to the mouth of the South Snowball Creek and Williamson Flat.

In the reverse direction. Follow the true right of the Joe through a series of small clearings and cross the South Snowball Creek. Sidle up though beech forest, using old deertrails where they are useful, to a bench at 540m, drop abruptly into a chasm and climb straight out the other side. A further gradual climb is followed by a sharp drop through bluffs to a grass flat above a gorge, about 3.5 hours from Williamson Flat.

From here, an exasperating sidle leads through slips and guts, utilising the river where practical, till easier travel returns at about E39 470 298. From the small clearing here, a short stretch leads along close to the river before the bush is again entered, 500m beyond. Follow gentle bush slopes, gaining height above the river to Victoria Creek at the 720m contour, and cross it diagonally upstream. Sidle on up the Joe Valley, keeping at about 740m. The river rises to within about 30m of the route at

E39 465 270. Continue through open bush, small clearings and swamps, over a short gorge, and out to the ribbonwood glades leading up to the Victor Joe junction.

Times: Victor Creek to Williamson Flat, 9 to 11 hrs; In the reverse direction, about 11 to 13 hours.

DESTINY RIDGE Joe Glacier to Olivine Ice Plateau

From the Joe, Destiny Ridge is usually approached from about E39 450 260, but it can also be approached for almost 2km up valley. From the lateral moraine on the true left of the Joe glacial flats, climb tussock, scree and snowslopes. Gain the main ridge between Twin Icefalls and the Passchendaele Glacier as soon as possible after reaching the snow. Broken rock bluffs on the face at about E39 440 267 are very impressive close up but are worth avoiding. The ridge is followed to a rock outcrop at the 2080m contour, which may be passed on the Passchendaele Glacier side. From here or above, depending on ice conditions, a traverse around the face of Mt Destiny leads to Solution Col. Alternatively, Destiny itself may be traversed, but a schrund near the top can sometimes give problems. Descend to the névé of the Memorial Icefall and traverse to the NE end, where moderate snowslopes lead down to the Plateau.

Caution. This is only a route for climbing parties; Solution Col is over 2000m.

Time: 6 to 8 hrs, plus time required to camp on, dig into, or leave the Plateau.

DESPERATION PASS

Recession of the Joe Glacier makes Holloways original line (NZAJ 1936 and Alexander, NZAJ 1955) impractical. However the pass has been crossed more recently (1984) using a slightly different line that descends the snow gully off the pass, sidles to the Dilemma Glacier basin and then descends steep tussock ledges and loose eroding boulder and scree to the Joe Glacier on the true left of Dilemma Stream. This is a poor route as some of the lower slopes are subject to rockfall. For climbing parties only.

O'LEARY PASS Joe River to the Dart

This is an extremely steep and treacherous route that must be approached with great care. It requires an excellent head for heights, is for climbing parties only, and only described as a route out of the Joe. Two mostly gravel streams drain the gulch 1.5km west of O'Leary Pass. One leads to Victor Creek and the other to the Joe:

1. From the upper Joe at E39 458 259, head up at the back of the flat in bad scrub under bluffs, on the true left of the creek draining from the Gulch. Stay against boulders and head through patches of beech (much more open) to sidle into the creek 150m distance from the flat, above the second set of boulder falls where the creek levels off in gravel. Follow the streambed up and cross to the Victor Creek branch at about the 960m contour (to avoid a boulder).

2. From the Victor Creek bivvy rock cross the clear Victor Creek and follow up the bouldery creek bed into the gulch with digressions into the scrub to pass big boulders as necessary. Be aware of potential stonefall.

From the exit point at E39 462 255, about 100m distance before the headwall, two routes have been used, both of which gain tussock slopes on the west (Joe Glacier) side of the gulch. One leads up onto the spur with some very steep and exposed sections on short grass increasing the exposure. The other is a more complex route, easier to locate from above than below. It sidles generally across from the exit point tussock shoulder at the 1200m contour, connecting sloping benches, rockslabs and gullies. (Beware with contour heights across the Joe. Some are wrong). Then it crosses two streams close together between waterfalls, before climbing an easy rock slab to much better going in long tussock beyond at E39 459 255. A slip on either route would probably be fatal, and neither route is easy to protect with a rope, though many parties may find they want such support.

Once easier tussock slopes west of the slip are reached, the crux is passed. Above here, there are again two options. On the original route, traverse just above the headwall in tussock and approach a higher bench beyond, just under an 'eyetooth' of rock at E39 464 253. Care is still required, but travel is not difficult under normal conditions. Travel then becomes very pleasant, gaining new benches with tarns and keeping up near the base of bluffs above as the route climbs east. The Main Divide is reached at pt 1843m, where there are more tarns in the tussock.

Alternatively from above the crux, a more direct approach can be taken to the Main Divide, leading up tussock benches to just west of Frobisher. Follow the Divide east to beyond the saddle. This avoids crossing tussock slopes above the headwall, but climbs 200m higher than the saddle.

Although it is possible to descend snow and sometimes minor rock steps from the pass to the basin of the Pass Burn, the easiest line descends snow and shingle slopes 1km east of the pass to the basin. Sidle down from about the 1400m contour south across easy tussock slopes and hummocks well to the true left of the Pass Burn to the bushline at E39 483 225 and drop down open easy bush to the Dart. Use the Cattle Flat bridge if the river is too dangerous to ford.

Time: Allow a full day from the Joe to the upper basins of the Pass Burn.

THE ARAWHATA UPSTREAM FROM TEN HOUR GORGE

WILLIAMSON FLAT TO MCARTHUR FLAT

Both banks can be used, but when descending, the true left is definitely preferable, as it avoids a major crossing of the Arawhata at McArthur Flat. Both sides are described.

ON THE TRUE LEFT, descending. At normal to low river flow the best option is to boulder hop from Williamson Flat to the final bluff just above McArthur Flat. This saves heaps of time but is rough and awkward in places. The first 1.5 hrs travel is reasonable, along big boulders. Then less than an hour of slightly faster, flatter river travel ensues, before the river drops more steeply and slow awkward travel in huge boulders encourages sidling. (A fair option). Down at E39 506 362 an oblong boulder on the true right juts into a blocky bluff on the true left (the last bluff) halting all further river travel. Return 150m on shingle upvalley, climb 100m (height) up an open washout gully, and sidle above this last bluff over a knoll at E39 504 361 before descending directly to the Arawhata River at the top of McArthur Flat. There is great camping on flats above the river here. It is possible to sidle much of the way if necessary, but vegetation is scruffy and travel slow. It isn't necessary to climb more than 200m above the river. Drop steeply through small bluffs to McArthur Flat.

Ascending. Once across the Williamson, there is an easy 10 min along the riverbank before climbing diagonally 100m or so, with mossy boulders/outcrops to thread through about two thirds of the way up, to gain the forested flat prominence at E39 504 361. From there, there is a slow steep sidle for 300m at the same level crossing two washouts ending in bluffs and descending to the river at the third. Travel upstream is slow in huge boulders, with tough bush sidles before a brief shingle respite at the junction of the tributary at E39 510 356. About 4 hrs to here. Beyond here, there is more bouldering and a few low bush sidles, but travel is now much better to Williamson Flat.

ON THE TRUE RIGHT, descending from Williamson Flat climb 100m and sidle generally at this height, with variations as necessary. Initially from Williamson Flat, 30 mins good open bush travel leads to a gulch with deep eroded banks at E39 512 354. Descend steeply, cross near river level and climb steeply up again. This process is repeated 30 mins later at E39 511 356. Beyond here, travel is slow steep and rough, with thick vegetation including lawyer. Drop sharply to E39 505 363 once close to McArthur Flat, where good travel on forest flats begins. Crossing the Arawhata here is marginal and should not be relied on. The 1994 storms brought down fresh slips on both sides of the river through here, requiring extra care in places.

Time: Williamson Flat to McArthur Flat, 5 to 6 hrs.

MYSTERY COL AND WHITBOURN SADDLE Arawhata to the Dart

This crossing involves major crevasse/icefall travel at the head of the Whitbourn Glacier, requiring good alpine skills and gear. From the Arawhata, two approaches to Mystery Col are described.

STOKES CREEK ROUTE. This offers a good line through to Mystery Col from the lower end of Mid Flat. Stokes Creek is ill defined and spread out in the bush and where it reaches the Arawhata as marked on E39 is surprisingly small. Enter the bush at Stokes Creek, E39 544 355 and follow up the shallow basin Stokes Creek is in towards the bushline. The bush is reasonably open. Continue to E39 550 350, where there are bluffs above directly ahead. Follow slopes up under the bluffs to the bushline, which is relatively free of scrub, at E39 553 352. Excellent travel in the tussock now leads up to Mystery Col, with great views across to Ionia on the way.

A tarn and good campsites exist on Mystery Col. In the 1930s Snow White ice was level with Mystery Col. Now there are 100m of slabby bluffs down to the ice on the corner under the col. However, it is still practical to access the glacier by sidling onto it along ledges from the col at the 1700m contour, heading upvalley. Small icefalls on the glacier can be quite variable though. To continue to Whitbourn Saddle, sidle SE from the col and then swing back west up little steps in the rock back towards pt 1812m. (The route down through here to Mystery Col would not be easy to locate from above. In either direction a recce would be useful. Alternatively the glacier or a long route via pt 1373m can be used).

WILLIAMSON FLAT ROUTE. About 250m NE of where North Snowball Creek leaves the bush there is another smaller creek. From there, climb through scruffy bush. An old blazed deer trail has completely overgrown, though recent blazes have been reported on this route. Continue to the bushline, which is mostly free of scrub. Mystery Col can easily be gained from here. However, the best approach from here to Whitbourn Saddle is to follow the main ridge to pt 1812m then pt 1928m on the true left of the Snow White Glacier.

The two routes from the Arawhata rejoin on this ridge. Higher, at 2100m, sidle the upper glacier under Pivot Peak to Whitbourn Saddle. Glacial conditions allowing, a high sidle just under 2300m, sweeps across to the south névé of the Whitbourn Glacier. Then snowslopes lead across to a gully that joins the glacier at the 1440m contour, E39 551 281. Alternatively, the glacier may be descended, but the upper Whitbourn can become very broken later in the season.

Time: The crossing from Williamson Flat to Whitbourn Flats requires more than one day. Potential campsites exist in the Mystery Col and Whitbourn Saddle areas. Allow about 4 or 5 hrs to Mystery Col from the Arawhata.

ARAWHATA BIVVY ROCK TO WILLIAMSON FLAT

Expect a bit of a scrub bash. Travel on the true right from the **Arawhata Bivvy Rock down to the flats at Twin Falls,** the old route, is slow, through thick scrub where deer trails are mostly overgrown. However, this is still the best approach (2000). Sidle out and across from the kitchen area through the scrub for a couple of hundred metres until a shoulder is reached before swinging down towards the beginning of the flats at E39 601 346. **Going up,** follow flats on the true left until opposite a small slip at this grid reference. Cross, ascend the slip, climb another 100m, then sidle, keeping up, on the remains of a trail, to the biv.

Other alternatives. The bouldery river isn't a flash route from the Rock downstream, but can be used, with a sidle required half way. Some prefer to cross and use the true left, where the distance through scrub to the start of the flats may be slightly less, but most parties will take 40 to 60 mins either side. The tussock flats beginning at E39 601 346 however, provide good travel. Pick up the top end of the flats on the true left. Cross back just before Twin Falls Stream comes in and stay on the true right to the bottom of the flats, where there are good fine gravel crossings.

From the end of the gravel flats, either side can be used. Currently, if the river is low/normal, the best side is the **true left,** travelling on boulders almost all the way to Mid Flat. About 4 or 5 times short sidles into the scrub behind boulders will be required, but there is no need to climb more than 30m above the river. At Mid Flat, the river is normally crossed twice, the second time back to the true left at Stokes Creek on a good fine shingle crossing.

Alternatively on the **true right** from Twin Falls flat follow the old route down the river bed as far as possible before getting involved with the scrub. Keep low. About 45 mins below the flats, beech forest is entered at E39 577 352, about 30m above the river and travel at this height above the river becomes a little easier, but there is still undergrowth and logs and banks etc. Dont climb too high. Useful deer trails exist in this central section under the beech forest. Descend the last 60m steeply to Mid Flat. Unless the river is very low, stay on the true right down to near Stokes Creek. Here, the river splits into two channels at the top of the next rough section and there is a good crossing to the true left.

Now on the true left and below Stokes Creek, just as the shingle riverbed turns into a gorge, ascend a lightly blazed deer trail (1998). This blazed trail can be hard to follow in places, but the forest is open and travel good. It eventually levels out and sidles on an excellent terrace about 150m height above the river until the blazes suddenly end above Williamson Flat. Good open travel leads directly down to the mouth of Phantom Creek. If necessary, the true right can be followed from Mid Flat to Williamson Flat too, but it is slower.

Williamsons is a wonderful, inspiring and scenic place to camp at. There is also a poor bivvy rock at E39 510 323 that would sleep one or two. It is a few minutes in from a clearing and is quite open. In 1965 a stretcher was carried down the true right of the Arawhata, from Arawhata Bivvy Rock to Williamson Flat.

Times: Arawhat Bivvy Rock to Twin Falls Stream, 30 to 60 mins; Twin Falls Stream to Mercer Stream, about 4 or 5 hrs; Mercer Stream to Phantom Creek, 1.5 to 2 hrs.

ARAWHATA SADDLE Liverpool Bivvy to Arawhata Bivvy Rock

Snow recession in lean snow years and in late summer increases the difficulty on this route with rock steps to climb instead of snowslopes from the Liverpool basin. In these conditions an easier alternative MATUKITUKI ARAWHATA CROSSING is described in the West Matukituki notes, P 81.

From Liverpool Bivvy, head NW through hummocky tussock country without gaining much height. After about 15 mins, cross the first stream off Mt Barff at the 1080m contour where there are cairns at E39 647 329. Climb out and sidle left of the small knoll ahead then bear right above a steep slabby drop to the next creek. Pick a route down to the creek carefully, and cross at E39 644 331 where there is a cairn on a flat slab of rock.

From pt 1386m in the Liverpool basin, a moraine ridge runs ESE. Descend the creek to the stream bordering this ridge without losing any more height than necessary, keeping at least above the 1060m contour. Cross and climb onto this moraine ridge. Often snowbridges upstream can be used to avoid

■ At Arawhata Bivvy Rock

getting wet feet. The moraine ridge has a good ground trail on it and is fast travel. The trail follows the left hand lower ridge at one point, and quits the ridge entirely at a cairn.

Head over onto old avalanche debris and rock slopes leading up the basin at E39 629 331. Continue up this usually snowy basin, or rock slopes nearby to E39 626 334, at approx the 1500 to 1560m contour. Then head diagonally right up to a knoll at the 1620m contour E39 627 335. The rounded snow slopes above can feel quite exposed with a heavy pack. Normally, parties then sidle left across moderately steep snow at about the 1800m contour to the Main Divide, about 200m NE of the saddle itself, depending on conditions. In the reverse direction, good confidence on moderate snow slopes is required. This eastern side of Arawhata Saddle requires alpine skills and equipment, and can be subject to avalanche danger.

The Arawhata (Western) side of the saddle is more straightforward. At E39 615 336, at approx the 1560m contour, there is a bivvy rock sleeping about 4. From the saddle, descend about 150m on easy shingle slopes to about the 1600m contour, veer right and descend slightly across easy grass terraces, heading up valley along the slopes of Barff. A few cairns may then be found leading down grass to cross the first large stream off Barff. Continue to sidle down towards the Arawhata descending an open gully and keeping out of scrub virtually all the way to the Arawhata at E39 612 348.

Comments on the route down the bed of the infant Arawhata to Arawhata Bivvy Rock are a guide book writers nightmare. Some are certain travel is generally best on the true right. Others use ribbonwood benches on the true left and say that travel was okay there. Some use the river where possible, and advise that sidling the last section is reasonable on the true left through open patches in the scrub. Someone else suggested the same, but sidling the last 500m on the true right. Generally, they all agreed that the stream banks are extremely scrubby and slow, and the river bed itself is slow, bouldery, and bad news, especially if the stream is up. Except for someone who found boulder hopping in the river bed down to Arawhata Bivvy Rock okay … Stream levels and who is in front will probably determine where your party goes. If you want my opinion, I'd head down the river bed, sidling on the true right as necessary.

Arawhata Bivvy Rock is a huge boulder that sits right in the valley. The bivvy is a dry area under this boulder on the true right of the river. It is well established, currently has a log book and could sleep a dozen or more, but is set up for about half that number. Logbook figures indicate that about 4 parties visit per year.

Times: Liverpool Biv to Arawhata Saddle, about 5 hrs; Saddle to Arawhata Rock, 3.5 hrs.

THE SNOW WHITE GLACIER can also be approached from Arawhata Saddle. There are several routes, but none of them are easy, and they all require transalpine skills and gear. The key to the best route is an unpromising looking rock gully at E39 612 336, running between the 1550m and 1650m contours. About 100m before the lip below Arawhata Saddle, ascend a small scree slide and continue across a crack system, climbing slightly to tussock slopes above. From there, descend and cross the creek draining Liverpool Glacier and sidle across to reach the Snow White Glacier at the 1400m contour. Travel up the icefall on the Snow White Glacier is only sometimes feasible. In good conditions, Mystery Col can be accessed from the glacier along rock ledges at the 1700m contour. A route involving the ridge to pt 1822m on the true left of the Snow White may be an alternative, but parties in this area will need to be very self reliant. Given good conditions, the route connects with Whitbourn Saddle, Mystery Col and the Arawhata.

WAIPARA SADDLE Arawhata Bivvy Rock to Waipara River

Follow the river from Arawhata Bivvy Rock through the scrub and sidle up shingle and boulder slopes directly under pt 1511m to Waipara Saddle. From the lowest point, traverse left (NW) about 100m, follow down the tussock edge and then a 60m slab, that leads diagonally down into the loose gravel gully draining between the saddle and pt 1511m. Watch for stonefall in this. A small scramble is required from the bottom of the slab to the gully. This gully can be followed down to the Waipara, sidling a waterfall on the true left, and keeping to the streambed most of the way, to emerge beside Bonar Lake. However, an easier alternative is to leave this gully at about the 1240m contour and sidle west to descend the gravel stream bed of The Wilson.

Time: Arawhata Rock to Waipara Lake, about 7 to 8 hrs.

WAIPARA VALLEY Arawhata confluence to the lake

From Waipara Hut, (see lower Arawhata Valley), follow up the true left of the Waipara to where the first real problems begin at about Saddle Creek. Throughout, in general, stay within 50m of the river as much as possible, and don't climb too high as some slopes have thick undergrowth and big boulders to negotiate. From about E38 664 522 excellent river travel continues upvalley, with good deer trails cutting the bush corner at E38 675 521. Somewhere between Sutherland and Campbell Creeks, parties normally cross the Waipara to the true right, with usually good river crossing sites just above Sutherland Creek and at the Campbell Creek flat. Travel on either side between these points is mostly easy, with a slightly rougher section on the true left for about 400m centred at E38 679 510. (If forced to continue on upvalley on the true left, which was the original route up the Waipara, when climbing over the Ratlin Water bluff keep away from the river when descending off the bluff upstream).

Mostly excellent travel on the true right above Campbell Creek leads to Apparition Spur. Enroute, a slightly rougher section of about 500m begins at E39 675 488. About 100m to 200m below Ratlin bluff return to easier travel by the riverbed again. Cross below Apparition Spur to the true left again, then cross back to the true right above it. Good easy travel now leads up to the Companion Ladder Rapids. A deer trail enters the bush on the true right 150m below the start of the rapids and goes all

Approaching Arawhata Rock in the upper Arawhata.

the way to large flats above them (1990). Do not drop off the trail early, but stay on it until sure the flats can be accessed. The Funnel enters the flat as a rock tunnel. Travel to the glacial lake is reasonably easy now, more or less following the river. The top section below the lake is a little rocky. If using the true left, be aware that the Bascand is bouldery and can be hard to cross. There are excellent campsites by the lake.

Times: Waipara Hut to Apparition Spur, 9 to 11 hrs; Apparition Spur to the Lake, 9 to 11 hrs.

APPARITION SPUR and variations have been used occasionally by transalpine parties for many years to access Cloudmaker Lake and the Haast Range. This is a long climb in thick ('but fairly easy going') bush, with thick ('but okay, sort of') scrub at the bushline, and lots of speargrass (*Aciphylla*) in the tussock. The spur is mostly dry, but there is a deer wallow that should provide reasonable water at 740m, E39 667 458. Apparition Spur can be approached up the small unnamed creek draining it from the northeast and climbing onto the spur itself at the 420m contour, E39 660 466. Above bushline, just before a prominent pinnacle at the 1220m contour, traverse right for a few hundred metres. Schist slabs cut across the tussock slopes at about the 1360m contour, but routes following tussock cracks and described as 'not for the fainthearted', exist through these slabs, very roughly in the general region of E39 678 453 that give access to the basin above. It will pay to recce a route through these last few hundred metres without a pack. More than one party has used a rope here. An alternative approach leaves Third Mate Creek at about the 440m contour and follows up the spur to the north before joining this route just above bushline. This is a very full day from the Waipara.

Alternatively from the Waipara, **the spur north of The Rudder** provides better access to the Haast Range. The scrub zone is minimal and there are no exposed slabs to cross. The spur peters out in a basin at 1200m to 1300m on slopes south of the west ridge of Stargazer. Pick a line up to the west ridge of Stargazer, where it joins the standard route along the Haast Range at the 1340m contour. See the Southern Haast Range notes below.

THE SOUTHERN HAAST RANGE

For the northern Haast Range see Lower Arawhata Catchment notes. Heading south on the range, to bypass the prow of Corner Post, sidle tussock slopes on the Waipara side to 'Rock Wren Gully' beginning at F39 707 483. This gully is steep and in places exposed. Partly it is in a gravel gully with one or two small steps and partly on short tussock nearer the ridge. But it does give reasonable access to the range above at F39 709 480. From here, the range, and then snowslopes overlooking the Waiatoto lead up to a col at E39 701 472. This is easily crossed to a snowslope leading down towards the head of isolated Cloudmaker Lake. There is a rock biv (sleeps 3) in Third Mate Creek, the largest rock in the valley near here at E39 683 451, between the two streams shown on the map. From E39 680 449 in Third Mate Creek, climb a shoulder and cross the more challenging and steeper Cargo Creek at about the 1400m contour on old snow avalanche debris. Then descend along a tussock shelf to reach the west ridge of Stargazer at about the 1320m contour. Follow up the ridge and shingle beside it to the ice puddles of the Suet Glacier. Continue across the Dipso and more substantial Iso Glaciers to access Colin Todd Hut. This traverse requires good transalpine skills and gear.

Times: From about pt 1594m north of Corner Post to Cloudmaker Lake, about 4.5 hrs; Cloudmaker to Colin Todd Hut, about 7 hrs.

'The barometer doesn't affect the weather much on the coast.'

—Charlie Douglas.

WAIATOTO VALLEY

Draining the Volta Glacier under Mt Aspiring, the Waiatoto is a very big river. Its opaque gray glacial waters are seldom easy to ford and great care should be taken. Although the Waiatoto is negotiable to the head via either bank, travel is slow off the main route, difficult in the Selbourne Spur region and a sidle is also required on the true right just below the Drake. Flats in the valley are farmed under a grazing license held by Mr. Kim Landreth (Ph 03 750 0129) who also owns the huts. Contact him for access permission. Cattle are moved along a bulldozed track that forms the main route up valley as far as the Drake Flats. However, this bulldozed track crosses the river twice, the lower crossing being especially deep and dangerous and impractical on foot. Also, the track up the Waiatoto to Caseys has side creeks which back up if the Waiatoto is high, causing long detours into the bush to cross them.

To avoid the lower crossing at Long Beach, parties usually take a jetboat up to about Murky Gully. For this service contact Neil Ross or Roger Crow, Waiatoto River Jet (Ph 03 750 0780 or 0800 538 723). They are based behind the DoC Centre at Haast in the Red Barn. They can carry up to 10 people and packs, charge approx $350 per hour, and the trip takes about 45mins. John Nolan (Ph 03 750 0822) may also be able to offer jetboat assistance. Planes can sometimes be chartered to fly into gravel beaches in the valley depending on conditions. Helicopter operators such as Morgan Saxton (Ph 03 750 0866) by SH6 regularly fly parties to a wide variety of places including the Waiatoto, and are very familiar with the region.

JACKSON BAY ROAD TO DRAKE FLATS

Take a jet boat to Murky Gully and pick up the cattle track on the true right there. (For completeness, the ground route turns off the Jackson Bay Road on the true left of the Waiatoto and follows a

■ Across the Waiatoto to Mt Castor and other peaks on the Main Divide from the Haast Range.

2WD road to a farmgate, just before Nolans Creek. Beyond here, a bulldozed track leads to Nisson Farm flat. The Waiatoto is tidal to about this point. Bush sidling is necessary opposite Caseys Farm flat where the trail is interrupted by deer pens and riverbank erosion. Beyond here, the bulldozed cattle track leads on to Long Beach, where it finishes on the true left riverbank at about F38 786 782. The river here is too deep, discoloured, swift and dangerous to cross on foot, barring further progress.

Taking a jetboat up to Murky Gully is the practical and sensible solution.

The cattle track begins again on the true right, as marked on F38 Ed 1. Follow along the bulldozed cattle track to Caseys Flat Hut (locked, Kim Landreth, emergency use only), and on up to Axius Flats, where there is a fair but sometimes deep crossing of the Waiatoto back to the true left. (If the crossing is at all questionable, it is quite practical to stay on the true right all the way to the Bettne in the head of the valley). The bulldozed cattle track continues from the Axius Flats on the true left and ends at the Drake Flats. An old walk-in freezer serves as a hut at the top of Ferny Flat near Gloomy Glen on the true left of the river beside the bulldozed track. It is about 40 mins up from the Axius Flats.

There is a very good crossing of the Waiatoto 300 to 400m upstream from the Drake confluence, giving access to the true right of the Waiatoto again and Drake Hut (open, sleeps 3 or 4, rough but okay), getting on for 1km upvalley from its marked position on F38. There is a slip behind it.

When descending the valley, staying on the true right from the Bettne down to Murky Gully is a good option. Travel is reasonable with no great climbs being necessary. Jetboats intermittently visit as far up as Murky Gully in summer. Rampart Cliff further down on the true right is easily negotiated along a ledge some 40 to 80m above the river heading SW. At normal river levels, boulder hopping to F38 765 788 is good. Beyond there, a DoC stoat trapping track can be used to approx F38 757 805, where it ends on the riverbank (it is part of a loop track to Gus Hollow, returning along the toe of the hill to the Waiatoto). From F37 757 805 to the Waiatoto bridge is mainly hard going through thick supplejack, swamp, and buttressed treetrunks. Stay as close to the river as practical, until, beyond deer pens at F37 746 813, it is possible to wade at the rivers edge to the track on the true right that leads to the bridge.

Alternatively, on the true left if the river is up and cannot be crossed, it may be necessary to bash on down from the Axius Flats to Murky Gully, to pick up a jetboat. From Shady Nook, Balustrad Bluff can also be crossed if necessary.

Times: Waiatoto Bridge to Long Beach ford, 3 hrs; Long Beach to Caseys Flat Hut, 2 hrs; Caseys Flat Hut to Drake Hut along the 'track', about 7 hrs; Staying on the true right, about 10 hrs.

DRAKE FLATS TO THE HEAD

From Drake Flats, if heading over Pearson Saddle, the true right is now usually followed. Travel is reasonable all the way (Donald Hut has gone) until a slower, more awkward spot at F38 731 542 where there is a small climb and sidle in scrubby bush. Beyond here, still on the true right, good travel mostly on riverstones leads almost to the Bettne River, where huge boulders and a cascading Waiatoto are truly impressive. For route notes to Pearson Saddle, see below. The Bettne River is difficult to cross in its lower reaches, for anyone contemplating continuing up valley on this side. The Bettne can be crossed at a grass flat at the 640m contour, though.

Alternatively, from Drake Flats, if heading to the lake in the head of the Waiatoto, the true left of the Waiatoto is usually followed upstream. Travel is not difficult up to Bonar Flats. The Log Cabin on Bonar Flats was swept away by the huge flood generated by a very big rockfall into the lake at the head of the valley in 1978. If required, a reasonable shingle weir crossing of the river can sometimes be found in the vicinity of Bonar Flats or even 1km above, but the Drake Flat crossing is best.

From Bonar Flat, travel is generally easy beside or close to the river on the true left up to where the river crosses the 400m contour. Before this however, leave the river and climb the gravel stream at F39 725 470 to the 600m contour. Sidle across to a tarn F39 721 464 and on to the Splasher at the same altitude. Follow its gravel streambed SW up valley and look for a route through scrub to the gravel flats by the lake, possibly leaving the stream at the 700m level. Be especially careful with route choices through here as there's a lot of scrub about.

Alternatively, the riverbed may be followed on the true left from the Bonar Flats to the head but travel is difficult in huge boulders. The lake flats are an inspiring place and the head of the lake can be approached along low scrub and scree slopes on the eastern side. Although it is possible for climbing parties to gain the Volta Glacier from here, overlapping bands of schist slabs at the 1200m contour make that a difficult proposition.

Times: Drake Hut to Bonar Flats, 5 hrs on the true right, less on the true left; Bonar Flats to the Bettne on the true right, 2 to 3 hrs; Bonar Flats to the lake on the true left, 6 to 7 hrs.

PEARSON SADDLE South Wilkin to the Waiatoto

The full crossing is difficult. About 1km upstream from the Wilkin Waterfall, old deer trails lead west to Pearson Saddle on the Main Divide. From the saddle, follow the Divide to the south, climbing towards the 1500m contour, before descending across the basins of Jimmy Creek and

■ The Waiatoto slopes of Pearson Saddle viewed from the Haast Range. Routes into the Waiatoto and around to the Purity Glacier are shown.

■ The upper Te Naihi and Lake Axius from Mt Achilles.

climbing up to a prominent shoulder F39 768 474 at the 1500m contour, visible from the saddle. Some prefer to drop into the tussocky Pearson Basin en-route, descending from the Main Divide at F39 781 471. Others prefer to sidle above 1400m, but this higher line especially can be subject to significant avalanche hazard from snow slabs sliding off ledges below Beauty Ridge during summer.

From the point on the prominent shoulder mentioned, climb about 120m height further up the ridge to the 1620m contour, partly in big old deer trails above big bluffs. Then sidle around to F39 760 473 and descend tussock steeply to the bench at the 1360m contour, F39 756 472. This bench forms into a ridge at F39 753 470 between the Bettne and Pearson Rivers on the lower (NW) side of a deep and precipitous gut. (The gut drops off into the upper Bettne River). The route follows this spur between the Bettne and the Pearson Rivers out towards pt 704m. The bushline above the Waiatoto, near the Bettne, will be reached 4 to 5 hours from Pearson Saddle. A descent may be made down the large rockfall on the Pearson side of the ridge, giving clear travel for the first 120m.To proceed down the Waiatoto, descend the bush ridge between the Bettne and the Pearson over pt 704m. In its lower reaches the Bettne is difficult to cross.

To proceed up the Waiatoto in the direction of Mt. Aspiring, an easy descent of 250m in bush leads to a grassy flat at the 660m contour in the Bettne, at the foot of a series of waterfalls which cascade 800m from the Purity Glacier. Cross the Bettne at the flat, then descend through rough thick bush and boulders. There is further information in the NZAJ, 1949.

Time: Wilkin Waterfall Flat to the Waiatoto, allow a 9 to 11 hr day; In the reverse direction, allow a longer day or split it into 2.

ACCESS TO THE VOLTA GLACIER from Pearson Saddle. For equipped transalpine or climbing parties, a route exists from F39 760 473 on the Pearson Saddle route at the 1600m contour around to the upper Purity Glacier. Sidle SW across short tussock slopes at about the 1500m contour. Several streams and gulches will require dropping packs and looking around for the best line. Midway, several creeks come together and are best crossed at the forks. These slopes are exposed and care is required, see photo P 156.

Reach the corner on the ridge F39 756 465 at the 1600m contour. Below, there are big bluffs. Above, the ridge crest becomes rocky and difficult. A small snowbank here may need to be descended or sidled under. A careful recce will reveal a couple of moderate to steep gravel gullies to cross to easy gravel benches above the Purity still at the 1600m contour. There may be a cairn or two here. Sidle across snowslopes under Beauty Ridge to the upper Volta Glacier. The route across these snowslopes will depend on the season, and parties will need to be equipped for glacier travel. Good visibility is required to negotiate this route. There is now a lake in the Purity.

ONTO THE HAAST RANGE

From Bonar Flats, to gain access to the Haast Range, follow up the Waiatoto to a stream at about F38 740 506. Head up this stream. Travel is very pleasant for the first 30 mins. There are some large boulders to scramble around, but travel is otherwise fine until a fork in the stream (unmarked on F38) at about F38 733 507. It is recommended to use the bush on the true right of the stream from this point, which should give access up a vague spur right to the tussock, avoiding scrub at the 950 to 1100m level. Cross a tussock bench at 1160m; steeper tussock above leads to a higher basin at 1400m and the Haast Range. This route can be used to cross to the Waipara by using the long ridge above Campbell Creek. Bush travel along this ridge is reported to be fairly open.

TE NAIHI VALLEY Waiatoto to the Headwaters

From the Axius Flats, follow the true left bank close to or in the riverbed. Opposite the word rapids marked on F38 Ed.1 travel in the riverbed becomes impractical and a slow arduous sidle through the bush for an hour or two is necessary. The Te Naihi Hut is still standing and useable. It has an open fire, sleeps one or two, and its location is correctly marked. Continue on the true left up to more flats at Calliope Creek. Cross, and follow the true right bank, climb over a bushy knob at pt 438m and descend to the head of the gorge where the river is forded to a small flat on the true left. There is a bivvy rock in the bush, 200m up valley from the head of this flat.

To approach the tops climb the spur on the true left of Bosky Gully. There is a bluff in the bush on this spur at F38 848 652 that some have had difficulty with close to the stream. It is suggested that this bluff might be easier to ascend/descend 150 to 200m south of Bosky Gully, leading up or down a spur from about F38 843 651 on the flats. This route is steep in the bush but emerges onto a scrubless bushline at 1060m, F38 855 652. From here, tops routes lead to several catchments. There is a tarn on the ridge at F38 857 651.

Time: Axius Flats to Bosky Gully, about 6 hrs; Bosky/Te Naihi Junctn to the bushline, about 4 hrs.

ACCESS TO THE MUELLER VALLEY. From the Bosky bushline continue up the spur to the ridge near pt 1722m. Descend rounded bedrock to Dispute Lake and sidle out on the true left past a tarn to the ridge at the 1500m contour. Stay on the true left to the head of the Mueller. See P 162.

ACCESS TO NEWLAND PASS. From the Bosky bushline, it is necessary to climb the spur to the 1500m contour, to avoid narrow deep schist gullies before a descent can be made to the tussock flats in the upper Te Naihi at the 1220m contour. Follow up the true right, cross under pt 1431m

Mt Alba and the head of the Te Naihi Valley from Mt Dispute.

and climb to pt 1581m. The lake outlet and NE side can now be traversed to Axius Glacier and Newland Pass. The descent to Newland Stream is steep, difficult and suitable for alpine parties only. For a description in reverse, see Newland Stream, Wilkin Valley, P 96.

ACCESS TO TE NAIHI SADDLE AND THE SOUTH BRANCH OF THE TE NAIHI. From the Bosky bushline, follow the above route to pt 1581m. Continue along the ridge, then traverse across tussock slopes to Te Naihi Saddle. Climb/sidle the SW slopes of Mt Achilles to the Divide. From pt 1606m a fairly easy descent up valley leads to the South Branch at the 1220m contour. Alternatively, traverse Mt Axius towards the rocky outcrop of pt 1840m, leave the ridge at the 1500m contour and descend an ancient slump that avoids scrub to the flats at F38 849 605. Saddle to flat, 2.5 hrs. Descending south directly off Te Naihi Saddle involves steep schist slopes and is not recommended.

There is a bivvy rock under the bluffs on the true left of the stream south of Te Naihi Saddle at the 1300m contour, F38 867 619, and 4-500m downvalley from the falls. Travel down valley from this bivvy rock is straight forward, sidling the stream at the bend on the true left, to the tussock flats (pt 961m) under Drake Saddle. See the Drake Valley for crossing notes.

TE NAIHI RIVER TO LAKE CASTALIA

From Te Naihi Saddle, or the Te Naihi River South Branch, the Divide can be traversed by alpine parties south to Lake Castalia. There are tarns just north of pt 1640m, pt 1606m, and other spots along the Divide to just north of The Sentinel. The route from the Te Naihi South Branch Flats begins on the downstream end of a rockfall at F38 851 604. Roughly 20 mins up, keep to the more stable far left edge (looking up). Continue up into the tussock, trending upvalley past a bluff to the Main Divide near pt 1865m (2.5 hrs climb from flats). On the Divide, a steep section north of pt 1841m requires care but isn't too difficult. The Sentinel is sidled at the 1800m contour and Leda Peak about 100m below the summit on snowfields leading to pt 1821m.

Descend to Lake Castalia from pt 1715m, being careful to find a reasonable route through slabs to the shingle slopes below. To do this, cruise down off pt 1715m to the 1640m contour, and sidle for 10 mins at this height across snow, then rock, (above bluffs) to where 10m of slabby ledge gives access to a gully (watch the loose rock) at F38 849 574. This is the crux, and a rope may be handy. Continue down rocky scree to the lake then sidle on the east side of it, to pick up the cairned track down the North Wilkin on the true left. See P 95.

In reverse, climb east from Lake Castalia up to the top of the scree and find a gut leading through bluffs to shattered rockslopes above. Traverse along the range from pt 1715m towards Leda Peak, sidling 100m below the peak itself on snowfields to the east. The crest of the Divide can now be followed to Mt. Achilles, and with care bypassing a step of rotten rock beyond it, Newland Saddle. A steep section just north of pt 1841m requires some rock scrambling. A descent from near pt 1865m can be made into the top flats of the Te Naihi (See above). Alternatively sidle across the slopes under Mt Achilles to Te Naihi Saddle, connecting with other routes to the spur beside Bosky Gully and the Te Naihi. The crossing will take a full, fine day.

Caution. This route traverses the Main Divide and requires moderate alpine skills and equipment.

DRAKE SADDLE (PT 1706M) Te Naihi to the Drake

From the upper Te Naihi River flats (pt 961m), Drake Saddle (pt 1706m) can be crossed to flats in the upper Drake River. The higher slopes are a steepish mix of tussock, scree and small bluffs. Follow a gravel creekbed through scrub from the bottom of the Te Naihi flats to tussock above them, then sidle north at about the 1250m contour to a gully at F38 832 608 (the third main creekbed). Above here, initially the creekbed, then a minor spur, lead to pt 1706m on the saddle.

To descend to the Drake, sidle slightly left down scree and easy going to F38 820 604, then right in tussock as small streams drop in falls over bluffs forming above. Continue NW on slopes between bluffs and get into a shingle gully. Some scrub bashing will usually be necessary along the river bank to reach the flats in the Drake at the 880m contour.

Times: Te Naihi flats to saddle, 2.5 hrs; Saddle to Drake River, 3 hrs.

DRAKE RIVER Headwaters to the Waiatoto

When leaving the upper flats, stay on the true left close to the river, until the bush is entered at about the 860m contour. Keeping height, sidle left on old deer trails, cross a creek, then descend to the Spanking Stream forks. Travel on down the true left, between 10 and 80m above the river, using old deer trails where possible.

Cross the clear stream draining Castor and Pollux (which can be used to climb these peaks via a steep tussock spur at F38 784 584 and the slabs of Pegasus). Pleasant travel on down the true left leads through swampy clearings, bush flats and occasionally along the river stones. When the river drops, try to follow old deer trails close by, though it will be necessary to be 100m above the river in places. Two or three slabby slips can be sidled near the river. There are more small flats down near Sundown Creek.

Guardian Gorge can be passed on both sides. Continuing on the true left, one option is to sidle away from the river where scrub permits on old deer trails then descend screes or creekbeds to river level again and repeat the process to about the 220m contour. Here, sidle out towards a spur on the true left then cut back directly towards Roaring Creek at the bottom of the gorge.

Times: Upper Flats to Castor Pollux stream, 5 hrs; Castor Pollux stream to Waiatoto, 5.5 hrs.

TURNBULL VALLEY

ROADEND TO THE MUELLER JUNCTION

Follow the road on the true right (north bank) of the Turnbull River to the locked gate marked on F37. The gate is controlled by Westpower and Kim Landreth (Ph 03 750 0129), who runs cattle in the Turnbull Valley. Permission is required to enter the Turnbull Valley, and stock in the narrow valley further up means it may be closed. The road continues up the Turnbull Valley (great blackberrying) past the Powerhouse to where a bulldozed cattle track, not marked on the map, heads east from the road, 300m before the roadend intake at Venture Gorge. This point is 100m before a rockslab through which the pipeline runs on the Turnbull River side of the road.

The bulldozed cattle track is easily followed through the bush onto a terrace, across it, over the saddle at the 300m contour and down to a small clearing. It passes straight across this into bush again and soon finishes on a river bank strip of grass, at the start of the Turnbull flats, 200m before the river curves left into a gorge. In wet conditions, upper bits of the track may require wading. **Coming down valley**, look for blazes on a large silver beech about 50m before the end of the grassy terraces by the river. These indicate the track beginning on the true right, at F37 859 827.

Tramp up the flats if the river is low without disturbing any stock, otherwise follow the river terrace around through forest and small clearings to the quite serviceable Turnbull Flats Hut, (open fire, 2-4 bunks, Kim Landreth), an old musterers/hunters hut. Continue up to the forks, crossing to speed up travel and utilise flats. The river is normally clear, green and crossable, but the true right can be followed all the way if necessary.

Times: Locked Gate to Intake turnoff, 1 hr 20 mins; Turnoff to the Hut, 1.5 hrs; Hut to the forks, about 2 hours.

TURNBULL RIVER Forks to the head

This is a route only. Follow the true right bank to Io (Ossify) Creek, mixing boulder and bush edge travel to Adieu Creek, then sidle Uproar Gorge at least 50m above the river in good open beech forest with no boulders. Cross the Turnbull River at Io Creek and follow the river on the true left. Cross again below Accident Creek; the true right is now travelled to the head, and in fact the whole valley could be traversed on this side if required. There is a huge bivvy rock about 150m above the junction of, and between, Cache Creek and Turnback Torrent. refers to the streams as named on the metric F38 map. The same names are applied to quite different creeks on the older Inch to Mile series.

Times: Forks to Io Creek, 1.5 hrs; Io Creek to head, 3 hrs.

CROSSING THE BROWNING RANGE Io Creek to Franklin Creek

This can be made into a very satisfying, moderately challenging 3 day round trip with excellent views, crossing the Browning Range at the 1500m contour. It is not marked. Sidle up Io Creek on the true left, about 50m above it in open beech forest, well back from the river, to flats. Continue on the true left to Commotion Creek, ascend this creek to the 520m contour then climb the steep spur on the true right of it to a basin at about the 840m contour marked as scrub. The scrub is stunted beech and is sufficiently pocketed with rock outcrops and tussock clearings to give good travel. Swing diagonally NE to circumvent bluffs, then sidle above them to the Browning Range at the 1500m contour, overlooking Whirlwind Water.

Initial bluffs on the eastern side are reasonably easy to descend, but snow can last here till late summer and should be prepared for. Sidle at the 1400m contour around to the slopes above Quiet Hollow

Looking down the Mueller Valley from Mt Dispute.

and descend the gully system to the bushline. Descend the spur between Whirlwind Water and Quiet Hollow down steep but open easy bush to the top flats in Franklin Creek.

Lumpy tussock here doesnt offer good campsites. Cross to the true right and follow down the Franklin about 20m above and well away from the creek in the bush. There are some stunted patches of forest. Just before Meteor Torrent comes in on the other side of the Franklin, climb to the 400m contour on the true right and descend the spur to the basin south of Franklin Creek, staying close to the creek, to eventually emerge at Franklin Hut (4 bunk, open fire, possibly locked, belongs to Noel Gray). Thick undergrowth makes for slow going at the bottom. See Okuru Valley notes.

Times: From the flats in Io Creek to Franklin Hut can be done in a very long day. Descending the gorge on the true right from Meteor Torrent to Franklin Hut takes 1 hr 45 mins.

MUELLER VALLEY Turnbull confluence to the head

The route to the head of the Mueller is through rough going, with big boulders choking the bush and riverbed, particularly in the lower sections. Follow the river until the flats finish at F38 867 772 then head away from the river on the true left, climbing quickly to the 300m contour to bypass a gorge. In the 1990s (with care), there is still a followable animal trail much of the way through this gorge. The route descends and crosses to the true right above the gorge at about the 320m contour F38 864 768.

Stay close to the river bank up valley, using flats and gravel where practical to the base of the next cataract, which lies between Deep Down Creek and Re echo Ravine. Here, there is a spray soaked open area which would be dramatic in a flood. Continue up the true right of the cataract through a boulder bash in forest close to the river, below bluffs on the spur. Above the cataract, quickly return to the river where travel is easy. If river levels make crossing tricky, cross to the true left at the best place that can be found, as it is also a good option to continue to Quail Flat all the way on that side, passing a lake enroute at F38 850 739.

Alternatively, continue on the true right to a small flat just below Betsy Jane Creek, cross to the true left to pass through Presto Defile near the river. (Presto Defile cannot be traversed on the true right). Above Greasy Gulch, it is easiest (but not essential) to cross to the true right again to avoid boulders, scrub, and a minor cataract to Quail Flat. Quail Flat Hut, built by Mike Palmer for deer recovery in Feb 1967, is not where marked. It's actually at F38 847 707, still on the true left but 400m upstream. Originally, it had a shower and wetback stove that worked. It is of historic interest as one of the few tangible remains from a rich and romantic part of our back country history, but with a snow damaged and leaking roof, it is now only emergency shelter at best.

Travel up Quail Flat beyond the hut (another hut marked by Emily Stream doesn't exist) continues to be good until tall fern slows progress towards Crevice Gorge. When viewed from the downstream end, it is easy to see how Crevice Gorge got its name. Follow deer trails on the true left up onto the ridge at the 660m contour then descend off it away from the river until on flatter ground upstream, sidling to the first small tussock flat at F38 860 686, and then descending the next big creek east to the river. If the river is low, some may prefer to return to the riverbank sooner. Continue to Alpine Flat, which provides good travel. Beyond the flat, set in dense scrub and bush, there is an old, stone walled hut. It still has a good roof and offers fair shelter but its concrete floor can flood. It is about 10m above the river, well back from it, and would sleep one or two. It too was built by Mike Palmer.

The river is now small, and vegetation thick. The river boulders can be followed to a tiny flat at the 760m contour and a waterfall beyond which has to be sidled. From the 900m contour in the riverbed, take the easiest line on the true left until the riverbed is impractical. Bash up the easiest looking line through minor leads in thick scrub up an old slip. The top of this slip leads to blocky schist outcrops on the spur at about the 1240m contour, roughly 150m above and north of the waterfall.

The easiest line to the lakes under the Dispute Glacier continues generally up the spur to the NW still on the true left, to bypass a second fall. These moderately steep slopes lead to easier travel on rounded bedrock at about the 1500 to 1600m contour and a long easy sidle past a tarn at 1570m to Dispute Lake below the glacier. There are exilarating, but exposed campsites here. Pt 1722m on the Selbourne Range is now easily accessible, offering great views of Mt Alba and Lake Axius. Routes from this point connect with the Te Naihi, Newland Pass, and the Drake. Mt Dispute can also be climbed and offers good views onto the riverflats, Emily Torrent and Shady Ravine as well.

Times: Turnbull Junction to Re echo Ravine, 3.5 hrs; Re echo Ravine to Quail Flat Hut, 5 hrs; Hut to the 760 m contour flat (head) 5 hrs; Head to Lake Dispute, 4 hrs.

Before success chopping wood, after success chopping wood.

—Buddhist proverb.

OKURU VALLEY

ROAD TO THE NGATAU FORKS

Turn off the Jackson Bay road and follow the road on the true right (north bank) of the Turnbull Valley up to the locked gate marked on F37. Park here. Continue for 600m beyond the gate to a second locked gate on a side road to the left. It is only 3km further along this road to where the bulldozed track up the Okuru begins on the right, but this part can be driven with permission. The first locked gate was installed by Westpower, and the second belongs to Noel Gray, who keeps a key for both. Noel Gray (Ph 03 750 0765), who lives on the North Turnbull Road, runs cattle in the Okuru Valley. He should be contacted before entering the lower valley. Gate keys can sometimes be borrowed, but it needs to be appreciated that use of the key is a privilege, not a right.

The bulldozed track leads to a spectacular bend called the Boil Hole on F37. Above here there are some very attractive sections of river, with big boulder islands and deep pools. Continue up the true left of the Okuru to cross (not usually difficult) above a big clear green pool, as marked, to the true right. Spasm Hut (may be locked, Noel Gray; about 4 bunks and open fire) is about 2km up valley on the true right as marked at F37 922 862.

About 1km up valley beyond the hut, cross to the true left again and continue on shingle and cattle tracks. The big flat opposite Retreat Rivulet is locally known as Muster Flat. At the head of this flat, cross the river and use the cattle track through bush on the true right to the Franklin Flats. Recross to the true left on these flats. Franklin Hut (4 bunk, open fire; Noel Gray) can also be reached if necessary from the road without crossing the river with only one small bluff to negotiate. Upstream from the hut, the true right offers better travel on shingle flats, particularly towards the Ngatau Forks, where a spur descends steeply 500m below Ngatau Forks on the true left. For an account of crossing the **Browning Range** from the Turnbull via Franklin Creek, see P. 161.

Times: First locked gate to Spasm Hut, 3.5 hrs; Spasm Hut to Franklin Hut, 3 hrs; Franklin Hut to Ngatau Forks, 1.5 hrs.

NGATAU VALLEY Headwaters down to Ngatau Forks

The standard approach throughout the valley, where the river cannot be followed, is to sidle through bush on the true right, following light deer trails. The riverbed can be travelled from Hailstorm Gully down to Flicker Creek, although the river drops quickly through this section. At Flicker Creek the boulders become smaller and the river levels out. At stream junction F38 943 718, on the true left of the main river channel, there is a flood channel creating a small island in the riverbed. On the true left of this flood channel, there is good camping on a grass flat. River travel is easy below here until Deepworn Torrent, when the Ngatau enters a small gorge and river travel becomes difficult.

From Deepworn Torrent, sidle out on the true right, where light deer trails should be of use and in less than an hour return to river travel at about the 280m contour. Easier going leads to another small gorge to sidle at the 240m contour. Below this small gorge, there is a large flat offering good campsites at the bottom of Tinkle Rill, where the old Ngatau Hut used to be. The river gorges again below this large flat, but look for an animal track on a terrace on the true right and follow it to stream junction F38 993 755. The river is now out of a minor gorge and a small flat extends downstream for a short distance with open travel.

At F38 998 758 the river gorges again and another sidle on the true right is required (following a good trail), emerging on a huge slip at F38 009 760 which appears to have dammed the Ngatau at some stage. At the downstream edge of the slip, pick up an animal trail that leads through bush to the flood channel at the forks and the broad shingle bed of the Okuru beyond.

Times: Shelter Ravine to Twinkle Brook, approx 5 hrs; Twinkle Brook to the Okuru, 4 hrs.

UPPER OKURU Ngatau Forks to Headwaters

The upper Okuru has developed a reputation for slower and rougher travel than most parties expect. One of the easier routes follows the true left up as far as a good river crossing point just above Turmoil Torrent, then follows the true right to Princes Creek. The true right can also be followed all the way and is mostly a high bush sidle (the original route). This is also a good line.

Note that travel on the true left becomes impractical at bad bluffs and guts near Arcade Creek, and that although travel upstream beyond the crossing point is faster on the true left initially, it ends in a cul-de-sac of boulders where the river cuts into bluffs and crossings are very bad.

Cross the Okuru to the true left just above the Ngatau Junction as crossing is more difficult in boulders up towards Hesper Spur. Travel from the Ngatau Junction to Hesper Spur is easy and will take about 20 mins (on either side). Where a bush sidle is required on the true left, the forest offers open travel. The river then gorges under Hesper Spur and travel becomes generally slow. Continuing on the true left, follow along the river boulders until about 100m upstream of a bluffline off Hesper Spur that descends to the riverbed at about F38 019 760. Big greasy boulders block further travel in the riverbed here. Climb about 20m height up the bank and sidle in bush upvalley, keeping this distance above the river, but under bluffs above, before returning to the riverbed again at about F38 022 758.

A mix of riverbed boulders and gravel fans can now be followed upvalley, with a bush sidle or two required depending on conditions. Both Turmoil Torrent and the stream downvalley from it end in gravel outwash. Between them, tiny grass clearings in open scrub exist at F38 025 757 about 100m back from the river. From Turmoil Torrent, boulders lead to the Okuru River crossing point at F38 031 754. The crossing, at the bottom end of a long deep blue pool, is on fine shingle, flat, shallow and normally easy.

Once on the true right at the crossing point, a bush sidle is required to continue upvalley. With care, a good deer trail which climbs steeply uphill can be picked up near the crossing, giving good travel initially (1998). However, some sidling from here upvalley is thick and scrubby, across old slips and steep slopes. On the corner at F38 037 753 the river cuts into a bluff which can be passed about 50m above the river. Return to the riverbed again at about F38 038 753. The river eases off above here and boulder travel on the true right is reasonably easy to Princes Creek.

If staying on the true right from the Ngatau to Princes Creek, the best route is to climb from the last goodriver terrace 150m or so up on deer trails, sidling the steep spur before openings at Chromite Creek are reached. Then more high sidling above the Okuru (100m or so) gives reasonable going on trails to Princes Creek confluence (1998).

There is a reasonable campsite on the true left of the Okuru opposite the Princes Creek junction, but beware of being trapped on that side by rain. Alternative sites exist on the true right of the Okuru, but above rather than below the Princes Creek junction.

The Okuru above Princes Creek consists of alternate sections of boulder hopping, huge boulders and rough going where the river drops rapidly. For the most part, travel is up the riverbed though sidles are necessary from time to time. Sidles tend to be brief, and the best approach is to take what appears to be the easiest line keeping as close to the river as possible to avoid thick bush and scrub. When travelling up valley, be careful not to be forced by bluffs on the true left into difficult river crossings.

From about F38 051 720, a variable deer trail on the true left can be picked up (1998) leading over bush terraces and small swampy grass clearings up to 150m distance from the river. This trail continues through the bush to extensive grass flats beginning at F38 041 719. These grass flats extend for a kilometre upvalley. The F38 Ed.1 marking of these flats as scrub is incorrect. Good campsites can be found on these flats, including at the top end on the true right close to the beech forest. Douglas Pass to Howe Creek is covered in the Howe Creek, Burke Valley notes. Maori Saddle is covered in Blue River notes. Princes Creek to Mueller Pass, see P 168.

Times: Ngatau confluence to Princes Creek, 5.5 hrs; Princes Creek to the upper flats, 6 hrs.

EMILY CREEK Okuru to the headwaters

Emily Creek descends to the Okuru Valley through a deep canyon. To access the upper reaches of Emily Creek from the Okuru, ascend Ironstone Spur. This spur is steep but open and can be followed from beside Emily Creek at F38 016 777. Follow up the spur to the 440m contour. Right on the ridge at the northern end of a small saddle at this contour, there is a small cairn. This is the second or third time the ridge has flattened off and takes longer to get to from the Okuru than might be expected.

Sidle from the cairn across moss carpets under open bush, keeping the same height heading up valley. Travel is excellent for the first half of the sidle to the open gully marked upstream, but the second half is thick, ferny and slow. The open gully is reached at F38 022 787, 50 to 100m above its Emily confluence. Cross the open gully and re-enter the beech forest, following up a rib to flatter going upvalley. Travel is not brilliant in places, due to ferns and thick bush, but its no worse than the second part of the sidle to the open gully. Follow the lip where contours ease off, crossing small gullies as necessary, to sidle back to Emily Creek at F38 028 794. The valley opens into scrub here, with easy travel on boulders up the creekbed. There are no good campsites in this scrubby basin.

Times: Okuru to the open gully at F38 022 787, 2.5 hrs; Open gully to upper basin at F38 028 794, 1 hr 20 mins.

EMILY PASS Emily Creek to Roaring Swine

Emily Creek Side. Easy boulder hopping up Emily Creek leads from F38 028 794 to F38 031 800. Above here there is a difficult waterfall/cataract to bypass. The lower bluffs on both sides are covered in leatherwood, with beech forest higher up. Although the falls can be bypassed on both sides, the editor has no good route to offer past them. One option, a bit of a grovel, is to follow ledges up on the true left, cross, continue in scrub at the edge of the falls on the true right, cross on greasy rock and follow the stream on the true left to the beech forest. The true left can now be climbed (very steep for 50m) up a forested bank to easier and flatter travel on a bush terrace above the falls. Above the falls, the creek itself is cut into a deep trench that is not easy to get in or out of, though it is easily crossed nearer the pass. Emily Creek begins by draining bluffs on the eastern side of the pass. It then flows across a bush basin at the pass before descending into the trench mentioned above. This means water is available for camping. On the western end of the pass there are tarns and tussock clearings. (There is about 100 to 200m of scrub to ascend to access continuous tussock on Rotten Ridge from the clearings).

Roaring Swine Side. On the Roaring Swine slopes below Emily Pass, a stream drains down towards the left into the head of the valley, as marked on F37. It is possible to descend in the bush either side of this stream (the stream itself is waterfally). On the true left, keep your height above the stream and sidle well towards the left (NW) into the head of the valley. Some of the slopes are heavily covered in leatherwood under the beech forest and once-heavy deer trails are now overgrown.

On the spur on the true right of the stream, keep towards the stream side of the spur, and descend the last bluff with the aid of a broadleaf (Griselinia) bush near the stream at F37 035 807. Be careful to avoid all slopes NE of this spurline as they end in bluffs. From F37 035 807, much of the creek can be travelled, but there are some essential sidles to avoid jumbles of huge greasy boulders. The thick bush up here offers only slow travel. It may be possible to make use of the gully at F37 036 810 which is open and offers good travel. Continue down the creek, on boulders where possible and sidling where it is not, to the flats.

Times: Emily Creek basin to Emily Pass, 2.5 hrs; Emily Pass to F37 035 807 in Roaring Swine, 1.5 hrs; F37 035 807 to the main flats in Roaring Swine, a good 2 hrs.

ROARING SWINE CREEK Road up to the main flats

The Haast Pass Highway bridge crossing Roaring Swine Creek is labelled Gap Creek. There is a carpark area on the upstream, true right bank. From this carpark, follow a lightly blazed and paint sprayed ground trail through bush up valley on the true right, initially about 5 to 10m vertically above, and close to, the river. At about F37 063 855 there is a messy area of tutu, with an old slip and boulders to travel through. Pick up the lightly marked route on the terrace edge, further from and higher above the river now and stay on this terrace edge as it climbs to 100m height above, and 150m distance from, the river. A steep sided creek at about F37 058 848 can be crossed up or downstream. Upstream is easier. As the flats are approached, the terrace runs back towards the river edge and the lightly marked trail still on the true right, follows the lip 10m above the river for the last 10 mins to the flats. Follow fine gravel in the riverbed upstream to the flats, crossing as necessary.

To descend to the road from the flats, follow the river to the end of the flats and fine gravel crossings to where boulders begin at F37 054 845. Scramble onto the terrace there on the true right where there are a few old blazes and red spray spots on trees to help give a line. Follow them and a light ground trail along the bank, head slightly up, keeping on easy going across an old fan under the trees, then swing back towards the river as open travel allows. Below here, the line generally follows the lip of an old terrace, keeping off steeper scrubbier slopes below that drop into the river. Lower down, cross an old slip F37 063 855 and return to within sight of the river, where the last few 100m of ground trail gives good going to the carpark.

The best campsite on the flats is probably at F37 047 831 between a side creek off Grandeur Cliffs and the Roaring Swine. To approach it, follow up a side creek, and at the end of a long gravel straight swing 15m towards the river, where dry, mossy flats will be found in *Coprosma* alcoves (1997). Other attractive sites are fine in good weather, but are very prone to river flooding.

Times: Road to flats, 2 hrs; Flats to Road, 1.5 hrs; The flats will take 45 mins to traverse from end to end.

ACCESS TO THE MARK RANGE

The Mark Range is rugged and untracked, with travel on the range itself slow and bouldery. A spur from the Okuru Valley, beginning on the true right of Lindsay Creek, offers reasonable travel to bushline where there is stunted beech, but not much scrub. This spur can be used to access the Lindsay Glacier and Staircase Creek. Staircase Creek is reported to be negotiated largely in the stream itself up valley from Lake Douglas to Lather Creek, where there are good campsites on the true left. Lake Douglas can if necessary be sidled around both sides close to the lake in thick, rough bush. Strata Falls can be passed on the true right, beginning up an indistinct streambed 150m back from the falls. Head for a rockface about 250m back, sidle right (looking up) about 150m to bypass bluffs, climb up 15m in scrub and head only gently down, crossing a couple of creeks, to tussock above the falls. From here to Mistaken Saddle is a delightful stroll. Beyond here, the tops are rocky and difficult alpine travel.

From the Haast Pass Highway, pt 1461m near Mt Mark can be approached up a spur on the true left of Greenstone Creek. This provides steep but reasonable travel to the tops, with less scrub than in other parts of the range at the bushline.

PRINCES CREEK

From Mueller Pass (see P 170) follow open grassland down on the true right until it finishes, then cross Princes Creek. A good deer trail leads down the true left from the bush edge, generally keeping about 50m distance from the creek, to a big gravel fan at a side creek, F38 061 762. There are open campsites here in all but very bad floods. Good going continues with the gravel, but then the valley closes in.

As the river becomes impassable at about F38 056 758, with bluffs on the true right, climb out on the true left gaining about 50m height. A reasonable deer trail may be followed for parts of this sidle downstream. This sidle is the slowest (it will take the best part of an hour) and the bush the thickest on the whole route down Princes Creek, but it isn't too bad. Towards the end of it, a good deer trail leads down the spur between the river and a creek shown on F38, arriving at forks with the river at F38 052 757. (Use it going upvalley, too).

Easy travel for 400m down the riverbed leads to Cranny Creek, where Raolia carpet mats almost break into flats. Below Cranny Creek, the river descends into boulders again. Sidle out on the true left on scrubby pepperwood (*Pseudowintera* sp) terraces and stay close to the river, following an intermittent trail along the riparian strip. This trail improves, then leads back to a calm river with good going along the stones below the boulders. Continue down the riverbed, or on the openly forested terrace on the true left beside it, (as approriate) to the forks.

Time: Mueller Pass to the Okuru, 2.5 hrs.

... rain and hail came in a drumfire over the low rocks, the wind stepped up to 50 knots, and the first rips showed in the tent. The rain came in. Things were getting just a little unpleasant. ... the ridge beside us, suddenly glowed with an aura of uncanny light. It was blue-purple. Our ice-axes hummed. The flash and impact of lightning shook the ridge; the thunder came with the synchronous crash of cymbals ... For the rest of that night, and the following six days and nights, we shivered in soaked bags ...

—Paul Powell stuck in a snowcave after their tent ripped to bits on the Volta Glacier, Jan 1965.

A few wet days must be expected, perhaps as much as a week, but even if the bad weather should continue for a fortnight there is no need to give up hope. The second week may be the worst, and by the third some definite improvement usually takes place.

—GM Moir.

By Christmas, I'm wet!

—Arawhata Bill.

THE BURKE VALLEY

PLEASANT FLAT TO THE MONUMENT (HOPE/BRANCH FORKS)

For much of its length, the Burke flows through a canyon, making a bush sidle on the true left necessary. Although travel is not fast, the forest isn't generally too thick or difficult. Remember though, this is Westland. Occasionally, parts of the old track, originally blazed then marked with red and white permolat, are followable on the route described, particularly around Strachan Creek. Normal to low flow in Strachan Creek is essential to negotiate the Burke Valley.

There are two approaches to the valley from the Haast Pass Highway, SH6.

1. Approach the Haast Riverbed from the highway down a short access road, opposite the gravel stockpile marked at G37 188 806. If the river is low, cross just below the Burke/Haast confluence to the shingle beach on the true left of the Haast, 100m below the Burke junction. Judge this crossing carefully, as it is often clear but deceptively deep and watch for holes in the rapids, especially on the true left.
2. This route removes the need to cross the Haast. From Pleasant Flat Shelter, go about 50m towards the river and follow a track to Muir Creek. Leave the track and cross Muir Creek, then pick up a trail that leads through a long, curving grass tongue in beech forest to the top of an island in Mather Creek and 200m up from the Haast. The most straightforward option from here is to descend and continue along the Haast Riverbank, mostly on gravel. There are a couple of small scrambles to avoid eroding banks and then the shingle beach, 100m below the Burke junction, is reached about 40 mins from the Shelter.

From this shingle beach at the confluence, follow up the spur on the true left overlooking the Burke. Old blazes and intermittent orange markers lead over a minor knoll at the 180m contour. Descend off the knoll to the first creek, and follow just above the lip of cliffs overlooking the river. The route generally follows this lip to beyond Strachan Creek. Cross 2 or 3 more creeks, following a lower terrace until it finishes at approx G37 171 803. Climb up a spur (some old good blazes) and then sidle over the top of a high drop. Here, parties are at least 100m directly above the river and travel in the beech forest is more open. Traverse down again to follow the lip about 40m above river level, sidling up valley, and crossing small creeks (take care: some of them are very slippery and go straight into the gorge). Then climb again, still following the top edge of bluffs directly above the river. As Strachan Creek is approached, intermittent markers may be seen swinging towards this creek across a high terrace, to reach the old Strachan Creek bridge site 150m distance upstream from the Burke/Strachan confluence.

The wires on the old bridge have been cut, making a crossing of the Strachan canyon necessary. This will take about 30 mins. There is a fair crossing (the best for a couple of kilometres upstream) about 60m upstream and just visible from the bridge site. But the crossing is not accessible along the bank from the bridge site on the true left (except in very low flow). Instead, go 100m (distance) up the edge of the spur overlooking the Strachan from the bridge site where there may be white plastic on a tree. Descend a very steep gully into ferns and continue down directly to the creek, then cross. The boulders are very greasy and the runout poor. On the true right of the creek, climb 5m then sidle across to the old bridge site in a slippery, festering green jungle. The bush is very thick, but keep above the greasy moss walls of the canyon itself.

On the true right of Strachan Creek, from permolat at the old bridgesite 30m above the creek, sidle down towards the river, then swing upvalley, following the edge of small terraces overlooking the river at the 260m contour. Continue to at least Hidden Rivulet, where in low conditions river travel becomes practical much of the way to the Howe, sidling as necessary. Where the Howe joins the

Burke, gravel makes a small flat under the trees on the true right. About 200m upstream from Howe Creek, the river gorges. In low/normal conditions, climb out on the true right, and sidle in open beech forest to Cowan Creek. In low/normal conditions, the riverbed can then be followed pretty much up to the Monument. However there are other options from Cowan Creek, too.

1. Return to the true left after about 15 mins and follow the true left most of the way up to the Monument. The track that once led through here has now virtually gone. At F38 082 783 a red/white marker on a tree by the river indicates a good crossing to the true right. Cross. Fast travel on the true right leads upvalley over an open bush flat, returning to the river edge at F38 080 783, where another red/white marker indicates a good crossing back to the true left. This avoids a slow awkward section on steep banks by the river on the true left. Travel is now all on the true left to the Burke Monument, through reasonably open but bouldery forest, taking about 45 mins from the crossing. There are 3 streams en-route, and they are all best crossed close to the river, to take advantage of good travel on long narrow terraces in the forks of each.

2. Continue on the true right through mostly open forest up behind pt 510m, (this route was once blazed), rejoining the river at F38 080 783. Cross to the true left and continue as above. At the Branch/Hope forks, there are good campsites on the grass flats on both sides of the Burke. The concreted memorial plaque, in a small grass clearing screened from the Burke by a strip of beech trees, is in memory of Brian Grady, accidentally killed near there in April, 1949. It is at F38 070 780.

Descending from the Hope/Branch forks, follow deer trails into the bush from flats on the true left. Keep on terraces above the river, descending to cross each of three streams near the river and then crossing the river itself at F38 080 783 to the true right. Follow one of the two routes described (or the riverbed) down to Cowan Creek, sidle to just above the Howe and continue in the riverbed or sidling, down to The Twirligig, where there is a grassy flat. Fairly good travel on bush terraces continues on the true left, generally following the old trackline.

Approaching Strachan Creek, swing up the terrace towards the Strachan Valley. The old bridge site is about 150m upstream from the Burke confluence, and the crossing of Strachan Creek 60m distance above that again. Stay on easier going above bluffs directly overlooking the river past Churn Rapids, and continue to keep generally on this lip downstream. The river noise fades into long calm confined pools near the Haast, and along here climb up over an open bush knoll and follow odd markers down the spur beside the river to its confluence with the Haast.

Times: Burke/Haast confluence to Strachan Creek, 3.5 hrs; Strachan Creek to Howe Creek, 6 hrs; Howe Creek to the Monument, 3 hrs.

MUELLER PASS Hope Creek (Burke) to Princes Creek (Okuru)

The open forest canopy between Hope Creek and Mueller Pass is a mix of silver beech and Hoheria, but it is the dense, deep understorey of prickly shield fern (Polystichum sp) that is the problem for trampers, making travel slow and arduous. Probably the easiest way to the pass currently lies along the SE side of the Hope Valley. An easily followed gravel creekbed, not shown on the map, joins Hope Creek at F38 068 776. Follow this up under the forest to about F38 066 774, then swing across a gentle fan under the trees, heading for the clearings that begin at F38 065 772. **(In the reverse direction,** from this grid reference, head across and slightly up towards the creek that feeds into Hope Creek from the SE. Easy travel then leads down the creek to the Burke).

The open area shown on F38 is mostly boggy grass, and offers good travel. The pass area is not known for good campsites, but there is dry ground on old mossy alluvium on the true right of Princes Creek at the southern end of the flats that would be fine to camp on.

A permolat route once crossed the pass, but is now so overgrown as to be useless. However, for the record, there are still some markers on the Hope Creek end of it (1998). To locate them, follow up open flats in Hope Creek to the junction at F38 067 776 and continue up the confined true right creek heading towards the pass for 100m. Here, red/white markers on a Hoheria overhanging the creek indicate where the marked route leaves the creek on the true right and disappears into hectares of deep prickly shield fern. There are a few more markers on beech trees here and there, but then they are lost altogether. There is no ground trail. If using this route, continue on a line straight to the pass, where grass clearings begin as shown on F38 after about 45 mins in fern. Avoid using routes closer to the western slopes, as the fern is deeper and a small drain there is full of blockages and deep holes, offering slower travel.

Time: Hope/Burke Forks to Mueller Pass, 1 hr.

HOWE CREEK

Traditionally, use the true right bank to the first flats (at about the 500m contour), then the true left to the upper flats just above the 600m contour. Recross to large clearings from which the head of the valley can be seen. There is a dry bivvy rock estimated about 4 hrs in, on the true right. Travel from the beech forest to up under **Douglas Saddle** is not particularly difficult, with the streambed offering good going much of the way, avoiding almost all scrub in the upper basin (1998). There is a small open flat above the bushline on the true right at F38 077 714. Other sites to camp on also exist, such as the carpet mat terrace by the stream at F38 067 718, under the pass.

A SADDLE TO THE FISH from the Howe is relatively straightforward. Follow the spur at G38 102 738 up to bushline. Continue in tussock to near pt 1620m before descending into the Fish River true right branch.

DOUGLAS SADDLE

A relatively good route exists from the upper Okuru flats to Howe Creek over Douglas Saddle. From the end of the upper Okuru flats at F38 042 719, sidle down the Okuru on the true left. Follow deer trails where possible, up to 150m back from the river. The trails lead through discontinuous swampy grass clearings en-route. A trail leads back to the river as the country steepens. At F38 051 719 a small bush covered stream enters the Okuru from the true right. At F38 053 721 a larger stream enters the Okuru on the true right and has an open gravel bed. Between them the river flows peacefully through small stones and is easily crossed.

Cross to the true right of the Okuru between the streams and climb steeply in scruffy bush to a terrace at the 680m contour. The terrace and spur above now offer excellent open bush travel to bushline. At about the 940m contour on the spur, sidle east across to a grassy tongue down which a stream flows. This tongue descends into the bush and is visible from the upper Okuru flats. Cross to the east side of this tongue. Follow a stream up in the open to where a band of scrub crosses slopes above the bushline at the 1100m contour. Here, at F38 058 715, a narrow lead of carpet grass winds up through the scrub to the tussock and the start of several small slips that extend across towards Douglas Saddle. Sidle across 300m, reaching Bright Water at the 1130m contour.

From Bright Water, sidle 50m north across tussock slopes to access a gully. This gully leads 100m directly up to the ridge at F38 062 716, the low point at the extreme southern end of Douglas Saddle. Although steep, the gully is sheltered and has plenty of tussock in the upper reaches. Although care is required, it is not exposed. Follow the range crest north for 100m, then sidle on the Howe side, to follow the tussock spur down to F38 066 718. There is a reasonable campsite by the upper Howe Creek at F38 067 717 and others downvalley at F38 077 714 where there are small flats. Although F38 marks all the upper Howe here as scrub, there is actually only scattered scrub and travel down the open gravel streambed to bushline is all easy.

■ Flats in the upper Okuru from Maori Saddle. The route to Douglas Saddle is shown. *John Fox*

In the reverse direction, to cross from the Howe to the Okuru. From F38 066 718, climb to Douglas Saddle and head south to F38 062 716, just before the range rises in scrubby walls. Descend the gully towards the Okuru, cross Bright Water and sidle SW for 300m at the 1120m contour. Find a thin lead down through scrub to an open grassy streambed. Sidle out on the true left and follow the spur down through open bush to the Okuru at F38 052 720. From the Bright Water, other routes can also be taken into the Okuru.

Times: Okuru River (F38 052 720) to Douglas Saddle, 3.5 hrs; Douglas Saddle to the upper Howe, 30 mins; Upper Howe to Douglas Saddle, 45 mins; Douglas Saddle to the Okuru River, 2.5 hrs.

BRANCH CREEK Monument to head

From the Burke Monument, begin up Branch Creek on the true right to avoid a bluffy sidle on the true left. About 250m up from the Monument, cross at the bottom of a pool and sidle into open bush. Excellent travel on the true left now leads upvalley on gently rising slopes then a terrace, before dropping about 15m to the river edge at F38 067 787. From here, flats can be followed upvalley. Initially cross to the true right, then cross back and follow the true left along grassy banks towards Top Brook forks. From a terrace above the river at the top end of the swampy open clearings marked on F38, descend through a narrow strip of bush to the riverbed again. From here, 200m of easy river stones lead to the forks. Travel to here is fast and pleasant. (Top Brook descends to the Branch as an open gravel bed offering easy access to its head).

To continue up Branch Creek, cross Branch Creek to the true right. Climb the spur between Top Brook and the Branch to the 560m contour on the terrace above. Sidle up the Branch on this terrace, dropping slightly to river level just below the corner at F38 066 796 to bypass a deeply incised gully. Travel in the riverbed for 150m to bypass this gully is easy. Immediately past the gully climb to a terrace at F38 067 797, still on the true right. This terrace, which is 20m above the river, has a small tussock and bog clearing on it, fringed by beech from the river. Travel upvalley on the true right under the beech from this clearing is slow and uninspiring through thick prickly shield fern for 500m. From this clearing, there may be better travel under beech forest on the true left of Branch Creek. From F37

069 802, the true left certainly offers good travel about 30m height above the river, where there are connecting corridors of beech forest along the lip of a terrace overlooking the river. This continues upvalley on the true left to open grassland at the start of the top flats.

Descending. From the top flats, follow the grass fan down on the true left and enter the beech forest 60 to 80m distance from the river. Keep under the beech and continue on the true left as far as possible. Cross to the swampy clearing at F38 067 797 on the true right. Descend off the end of the swampy clearing down to the river and follow the bank for 150m past an incised creek. Sidle out onto a terrace through open forest and follow it easily down towards Top Brook and the forks.

Times: Monument to Top Brook, 1hr; Top Brook to top flats, 2.5 hrs.

HEADLONG SPUR Cache Creek to Branch Creek

Branch Creek can also be approached directly from the Haast Pass Highway at Cache Creek by experienced parties. About 100m towards Haast along the road from Cache Creek, enter the bush and climb steeply on surprisingly good deer trails to flatter travel between the 100 and 200m contours. Bluffs at the 200m level are difficult to bypass, but greasy banks can be ascended about 400m from Cache Creek. Other, better lines may exist through this band. Once above this bluff, sidle over to Cache Creek at about the 300m contour, where good deer trails lead up through open forest right beside the creek. As the creek steepens again, follow the trails on up the spur, being careful not to be led too far away from Cache Creek. At about the 780m contour, a bluffline on the Cache Creek side of the spur at F37 073 849 pushes parties up a tiny gully on good deer trails, out of the forest into open subalpine scrub and stunted beech on a large flat area leading to pt 805m. Follow heavy old trails across this boggy, stunted beech and scrub area west of pt 805m and descend to the flats in Cache Creek where there are campsites.

From F37 073 845 on the flats in Cache Creek, pick a route past leatherwood through to the spur itself again and follow the spur up to the tussock. Travel is relatively easy under open beech forest, with only the occasional block of rock to clamber up. The treeline is free of scrub bashing and travel above it in the tussock is open and easy. A couple of steeper bits are easily bypassed a little below the ridge on the Cache Creek side. There are no campsites at the bushline, but tarns and campsites exist on the pass at F37 069 832. There is also a tiny tarn at F37 066 835.

The head of Branch Creek down to the top flats is gorged and waterfally. To descend from Headlong Spur to the flats, either:

1. Follow an old deer highway to pt 1460m and descend the spur off it to F37 068 820, or
2. sidle down the true right, keeping at least 50m in height above the creek. There are several steep, awkward little gullies to cross on this latter route. There is open scrub to descend for the last 100m to the flats on either route. The route down Branch Creek to the Burke has been described above in reverse. Although this route can be used in reverse, be aware that it may be difficult to find routes down through the bluffs from about the 300m contour to the road.

Times: Road to flats in Cache Creek, 4 to 5 hrs; Flats in Cache Creek to bushline, 2 hrs; Bushline to top flats in Branch Creek, 2hrs.

OTHER BURKE TRIBUTARIES

STRACHAN CREEK headwaters are accessible on the true left. Climb high to avoid a gorge.

TWIRLIGIG is entered by climbing the main spur on the true right bank for 1 hr, then sidling to the flats; about 3 hrs from the mouth. There is a good bivvy rock opposite the first clearings on the true left bank, about 100m from the river.

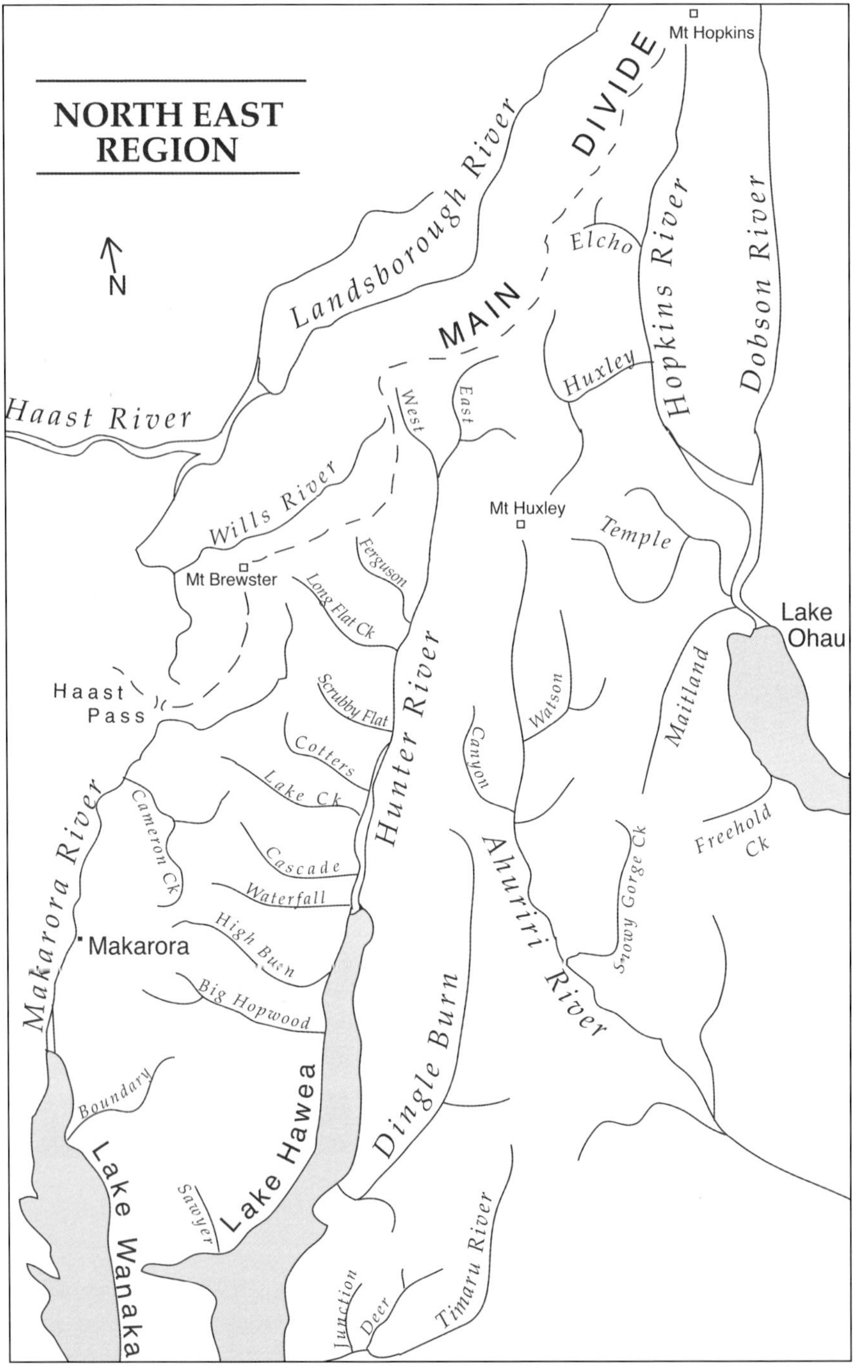
NORTH EAST REGION
N
Mt Hopkins
MAIN DIVIDE
Landsborough River
Haast River
Elcho
Hopkins River
Dobson River
Huxley
West
East
Wills River
Mt Huxley
Temple
Mt Brewster
Ferguson
Long Flat Ck
Lake Ohau
Haast Pass
Scrubby Flat
Hunter River
Watson
Maitland
Cotters
Canyon
Lake Ck
Makarora River
Cameron Ck
Cascade
Waterfall
Ahuriri River
Snowy Gorge Ck
Freehold Ck
High Burn
Makarora
Big Hopwood
Dingle Burn
Boundary
Lake Hawea
Lake Wanaka
Sawyer
Timaru River
Junction
Deer

PART 3: THE NORTH EAST REGION

Makarora to the Dobson

INTRODUCTION

Generally, route information in each catchment begins with a description up the main valley and over the pass at the head, followed by the major tributaries and side routes.

This is an area of long valleys with flats, beech forested sides and craggy mountains, particularly to the north. Peaks like Brewster and those in the head of the Hopkins are reasonably well glaciated. Parts of the region, like the Hunter Valley, are seldom visited, offering some superb tramping options for those wanting to get away from it all. The country is ideal for those wanting to plan their own trips, with much easier travel and escape routes available than there are to the west of the Divide. This is mostly public land, vested in DoC, but outside of National Park.

The more popular routes in the area are up the Makarora Valley, Canyon Creek, the Ahuriri, Temple Stream, the Huxley and Hopkins. Round trips are sometimes restricted, due to the semi-continuous high ranges between the valleys. DoC and other facilities are inherited from a more traditional New Zealand outdoor culture; no frills, and quite satisfactory as they are, provided they are looked after. There is a DoC office in Twizel, Ph 435 0802, and DoC Visitor Centres in Wanaka, Makarora and Mt Cook.

The weather is generally drier, being east of the Divide, but thunderstorms and rain can occur at any time of the year. Snow lies on the valley flats for extended periods in winter and some areas like the Temple/Huxley are very prone to major snow avalanches well down into the valleys, particularly from August to November.

Bedrock varies from metamorphic schists in the south, to shattered sedimentary greywackes in the north. Relatively open beech forest extends throughout the region. Silver beech predominates in the Makarora Valley and close to the Divide, but as the country dries towards the east and north, this quickly changes to mountain beech then tussock. Red mistletoe, (*Peraxilla* sp), is still common in many areas, particularly growing on mountain beech. There are yellowhead populations in the Hunter often associated with flocks of brown creepers. Keas are around and rockwrens can be found at places like Wilson Pass, but the bush can be unusually quiet here at times. Canadian geese and paradise ducks are common on the river flats.

For further information, see the *1956 NZAJ*, p 437, Spotlight on the Ohau Valleys. Those interested in climbing should consult the excellent guide by Ross Cullen, *Barron Saddle to Mt Brewster*, published by the NZAC in 2002. DoC also produce a useful booklet entitled *Tramping Guide to the Makarora Region.*

Other trip possibilities include;

- Wills/Hunter/Makarora circuit with various options, 5 or 6 days.
- Temple/Ahuriri/Maitland, 4 or 5 days.
- Huxley/Brodrick Pass/Landsborough, 5 days.
- Cameron Creek/Hunter/Wills, 6 days.
- Freehold Creek/Lake Dumb-bell, 2 days.
- Dasler Pinnacles, 2 days.
- Canyon Creek, 2 days.

UPPER MAKARORA VALLEY

This valley is a little demanding to enter, but it is tracked to a pleasant little hut in wonderful surroundings. It can be visited as a two day trip up and down the valley or as a round trip using more adventurous and untracked routes to Scrubby Flat Creek and the Wills, or Brewster Bivvy, taking several days. It is superb tramping country.

DAVIS FLAT TO MAKARORA HUT

At the bottom end of Davis Flat there is a roadside tracksign on the true left of the river a few metres down from the roadbridge. Follow this track up the true left of the Makarora and cross Stewarts Creek to its true right on the bush flat below the falls. Alternatively, this spot can be reached by fording the Makarora from the Davis Flat carpark and following a short link track through the bush. The track now climbs very steeply for 20 mins, then sidles up beside a long trough leading to the lip of the Makarora Gorge, about an hour from the road. From the lip, the track leads along the valley wall in a steepish descending sidle, reaching river level after 45 mins beyond a big slip. A further half hour through patches of bush, clearings and slips just above the river leads to the first sizeable flat. Generally easy travel, mostly in the bush, leads to the main flats and near the top of these, Makarora Hut (4 bunks, pot belly stove, DoC cat 3). The true left is followed all the way, but if the river is low some crossings will make travel up the flats above the gorge easier.

Time: Davis Flat to the hut, 5 to 6 hrs.

STEWARTS CREEK, a tributary of the Makarora River, provides the easiest access to the lake at the head of Lake Creek. From Davis Flat, head up the main Makarora Valley track until G38 177 686 is reached. From here, head up the bushed face on the true right of Stewarts Creek until pt 1207m is reached. Travel south over open grass until a ramp at about G38 188 672 leads into Stewarts Creek. A small deep gorge at G38 196 654 is passed on the true right.

MAKARORA HUT TO THE VALLEY HEAD

To reach the head, cross the river opposite the hut and at the top of the flat climb a bushy spur on the true right to avoid a short gorge. Recross above the gorge. After half an hour, bypass a steep cascade with large boulders on the true right and again cross to the true left near its lip. Don't cross too soon though, as there is a side creek with waterfalls to pass first. The extensive flats in the head soon open out with Mt. Brewster rising above to the left, 3 hrs from the hut.

For crossings to the Hunter Valley, see Hunter Valley notes.

MAKARORA HUT TO BREWSTER HUT

It is also possible to ascend the stream east of Mt Kaye, cross the Divide, and sidle to the Brewster Hut ridge, offering a round trip. From the Makarora River, open forest leads to pt 777m and the open streambed draining Mt Kaye. Easy travel leads up to and through the tussock and scree of the basin. Rock outcrops need to be crossed between the 1500 and 1700m contours to snowfields higher up. These lead to the ridge a few hundred metres north of Mt Kaye. Sidle on open rocky slopes, at the 1800m contour, right across to the Brewster Hut ridge before descending to Brewster Hut (4 bunk, no cooking facilities or stove, DoC cat 3). See Brewster Hut and Glacier notes.

Caution. This unmarked crossing requires good visibility, alpine skills and equipment to cope with small but permanent snowfields. Significant avalanche hazard can exist, mostly in winter and spring.

Time: Makarora Hut to Brewster Hut, about 5 hrs.

EASTERN TRIBUTARIES MAKARORA VALLEY

CAMERONS CREEK

Normally this valley is visited as a 2 or 3 day trip in and out, but there are other options, such as crossing to the High Burn in the Hunter Valley. Camerons Creek has a spectacular lower gorge. A track leads up through it to a hut on pleasant flats in the South Branch. One or two slips and bluffs require confidence and care, but the track is generally fine.

Note that the trackline is incorrectly shown up the Camerons Valley on G38 Ed.1. The track actually crosses the river at G38 154 643, about 700m further upvalley than shown, in a confined area between bluffs. Rain at the hut may mean an extended stay.

HAAST PASS HIGHWAY TO CAMERON HUT

From Cameron Flat beside the Haast Pass Highway a gravelled track leads up the true right of Camerons Creek to a lookout point, and the marked track begins from there. The marked track climbs steadily into the gorge, crosses a small creek and climbs to a small corner, just beyond which is an older slip on a bluff. Once beyond the gorge, the track sidles down to easy slips near the river. A good shingle crossing leads to the true left at G38 154 643. A short sidle leads to small flats. Where the upper gorge starts, the track swings to the right and climbs, crossing a newer slip in one place. Once around into the South Branch it levels off before descending to the top flat. Cameron Hut, (4 bunks, pot belly stove, DoC cat 3), is 15 mins further, still on the true left.

In the reverse direction, take care to follow the track markers all the way.

From the hut in late summer, competent and experienced parties can traverse along the McKerrow Range basins to Mt. Shrimpton and follow down the tracked spur to Makarora, but don't underestimate the steepness of the descent off Mt Shrimpton.

Time: Cameron Flat to Cameron Hut, about 6 hrs; 1 hr less in the reverse direction.

THE SOUTH BRANCH HEADWATERS can be approached from Cameron Hut. From the hut, provided the river is low, follow the river upstream into the gorge. At least two and usually three sidles are required. The longer first one (about 300m distance) sidles a gorgy section where travel in the riverbed is not practical, and the second one sidles a small waterfall further up at about G38 158 600. All sidles are on the true left, and none should require climbing more than 60m above the river. Up valley from the forks at G38 161 597, there is a third sidle, this time on scree slopes on the true left. Above this, cross Cameron Creek at G38 162 596. The true right can now be followed up to the flats.

In the reverse direction, heading down valley into the gorge, parties begin on the true right, crossing to the true left on a corner just before the river begins to drop seriously. Allow 2.5 hrs up and 2 hrs down the gorge. Avoid this gorge if the river is at all up.

Continuing up valley, tussock flats now lead to forks at G38 163 586. Either the spur on the true left, or terraces on the true right can be used. *Dracophyllum* scrub is open, low and offers easy travelling. For crossings to or from the High Burn, see Hunter Valley notes.

THE SADDLE AT PT 1547M gives reasonably good access to upper Cascade Creek. On the Cameron side sidle up a spur on the true left of the stream draining the saddle. Sidle off the spur into the stream at about the 1240m contour and continue near the stream, still on the true left to the upper basin. On the Cascade side, sidle into beech forest on the true left.

THE NORTH BRANCH HEADWATERS are thought to be approachable from the North/South confluence directly up the gorge, which is steep and bouldery, on the true right. However, there is no recent confirmation of this. Crossings can be made into Stewarts Creek from the head of the true left branch by experienced parties. If descending from the North/South confluence at G38 165 624 to the road, continue down the river for several hundred metres before climbing up to the track, to save unnecessary climbing. This route into the North Branch should only be considered by fit, experienced parties.

MCKERROW RANGE ACCESS

MT SHRIMPTON TRACK

A signposted track begins from the Nature Walk near Makarora Visitors Centre. Markers lead across bush terraces towards Pipson Creek then climb steeply through silver beech forest to the bushline, which is relatively free of scrub. Note the track entry into the bush for the return; it is only lightly marked. The tussock spur continues to the McKerrow Range and Mt Shrimpton, and offers great views across the Makarora Valley.

Time: Road to the bushline, about 2 hrs.

BOUNDARY CREEK

Boundary Creek now has legal public access to it thanks to the tenure review process and is a useful access to and from the McKerrow Range. Please make sure any farmgates are left as found. Flats up the valley make a great day or overnight trip. At the mouth of Boundary Creek, by Lake Wanaka, there is an excellent DoC campsite set amongst mature kanuka with toilets and a picnic shelter.

A DoC sign marks the start of a bulldozed track from SH6, opposite the campground turnoff. This winds up the spur on the true right of Boundary Creek, offering great views on the way, to a second sign at a track junction at about the 840m contour. Here, the Boundary track begins to sidle into flats in the creek. Only 300m beyond the junction sign, at a strip of beech forest, there is shade and a cool creek. The 4WD becomes distorted in slips, but is followable to the flats, which can all be traversed on the true right. Silver beech forest and campsites surround forks at the top of the flats.

Big Hopwood Burn and the Shrimpton tops are accessible from the upper valley. There are a number of crossings and interesting tops basins that competent parties can link together from here along the range. However, some of the passes may require basic alpine skills and equipment. To access the head of the valley from the flats, climb onto a narrow spur between the two branches. From right at the forks, climb up through open beech, scree, and *Dracophyllum* scrub, tending towards the slopes above the true right branch. Animal leads sneak over a minor rock rib that interrupts the climb up to the crest of the spur. This spur provides good going, and gives access to both branches. Continuing up the **true right branch** beyond the spur is straight forward.

Crossing to the Big Hopwood. From the spur, descend easily to the **true left branch** streambed. From there, follow the spur on the true right of the main stream (which is in a gut) up to the 1340m contour, where the ridge flattens at G39 127 473. Steep grassy slopes lead down to a side rib which is followed downvalley to the streambed again above the cataract. The stream or easy sidling closeby leads on upvalley. The range south of pt 1965m can now be accessed and crossed, and a route NE follows a bench to meet a spur off pt 1965m at the 1400m contour. A rib heading NW then NE leads down to the hut in Big Hopwood. Below the 1000m contour, this rib is thick manuka, and a better route probably exists in this lower section.

Times: SH6 to the top of the flats in Boundary Creek, 4 hrs; Top forks to Big Hopwood Bivvy, 9 hrs.

■ Looking across the Makarora Valley to Mt Brewster from the saddle with Scrubby Flat Creek.

SAWYER BURN AND SENTINEL PEAK

This is an excellent day trip from the popular Kidds Bush camping ground, by Lake Hawea. Kidds Bush is 6km along the Hunter Valley Station access road (Meads Road) from SH6. This patch of mountain beech forest is a popular DoC campsite, with toilets and a wonderful Shelter built in 1993 with a bequest from a farmer.

Opposite the entrance to the campground, a well signposted and graded zig zag track marked with red and white permolat climbs to the bushline. There are good views over Lake Hawea from here. The track, marked intermittently with steel standards, then sidles above the bushline at about the 900m contour, keeping mostly level, to Sawyer Burn Hut. This is an old fencers' hut from the 1960's at the bush edge in the first tributary of the Sawyer Burn on the true right, as marked on G39. Though in poor condition it still provides shelter for 2 or 3 people.

To continue to Sentinel Peak from the hut, descend 30m to the tributary, cross it and head up through open bush to the big snowgrass basin west of the hut. Ascend this basin to the SE ridge of Sentinel Peak. Near the top of this ridge, angle out under the south side of the peak and climb a small gully to the ridge crest 200m east of the peak. There remains a short scramble to the top.

Times: Kidds Bush to the bushline, 1 hr; Bushline to Sawyer Burn Hut, 1.5 hrs; Hut to Sentinel Peak, about 4 hrs up and 2.5 hrs down.

'I once laid a large noose flat on the ground with a string attached and a piece of white paper in the center. Standing back a few yards I waited in hopes the bird would see the paper, but they also saw the noose and not one would cross the unknown danger they walked around it in a critical manner, looked at me and skirled. At last a more adventurous one suddenly grabbed the line I held in my hand, gave a jerk which carried the noose away from the paper, which was at once carried away with a triumphant yell.'

—Charlie Douglas describes being outwitted by keas.

THE HUNTER VALLEY

Few visit the extensive Hunter Valley. It is a place for longer, more relaxed trips in relatively isolated country. Travel in the main valley is easy, but most of the tributaries on the true right descend through deep wild canyon gorges. Fishers and hunters sometimes fly into strips at Forbes Flat and Fergusons by plane from Makarora, or else 4WD in. It is less frequented by trampers even though a variety of side trips and crossings are available.

Alternative access to the upper valley is over passes from the Wills and Makarora valleys, though these are high untracked crossings that will frequently require an ice axe. Crossings can be combined to form challenging round trips from SH6, the Haast Pass Highway.

The mid to lower reaches of the Hunter Valley are leased by Hunter Valley Station on the true right and Dingle Station (in tenure review) on the true left. Hunter Valley Station may have a closed period during the lambing/calving season. The road into the lower Hunter, Meads Road, starts at the Kidds Bush signpost near the Neck between Lakes Hawea and Wanaka on SH6. It leads 10km around the lake to Hunter Valley Station Homestead, (Mr Taff Cochrane, Private Bag, Wanaka; Ph 03 443 1241) beside the Bee Burn. There is a locked gate across the road at the Homestead. Parties intending to go further need to obtain permission in advance. Seek approval before using Station huts and information on the state of the road. An administration charge may be requested per vehicle. The public road ends just before Terrace Creek (Mill Creek).

HUNTER VALLEY STATION HOMESTEAD TO FERGUSON HUT

With Station approval, 4WD vehicles may be taken as far as Ferguson Hut. DoC discourages 4WD use beyond here. However, the 4WD track deteriorates with washouts a little past Boundary Hut, and Billy Creek is the limit without crossing the main river. Allow for considerable delays during bad weather and take vehicle extraction equipment. Some of the side creeks are rivers in themselves.

Beyond Terrace Creek, the road climbs almost 200m above the lake giving an excellent view. Mt. Strauchon is the prominent peak above the East Branch while Mts. Ferguson and Enderby rise to the west of the upper flats. The road then descends to cross the Fast Burn, the Little Hopwood Burn and the ravine of the Big Hopwood Burn. It continues relatively close to the lakeshore and emerges onto the valley floor between the High Burn and Waterfall Creek. A good formation continues as far as Boundary Hut.

The hut at the mouth of the High Burn on the true right is locked. The 2 bunk aluminium clad hut 500m north of the High Burn is an old Rabbit Board hut. It is unlocked and tidy. Boundary Hut, (unlocked, 10 bunks, open fire) is a Hunter Valley Station hut, as is Little Boundary Hut (unlocked, 2 bunk, open fire). Green Bush Hut, at the start of the 4WD track out to Dingle Station from the true left of the Hunter, belongs to Dingle Station. It is essential that parties granted the priviledge of using station huts leave them clean and tidy, with firewood replenished, taking all rubbish with them.

From Boundary Hut, the 4WD track crosses open grassy flats to Scrubby Hut (4 bunk, open fire, Hunter Valley Station). Permission needs to be sought to use this hut. The track continues in a rough state, crossing the river twice, to Ferguson Hut (4 bunk, open fire, DoC cat 3) 600m beyond Long Flat Creek. If Long Flat Creek is up, there is a foot bridge at the mouth of the gorge, as marked on G38 (Ed 1). For those on foot, the sidle on the true right of the Hunter just upstream from Billy Creek is straightforward, avoiding any need to cross the main river. Bull Flat Hut (2 bunk, open fire, DoC cat4) and correctly located on G38) is small and useable, but not flash. Don't rely on it; it may go.

Times: Hunter Valley Homestead to the High Burn, 4 hrs; High Burn to Boundary Hut, 2 hrs; Boundary Hut to Scrubby Hut, 2 hrs; Scrubby Hut to Ferguson Hut, 2 hrs.

■ The Hunter Valley from the Dingle/Ahuriri/Hunter divide.

Mt Brewster
Mt Tole
Mt Enderby
Mt Dechen
Forbes Flat
Ferguson Ck
Long Flat Creek
Scrubby Flat Creek

FERGUSON HUT TO THE EAST WEST FORKS

Note that the footbridge marked across the Hunter 1km below Forbes Hut was destroyed by the 1994 floods. There are now no footbridges across the Hunter. The Hunter is usually crossed upstream from Ferguson Creek by parties heading up valley. In normal and low flows this should not present a problem provided time and care is taken to select a good crossing above rapids where the river braids well, but remember this is a large river. If necessary, it is also possible to follow the true right to the Forks, but it is much slower, involving climbs and bush sidles. An old track once existed along here, but is now of little use.

Once on the true left, travel continues to be straightforward up flats to Mid Flat Hut (2 bunk, open fire, well maintained, DoC cat 3) on a prominent terrace 10m above the river. Continue close to the river around a neck of bush to Joes Flat. Cross Joes Flat to the top end where, 200m from the river, there is a lone mature beech tree beside a stream. Permolat markers here at G38 384 768 cross the stream to the bush edge and mark a cattle track through to Forbes Flat and Forbes Hut (excellent condition, 6 bunk, open fire, DoC cat 3). (**In the reverse direction,** clearings at the bottom of Forbes Flat 100m from the river lead to permolat markers and the same cattle track).

From Forbes Flat, either bank can be used to the Forks. The fastest route is to cross at the top of Forbes Flat and continue on gravel till the bush closes in and then use the old permolat track on the true right through open beech forest to the forks. Cross the West Branch here. The permolat and orange triangle markers begin right in the bush 'V' of the forks and lead to the East West track junction sign in less than 5 mins.

Times: Ferguson Hut to Mid Flats Hut, 1.5 hrs; Mid Flat Hut to Forbes Flat, 1.5 hrs.

WEST BRANCH

Numerous open gullys interrupt the marked route up valley, particularly towards the bushline. Some entrances are overgrowing and cairns may have been destroyed by winter snows. Look for permolat back in the bush again to be certain of the marked route.

From the DoC junction sign, follow the marked route up the Hunter Valley, West Branch, climbing then descending to a flat after about 50 mins. This flat was devastated in the 1994 floods and is now virtually all gravel. Cross the river (reasonable in normal conditions) picking up orange markers on trees at the riverbank on the true right only slightly upstream at about G37 391 819. (Should the river be up, parties descending can avoid this crossing by leaving the marked route and continuing to sidle along the true right through untracked open beech forest to the Forks)

Just beyond a small creek at the top of the gravel flats, the marked route climbs steeply for about 200m distance to avoid slips and sidles well above the river. The marked route generally keeps on the midslopes of large old revegetated gravel fans, between the river and spurs off the range. Where crossings of open or scrub zones are made, look for old cairns and cut scrub. At the first clearing, the permolat markers re-enter the bush across and a little upstream. At the second one, the marked route climbs 50m distance on the true left bank of a washout, sidles through scrub, then climbs a further 50m distance up a smaller, fresh gravel creekbed before sidling into the bush. The re-entry here is obscure, but there are permolat markers again from the tree edge.

The bushline, where there is a large orange triangle facing upvalley, is a short distance further on, 1 hr from the river crossing. The marked route then sidles through scrub. Permolat marking finishes at G37 383 833, but orange standards continue for a few hundred metres into the open, near a large rock.

Time: Forks to the Bushline, a good 2 hrs.

WILSON PASS Hunter to the Wills Valley

This crossing is an unmarked route and steep snowslopes may need to be crossed until mid January.

Wilson Pass is directly ahead from the end of the orange poles in the Hunter West Branch, and may be reached from there without descending to the river. This involves crossing a band of scrub where it is narrowest (100m), just below a lone beech tree at about the 1040m contour. Before and after are open, easy tussock slopes. Heading on towards the pass, climb diagonally up to a small shelf at the 1330m contour due east of the pass and still on the true right of the marked creek draining the pass. From here, a moderately steep rib that carries the remains of old deer tracks leads to the south end of the pass, and perhaps 20m above it. There are small tarns on the pass. From here, veer south (left) along a prominent tussock ledge without losing much height until a steep route is found leading down to G37 364 845 in the valley below. See the Wills Valley for more notes.

Time: Hunter Valley to Wills Valley, about 4 hrs.

THE UPPER WEST HUNTER VALLEY

To continue up the West Hunter from the orange poles, follow cairns and then sidle slightly down to the sloping terrace just above a tiny riverbend gorge. An old track enters the scrub at a cairn G37 381 838 and emerges down on the upper valley grass flats at the 950m contour, where there is a waratah, still on the true right. The old NZFS bivvy and bivvy rock opposite here have both gone due to river erosion. Beyond here, travel up valley is easy. However, a bluff on the true right makes it necessary to cross the river twice before tussock fans giving access to Lower Studholme Pass can be gained.

STUDHOLME PASS Hunter to the Landsborough Valley

Note. Based on early descriptions of the passes, and their relative heights, the marked positions of Upper and Lower Studholme Passes on map G37 appear incorrect. However, for ease of use, these route notes refer to the features as marked and named on the metric G37 map.

From the Hunter, the climb to Upper Studholme Pass (pt 1730m) is up moderately steep tussock slopes then scree. It is reasonably straightforward.

Crossings to the Landsborough from here should all be regarded as difficult. Mid McLennan Creek itself is badly bluffed and needs to be avoided. However, the spur between Border Creek and the short South Branch of McLennan Creek provides a steep but mostly good route through open beech forest down to the river. This spur is usually accessed from the upper McLennan Creek basin, where there are good campsites near the bushline. There are a couple of ways through the bluffs from the creek to this spur with pt 1174m on it. Probably the best route heads up through a tongue of bush to about G37 337 872 and about the 1200m contour. From here a scrubby ledge leads up to the west and the 1300m contour on the ridge itself. Descend, making sure to get on the Border Creek spur lower down. An alternative is to sidle from the tussock/bushline in upper McLennan Creek west across very steep bush faces to pt 1174m. Below bushline, a schist gorge makes crossing McLennan Creek impractical.

In reverse, from the bottom end of Harper Flat, head up McLennan Stream for about 1km to a stream junction marked at G37 317 895. There is no actual sidestream here, but head into the bush and sidle onto the prominent bush spur immediately NE of Border Creek. This spur provides good open travel up to a knob at 1174m. Continue up the ridge through tight scrubby forest until above bushline. At about the 1300m contour on the ridge, follow a sloping scrubby ledge down to the 1200m contour at about G37 337 872, and descend a tongue of bush into McLennan Creek. Crossing Upper Studholme Pass from here is straightforward. Follow tussock slopes above the true right of McLennan Creek, cross a narrow rib around some gentle slopes into a basin below the pass, and continue on scree slopes to it. The descent into the West Hunter is over moderate slopes where it is easy to avoid the occasional steep bit.

A good daytrip from the West Hunter leads up to Upper Studholme Pass, over Watkins Dome, descending from the saddle about 300m north of it back to the Hunter.

EAST BRANCH

From the DoC junction sign at the forks, red, white and orange markers follow a terrace above the gorge on the true right. They climb steadily before sidling and leading down to finish by the river at the lower end of an extensive gravel flat at G37 410 823. Extensive gravel movement in 1994 floods means that the track for all practical purposes has gone beyond here, although permolat is visible occasionally on trees upstream. The East Hunter Bivvy has also gone. The valley beyond here is, however, fairly easily traversed near, or at river level to the head, mainly on the true right and entirely if necessary. Where river travel becomes impractical, old ground trails are followable close by.

There is one small exception. Just beyond a fenced animal exclosure plot G37 414 850 on the true right, continue directly up valley across a tussocky fan rather than stay close to the river. This is an obvious line on the map too, leading back to the riverbank at the last significant bend in the valley. The upper valley is pleasant and dominated by Mt Strauchon. Alpine routes have been used from the East Hunter to Brodrick Pass.

Returning down river should present no problems provided the start of the marked route is found on the true right at G37 410 823, (orange triangles on trees) shortly before the end of the gravel flat.

Times: Forks to the gravel flat, 2 hrs; Gravel flat to the head of the valley, 2.5 hrs.

FERGUSON CREEK

The route marked on G38 Ed. 1 is incorrectly shown. It begins closer to Ferguson Creek and crosses to the true right 300m upstream of the marked position. This marked route, described as at 2002, is not being maintained. A red/white permolat marked route begins at G38 347 723 at the toe of a spur on the true left of Ferguson Creek close to a dry flood channel. Follow the marked route up to pt 683m where it traverses mossy rock knolls and open glades amongst mountain beech forest, with excellent campsites and a small tarn at the far end. About 5 mins further, a creek is crossed before the marked route descends and sidles to the first major stream on the map.

This and the next stream up valley are open winter avalanche runnels. Cross the first stream horizontally and descend along a scrub terrace on the true right side. Sparse and obscure permolat markers lead down into the bush and sidle across a shallow gully with windfall before climbing about 80m to cross the spur between the two streams at the 760m contour. Where the marked route emerges on the bank of the second stream at G38 347 743, there are permolat markers on a snapped off beech stump, 50m above and 150m distance up the stream from Ferguson Creek.

Descend the open stream to the river and go up the stones 200m. Cairns may be visible. Look for a line of markers 10m up on the opposite (true right) bank of Ferguson Creek on trees at the top end of a slip indicating to cross. This crossing is not very good. A much better crossing exists 250m further upstream, requiring a fairly easy sidle (no markers or track) to reach it. Once across, climb 30 to 40m to the route markers on the true right.

This next section on the true right crosses scrubby avalanche fields and bush tongues where the marked route is easy to lose. Keep down towards the river edge if this happens. Red and white markers continue in the forest again. At a small gravel flat at G38 334 754, where there are big bluffs on the true left devoid of forest, pick up battered markers by the river on the true right, on gravel flooded trees. Follow them up a bush fan and sidle about 100m above a small gorge before dropping to the river edge again at the start of the main flats, still on the true right. The exNZFS bivvy marked on G38 was removed by DoC in 1996.

In the reverse direction:

1. Pick up the marked route at the bottom of the flat near the river on the true right.
2. Be careful to cross Ferguson Creek as noted.
3. Once on the true left of Ferguson Creek it is necessary to climb and sidle to avoid a bad gorge. From Ferguson Creek, climb 150m distance up an open side stream to G38 347 743 and pick up permolat markers on a tree stump on the true left of the stream at about the 740m contour.
4. Look for cairns and markers in the next open stream down valley at the top of a narrow line of schist slabs on the true left of the gully. Follow the marked route which improves from here out.

Times: Ferguson Hut to beginning of track, 30 mins; Hunter Valley to start of main flats (near old Bivvy site), 4 hrs.

WILLS PASS Ferguson Creek to the Wills River

Open flats lead to a tiny gorge at G38 327 776 which is easily sidled on the true right about 30m above Ferguson Creek. From the upper flats, where there are excellent campsites, the pass can be seen. The pass can be accessed from the head of the valley. Alternatively, a spur to the west of the upper flats can also be used through the bush to access tops basins at roughly G38 321 785, and the Main Divide SW of the pass. To reach the Wills, either descend good tussock slopes west of Safe Creek, then scrub and a bush spur (which becomes a face lower down) to emerge more or less opposite Dredge Creek, or as follows. Follow the Divide south from the pass to the 1700m contour and sidle across at that height roughly to the spur on the true right of Tole Creek. Pick a careful route into the initially steep gravel bed of Tole Creek on the true right, and follow it to the valley floor. Be aware that the gully can be subject to loose stones from above, particularly in wet weather.

LONG FLAT CREEK

A marked route starts behind Ferguson Hut and leads across a bush fan to the Long Flat Creek bridge at the mouth of the gorge. Beyond here, the track marked on G38 is incorrectly positioned. The marked route instead gains 150m altitude up the spur on the true right, then descends abruptly to near river level before re-climbing 70m and sidling at roughly that height. About 10 mins before the open creek on the corner, there is a good 4 person bivvy rock visible from, and just below, the marked route in the bush. Water is a few minutes away though.

At the creek on the corner, G38 322 701, there is sloping open ground (the result of winter avalanches). Cross it to approximately the same altitude and pick up more red/white permolat at the bush edge again. Continue sidling on the marked route to the second open runnel which is more ferny and scrubby, and cross at approximately 100m above the river. The marked route again re-enters at the same height and sidles to G38 311 712 where an early 1990s re-marking of the route finishes near the river. Beyond, the route is followable (1996) to G38 305 720, but is overgrowing fast. Alternatively, travel is not difficult along the riverbank, involving few bush sidles. The ex-NZFS Bivvy located at G38 304 726 was removed by DoC in 1996.

Time: Ferguson Hut to site of removed bivvy, 4.5 hrs.

LONG FLAT SADDLE Long Flat Creek to Wills River

Continue up the flats in Long Flat Creek, crossing and re-crossing as necessary until the true left provides the easiest travel to the saddle, best gained at its east end. The route to the Wills is initially down tussock slopes to a basin at the 1400m contour then it negotiates a bluff and sidles to the spur on the true right of Fleming Creek. At the 1260m contour, G38 262 782 there is a bivvy rock, sleeping about 4. A steep descent through rough bush ('bloody awful'), with several bluffs bypassed well away from Fleming Creek, leads to the Wills Valley floor between the hut and Fleming Creek.

SCRUBBY FLAT CREEK AND SADDLE

Although in better condition than the late 1980s and now quite followable (2002) there is some windfall to negotiate and care is required in some quite steep places. This is a marked route rather than a track. Re-marked with permolat and orange triangles in the early 1990s, this route begins at a sign near the bush edge on the true left of Scrubby Flat Creek, G38 318 651. Initially it climbs a good 200m up the Hunter face of the corner spur before crossing into the Scrubby Flat Creek gorge and climbing further. At about the 700m contour, it sidles across towards the river then climbs again, keeping 100m above it. The markers finish at G38 301 659, 50m above Scrubby Flat Creek on the true left at the bush edge. Here, a small gravel creekbed marks the start of more open travel up valley. A further 500m sidling on mainly gravel slopes, not difficult, leads up to the flats. Note the grid reference for finding the track if heading down valley.

Travel up valley from here is straight forward, and leads to a 1570m high pass at G38 276 688. (With a great view of Mt Brewster). From this tussock pass, tussock gullies lead through small bluffs onto easier slopes. The spur directly off the pass between two creeks gives generally good travel to the Makarora Valley floor at the very top end of the main flats, G38 262 698.

Times: Track sign in the Hunter to the flats, 2.5 hrs; Allow a full day to cross from the Hunter Valley to Makarora Hut. (about 8 hrs).

COTTERS, LAKE, CASCADE, AND WATERFALL CREEKS

These all have very rugged gorges in their lower reaches and old marked routes are now overgrown and not generally followable. There are no plans to maintain them. None of these lower valley routes are recommended, and are suitable for experienced and competent parties only. The heads of the valleys are great though, and can be linked together by tramping/transalpine parties from Boundary Creek through to Lake Stream and further.

COTTERS; A very old NZFS track marked with white permolat once led up the minor creek at G38 290 614, climbing to avoid the bottom gorge then descending through broadleaf and scrub back to the stream, crossing and continuing up valley on the true left. It is now virtually unfollowable and only of historical interest.

LAKE CREEK; Much the same applies to the route into Lake Creek, although the line up a scrubby face beginning at unotrusive markers 200m down the Hunter Valley on the true right of Lake Creek has been more recently marked with permolat. It finishes at about the 760m contour in tall kanuka at a red permolat marker declaring go straight up for 250m. Above is more scrub then open country with heaps of spaniard. There is a very old cairn on the pt 1670m ridge at about 1000m, but the route into Lake Creek from there is completely overgrown.

Sidle across 300m through untracked scrub then force a route directly down to the valley floor through dense scrub filled gutters. Once in Lake Creek, the easiest route is to boulder hop up the creek. Traces of the old track may be found on bush terraces by the river. For a km below the lake outlet there is very dense scrub. This is best avoided by keeping in the riverbed. This route is hard. The true left through this lower gorge is not an option.

There are reasonable campsites scattered along the lake flats, and a couple of sheltered ones under beech trees along the lakeshore. Traverse the lake on its southern side. Above the lake, the valley leads to an easy pass into Stewarts Creek and very pleasant tussock basins. See upper Makarora Valley notes.

Times: Hunter Valley floor to Lake Creek outlet, allow at least 7 hrs; Lake Creek outlet to Davis Flat, allow 7 hrs.

CASCADE CREEK; has the remains of an old NZFS track on the true left up a spur overlooking an impressive canyon; it sidles at about the 600m contour up valley until it is completely obliterated by extensive windthrow and snowbreak at about G38 264 568. However, upper Cascade Creek is an attractive beech forested valley with extensive grass flats from about G38 223 584 to G38 219 595. These open flats are not shown on G38. In the head of the valley, the open avalanche trimmed sides of a stream at G38 213 608 can initially be followed up. Further up it is necessary to take to the spur on the true right, and this leads to the tussock tops which can then be traversed to cross the range to Lake Stream.

A crossing just north of pt 1945m can then be made to Lake Stream. To descend to Lake Stream, follow a tussock rib on the true left of the stream draining pt 1945m. Cross the stream at the 1320m contour and sidle on across to an old slip creek at G38 240 623 and the lake edge. Stewarts Creek is also directly accessible from pt 1945m along the range.

Lake Stream. Looking towards the Hunter Valley from the Young Range.

WATERFALL CREEK; is very gorged and rugged, though in the past, NZFS had a track on the true left that climbed to the 1000m contour on the Hunter slopes. It is now overgrown.

HIGH BURN Lake Hawea to the main flats

Cattle are farmed in the upper High Burn. The cattle trail offers good travel, but parts of it are indistinct. From the Hunter Valley vehicle track, follow up the gravel bed of the High Burn. As it narrows, pick up the cattle trail by the stream on the true left at about G38 246 503. Sparse old white permolat markers follow along the true left riverbank and then the cattle trail climbs through beech forest away from the river slightly before descending to a small grassy flat at the river edge. Cairns indicate a poor crossing of the High Burn. Cross at G39 235 500.

The cattle trail then heads away from the river on the true right through bush to a swampy clearing before climbing for 50m (height) through kanuka scrub. White markers are very sparse on this part of the route and the cattle trails tend to spread out. Just below a knoll, the cattle trail swings on upvalley again and further upvalley the kanuka gives way to open grassy corridors and pasture. The ground trail sidles across to river level and continues up the river bank to a bluff where the cattle make two crossings of the High Burn within about 100m. Follow them, crossing twice.

(However, these crossings can be avoided if the river is up by traversing a small ledge 5 to 10m above the river on the true right for 50m distance. The scrub is scratchy and packs need to be passed at the top end. Normally, the two crossings will be easier). At the upper of the two crossings, a good cattle trail commences at the river edge, G39 221 501, on the true right, and continues generally not far from the river to Lower Burn Hut (3 bunks, open fireplace, okay but not flash, Hunter Valley Station) at the bottom of the flats, G38 214 505.

Time: Lake Hawea to the hut at the bottom of the main flats, 2.5 hrs.

HIGH BURN SADDLE (1166M) High Burn flats to Cameron Creek

From Lower Burn Hut, grass and matagouri slopes, gravel and bush fringes, then open flats, provide easy travel to the Upper Burn Hut, located at the edge of silver beech forest, G38 174 554, not as marked on G38 Ed.1. This old hut is in very poor condition, and camping will usually be preferred, but it may still be welcome in rain. It has 3 wire bunks. Winter snow has stuffed the chimney.

Open *Dracophyllum* scrub provides easy travel to the top flats under pt 1166m saddle. From G38 155 563, a grass and scrub slope runs up towards the west under a line of bluffs. It doesnt look promising. From this slope, a good short line cuts back NE between bluffs and rock shards at the 1100m contour, G38 154 564, climbing just above the upper beech trees on the bluff. This is a good, safe route that cattle have used, with waratahs and wire higher up indicating the route is the right one. There are tarns on the saddle.

If descending from the saddle on the High Burn side, look for a fence parallel to and only 50m from the range crest, across easy tussock slopes at the western end of the pass. This waratah and wire fence runs for perhaps 100m along the top of a bluff and is the key to finding the route through the bluffs from above. Follow it to the SW and the trail from the end of it leads down through the bluff to easy slopes in the High Burn.

On the Cameron Creek side, there is an easy descent to the basin down tussock. See Camerons Creek for further notes.

Times: Lower Burn Hut to Upper Burn Hut, 2 hrs; Upper Burn Hut to upper Camerons, 1.5 to 2 hrs.

The head of the High Burn.

BIG HOPWOOD BURN

The track marked on G39 is not followable. Instead, an old marked route goes up the true right bank. This overgrown marked route starts about 1km south of where Big Hopwood Burn crosses the road, behind an ex-NZFS Base near some cut larches and may be signposted. The marked route goes up about 300m onto terraces and then follows these manuka clad terraces into Big Hopwood Burn. The marked route stays on the true right about 300m above the river. It has had no maintanance for nearly 20 years and is quite overgrown. The marked route finishes by the stream at G39 206 469, just down from a side creek. The true right can be used from there all the way up to the hut on open going, using gravel and flats. The lower valley is mountain beech, with mistletoe on it, but about 1km down from the hut, silver beech takes over up to the bushline.

The small, pleasantly sited hut (1 bunk, DoC cat 4) at G39 168 496 is occasionally used by hunters and trampers.

Time: Road to start of open stream travel at G39 206 469, 4 hrs; G39 206 469 to the hut in the headwaters, another 2.5 hrs.

A route exists from the **North Branch of the Big Hopwood Burn over the range towards Makarora.** It leads from the old hut site (ruined) at G38 152 519, over the McKerrow Range to the Mt Shrimpton/White Creek face above Makarora. This was used in the past as a route to take sheep into the Big Hopwood. Other routes lead to Boundary Creek (see Boundary Creek notes) and the High Burn.

To cross from the Big Hopwood Burn to the High Burn. This unmarked route has lots of scrubbashing potential, but it's almost all avoidable. From forks at G39 152 532, go up the beech covered spur to the north to about the 900m contour and sidle across just inside the bushline up the side-valley to G39 153 533. Cutting across through relatively open scrub should lead in a hundred metres to a tiny open creek. Ascend this thin gravel creekbed in the scrub and then open tussock leads to where travel flattens off on the continuous tops. Cross the ridge at G38 159 544, head NE across benches to about G38 163 548 and cut back to the right (south) down to a grass basin.

Time: About 6 hrs from the Big Hopwood Burn to the High Burn.

Eastward the downs rose, ridge behind ridge into the morning, and vanished out of eyesight into a guess: it was no more than a guess of blue and a remote glimmer blending with the hem of the sky, but it spoke to them, out of memory and old tales, of the high and distant mountains.

—JRR Tolkien.

THE DINGLE BURN

Draining into Lake Hawea from the east, this valley is popular for hunting and fishing. Most of the forest is dry mountain beech. Red mistletoe (Peraxilla sp) is not uncommon in the beech, especially around Top Dingle Hut. 1990s storms bought fresh shingle down the streams and there are also patches of windthrow/snowbreak in the forests. Recent purchases and tenure review means that all the upper Dingle is now public property vested in DoC. The area can offer interesting trips 2 to 5 days long, particularly when the weather doesn't allow for trips further west.

There is a public road as far as Timaru River. Beyond Timaru River the road is private, rougher, and more suited to 4WD vehicles. It belongs to Dingleburn Station from whom permission is required to use it (the Mead family, Ph 03 443 1558). Ring in advance. It should to be appreciated that use of the road is at the discretion of the Station, and that care needs to be taken on it. Dingleburn Station is presently in tenure review.

The upper Dingle is accessed fairly easily over the 1448m saddle from the Ahuriri Valley and is described over the page. The upper Ahuriri is now all public conservation land.

DINGLE BURN STATION TO BUSH HUT

The road finishes at the Dingle Burn woolshed. The house is up to the right, about 250m away. With permission, go through a gate with a Bottom Dingle Hut sign on it just to the right of the woolshed and across to a stream, where the high and low routes to Bush (Bottom Dingle) Hut divide. For the low route, sidle down to the river and then cross as required up the gravel riverbed. This is the best option at low river flows. Alternatively, for the high route, cross the creek and follow the 4WD track up a spur, following occasional red and white topped waratah poles put in by the Forest Service, to a terrace at the 500m contour, as marked on G39. Head up the terrace. Sidle at that height through grass and low bracken following the poles then markers once the track drops into the bush and crosses a small creek. DoC has recut and marked the track from here upvalley (2005). Beyond the creek, the track leads down a spur, sometimes on bare steep clay to the shingly stream draining Mae West Biv near its confluence with the Dingle. It climbs again then sidles steadily at about the 600m contour before dropping to cross the last creek with a minor sidle beyond to Bush Hut. Bush Hut (6 bunk, open fire, DoC cat 3), is situated in a small grass clearing surrounded by beech forest.

Times: Roadend to Bush Hut, low route, 2 hrs; high route, 3hrs.

BUSH HUT TO COTTERS HUT

DoC has (2005) remarked and recut much of the track up the Dingle. However, a slip at G39 311 403 creates problems, and the track here is not useable. The slip has been crossed a little over halfway down to the river from the track, but is easier to avoid altogether by climbing above it in the bush. DoC will mark and cut a new track in this area, but not until sometime in 2006. The trackline shown on G39 between Bush Hut and the slip isn't accurate either. From Bush Hut, the track climbs steeply then steadily before sidling a little above the 700m contour. It descends to cross the first major stream at G39 308 393, climbs over a rib to the next branch, then climbs to about 760m again, shortly before the slip. At LOW riverflow, from Bush Hut competent parties can also follow the main river up then climb up to the Cotters Terrace, but there are small gorges and numerous crossings involved. Cotters (2 person upright bivvy, open fire, DoC cat 3) is in good condition. It is located 100m south of its marked position on G39 Ed.1, in grass at the bush edge, on the extensive airstrip terrace.

Times: Bush Hut to Cotters Hut: in the riverbed, 3 to 4 hrs; On the track, 4 to 6 hrs, depending on the slip.

Looking up the Dingle to the top forks

COTTERS HUT TO TOP DINGLE HUT

Travelling upstream from Cotters, descend the two grass embankments at the top end of the airstrip to a side creek, 50m from the Dingle Burn. Cross this creek here and follow the permolat markers leading through the bush to tussock fringes beside the river and continue on open going up the gravel riverbed. When the valley closes in, stay close to the river till the stream beside Ben Avon Hut is reached. Follow up this and climb onto extensive grass terraces. Ben Avon Hut (4 bunk, open fire) is situated at the bush edge, on the terrace in a grassy alcove facing down to the river, approx as shown on G39 Ed.1. About 500m up valley from the hut, a line of matagouri can be crossed with care on cattle tracks at the 780m contour. From there it is straightforward grass and gravel travel with no river crossings to Top Dingle Hut. (6 bunk, open fire, DoC cat 3).

Time: Cotters Hut to Top Dingle Hut, 3.5 to 4 hrs.

1448M SADDLE Top Dingle to Ahuriri Base Hut

Enter the bush approximately 200m up valley from Top Dingle Hut and follow a small stream draining from the tops. Occasional bits of blue ribbon and blazes may be seen on the true left of this creek. Cross to the true right at the 980m contour and climb steeply in open beech to the bushline at the 1080m contour, G38 356 534. From here, the route climbs and sidles through tussock towards the saddle at pt 1448m. Above the bushline, there are a couple of iron standards to help identify the route to the start of the bulldozed track. The bulldozer line descends as marked on G38 to the Ahuriri Valley. The track is signposted from the Ahuriri road.

Time: Top Dingle Hut to Ahuriri Base Hut, approx. 3.5 hrs.

CROSSINGS FROM THE DINGLE BURN

1. **TO LAKE HAWEA AND THE HUNTER.** High and exposed crossings can be made to the head of Lake Hawea and the Hunter Valley. From Top Dingle Hut head up the west branch, sidling under open beech on the true left when the bush closes in. This leads easily to scree beyond the treeline. Easy slopes lead to the pass at G38 319 552. From here, sidle north and descend slopes into the upper Green Island Bush Stream. From here, pick a line through beech to the prominent spur on the north side near pt 1199m. Descend the nose of the spur to the Hunter flats (don't be tempted to shortcut. Slopes are densely scrub covered).

   Times: Top Dingle Hut to pass, 4hrs; pass to Hunter, 4 hrs.

2. **TO THE TIMARU RIVER.** The spur above Bush Hut, leading to pt 1703m, gives fair travel but is dry. To avoid some (but by no means all) of the windfall, go 20 mins up the marked route in the valley from the hut before heading uphill. The descent into the tussock headwater basin of Timaru River is open and reasonably straight forward. Allow a day for the crossing.

   An easier, alternative route follows an old bulldozed track up the open spur west of Mae West Bivvy (low roof, sleeps 2, no fire) from the Dingle farm terraces. Cross the range 100m west of pt 1600m and follow down an easy tussock rib to the bushline. Descend to forks in the stream draining pt 1600m and then follow the stream down to Top Timaru Hut. Allow a day for this crossing too.

TIMARU RIVER

Timaru River drains into Lake Hawea. In the lower valley, some of the mountain beech has been replaced by manuka, matagouri and briar rose. The valley is popular with anglers. It offers trampers trips from 1 to 5 days long. Timaru River can be approached by car around the lakeshore from Hawea Flat along the public, gravelled Timaru River road. Despite the sandflies sometimes being very bad, there is a sheltered and pleasant campsite with toilets at the mouth of the Timaru River, by the lake. Access to the campsite is by a side road to the left, 100m past the Timaru River bridge.

ROAD TO JUNCTION HUT

From the sign at the carpark on the true left of the Timaru River by the road bridge, a route marked by red and white permolat on steel poles leads up the riverbed, crossing as neccessary. This marked route is in poor condition since the 1994 floods, but remains well used by anglers. In normal to low flow, travel is easy, sidling loose slips and scree on the true left where the river climbs a little. Then the valley opens out again onto gravel flats around Junction Hut. (Dingle Burn Station, 4 bunks and an open fireplace). There isnt much dry dead wood nearby. It is an older station hut that is not well looked after by recreationalists, but would be welcome in the rain. If the river is flooded, it is possible to descend from Junction Hut to the road by sidling 300 to 400m up on the true right, but travel is rough and the briar rose thick.

Note. The metric map naming of Deer Spur Creek conflicts with the older NZMS 1 series map and local usage. Junction Creek joins the Timaru River at Junction Hut. Deer Spur Creek joins the Timaru River from the true right, 1.4km up Timaru River from the Junction Forks.

Time: Road to Junction Hut, 1.5 hours.

JUNCTION HUT TO TOP TIMARU HUT

The bushed section of Timaru River is confined and the river often gorgy. The marked route is overgrowing, but is still generally followable with care. From Junction Hut, gravel flats lead to a short confined beech forested section, easily traversed at river level, followed by more gravel flats. Travel is reasonably fast to here, at G39 242 244. Steel warratahs with red and white permolat lead onto a small terrace on the true left as marked on G39 and cross two streams to a larger terrace. Scrub regrowth further along this terrace makes the marked route challenging to follow in places, but it is possible with care (1996). Staying at about the 600m contour, the route crosses a stream then descends to the river at a creek, G39 269 250.

Travel is now slower most of the way to the bushline. Although this route has been remarked with permolat in the 1990s by DoC, it has not been recut and in places there is regrowth and windfall. In some places the ground trail itself is non-existent and the route crosses steep earth slopes requiring care. Generally, the marked route follows the true left, but crosses to make short detours close to the river on the true right about 3 or 4 times. It does not climb high on the true right anywhere.

Alternatively, the river is negotiable up valley at normal to low flows from G39 269 250, (though some scrambling around bedrock, thigh wades and many crossings are involved) to approximately G39 308 280, a point approximately 7 hours from Junction Hut. There are good campsites for 500m downstream of this point.

Above here, the marked route is reasonably fast travel again, and generally close to the river. At stream junction G39 311 292, there are more good open campsites. Beyond here the riverbed is confined in places and travel on the marked route 20 to 30m above the river on the true left is necessary. Where two streams join the river close together on the true left, G39 316 302, the track descends to the river but beyond the second stream, it climbs steeply back up 30m on the true left and sidles at this height, initially across steep slopes, to the bush edge. The river is quite gorged in this section. The small bluff at the bush edge is easily crossed about 30m above the river, by a minor climb and descent on grass to the riverbed on the upstream side. Open travel leads to Top Timaru Hut, (4 bunk, open fire, DoC cat 3) correctly located on G39.

When descending from Top Timaru Hut, pick up a routed signpost on a grass slope about 10m above the river on the true left just before the bush edge. Climb up across an easy bluff and descend to a tiny terrace at the bush edge, 20m above the river. Look inside the bush edge on the terrace for permolat markers at the start of the marked route.

If Timaru River is high, it is possible to climb above the bushline and pick up a 4WD track on the range between Timaru River and Breast Creek. This track can be followed out to Breast Hill, although it should be noted that this is a long detour.

Time: Junction Hut to Top Timaru Hut, 9 hrs.

TOP TIMARU HUT TO THE VALLEY HEAD

Travel in the upper valley is easy, on tussock grass and gravel. A 4WD track from the Lindis River over Mt Prospect leads into the Timaru River at the Top Timaru Hut. This track was re-dozed in the 1996/1997 summer. It doesn't cross but continues up the true left in the floor of the open valley. Part of the track has been eroded away by the stream here. In the head, this track leads over a high saddle by Mt Martha (which is quite approachable from here) to the Avon Burn and Ahuriri Valley— a possible escape route in case of high rivers, as no major stream crossings are involved.

Time: Top Timaru Hut to the valley head, approx 1.5 hrs.

CROSSINGS FROM TOP TIMARU HUT

1. **TO BUSH HUT IN THE DINGLE.** This crossing is normally approached from the Dingle. (See the description in the Dingle notes). From the tussock headwaters of Timaru River, a straight forward climb is made to pt 1703m. Descend the ridge out to 1490m and 1292m through

reasonably open bush, especially in the top section, crossing to pt 1040m to meet the marked route 500m or more distance upstream from Bush Hut to avoid areas of windthrow. There are no markers on this route. Allow one day.

2. **TO DINGLE BURN STATION.** From the hut, follow up the stream draining from the west to forks and climb the minor rib between them to the bushline. Continue up this easy tussock rib, sidling near the top to reach the range 100m west of pt 1600m. Descend to Mae West Bivvy then sidle west to the ridge that the map shows as open travel, passing pt 1246m on the way. (See Dingle notes).

TOP TIMARU HUT TO MOONLIGHT AND ROSES HUT

This route traverses high and exposed tops and requires navigational care and fine weather. Even as a summer route, an ice axe may be required. Follow up the stream beside Top Timaru Hut and climb out as per the Mae West Bivvy route onto a tussock rib. Sidle west to the ridge running off the range with pt 1428m on it. Cross this on tussock at G39 301 313 or shingle at G39 297 317. Sidle across upper basins, gaining height to cross the next ridge at G39 280 310, 400m NW of Maungatika Peak. This ridge is the crux of the crossing and requires care with navigating.

Descend shingle and small bluffs to the tarn marked at the 1500m contour before climbing to cross a small spur at about G39 267 305. Sidle across scree under bluffs to the creek draining east from pt 1675m and cross the saddle (G39 257 304) at the head of it. Note that there is a slightly lower saddle close by on the main range itself, which is ignored. Descend a high basin and sidle down tussock slopes on the true left to bushline, crossing to the true right at about the 960m contour. Sidle above the bush at the 1000m contour till the side creek before Moonlight and Roses Hut is reached.

Cross this bushed gully to Moonlight and Roses Hut (Dingle Burn Station, 4 bunk, open fire), situated as marked at the bushline, set in an alcove.

Time: Top Timaru Hut to Moonlight and Roses Hut, allow a full day.

JUNCTION HUT TO MOONLIGHT AND ROSES HUT

Follow up the stream beside Junction Hut that drains Dingle and Corner Peaks. (G39 Ed.1 calls this Deer Spur Creek, but it is actually Junction Creek). After 20 mins, the wide gravelled stream becomes confined and many crossings will be made, but travel remains straightforward. Further up the stream, the valley opens into extensive gravel flats again, leading to major forks.

From the forks, continue up the Dingle Peak branch to the NE. Easy but confined travel for 1.2km leads to forks near the bushline at the 740m contour, G39 217 275. From here, or a little further up the main stream, climb NE between the forks to the bush edge on the true right, bypassing pole beech regrowth, to open, easy grass travel behind the bush. Sidle into and cross the main stream above the bush at the 1040m contour then climb to the saddle 750m distance west of Moonlight and Roses Hut. Though not quite visible from the saddle, the hut is easily seen by descending 100m and is located as on G39 Ed.1.

A 2nd alternative route to Moonlight and Roses Hut involves climbing the open spur behind Junction Hut to the 800m contour. Cross the ridge here and sidle gently up to the 1100m contour along the east side of the ridge, just above the bushline, before descending 100m to Moonlight and Roses Hut, tucked in its alcove at the bushline.

A 3rd alternative route to Moonlight and Roses Hut follows a stream 1.5km further up Timaru River at G39 223 241. (Although this stream has no name on G39 Ed.1, it is in fact the original Deer Spur Creek). At normal to low flows, easy travel leads up the creek bed to forks at G39 249 280.

Then climb west up a spur, initially on scree then under open beech forest, to the bushline. Sidle upvalley to Moonlight and Roses Hut, keeping within a few hundred metres of the bushline. The old permolat track shown on G39 Ed.1 sidling up this stream is overgrown.

Time: Junction Hut to Moonlight and Roses Hut, 3.5 hrs.

DINGLE AND CORNER PEAKS

These can be approached as a fit, long summer day trip via the Timaru River and offer magnificent views. From Junction Hut, continue up the gravel stream draining the two peaks. Gain a leading ridge between the main forks and follow it up through open, dry bush into the tussock. Continue over pt 1070m to the range between the peaks. The west ridge of Dingle Peak is a straightforward climb, mainly on shingle slopes. Descend this ridge to the col between Dingle and Corner Peaks. Corner Peak is approached up an obvious tussock shoulder. There is a spectacular view of the Lake Hawea country from this peak. The ridge leading south can be followed all the way back to the Timaru River roadbridge, but it is much more difficult than the ascent route described. There are a couple of tricky rock knobs and a section of ridge which are easier to turn on the Junction Creek side, but animal tracks should show the way around any difficulties.

Times: Junction Hut to Dingle Peak, 3 or 4 hrs; Dingle Peak to Corner Peak, 2 hrs; Ridge traverse from Corner Peak to the road, 4 hrs.

DINGLE PEAK can also be approached from Moonlight and Roses Hut. Wander up tussock slopes behind the hut and cross the ridge at G39 227 297, then sidle to the main range at G39 225 300. Traverse Dingle Peak on shingle slopes on the north side. It is also possible to continue to Corner Peak from here. This route to Dingle Peak has severe avalanche hazard in winter and spring, and is really a summer and autumn route only.

■ The upper Ahuriri Valley from a clearing on bush slopes below Mt Barth.

THE AHURIRI VALLEY

The upper Ahuriri has attractive beech forested slopes set between upland valleys of grassy flats and glaciated peaks like Mts Barth and Huxley. Birchwood Station at the roadend was bought by the Government in 2003. This wonderful addition to our Conservation lands ensures public access to the Ahuriri Valley, its side valleys and the saddle to the upper Dingle (which was also included in the purchase). To approach the Ahuriri Valley, turn off the Lindis Highway at an AA sign to Ahuriri Conservation Park, where the highway leaves the Ahuriri River and swings left towards Lindis Pass. A good gravel public road leads to the Birchwood homestead, and although it slowly deteriorates beyond here, DoC intends to maintain this road to the barren carpark and locked gate 20mins walk short of Canyon Creek. Reasonable clearance is required under cars between the Homestead and this carpark.

AHURIRI BASE HUT TO THE HEADWATER

From Ahuriri Base Hut (6 bunk, stove, DoC cat 3), travel up valley is straightforward and needs little explanation beyond the map. Canyon Creek has no bridge, but is not normally difficult to cross. Shamrock Hut (2 bunk, open fire, DoC cat 3) is at the edge of open beech forest on the true right of the Ahuriri River. Hagens Hut (4 bunks, open fire, DoC cat 3) is also on the true right, just up valley from the first big creek past Canyon Creek. Travelling up valley, parties can easily miss Top Hut (2 bunk, open fire, DoC cat 3) on the true left, as it is set back in an alcove of celery pine at the base of the hill under the last patch of beech forest.

Beyond Top Hut, travel to the head of the valley is easy, generally keeping to the true left, but crossing in places. Scrub can mostly be bypassed in the riverbed if necessary. At the head of the valley, the south face of Mt Huxley is very imposing. Slabby bluffs in the very head, SW of Mt Huxley, make a crossing from here to the Hunter Valley impractical. However, there is a good semi-alpine crossing to the Temple Valley.

Times: Ahuriri Base Hut to Shamrock Hut, 2.5 hrs; Shamrock Hut to Hagens Hut, 1.5 hrs; Hagens Hut to Top Hut, 1hr 20 mins; Top Hut to valley head, 1 hr 15 mins.

CROSSING THE BARRIER RANGE FROM THE HEAD OF THE AHURIRI

TO THE SOUTH TEMPLE. From the head of the upper Ahuriri Valley, follow up a tiny creek at G38 444 749 through bluffs. Climb out on the true right of the creek onto a spur leading into the basin under pt 2058m. There are wonderful but exposed late summer campsites here at about the 1560m contour. Scree leads up to the Barrier Range at G38 460 752. The descent to the South Temple Valley is generally obvious and will usually involve snowslopes followed by bedrock gullies leading down left to scree slopes.

In the reverse direction, from the South Temple, climb up through tussock and rock gullies, or follow scree, beginning at about G38 467 752 to the saddle. See Hopkins Valley notes. It is also possible to cross over the range near pt 1965m to a western tributary of the South Temple.

Time: Ahuriri head to South Temple head, allow 3 to 4 hrs.

TO THE SOUTH HUXLEY. The Barrier Range can be crossed at pt 1884m. Although there are varying views about this crossing, it is regularly used and is a reasonably good route. The narrow gully on the South Huxley side is moderately steep near the top, but not excessively so. Beware of loose stones in late summer. Access on the Ahuriri side is fairly easy. When descending to the South Huxley, it is best to sidle up valley to avoid scrub. See the Huxley in Hopkins Valley notes.

CROSSING TO THE HUNTER VALLEY DIRECTLY

There are no easy routes from the upper valley. An alpine route that has been used follows. From G38 424 700 in the Ahuriri, climb generally north to a shoulder at G38 424 706. After the first 15 mins, travel is on talus slopes amongst scrub. Descend from the shoulder on scree and cross a stream to the north. Now begins a long tussock sidle up to another shoulder at G38 419 719. Sidle over rock and snow to the next shoulder, near the bluffy outlet to a large tarn. Descend rubble from the shoulder to near the tarn outlet. Ascend the valley past the tarn to snow slopes and the range at G38 408 718. The Hunter side is easier and shouldn't present problems for experienced parties. See p192 (via Dingle) and Little Canyon Creek notes, p200 for easier crossings downvalley.

WATSON STREAM

There are extensive open basins in Watson Stream above the bushline. These can be reached from the Ahuriri by climbing and sidling on terraces just under the 1000m contour on either side of Watson Stream. On the true right, climb open bush slopes from the Ahuriri to the terrace with a tarn clearing NE of pt 1003m. Although there is some windthrow further up Watson Stream along this bush terrace, travel to the bushline is not difficult. On the true left, travel is through lanky grass and scrub on old stock tracks.

Travel up the main Watson Stream from the bushline is open and straightforward. Watson Stream also has a major tributary entering from the true left, just under the 1000m contour. A gorge in this tributary is easily bypassed on the true left on open grass slopes. The gorge is deeply incised, and worth a look at about G38 444 634. Above the gorge in this tributary, there is access to the South Temple and Maitland Streams.

Time: Ahuriri Valley to the bushline, 1 hr 45 mins.

CROSSINGS FROM WATSON STREAM

TO THE SOUTH TEMPLE. A gravel col (snow here earlier in the season may require an iceaxe) between pt 2222m and pt 2090m leads to a stream draining down to South Temple Hut. From the bushline, sidle on the true right through beech forest and at stream G38 498 689 climb up to the ridge at G38 499 692 and follow it down to the forks. See Hopkins Valley notes, P 204.

TO MAITLAND STREAM. On the Watson side access is straight forward up to the Barrier Range crossing at G38 469 625. If necessary, the creek on the way up can be crossed easily at G38 463 628. Beyond here, there is a long slog up dry shingle to the saddle. At about the 1700m contour on the Maitland side, carpet plant mats in small basins and water in small creeks make a high campsite an option. The basin begins steeply below here, but it is not difficult to descend, keeping on the true left towards the bushline. Cross to the true right at the 1100m contour and sidle through beech forest to an open bush rib at G38 492 609. At the 1000m contour, swing across towards Maitland Hut through less open bush, but still offering reasonable travel. See Maitland notes in the Hopkins Valley.

Time: Watson Creek bushline to the bushline in the Maitland, about 4 hrs, and a further 40 mins to Maitland Hut.

SNOWY GORGE CREEK

To reach the Maitland Stream from the Ahuriri, follow the true right of Snowy Gorge Creek until Snowy Gorge Hut is reached. Initially, use terraces 20 to 60m above the stream, but sidle into the open streambed further upvalley as flats allow. Travel is easy, through grass and open tussock with little speargrass. The speargrass and bouldery jumble on the true left downstream from the hut is also quite negotiable, but is more difficult. Snowy Gorge Creek Hut (5 bunks, no fire or cooking facilities, DoC cat 3) has been rebuilt by DoC and is in excellent condition, in a pleasant grassy basin. It is hidden from downstream and the riverbed behind a pile of boulders, at pt 1125m.

CROSSING TO THE MAITLAND. From the hut, follow up the flats and climb in open tussock and bog cushions to the saddle at pt 1352m. At a pinch, campsites exist near and on the saddle, with water not far away on both sides. From the saddle, follow the creek down into the Maitland, sidling close to the creek on the true left as necessary. The speargrass (*Aciphylla* sp) zone, between the 1100m to 1300m contour, is best sidled where necessary on the true left too. A gravelly stream from the true left crosses the last tussock flat just before the bushline. Cross it, climb onto a terrace at the bush edge, and pick up an old permolat marked route on the true left that sidles through the bush to Maitland Hut. See Maitland notes in the Hopkins Valley.

Times: Ahuriri to Snowy Gorge Creek Hut, 5 hrs; Snowy Gorge Creek Hut to pt 1352m Saddle, 1 hr 15 min; Saddle to Maitland Hut, 2.5 hrs.

CANYON CREEK

Follow the 4WD track up towards Little Canyon Creek. At about G38 375 589, pick up markers just inside the open bush on the true left of Little Canyon Creek. Follow them up onto a spur at the 900m contour overlooking the main Canyon Creek and on the true right of it. Where the spur begins to climb steeply up, the marked route sidles off it and down to the gravel riverbed. Follow up the marked track and in places the riverbed, staying on the true right.

The waterfall bluff halfway up the valley is usually bypassed on the true right. The route is lightly cairned. Between the waterfall and the scree on the true right downvalley, four side creeks are marked on G38. Cross the first two creeks marked and continue to the third, G38 368 626, but don't cross. Instead, climb up the bedrock on the true right of it sidling downvalley over a rib and cross the second creek again up there. Continue up the rib on the true right of the second creek in short scrub on a ground trail until above the bluffs. Cross the second creek again, and access a minor saddle upvalley at the 1200m contour. The ground trail continues up easy tussock slopes to the rim of the basin at about the 1280m contour, still on the true right at G38 367 630. A bivvy rock (sleeps 3) lies in the upper basin on the true right of the creek, at about G38 382 642, but it is not entirely weatherproof. This tussock basin under a glacier and Mt Barth is a great location.

CROSSING TO THE AHURIRI VALLEY from the head of Canyon Creek makes an easy weekend round trip. However, a recent massive winter snow avalanche has devastated beech forest on the route beginning at G38 402 642 and extending for 300m north to the descent gully to the Ahuriri. From approx G38 383 640 climb tussock and old scree slopes to near the dividing ridge. Head south in undulating short tussock basins to G38 389 632 and follow down on the true right of the marked stream into a tussock basin at the 1340m contour. Cross the stream to the true left and sidle down, heading upvalley under bluffs at about the scrubline, onto forested benches at about the 1160m contour. Follow the benches north avoiding the worst of the avalanche debris, keeping height and crossing a creek or two en-route until overlooking a major open streambed. Descend this easy creek to the valley floor at G38 407 646. Beware of dropping down too soon, as there are numerous bluffs to bypass all the way down through the bush to the flats. Some of these little bluffs extend for some distance.

Times: Ahuriri Valley to Canyon Creek Basin, 2.5 hrs; Canyon Creek basin to Ahuriri flats, about 3 hrs.

LITTLE CANYON CREEK headwaters can easily be approached from the Ahuriri by sidling through the short section of bush in the valley on the true right. Keep above the gorge itself, where open beech forest slopes offer good travel. The bushline is pretty much free of scrub. The basin above here is all stones and scree; even the stream disappears underground within a kilometre of the bushline, making a waterbottle very handy. It will take about 1 hr from flats by Canyon Creek to bushline.

CROSSING TO THE HUNTER. A long, but safe and easy plod, mostly on gravel, leads from the bushline in Little Canyon Creek up to the crossing point on the range 200m south of pt 1883m. There is a small tarn at G38 341 609. From the range crest 200m west of pt 1883m, overlooking the Hunter, head NW across a basin under a gnarly bit of ridge, then pick up the ridge and suss out the best looking line on down to the Hunter flats. This is a long grunt on tussock if approaching from the Hunter. Those with climbing skills can sidle south along the Hunter faces of the range and return to the Ahuriri via the head of the Dingle Valley and the saddle at pt 1448m, making a good weekend trip. To reach the Hunter Divide from the Little Canyon/Canyon Creek confluence will take about 4 hrs.

Brodrick Pass from the North Huxley side. Mt Strauchon to the left.

THE HOPKINS CATCHMENT

In the Hopkins Catchment, there are two valleys that are passed on the way to the roadend; the Maitland and the Temple. They and the Ohau Range are covered before moving on to the main Hopkins Valley. For access to the Hopkins Valley and its tributaries, turn off SH8 at the Lake Ohau Skifield junction sign and follow the road around the SW shores of Lake Ohau. The seal ends at Lake Ohau Lodge, but a reasonable gravel road leads to a DoC carpark a few hundred metres past Huxley Lodge where there is an intentions book. Beyond here, the condition of the last 5 or 6km of public road leading to the old carpark 2km from Monument Hut varies, and is currently (2004) only suitable for fully 4WD vehicles. This section can be subject to river flooding and is only roughly maintained. Along the road in, there are good campsites at Lake Middleton and Round Bush beside Lake Ohau, but the roadend itself can be a little bleak. Most huts and facilities in the Hopkins have been recently upgraded by DoC.

FREEHOLD CREEK TO THE OHAU RANGE

This is a great area for day or weekend trips, including family trips, though there is a bit of climbing involved. Once in the subalpine basins of the range there are numerous tarns and campsites, with interesting rock outcrops, pleasant streams, bog cushions and short tussock to travel through. Speargrass begins above the bushline, but peters out at about the 1300 m contour.

Tracks lead to Freehold Creek from the skifield road and the road along the lakeside. From a major DoC sign at H38 551 583 by the Ohau Skifield road, markers lead across the toe of the hill to a signed track junction on the true left of Sawyers Creek, H38 554 559. Alternatively, from the lake road, turn off onto a side road to the Glen Mary Ski Club Hut (private) just after a cattle stop. Occasional green and yellow markers lead from here along a 4WD track up to the same track junction mentioned earlier beside Sawyers Creek.

The track crosses Sawyers Creek on a bridge and continues south on flats at the base of the hill to beech forest by Freehold Creek. The track now swings upvalley. A few hundred metres up, it crosses to the true right of Freehold Creek on a good bridge and follows up beside the stream through open forest to the bushline. The track finishes here, about 10m from the stream, still on the true right. A ground trail continues from the bushline, keeping about 7m above the streambed, but peters out after a distance of about 300m. Travel is not difficult. To the south, the lake at height 1514m is easily accessible and surrounded by tussock. The tops here are very pleasant, offering some wonderful trips.

To approach Lake Dumb-bell, climb to the tarn at pt 1479m, continue up past pt 1922m, then descend towards the outlet. Alternatively, sidle between H38 517 557 and H38 511 565. There are campsites by the lake at H38 511 577 and H38 512 579. Mt Sutton and the skifield can be approached from Lake Dumb-bell outlet via a sidle and final scree gully up to the ridge at H38 515 594. Snowy Gorge Creek and Maitland Stream can also be approached from Lake Dumb-bell, by descending the stream draining the lake. Speargrass is a nuisance below the 1380 m contour, but travel is reasonable.

Times: Lake Ohau Skifield Road to Freehold Creek, 1 hr; Glen Mary Ski Club Hut to Freehold Creek, 45 mins; Up Freehold Creek to the bushline, 1.5 hrs; Freehold Creek bushline to pt 1479m, 1 hr 15 mins; Pt 1479m to Lake Dumb-bell, 2 hrs; Snowy Gorge Creek Hut to Lake Dumb-bell, 4.5 hrs.

SAWYERS CREEK can be used as an alternative descent route from Lake Dumb-bell back to the road. From the lake, climb to the range 300m distance south of Pinnacle, where stones have been laid out as arrows on the shingle. Descend easily into Sawyers Creek. There are campsites up here at the 1600m to 1700m contour, with water close by in idyllic mossy banked streams. Descend the rib between 2 gullies, and sidle left from about the 1340m contour before the rib finishes. Sidle down to a bench about 15m above the stream and continue down the true left on a light trail on this bench, between scree and scrub. Continue in this zone past the first patch of beech to the bushline proper before descending to the creek. This route mostly avoids both scrub and speargrass. Travel down through fairly open bush, and climb out on the true left onto the open grassland and follow this about 200m down to the track junction.

Time: Descending Sawyers Creek from the range to the road, 3.5 hrs.

MAITLAND VALLEY

The Maitland offers accessible round trips from 1 to 4 days long. Forests are mountain beech. This area, along with the Ohau Range, can offer pleasant trips when rain engulfs ranges further west. Permission for tramping access to the Maitland Valley needs to be sought at Lake Ohau Station (Mr Weatherall, ph 03 438 9663). During lambing, access is closed. From a DoC sign by the road 300m past Lake Ohau Station, a 4WD track, marked on H38, climbs onto the airstrip terrace and sidles high above the Maitland on the true right.

Near the end of the 4WD track, a track recently recut and marked by DoC sidles across scree and ribs of trees at the 1100m contour, marked by poles and permolat. A bush knoll at H38 519 632 is called the Beehive. The track descends before the Beehive, into a basin at H38 522 638 and at about the 920m contour enters the beech forest and sidles up valley, gradually descending to open flats in the riverbed at H38 509 630. Take care to pick the track up here on the return. The Maitland Valley, like the Temple Valley next door, suffered severe flooding and gravel movement in the 1994-5 summer and in places the riverbed is strewn with gravel and toppled trees.

At H38 501 610 the track crosses to the true left. It then climbs through the bush to a beech forested terrace, emerging on a pleasant grass clearing 40m above the river where the tidy Maitland Hut (4 bunks, open fire, DoC cat 3) is sited.

Beyond the hut, the track continues to the bush edge on the true left. Open tussock travel up the stream, sidling on the true left as necessary, leads to a saddle at 1352m. Up the Maitland, there is a band of speargrass between the 1050m and 1250m contours but these are mostly avoidable with care. The descent to Snowy Gorge Creek Hut at G38 465 531 is straightforward. This hut (5 bunks, DoC cat 3) has been rebuilt. See Snowy Gorge Creek notes in the Ahuriri.

Times: Lake Ohau Road to Maitland Hut, 4.5 hrs; Hut to Snowy Gorge Creek Hut, 4 hrs; Hut to Pass at G38 469 625, 2 to 3 hrs.

DUMB-BELL LAKE can be approached from the upper Maitland and a crossing of the Ohau Range made to Freehold Creek. Speargrass is a nuisance in the stream draining Lake Dumb-bell below the 1380m contour. See Freehold Creek notes.

WATSON STREAM can be approached from the Maitland over high open tops. From Maitland Hut, sidle across to the spur overlooking a creek at G38 495 610. Follow up this spur, sidling into the creek at the bushline and crossing to the true left. Ascending to the upper basin and pass at G38 469 625 is straightforward. Small gorges in Watson Stream can be sidled easily on the true left. See Ahuriri Valley for further notes.

TEMPLE STREAM

The Temple offers pleasant, accessible beech forest tramping, but most round trips will involve high (~2000m) crossings. DoC managed public land begins at the Temple Valley roadend where there is a carpark, open shelter, and toilets at the bush edge, 5 mins below the North South forks. From the carpark, there is a marked track to a scenic viewpoint above bushline on Ram Hill. Wasps can be a problem in summer. Major storms in 1994-5 flooded much of the Temple Valley with fresh gravel, burying forest flats and redirecting the river.

NORTH TEMPLE STREAM

To reach the North Branch headwaters, cross to the true right near the forks and follow the partly marked route up flats until the bush closes in at H38 541 746. A good track, marked with orange triangles, enters the bush on the true right near river level to avoid the gorge and climbs steeply to emerge in the top basin. **In the reverse direction,** the track enters the bush on the true right about 25m above the stream. The hut marked on some maps in the North Branch has now gone. However, there is a DoC campsite with a toilet and fireplace beside a large rock at the bushline on the true right of the North Temple.

From the head of the North Branch, a steep narrow rocky gut, easier than it looks, can be ascended to the main col (locally known as **Gunsight Pass**) between Bruce and Belfry peaks. Scree slopes lead to the South Branch. This crossing is not recommended in winter or spring as the gut is a natural avalanche chute. Beware of stray rocks, too. Times: Carpark to the bushline, 1.5 hrs; North Branch crossing to the South Branch, 3 to 4 hrs.

SOUTH TEMPLE STREAM

The South Branch is more open, with a greater variety of scenery than the North Branch. The track leads up the true left through open bush and flats to opposite the South Temple Hut (6 bunk, stove, DoC cat 3). Floods in th 1990s threatened the hut so DoC shifted and rebuilt it closeby. There is no footbridge over the river here, as the same floods destroyed it. The track beyond the hut has been obliterated by floods for the first 2 km. Both banks can be followed, but at normal river levels the gravel riverbed gives the easiest travel, crossing as necessary. Above G38 495 715, the track becomes useable again and follows the line shown on G38 Ed.1.

The track does not end as shown on the map though. Marked by small cairns and an occasional pole, it continues through scrub, remaining between the two streams to the 1060m contour. It then crosses the stream to the west and curves up behind the small tarn to emerge close by on the gravel river bank at G38 487 743. Watch out for this poorly marked entrance coming back. The approach to the upper basin draining from the west is now straightforward in the gravel streambed.

Times: Carpark to South Temple Hut, 3 hrs; Hut to the upper basin, 3 hrs.

CROSSING TO THE AHURIRI. The saddle at G38 460 751 to the Ahuriri is approached from the South Temple either up scree (watch for loose stones), or tussock and rock steps followed by snowslopes, depending on conditions. An ice axe will often be required. The descent to the Ahuriri is reasonably straightforward. See Ahuriri notes.

CROSSING TO THE SOUTH HUXLEY. The South Huxley can also be approached from the head of the South Temple. Ascend to G38 460 751 as above. Sidle across to a col overlooking the South Huxley, pt 1884m. Initially the gully into the South Huxley is confined and steep, but it quickly improves. Beware of loose stones, particularly in late summer. See Ahuriri and Huxley notes.

CROSSING TO WATSON STREAM. In normal conditions, a straightforward (mostly gravel) route exists from South Temple Hut over a high col near Mt Maitland, between pt 2222m and 2090m. An ice axe could be useful in snowy conditions. See Ahuriri notes, P. 198.

THE MAIN HOPKINS VALLEY Roadend to Elcho Hut

From the carpark about 300m past Huxley Lodge, a 4WD track continues about 6km to Monument Hut (6 bunk, stove, DoC cat 3, and recently done up) and the cairn the hut is named for. About 200m downstream from the hut is a picnic site. A track sign here indicates an old benched side track up through forest to a lookout, taking about 1hr. Several options exist for heading on up valley, depending on conditions. From Monument Hut, to avoid crossings, a track begins sidling through beech forest up valley on the true right 10 to 30m above the valley flats. Cattle tracks and markers lead to grass flats again, at H37 543 830. Alternatively, in low river conditions, the flats can be followed, crossing a side channel of the river twice, but essentially staying on the true right.

To cross the Huxley swingbridge, look for the sign at the bush edge, Huxley Forest, 300m before the Huxley River. This marks the start of the permolat track to the bridge, which takes 15 mins. Across the swingbridge, the tracks on the true left of the Huxley are incorrectly marked on H37 Ed.1, and can be a little confusing. From the bridge, climb up a short distance to a track sign where the track splits. The track to the left is the fine weather track for those going up the Huxley Valley. It descends to the start of shingle up valley at H37 538 848.

The track back to the Hopkins continues to climb straight ahead uphill to a clearing at pt 688m where there is a second junction sign. Here, another track leads off to the left and descends to grass flats in the Huxley at H37 536 849 and this is the Huxley wet weather track. To continue up the Hopkins, follow the other, lightly marked, right hand track along the side of clearings and through open forest to flats in the Hopkins again. (If coming down the Hopkins, the track leads into the bush at a signpost on grass slopes 200m north of Huxley River at H37 545 855).

Open flats now lead up valley to Elcho Hut (12 bunk, open fire, NZAC, $10 per person/night). In case of flood conditions, there is a swingbridge over a stream at H37 550 899 en-route. It is 100m downstream of its marked position, with an overgrowing track to and from it.

In low river conditions, an alternative route from Monument Hut to Elcho Hut crosses the Hopkins to Red Hut and crosses back upvalley following flats. This can be marginally faster. Red Hut, built in 1916 as a Station Hut, is very well maintained and has 2 rooms (DoC cat 3, 12 bunks, stove).

Times. Roadend to Monument Hut, 25 mins; Monument to Huxley Bridge, 1 hr 15 mins; Bridge to Elcho Hut, 3 hrs.

ELCHO HUT TO DODGER HUT

From Elcho Hut, if conditions permit, cross Elcho Stream and its gravel fan directly to Apricot (Cullers) Hut on the true left. This will take about 30 mins. Apricot Hut (4 bunk, open fire, DoC cat 3) stands on a grass terrace alcove, tucked against the bush as marked. Alternatively, if Elcho Stream is up, the Elcho swingbridge can be used to continue up the Hopkins Valley. The bridge track begins at a sign near Elcho Hut and has been recently recut and marked on both sides of Elcho Stream.

From the Elcho, to cross the Dodger Bridge over the Hopkins, continue up the true right of the Hopkins to the end of the flats. Where the bush meets the river, permolat markers lead up over a small spur into the marked stream immediately below the bridge. Between this stream and the bridge is a high, eroding gravel slip. This is best avoided by descending the creek and following along the riverbank to the bridge. Watch for falling stones. The bridge itself is not threatened by the slip. Alternatively, if the river is not up much, the river bank can be negotiated from the flats up to the bridge, saving a small climb. Follow the terrace edge beyond the bridge on the true left to Dodger Hut (4 bunk, open fire, DoC cat 3), situated in a grassy alcove backed by celery pine and beech.

Times: Elcho Hut to Apricot Hut, 30 mins direct, or 1 hr 15 mins via the bridge; Apricot Hut to Dodger Hut, 2 hrs.

DODGER HUT TO RICHARDSON GLACIER

From the head of Dodger Flat, the route follows the riverbed on the true left and is rougher going, but not difficult. Erceg Hut (4 bunks, DoC cat 3), is situated on a scrubby terrace well above the river itself. Cairns and an iron standard in the riverbed at a creek junction where the Hopkins turns left mark the start of the climb to the hut. The route to the Richardson Glacier continues on the true left. On the grassy river bank around the corner from the final flat are the Richardson bivvy rocks. These consist of several scattered smaller bivvy rocks rather than one large boulder. Together they could sleep up to 5. From here, the Neumann Range slopes are easily accessible and offer wonderful views across to the Main Divide.

There are no tramping routes from the head of the valley. Charity Col can be crossed to the Landsborough by climbing parties, but the ascent on the Hopkins side is moderately difficult with added danger of rockfall. A similarly difficult crossing to the Dobson exists; Tragedy Col. See Neumann Range notes below.

Times: Dodger Hut to Erceg Hut, 3 hrs; Erceg Hut to Richardson bivvy rock, 1 hr 20 mins.

THOMSON STREAM

This enclosed alpine valley could be camped in or visited as a day trip. A marked route leads into Thomson Stream. The entrance to it is well cairned on the true left at H37 591 977. Marked with permolat, the route climbs over pt 1032m, crosses a clearing with a view of the east ridge of Mt Ward and continues through forest towards Thomson Stream again. The end of the marked route is a little obscure. It finishes at about H37 583 985, upstream from a prominent spur.

From here, travel to the head of the valley is easy on boulders on the true left and easier still on a terrace on the true left at about the 1160m contour. There is a pond rather than a lake in the head of the valley, surrounded by high mountain walls, which offer only climbing routes out. For climbers, it offers access to Mts William and Browning.

Time: Hopkins to pond in the head, about 4.5 hrs.

ELCHO STREAM

Tracks exist up to the footbridge on both sides of the valley. From the bridge, a good permolat marked route on the true left leads up to the forks, about 20 mins away. At the forks there are excellent mossy flats and alcoves by the track to camp on.

NORTH ELCHO STREAM

Beyond the forks, the marked route up the Elcho on the true left continues in reasonable condition. It crosses small gravel flats, following the riveredge then climbs in the bush, staying about 20 to 30m above the river, and climbing in tandem with it. Red and white markers finish at the bush edge on the downstream side of a slip, 20 to 30m above the river, at H37 544 958. Beyond here, some cairns mark the route up valley, keeping within 30m of the river as it crosses a slip, a rib of bush and then another slip to the tussock. Continue up the riverbed on the true left. Elcho Pass can be used to cross

■ Across the Hopkins Valley to the Huxley from the Neumann Range below Mt Glenmary.

to the Landsborough by parties with some alpine experience and equipment. See Landsborough notes, P 222.

Time: Elcho Forks to the bushline, 1 hr.

SOUTH ELCHO STREAM

From the swingbridge, follow river boulders on the true right to the forks. This makes stream crossings unnecessary there. Alternatively, the track on the true left can also be used. From the forks, travel up the South Elcho is initially on the true right. Further up, there is usually snow avalanche debris to cross in the valley itself. Either side can be travelled in the mid section.

Those with some alpine skill and basic equipment can **climb out of the South Elcho and cross back into the Hopkins.** From about H37 510 923, climb out on the true left and cruise up into the upper basin. Scramble up rock and snow patches to the ridge at H37 531 914 (2100m) and follow the ridge SE, ending up by the small swingbridge at H37 550 891. Higher up, travel is sometimes easier on slopes on the NE side of the ridge than on the ridge itself.

Times: Elcho Forks to 2100m, 5 hrs; 2100m to footbridge, 3 hrs.

HUXLEY RIVER

This valley is a gem. Access is straightforward with basic huts in handy locations. The scenery is spectacular, but there is the disadvantage that for most parties the return will be back down valley. From the bridge across the lower gorge, follow either the dry or flood track up valley on the true left to the flats. Stay on the true left if the river is high, and follow a short sidle track through the bush where the river cuts in. The main Huxley Forks Hut (6 bunk, wood stove, DoC cat 3) and the small older hut behind it (2 bunk, DoC cat 3) are on a grass flat at the bush edge.

Time: Monument Hut to Huxley Forks, 3 hrs.

NORTH BRANCH

The gentle upper basin of the North Branch is a wonderful place with dramatic rock strata on surrounding ridges and plenty of campsites. There are various route options to Brodrick Hut from Huxley Forks, depending on conditions, but most follow the track that sidles on the true right.

From Huxley Forks Hut, follow the track to the bridge, cross and continue upvalley, sidling in and out of creeks along the true right. Major snow avalanches descend some of these side creeks in winter and spring, (be aware of this) raking scrub, trimming beech forest edges and keeping some of the stream banks open and grassy, where they would otherwise revert to scrub and bush. Look for cairns. At times the track is cairned along the riverbank, and at other times, climbs higher than the map shows (eg; between G37 480 848 and 478 858) but is well used and offers good going.

Alternatively, in normal to low river conditions, the riverbed can be used most of the way. When the track begins to climb, take to the river and boulder hop, picking the track up again upvalley. From G37 478 870, stick with the track on the true right, following it up through the bush for the last 500m to Brodrick Hut.

Brodrick Hut (6 bunk, stove, and recently done up by DoC, cat 3) is on a high terrace 80m above the river on the true right at the bushline and faces the upper valley and Brodrick Pass. From the hut, the upper tussock basin is easily reached on a cairned route through low *Dracophyllum* scrub at about the 1000m contour, still on the true right. From there, Brodrick Pass is readily accessible. See Landsborough Valley for crossing notes, p 222.

Time: Huxley Forks to Brodrick Hut, 2.5 hrs.

Brodrick Pass in winter from the south.

SOUTH BRANCH

The South Branch descends through a canyon with impressive walls making travel impractical on the true right below the bushline. An easily followed track leads along the true left. From Huxley Forks Huts, cross the bridge 5 mins upstream to the true right of the North Branch and follow a track back down to the forks. Major floods have built gravel up here, flooding bush flats and obliterating a section of track. Follow gravel flats up the true left of the South Branch to a stream junction at G37 489 834.

From this junction, markers climb 30m then sidle, climbing round a slip and descending to cross two open avalanche gullies. These two gullies form a catchment known locally as Chamois Creek. Once across the second gully, at G37 486 824, the track sidles out NE to a shoulder and crosses a bush flat behind a knob at the 900m contour. It remains on the true left to the bushline at G37 493 800.

South Huxley Bivvy (2 person, upright biv, DoC cat 4) in the head is correctly located on G38 Ed.1. It was built in 1961. Although there are bog pine shrubs nearby, the bivvy is in the open and visible from the river. Crossing the river here can be awkward. For access to the Ahuriri or South Temple, leave the valley at G38 461 771 beyond the scrub, to ascend tussock slopes into an upper basin. Above here, the narrow col at pt 1884m (Vee Notch Pass) can be accessed, depending on conditions. Beware of loose stones. See Temple and Ahuriri notes for further crossing information.

Time: Huxley Forks to South Huxley Bivvy, 3 hrs.

NEUMANN RANGE

There are no straightforward crossings of the Neumann Range north of Mt Glenmary. The Hopkins slopes are much easier than the forbidding Dobson faces, which are unrelentingly steep throughout.

TRAGEDY COL

This is a seldom used, difficult crossing requiring alpine gear, skills and confidence on steep ground. Tragedy Col was named after a fatal accident on the Dobson side in 1947. Some tricky route finding may be involved. It is best to ascend rather than descend the steep, exposed Dobson slopes. Watch for stonefall.

Waterfall Hut provides a convenient landmark for parties using this alpine crossing to the Hopkins. The route ascends a stream from the Dobson at H37 665 036, then follows up a steep grassy gully on the true left of the stream, passing left then right around a big rock near the top of this gully. An occasional cairn may be found from the top of the gully leading through to the top of the bluffs at the 1300m contour. Climb diagonally to the right up what is effectively a sloping shelf cut by several small streams and gullies, to the final snowslopes. Climb them directly to Tragedy Col. On the Hopkins side of the col, descend across easier slopes to Richardson bivvy rocks.

If approaching from the Hopkins side, it is worth spending some time to ensure a descent via the easiest snowslopes. Look for the small gravel outlier at H37 657 049 on the Dobson side and pick a snow gully down towards it from near the marked saddle. Beware of rockfall. The most unnerving part of the descent to the valley is getting off the tussock to the top of the steep grassy gully mentioned above at H37 661 039. This can involve vertical scrub or an exposed metre wide rock ledge.

DASLER PINNACLES AND BIVVY

The Dasler Bivvy at the bushline is accessible when the Hopkins River is low. Above it, there are sub-alpine basins to camp in and explore with dramatic pinnacles behind. It is a great place for sunsets. From the roadend, head up past Monument Hut. Cross the river upstream of the bluff on the true left. Red Hut, hidden by a shingle fan, is about an hour from Monument. Continue up the flats, sometimes following a 4WD track, for a further hour to the stream draining the Pinnacles.

DoC have been busy here too. From a track sign, markers are easily followed to the small, upright, Dasler Bivvy, called Cullers Biv on the door (sleeps 2, tiny fireplace, DoC cat 3). Initially, the track climbs steeply and then between the 1000m contour and the bivvy, the track is slightly further from the stream than is shown on H37. The track sidles out of the beech forest, crosses to the true left of the stream at hut level and continues to sidle 100m through scrub to the Bivvy as marked. The route to tussock above begins by the bivvy door and goes up open scrub on the bivvy spur to the tussock basin above. There are cairns and a ground trail in places. The slopes well above the bushline command a fine view. The summit of the Dasler Pinnacle is reached fairly easily by the broken north ridge during summer.

Time: Valley to Bivvy, 1.5 to 2 hrs.

LOWER NEUMANN RANGE CROSSING Red Hut to Jamieson Stream

This is a relatively straightforward crossing, but an ice axe and some alpine knowledge are required as it climbs to 2300m. It would make a great summer weekend trip. From Red Hut, climb the ridge overlooking the stream to the south through open beech forest to the bushline at H37 575 850. Climb through a break in the scrub, pass a knoll on the NW side and head NE up an open basin to overlook the stream again at the 1500m contour. Cruise on past the shallow tarn at H37 579 859 under the south face of Mt Glenmary to a Southern Lakes Helicopter landing site (possible campsites).

From here, the route slogs up loose gravel screes to the south, crosses a ridge, then descends to an unmarked but good tarn at H37 592 857 with open campsites. (This tarn can also be approached directly up the gully from H37 580 852). Climb to the range crest 300m SW of pt 2309m and descend, sidling left across benches to the snout of a small but nifty white glacier draining into the Jamieson Valley. Alternatively, cross over right up near pt 2362m, but up here, expect crevasse travel. There is good travel on boulders and in open beech down Jamieson Stream.

Time: Allow 2 days for the crossing.

DOBSON VALLEY

The Dobson is less spectacular and of less tramping interest than its neighbouring valleys and is less visited by trampers. However, it is popular with 4WD enthusiasts and hunters. Autumn and winter can be a pleasant time to wander up and down the valley.

From Twizel, the Glen Lyon Station road winds around the eastern shore of Lake Ohau, giving access to the Dobson Valley. Much of the valley floor is in Glen Lyon Station (Mr Wigley, ph 03 438 9644) and permission will be required to enter it. With permission, cars can usually be driven to near Irishman Stream, although muddy ruts not far from Irishman Stream can be difficult to negotiate. Good vehicle clearance is required and there are a couple of tiny streams to cross. A 4WD route leads right up to Reardon Hut, in the valley head, but this involves river crossings.

Alternatively, the valley can be approached from the Hopkins Road, near Huxley Lodge if the rivers are low enough to cross. No bridges cross the Dobson River.

The valley can be travelled on either side if necessary, but the usual route generally follows the line of the 4WD tracks marked on H37. From Glen Lyon Station, this follows the true left up the lower valley. There are no tramping routes out of the valley head, but brief notes on two alpine passes are included and a crossing lower down to Bush Stream on the Mt Cook road.

There are several **huts** in the valley as named and located on the map. All station huts will require permission from Glen Lyon Station to use. Details of the huts in the valley are as follows:

Looking down the Dobson from the Ben Ohau Range above Waterfall Hut.

On the true left,

Station Hut (8 bunk, open fire, Glen Lyon Station).

Waterfall Hut (4 bunk, open fire, DoC cat 3).

Reardon Hut (2 bunk upright bivvy, DoC cat 3), (spelt Readon on H37).

Stony Stream Bivvy (2 bunk, DoC cat 4) on the true right of Stony Stream, can be approached up the streambed.

On the true right,

Le Crens Hut (4 bunk, open fire, Glen Lyon Station, and recently done up).

Watson (or Grough) Biv (2 bunk upright bivvy, DoC cat 3).

Kennedy Hut (6 bunk, stove, recently done up by DoC cat 3).

Times: Glen Lyon Homestead to Station Hut, 5 hrs; Station Hut to Watson Biv, 1 hr; Huxley Lodge to Le Crens Hut, 3.5 hrs; Le Crens Hut to Watson Biv, 2.5 hrs; Watson Biv to Kennedy Hut, 2 hrs; Kennedy Hut to Waterfall Hut, 2 hrs; Waterfall Hut to Reardon Hut, 1.5 hrs.

CROSSINGS FROM THE DOBSON

CROSSING TO BUSH STREAM FROM THE DOBSON. From Waterfall Hut, follow a route on the true left (downvalley) side of the waterfall streams, through beech then untracked subalpine scrub to a tussock spur between tarn filled basins. This spur has pt 1786m on it. The saddle a few hundred metres north of pt 2172m provides gravel access to Bush Stream. Bush Stream offers straight-forward travel down to the Mt Cook Road if the stream is not up. On this route there is no snow in summer, minimal rockfall danger and no steep rock. **In the reverse direction,** the descent to Waterfall Hut may prove difficult due to routefinding among numerous small streams and waterfalls.

JAMIESON SADDLE on the Ben Ohau Range offers a high crossing from the Dobson to the Tasman Valley. Eroding rock and scree slopes create some rockfall danger, and the crossing to Bush Stream described above is generally a better and safer route. An ice axe and some alpine skills are necessary. From Reardon Bivvy, follow the river up valley. There is a reasonable campsite in the tussock at H37 699 090. Continue up a steep bouldery streambed which provides good going and climb out at about H37 711 103 (the 1400m contour) SE into a basin leading up to Jamieson Saddle. The final slope to the saddle is of large unstable blocks at a moderately steep angle. On the Birch Hill Stream side, keep over to the right until fairly well down. The climb from Birch Hill Station side is a steep grind with much loose scree underfoot in summer conditions.

BARRON SADDLE on the Sealy Range offers an alpine route between the Dobson Valley and Mueller Glacier. This is at the extremity of this guide and only a brief note to Barron Saddle Hut is included. Park staff at Mt Cook Visitor Centre should be consulted for current access information to and from Barron Saddle Hut (sleeps 8, kero stove, radio, first aid kit, DoC, cat 1).

From the head of the Dobson, follow up the moraine terrace to H36 684 111 and sidle north into a gully at about the 1500m contour. Climb up from about H36 684 114 towards the easy slopes SE of Barron Saddle. Watch for loose stones. On the Mueller side or along the Sealy Range, parties need to be equipped for crevasse travel.

Once a man has found the road he can never keep away for long.

—Tom Longstaff.

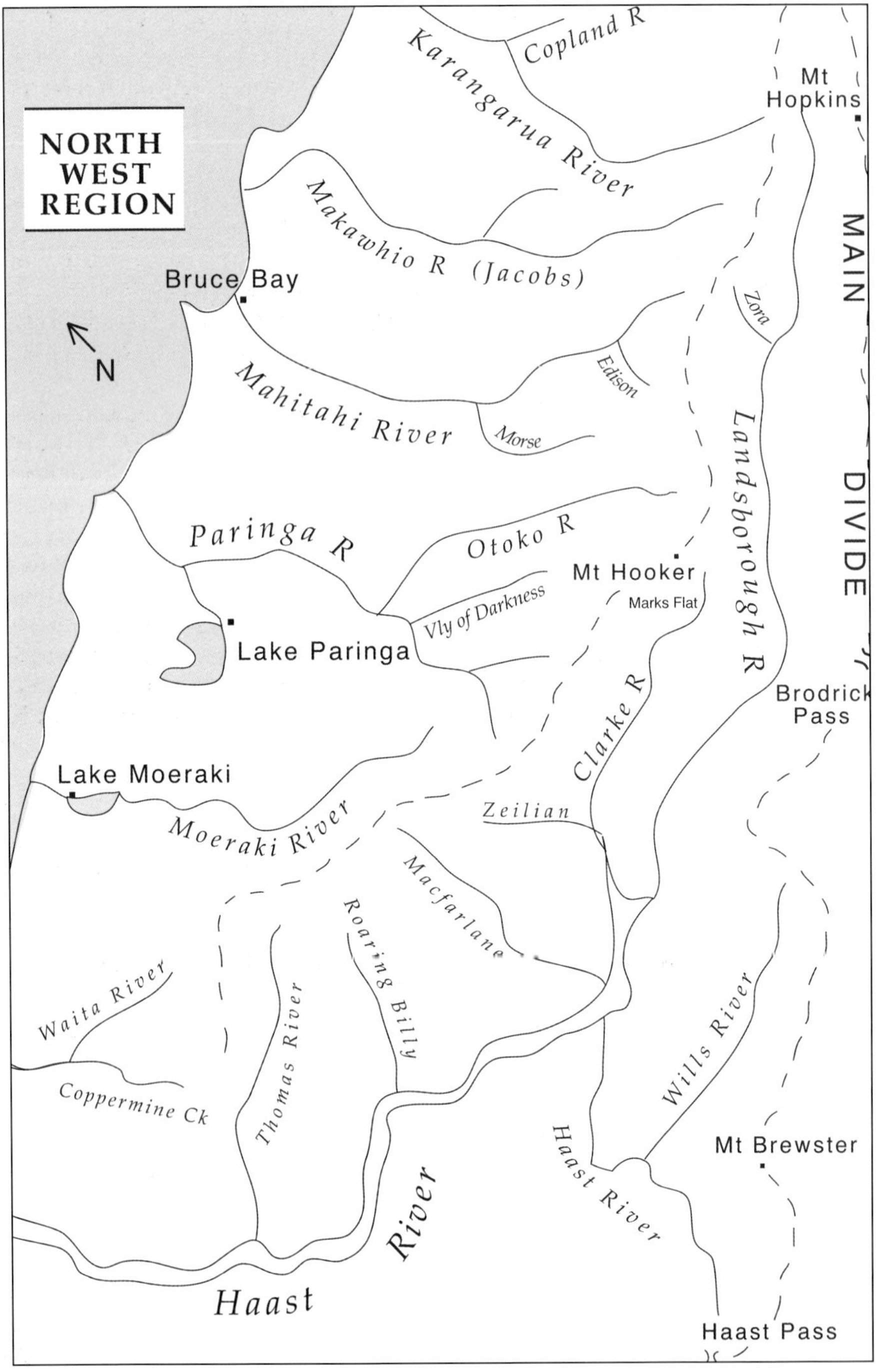
NORTH WEST REGION
N
Copland R
Karangarua River
Mt Hopkins
Makawhio R (Jacobs)
Bruce Bay
MAIN DIVIDE
Zora
Edison
Mahitahi River
Morse
Landsborough R
Paringa R
Otoko R
Mt Hooker
Marks Flat
Vly of Darkness
Lake Paringa
Clarke R
Brodrick Pass
Lake Moeraki
Zeilian
Moeraki River
Macfarlane
Roaring Billy
Waita River
Thomas River
Coppermine Ck
Wills River
Mt Brewster
Haast River
Haast River
Haast Pass

PART 4: THE NORTH WEST REGION

The Landsborough to the Karangarua

INTRODUCTION

Routes in each catchment generally begin with a description up the main valley and over the pass at the head, followed by the major tributaries and side routes. The heart of stormy South Westland, this region is characterised by green jungle and wild craggy peaks that even on a 10 day trip may never emerge from the mist. It is a land of high humidity, silty, bouldery rivers, and difficult travel, not to be taken lightly. It will only suit those with considerable experience and fitness, and is not an area to tramp alone in.

Beyond the roadedge, facilities are limited. They are no frills, but ideal as they are, provided they are looked after. There is a reasonable track into the Smoothwater, up the Moeraki, and over the Haast-Paringa cattle track. A good track also leads up to Brewster Bivvy. There aren't many others. Hunters fly in to use some huts as bases, such as the Thomas and Roaring Billy. Commercially guided rafting trips operate from Creswicke Flat down the Landsborough. Marks Flat in the upper Clarke is now part of a gazetted wilderness area. DoC Visitor Centres are located at Makarora, Haast and Fox Glacier.

The weather and climate are similar to the SW Region. High, unpredictable rainfall and sudden storms characterise the area. The bedrock is schist, a metamorphic rock, culminating in isolated peaks like Mt Hooker, which rears above the Otoko. The western valleys, from the Moeraki to the Karangarua, are wetter and more difficult to travel in than the Landsborough tends to be, but the Landsborough has its own problems in the difficult Strutt Bluff. Sheer river size often rules out river crossings.

Forests are thick and impenetrable to the west. Silver beech predominates in the south, with rata and kamahi taking over further north. The Landsborough Catchment is mostly comprised of beech, with lots of red lower down, and silver upvalley. Blue ducks love the place, as do kakas, bellbirds and higher up, keas.

Those interested in climbing should consult the excellent guide by Ross Cullen, *Barron Saddle to Mt Brewster,* published by the NZAC in 2002. DoC have useful information sheets available for some valleys.

Some trip possibilities, mostly strenuous, requiring good bush and often alpine skills, include;

- Haast-Paringa Cattle Track/Mateketeke tops, 3 days.
- Elcho Pass/Brodrick Pass, 5 days.
- Otoko/Clarke/Zeilian/Moeraki, 2 weeks.
- Huxley/Brodrick/SolutionRange/Marks Flat and out via the Otoko or Paringa or Moeraki, 2 weeks.

BREWSTER HUT AND GLACIER

This is now probably the most accessible glacier for tramping parties in the area. It is a great place for people of all levels of ambition and abilities to visit, from climbing Brewster to exploring the melt-water lakes of the glacial snout. The glacier is especially attractive, showing more white ice and less moraine than many others.

Stop at the Fantail Falls carpark on SH6, just on the western side of Haast Pass. Follow the falls track down to the riverbed and cross (wet feet) to the start of the Brewster Hut track, 100m below the falls on the true right. This marked track climbs steeply to bushline and continues to tiny Brewster Hut (4 bunks, no stove or cooking facilities, DoC cat 3) at the 1450m contour, beside tarns on a flat spot on the ridge with wonderful views. The Brewster Glacier is easily accessible by ascending to about the 1650m contour and sidling north through small bluffs and a rocky gully. Beyond the hut, watch out for mist obscuring the route. Mt Armstrong directly above the hut is also an easy scramble, offering great views. A route requiring transalpine experience and gear crosses to the upper Makarora River. See Makarora Valley notes.

Times: Road to hut, about 3.5 hrs up and 2.5 hrs down.

WILLS VALLEY Haast Pass Highway to Wills Hut

A signposted track begins at the Gates of Haast Bridge on the up valley true right corner. Initially, keeping its height above the river, the track crosses second growth on slip debris from a major rock avalanche in the 1980's. However, markers soon lead to the old benched track formation. This continues to the Wills/Haast confluence about 25 mins from the road. A bridge, now long gone, once crossed the Wills here, and the benched track continued to Haast Pass. The Wills Track instead swings left, climbing then sidling up the Wills Gorge on the true right. The track is rough, and keeps about 100m above the river on average. There is a ladder on the second slip (keep your height while crossing the slip) near the top of the gorge. After further sidling in forest, the track descends in a tongue of prickly shield fern beside beech trees and ends as marked on G38. Cross to grassy flats on the true left.

Large grassy flats extend up valley from here. Continue up the flats for about 40 mins to Wills Hut, crossing as necessary. Wills Hut (sleeps 4, pot belly stove, great condition, DoC cat 3) is on the true left on a grass terrace close to the bush edge, about 300m upstream from Fleming Creek, a little downstream of the mapped position on G38 Ed.1.

Time: Road to Hut, about 5 or 6 hrs.

WILLS HUT TO VALLEY HEAD

From Wills Hut, follow up the flats. Cross as necessary. From the end of the flats follow the true left up valley to the bushline. Opposite Dukes Creek, a good hour from the hut, the river runs through an impressive bedrock gorge. This is easily sidled in open beech nearby. Further up, at about G37 308 809 there are campsites in mossy glades near the river. Beyond here there is a gravel flat, above which the river climbs in boulders and it is necessary in places to sidle on bush slopes. Travel is time consuming and demanding, but not difficult.

Further up, boulders and scree near river level provide better going, with occasional climbs around big boulders. At the bushline, still on the true left, climb over a small shoulder about 50m above the river to avoid a big boulder and sidle open scrub on a reasonable deer trail down to the upper flats. Open flats lead from here to the head under Wilson Pass. About 100m upvalley from Cheap Creek, at G37 340 825, there is a poor bivvy rock, open to the SW, that would sleep 2.

Times: Hut to top flats bush edge, 3.5 hrs; Bush edge to head of the valley, 1hr.

Looking down the Wills Valley from the tops above Tole Creek.

WILSON PASS Wills to the Hunter

Steep snow on this crossing may make an iceaxe necessary until mid January. From the Wills, if the pass is snowfree, it is little more than a scree climb to ascend gravel and a rocky spur on the north side of the shallow gully draining the pass itself. However, the more usual approach, particularly if snow is lying on upper slopes, begins up a stream to the south. Draining from the south, a tributary under the pass swings west at G37 364 845. Follow this stream up, then climb on the true right of it and gain a tussock bench at about the 1500m contour. This bench leads diagonally left (going up), climbing only slightly to the south end of the pass.

The first 200m of the descent to the Hunter Valley is quite steep, but after that it eases. About 20m above and to the south of the pass, descend snow or scree and swing north to follow a rib on the true right of the stream marked on G37 draining the pass towards the Hunter. There is an old deer trail on this rib, which is tussocky higher up and rocky and steep towards the bottom. From the basin at about the 1340m contour, head diagonally down valley, crossing a continuous strip of scrub at the 1040m contour by a beech tree. Continue to the start of the marked route following cairns, poles, then a big orange triangle at the 900m contour, G37 383 834. See Hunter Valley notes.

Time: Head of the Wills to the start of the marked route in the Hunter, about 3 to 4 hrs.

OTHER ROUTES FROM THE WILLS VALLEY

THE BEALEY RANGE can be approached from either directly opposite Wills Hut or opposite Torrance Creek, down valley. In fine weather, the Bealey Range offers great views of Mt Brewster. It can be traversed for several kilometres and generally reasonable spurs with little subalpine scrub lead off it towards the Landsborough from the bush edge. Avoid travel in the creeks.

CROSSING TO LONG FLAT CREEK in the Hunter. Either follow Fleming Creek for 20 mins (not including the shingle fan at the bottom) then enter the bush to the east from a scrubby terrace, or climb directly up the spur between the hut and Fleming Creek. Continue up through the bush. The easiest travel through minor bluffs is about 200 to 300m from the creek. Once in the tussock sidle above the creek, negotiating a bluff, and continue to Long Flat Saddle. There is a bivvy rock

on the way up at the 1260m contour, G38 262 782, sleeping about 4. Descend from the east end of the saddle into Long Flat Creek. See Hunter Valley notes.

WILLS PASS TO FERGUSON CREEK in the Hunter. Climb the bush face opposite Dredge Creek. The face soon becomes a spur. Above the scrub, easy tussock leads to Wills Pass. From the pass, descend into the head of the valley. Alternatively, about 1km south of the pass, benches lead to a spur at G38 325 786, and the valley. See Hunter Valley notes.

TOLE CREEKBED offers open gravel and boulder travel up to the tops. Higher up, the creekbed is steeper, but there are reasonable routes out on the true right, a little above the bushline. Once in the tussock, sidles can be made to either Wills or Long Flat Saddles. Be aware that the gully can be subject to loose stones from above, particularly in wet weather.

LANDSBOROUGH CATCHMENT

The Landsborough River flows parallel to the Main Divide for more than 60km, and drains heavily glaciated peaks on both sides of the valley. It follows that attempting to ford the river in its lower reaches is always a very serious undertaking, never to be tried when the river is other than low. There is no easy way on foot into or out of the head. When the river is in flood routes up or down valley are impassable and alternative exits all involve high alpine crossings. Parties should familiarise themselves with as many routes in the area as possible. Over much of the valley, the true left is the better side to travel on.

There are few huts and tracks in the catchment. A small old hunters' hut at Creswicke Flat (Fraser Hut) has been recently maintained. A rafting company also has a semipermanent tarpaulin camp just below Harpers Bluff. An old A frame hut between the Landsborough and the Clarke Rivers, 200m south of the yards marked on G37, may be removed.

Jet boats can be taken to above Strutt Bluff, and sometimes further. For this service contact Neil Ross or Roger Crow, Waiatoto River Jet (ph 03 750 0780 or 0800 538 723). They are based behind the DoC Centre at Haast in the Red Barn. Other Haast jet boat operators may also be able to help. Helicopters are frequently used by hunters and others to fly into the catchment. Contact Morgan Saxton (ph 03 750 0866) based by SH6 near Haast township, amongst others, for this service. Planes can be chartered to fly to airstrips at Harper, Creswicke, and Toetoe Flats. See Paul Cooper (Southern Alps Air, Makarora ph 0800 345 666, $510 per planeload of 3 passengers and gear from Makarora) amongst others for this service. These days, many of the people visiting this catchment enter or leave by one of the services above, but not all. There are also commercially guided rafting trips during summer down the Landsborough from about Creswicke Flat, run by Queenstown Rafting.

HAAST PASS HIGHWAY TO CRESWICKE FLAT (Fraser Hut)

A gate 100m SE of the Pleasant Flat bridge on the Haast Pass Highway marks the start of a rough 2WD road to the Landsborough Homestead (at G37 252 856). This road leads down the true right of the Haast past a hunting lodge, generally following the bush edge into the Landsborough Valley and crossing numerous gravel fords en-route.

Either follow this road or cross the Haast River about 2km upstream from Clarke Bluff and approach the valley from that direction. There is also an airstrip 500m north of the homestead. The 2WD road ceases at the Homestead. Seek permission from the manager at Landsborough Station and be careful not to disturb stock. On foot or by 4WD, continue along the farm track up valley as marked on G37. Although the last kilometre is not marked, the farm track continues right to Strutt Bluff, keeping towards the bush edge.

If the river is low, the river can be crossed here, immediately below the bluff, on a reasonable ford. A second ford, not quite as good, leads back to the true left above the bluff. There is a better ford at the bottom of Harper Flat if necessary, but this will require bush sidling about 40m up for about 400m on the true right to get up to it. Strutt Bluff is one of two bluffs (Strutt and Harper) to negotiate on the true left if the river cannot be crossed. Harper Bluff is tracked and reasonably straightforward. Strutt Bluff is not and is much more difficult, particularly travelling up valley. Parties should carry a rope going either way. The route over Strutt Bluff previously described in *Moir's* and a more recent DoC pamphlet does not seem to have been used for many years. A recently used alternative is described instead, but it is very steep to carry packs over. It would be better used as an exit from the valley than to enter it by.

■ Left: The Landsborough Valley just above the Zora confluence. Pt 1550m to the left and pt 1845m to the right.

STRUTT BLUFF going up valley. Enter the bush near the river at the base of the bluff where the farm track finishes. Follow up the spur overlooking the river. Open beech forest gives easy travel to pt 384m beyond which is a saddle at G37 296 886. On the down valley side of this saddle is a small open Sphagnum swamp clearing marked on G37 that drains towards Quarry Creek. On the up valley side of this saddle drop 120m generally straight down open, very steep forest on a small rib between two shallow gullies, both of which develop into small slips. The steepness is such that the rib cannot be descended directly, but a careful recce should establish a useable line. At the bottom of the rib, where the forest finishes and the two slips join a short sidle to the right (looking down) leads to old mahoe, wineberry and nettle (*Urtica ferox*) covered scree slopes. The rest of the descent to the riverbank is reasonably open and easy with care.

STRUTT BLUFF going down valley. The steep section of this route is a little easier to ascend. As Strutt Bluff is approached from upstream, a clear saddle with sky visible low down behind silhouetted trees is seen ahead, 100m SE of pt 384m. Under the saddle, a very steep rib of bush flanked by recent slips, extends almost to the gentler shrub covered scree base. Follow a side channel of the river to the closest point underneath the saddle. Pick a route through the Mahoe and nettle up to the base of the steeper section and slightly left of the rib at G37 298 886. Don't allow nettle to force the party too far to the left (looking up). Check out a route climbing to the right up into the open bush on the rib. The rib remains partly eroded and very steep. Higher up sidle across a few metres into the slip on the right (looking up) and exit it on the right (looking up) again on a diagonal rock ledge in the bush near the top, when it is impractically steep to continue the last 20m directly up. From the saddle, easy travel in forest leads down the ridge to the farm track at the base of the spur.

Continuing up valley above Strutt Bluff, follow the true left beside the river to grassy Harper Flat. Continue up past the airstrip, along the river edge to the foot of Harper Bluff, where bedrock halts travel along the river bank. There is a small flood channel from the river here, under the trees. This dry gravel course cuts through the bush to Harper Flat. About 20m below the bluffs and the flood channel, close to the river on the true left, is a tarpaulin camp belonging to a commercial rafting company at G37 339 922.

HARPER BLUFF going up valley. A stoat trapping trackline has been marked over Harper Bluff, pretty much following the standard route described below. Find the markers on the corner and climb up the bush spur from roughly where the flood channel leaves the main river. They continue up the spur to the 380m contour where there is a definite saddle, 30 mins from the river and lead to the up valley lip where bluffs begin at G37 344 918. Here, antlers, old blazes and the markers indicate the start of the old blazed descent through bluffs, sidling down to the right from the lip. Follow the markers and blazes diagonally down to an old stable scree slope covered in waterfern (*Histiopteris* sp) under the forest at about the 300m contour. Descend, sidling right to the gravel flat slightly upstream by the river again.

HARPER BLUFF going down valley. Pick up the DoC stoat control track markers near the end of gravel flats and head up towards the bluff. They largely follow the old line through the bluffs as described below. Looking downstream from the gravel flat on the true left of the Landsborough River at G37 347 920, they aim for the base of a steep gully left of the bluffs, at about the 300m contour, G37 345 918. Here, a very small slip of vegetation at the base of the bluffs has exposed bare rock, and about 30m away, the markers, old blazes and cairns continue up and across to the right between bluffs towards the saddle, only 10 or 15 mins further on. Easy travel follows, following markers down the spur for 20 mins to the river edge and Harper Flat.

Alternatively, if the river is very low, Harper Bluff can be bypassed by crossing the river at the top of Harper Flat, sidling and crossing back to the true left near Larson Creek. The Larson Creek crossing though, is confined, swift and deeper than crossings down at Harper Flat, and some report it as impractical to cross even at low flows. Generally, the track described over Harper Bluff itself is much more preferable, reasonably straightforward and climbs no more than 200m.

Beyond Harper Bluff, boulder hop up the riverbed. There is recent windfall on some of the bush flats and an excellent campsite at G37 350 922 in an open glade. Travelling becomes easier beyond Golden Point. Fraser Hut (sleeps 4, open fire, DoC cat 4) is in the open on Creswicke Flat

Times: Pleasant Flat bridge to Strutt Bluff, 4 hrs; Crossing Strutt Bluff, 2.5 hrs, or 30 mins crossing the river twice; Strutt Bluff to Harper Bluff, 2 hrs; Crossing Harper Bluff, 1 hr 20 mins, or 30 mins crossing the river twice; Harper Bluff to Fraser Hut, about 5.5 hrs.

CRESWICKE FLAT TO ZORA CONFLUENCE

The true left generally offers better going all the way from Creswicke Flat to Romping Water in the headwaters, although the choice of route up valley will depend on trip plans and river conditions. River crossing options are usually very limited, and the true right has a messy bluff and Zora Creek to contend with. There is a good easy crossing up at Romping Water in normal conditions.

Lower down, in the central valley where the river is much bigger, if the river is not easily crossable and only one crossing is contemplated, Ford Flat probably offers the best option. Ford Flat is not named on G37, but is at approx G37 482 995. Creswicke and Hinds Flats also have reasonable crossing places. Travel on either side is mostly by the river with flats and occasional bush sidles. Some streams can be difficult to cross.

On the **true left** of the Landsborough from Creswicke to the Zora, travel is generally boulder hopping, grass flats, and open bush sidling, mostly by the river. From Fraser Hut to rafters Flycamp at G37 463 968 will take a good 2 hrs, and from there to Kea Stream will take another good 2 hrs. On Kea Flat, the remains of an old camp at G37 493 010 are stacked away in a box and may be of some use in an emergency.

On the **true right,** difficult stream crossings include Pass Creek, a stream at G37 499 028 just up valley from the slip mentioned below, and another creek at H37 527 052. Most have crossings a little upstream though. Zora Creek, which is considerably larger than the others, is bouldery and confined in a single channel near the river. Extensive ice fields in the headwaters mean it swells with afternoon snow melt. It can be particularly difficult to cross, is often marginal and requires considerable care. Many parties have had difficulties with it. The bivouac marked on ToeToe Flat true right appears to have gone.

On the true right of the Landsborough, there is also an active slip at G37 498 027, against which the river flows for 300m, necessitating a sidle at anything other than very low flows. This involves climbing up 150m, will take about 1.5 to 2 hrs, and although better avoided, is negotiable. Leave the river at the downstream end of the slip, G37 499 025. Climb steeply but easily through the bush for 35 mins, then when the slope flattens out, sidle and descend to the large stream upvalley. The problem is that this descent is very steep initially, and in one place ropes have been resorted to. The route drops into a vegetated gully and follows it straight down to the sidestream. Continue down the sidestream to the riverbed again at G37 499 028.

Time: Creswicke Flat to Zora Creek, about 9 hrs on the true left, and a good 10 hrs on the true right.

ZORA CONFLUENCE TO THE MCKERROW GLACIER

Either side can be used, but again, the true left seems preferable. Continuing up on the **true left,** apart from one small bluff at H37 577 081 below Arthur Creek, it is possible to sidle beside the river with very little need to enter the bush. This one small bluff can be passed relatively easily by a sidle around it in the bush (or if river levels are low, by crossing the Landsborough twice). Some major streams are crossed enroute. However, both the largest, the Rubicon and Le Blanc (Romping Water), are much easier to cross than the Zora. Just above the Le Blanc (Romping Water) confluence, the Landsborough itself can usually be crossed to the true right. Cross, and from about Fiasco Creek access the start of tussock benches about 60m above the river on the true right. These provide good

The upper Landsborough Valley from the slopes of Mt Fettes.

travel to the gravel flats under Karangarua Saddle. Here, the river runs hard against big slabby bluffs off Karangarua Saddle, making a crossing of the river back to the true left essential. Crossing is not normally a problem on the fine gravel flats. Eroding scree slopes lead to moraine on the McKerrow Glacier. All routes beyond here require alpine equipment and experience.

On the **true right**, beyond Zora Creek there is about 20 mins travel by the river until bluffs force a bush sidle. It should not be necessary to climb more than 60m above the river and in 30 mins or less the riverbed is reached again. Boulder hop on up until a huge boulder undercut by the river blocks river travel, about 400m before Struggle Creek. This necessitates a second bush sidle. Climb onto a bush terrace and follow it, overlooking the river. Then climb onto a higher terrace and follow it up towards the corner 150m below Struggle Creek. Continue about 40m above and overlooking the Landsborough, until the Struggle Creek junction. Finding a route down gravel banks into Struggle Creek may lead parties 100 or 200m up this creek first.

Easier boulder travel continues up valley, though there are a couple of boulders to sidle behind between Arbor Rift and Eager Creek. Whitcombe Creek is easily crossed on fine gravel flats upstream, where there was a lake in the 1970s. More boulder hopping and sidling leads to Fiasco Creek, above which there are good terraces about 60m above the river that lead to gravel flats under Karangarua Saddle. The route up the Spence past Scissors Peak to the Mueller Glacier is described on P. 171 of Ross Cullen's *Barron Saddle to Mt Brewster Guide*, published by the NZAC.

Times: Either side, Zora to Whitcombe Creek/Baffle ravine, about 5.5 to 6.5 hrs; Whitcombe Creek to McKerrow Glacier at base of the climb to Douglas Pass, about 6 to 7 hrs.

BIVVY ROCKS in the headwaters. The bivvy rock marked at H36 609 111 is 15 mins river travel beyond the slip upstream of Whitcombe Creek on the true right of the Landsborough. Here, 50m up valley from the guttery stream draining the Beith Glacier, perched on the edge of a terrace 25m above the river, is a large rock. Rockwalls help protect it from the south, from which it is exposed. It sleeps about 4, is cairned on top, and is known as Beith Rock.

On the true left of the Landsborough, there is a good bivvy rock 600m up Le Blanc Stream at H36 626 117 on a scrubby flat. It is quite close to Le Blanc Stream, on the true left opposite Romping Water and sleeps 5 or 6, but is exposed to the NW.

Another bivvy rock, difficult to see from a distance, but cairned on top, is on the true right of Repulse Creek.

The bivvy rock on the true right of Rubicon Torrent is accurately marked at H36 634 131, and is the largest rock in the vicinity. It has rockwalls on both sides and a cairn on top.

DOUGLAS PASS McKerrow Glacier to Christmas Flat Hut

Although this is probably the easiest route out of the head of the Landsborough, it is still an alpine route, climbing to over 2000m. Skills and equipment for that will be required and of course, fair weather. From the McKerrow Glacier, climb a series of slumping gravel benches up to Douglas Pass. Thats the easy part. Follow the ridge north up snow and rock bands to The Gladiator. Descend the ridge (slightly on the Douglas Valley side) to Mt Howitt, which can be bypassed 40m down on the north side and gain the ridge leading towards pt 1799m and The Pommel.

Between Mt Howitt and pt 1799m, descend a leading scree rib and sidle across some guts to about H36 634 160, then continue sidling down and west below Karangarua Saddle to stream forks at H36 621 154. From there stay in, or close to, the streambed below the bluffs. The going is bouldery, with a couple of short scrub bashes on the true right, but travel is otherwise reasonable down to the main forks at H36 617 159. Below these forks, travel down the infant Karangarua is easy. This is the best route and it avoids most of the thick scrub, but is not recommended after heavy snowfall as bluffs on the true left of the creek would be very avalanche prone.

Alternatively, a long descending sidle on gravel, then tussock leads towards a small spur on the true left of Baking Oven Creek, at about H36 621 170. Keep on the true left of this creek and its marked tributaries, looking for the easiest line in tussock and low scrub. The descent through this area isn't bad, but is too complex to describe in detail. Care needs to be taken not to get caught up in scrub and slabby bluffs. Hit the creek at the 800m contour below slabs and falls. Follow it down (easy) to Christmas Flat Hut. See Karangarua Valley notes.

Times: McKerrow Glacier to Douglas Pass, 1 hr; Douglas Pass to Mt Howitt, 2.5 hrs; Mt Howitt to Christmas Flat Hut, 3 hrs; Douglas Pass to Harpers Bivvy Rock, 1.5 hrs.

HARPERS BIVVY ROCK can also be approached from Douglas Pass. Descend to the north from the pass 100 or 200m distance, then cut back on slippery tussock and rock slopes to the right, descending to the stream at H36 664 164. Coming up from the bottom, pick up a cairn at the start of the route, about H36 665 165. Moss flats lead to Harpers Bivvy Rock (sleeps 6 easily, cairn on top).

Information beyond here should be sought from park staff at Fox Glacier. Although a difficult, eroding route has been used along slopes above Lake Douglas on the true right in the 1990s, it is not easy or always practical. The route out from Horace Walker Hut is a high level sidle in the tussock zone to an old marked track off the saddle east of Conical Hill. The river is very badly gorged. Or alternatively an alpine route leads over Welcome Pass, sidles to Scott Creek, and descends to the Copland.

ELCHO PASS North Elcho Stream to Kea Flat

This is an alpine crossing of the Main Divide and requires some alpine skills and equipment. From the upper North Elcho Stream (see Hopkins Valley notes) ascend slopes to a gully at H37 538 977. Continue up a moderately steep snow gully to flatter slopes at the 1740m contour. Alternatively, follow the stony slopes beside the gully, depending on conditions. Steeper slopes above lead to the pass.

On the Landsborough side, traverse north from Elcho Pass at about the 1940m contour to a ridge off Baker Peak. Descend this ridge between Kea Stream and McKerrow Creek. At about the 1700m contour, erosion on both sides of the ridge makes travel on the ridge slightly exposed and tricky, but it remains a reasonable route. There are poor but useable campsites and tiny tarns near the bushline at about the 1200m contour. From the bushline, follow the ridge to the west, keeping above bluffs that drop into Kea Stream, down to the Landsborough Valley.

Times: Allow a long day for the crossing.

BRODRICK PASS Brodrick Hut to Creswicke Flat

In 1896 D. Matheson of Freehold Creek, Lake Ohau, took horses over the pass and down to bushline on the Landsborough side. From Brodrick Hut, a partly cairned route leads through subalpine scrub and tussock terraces to about G37 472 881 at the start of the climb up to Brodrick Pass (see photo, P 200). Follow up tussock slopes on a spur overlooking a stream basin under the pass at G37 468 887. Continue up the basin, then sidle to the right (looking up) at about the 1560m contour, climbing to the pass.

To reach the Landsborough from the pass, descend to the right down scree and tussock on an old ground trail to upper McKenzie Creek. Boulder hop down the creek to the cairned start of a trail leading out on the true left at G37 448 910. This is a little before the first bush on the true right of the creek is reached. The trail climbs to the left through light scrub to a high terrace (campsites) then intermittent permolat markers enter the bush and a light trail leads up to a viewpoint on the ridge at G37 446 910. This ridge is narrow and steep sided, and descends from Mt Strauchon, separating the main McKenzie Creek from its true left tributary. About 20m below and before this viewpoint, the descent trail splits off and heads down the spur to lower McKenzie Creek. This trail follows intermittent permolat markers down the spur, finishing 300m above the forks in the true left branch of McKenzie Creek at G37 438 919. Follow the stream down.

In the reverse direction, follow McKenzie Creek up from Creswicke Flat until the creek forks at G37 440 921. Then, once beyond the cairn 300m up the true left branch, climb up the spur. Old blazes/permolat mark the route in places. Further up, the trail leads to an excellent viewpoint on the ridge, just above bushline. About 20m before the viewpoint, the trail sidles left, descending off the ridge into McKenzie Creek. Follow up this creek, boulder hopping. From well up the creek, a ground trail leads right through tussock and scree to Brodrick Pass. Brodrick Hut is visible from the pass.

From Brodrick Pass, sidle down to the right into a basin at G37 467 887, and follow the stream in this basin down. Before it steepens swing to the true right and follow down tussock spur slopes to the Huxley River. Head directly down to Brodrick Hut, following cairns through odd scrub bands. The marked track down valley starts behind the hut. See Huxley Valley in the Hopkins Valley notes.

From the McKenzie Creek basin, there is an alternative but poorer descent route to the Landsborough. Climb about 250m onto the spur on the true right of McKenzie Creek. Keeping on it, follow the spur down to the Landsborough. Where the spur divides at bushline, follow the northern spur. There are good campsites with fresh water on Brodrick Pass. There are also good campsites in McKenzie Creek in the vicinity of the bushline, both in the bush and in the open.

Times: Brodrick Hut to Brodrick Pass, 3 hrs; Pass to bushline, 2 or 3 hrs; Bushline to Landsborough, 2 to 3 hrs.

OTHER NOTES

Studholme Pass is covered in Hunter Valley notes and the Bealey Range in Wills Valley notes. **Surveyors Col** has been mentioned in previous editions as a Main Divide crossing point. This is not a tramping pass, and a poor transalpine route unless conditions are good. **Charity Col** is occasionally used by well equipped alpine parties. In the past, parties descending the stream from the Arthur Glacier have used the true left. A difficult alpine route has been used from the **Landsborough to the Mueller via Mt Scissors.** *Moir's* has got to stop somewhere, and this is it. See *Barron Saddle to Mt Brewster Guide,* by Ross Cullen, P 171.

ZORA CREEK

From its source in the Zircon Glacier, this creek meanders over glacial flats before plunging down through the wonderfully wild Zora Canyon to small flats again beside the Landsborough. A route on the true left of Zora Creek gives access to Mueller Pass and the Mahitahi Valley. Zora Creek is very confined and difficult to cross between the Canyon and the Landsborough.

From H37 547 067 near the Landsborough, climb a bush spur between two creeks on the true left of Zora Creek to bushline. Only one of these creeks is shown on the map. The spur is narrow and the bush thicker higher up. Sidle and descend north into a gully, (dont go too high) and follow up the true right fork when the gully branches at H37 550 073. In the streambed 40m height above the forks, there is an awkward rock slab to ascend or bypass on the true right. Above it, follow grass slopes up and sidle across above bushline between the 900 and 1000m contours before descending onto a shelf at H37 547 083. The route climbs a little to cross a gully then old trails lead easily through bluffs to the next ledge.

Continue north through a basin of tall tussock on this ledge to H37 546 091, where it is possible to sidle round on trails in front (west) of a knob through a tiny patch of open beech. Beyond this beech, descend as soon as practical to where the riverbed flattens off at about H37 547 093, offering reasonable travel by the river upvalley. Flats then allow easy travel to the head. Crossing the stream here is normally easy. For climbing parties, the glaciers on Mt Fettes can be approached by ascending a steep bouldery gully beginning at H36 553 117. See the Mahitahi Valley notes for crossing Mueller Pass.

Time: Landsborough Valley to the upper Zora flats, about 4.5 hrs.

ALONG THE SOLUTION RANGE

The Solution Range is strategically positioned for wonderful views of Mt Hooker. Much of the range is tussock from midsummer on, and the whole range can be traversed along the tops from the bushline to Mt Gow. Beyond Mt Gow, steep loose rotten rock towers make further travel along the range impractical.

There is also a section about 1.5 km NE of Mt Solution at about pt 1522m where the range cannot be traversed along the crest due to actively eroding rock. This can be bypassed with care about 60m down on steep gravel on the Clarke River side. Traversing on the Landsborough side is not feasible. Eroded, but more stable gravel slopes continue to pt 1530m, where tussock and easier travel begins again.

The bush ridge out to Clarke Mound from the tussock is mostly open beech forest. Long troughs in the ridge provide easy travel, but there is little water and care is required to not drop off to the side. A long ascent can be made to this ridge through sometimes steep but mostly open bush from the Clarke Valley at G37 335 956 to a saddle east of Clarke Mound. Approaches can also be made from the Landsborough.

ACROSS THE SOLUTION RANGE Toetoe Flat to Marks Flat

This is an excellent tramping route. Follow the broad, open bush face up from G37 456 969 at the back of Toetoe Flat. Other spurs at the bottom of Toetoe Flat can also be used. Gain the ridge to the NW and follow it up to its junction with the Solution Range at G37 435 980. The bushline is clear of scrub. Traverse the range NE to the saddle and descend a spur at G37 440 995 to Marks Flat. This spur is relatively free of scrub and has a good deer trail on it in places. See Clarke Valley notes.

An alternative crossing is also described, but in reverse. It finishes further up the Landsborough. From Marks Flat, use the same spur as above (beginning at G37 436 998), to reach the Solution Range. At G37 451 997 there is an excellent fine weather campsite beside tarns. From about G37 454 995, go SE straight down tussock slopes towards the Landsborough, past a group of tarns impounded behind slip terraces and into open forest. Continue down to reach the River at about G37 464 977. Note that above the bushline on this descent, a heavy deer trail leads NE through the tussock. Ignore it.

Times: Marks Flat Bivvy rock (most easterly one) to the Solution Range campsite, 2 hrs; From the campsite to the Landsborough, 3 hrs.

UPPER OTOKO PASS is a more difficult alpine crossing. It can be reached from Kea Flat by following up Pass Creek until a snowgrass spur on the true right leads up and into a snow basin. After a high sidle over steep slopes, a small spur leads to the pass. A high route to the pass has also been used, involving the ridge on the true left of Pass Creek and sidling under Mt Gorden. The Solution Range in this area is steep and eroding though, and the routes from Toetoe Flat or G37 464 977 leading over Lower Otoko Pass provide a much better line from the Landsborough to the Otoko.

THE CLARKE VALLEY

LANDSBOROUGH CONFLUENCE TO MONRO FLAT

This major Landsborough tributary can be approached from the Haast Pass Highway the same way as the Landsborough as far as the flats just below Strutt Bluff. However, crossing the Landsborough will be a major obstacle for most parties. Alternatively a jetboat can be used. See Landsborough notes. An A frame hut at G37 291 899, about 200m south of the yards marked on G37, may be removed. Follow the flats on the true left and cross the river to the true right at Rabbit Flat. The true right is now followed to Monro Flat.

The route continues through bush to the extensive grass flat below Rough Creek. Rough Creek Hut no longer exists. A door propped against a tree is the only indication of its past location at the top of the flat. Continue through a tongue of bush to the gravel flats of Rough Creek.

At G37 340 961 it will usually be necessary to climb up to a terrace and sidle upvalley. Cross a marked but unnamed stream (which reaches the Clarke at G37 344 962). Beyond this stream, follow up a gully to a saddle 300m north of pt 497m and descend to Davies Flat at the northern corner G37 358 968. Old blazes may be seen on this route. Another gorge needs to be sidled at the top of this flat from G37 366 968, climbing over a ridge at the 500m contour and descending to the valley upstream. Cross to take advantage of Monro flats if the river level allows. Murdock Creek and the Clarke River are similar in size at their confluence, but Murdock is more confined and difficult to cross. Continue up to Saddle Creek, staying on the true left if necessary.

Times: Landsborough confluence to Rough Creek, 4 to 5 hrs; Rough Creek to Davies Flat, about 2.5 hrs; Davies flat to Saddle Creek, about 3.5 hrs.

Across the Clarke Valley from the spur between Zeilian and Rough Creeks, to the Solution Range and peaks on the Main Divide.

MONRO FLAT TO MARKS FLAT

From here there are two routes to Marks Flat. The first leads up the gorge. The second leads up Saddle Creek.

THE GORGE is less fearsome than it looks. With a bit of care, a sidling ascent through bush on the true left, keeping 60 to 120m above the river all the way, leads through to Marks Flat without too much difficulty. Looking up the Clarke riverbed from the Saddle Creek confluence, bluffs can be seen on the true right. A little higher, on the true left, just the top of a bouldery slip can be seen. This old and largely stable slip extends from bluffs near the ridge to the river. It is easily crossed about 100m above the river at about G37 406 996. This is the key to the route.

Follow bush terraces beside the river until cataracts begin. Then climb, keeping about 60m height above the river, and more as the slip is approached. Cross the slip on old trails through short open scrub at about the 760m contour to the upstream edge. Cairns may be seen en-route. Climb this slip edge until at least 120m above the river at about the 860m contour. Sidle at this height in reasonable bush towards the flats upstream. Sidle across to the river at about the 900m contour, and continue up to the flats, climbing behind big boulders that drop to the river near the bush edge. At the start of the flats, scrub along the bank can partly be avoided by popping into the open bush fringe behind it for a few hundred metres.

SADDLE CREEK finishes by the Clarke in a flourish of gravel. The stream, however, is sidled through bush on the true right. Follow good ground trails up the spur between the Clarke and Saddle Creek to a terrace at about G37 400 990. Trails continue along this terrace, dropping to the main creek at the junction with Jack Creek, G37 412 984. Climb steeply up about 150m to a ledge (at the point where a pleasant creek crosses it). Helped by glimpses of odd, sparsely vegetated roche mou-

■ Marks Flat from snowline (G37 410 014) on the usual access route to Mt Hooker.

tonee outcrops marked at G37 421 988 and G37 425 988, travel is fairly easy through to the stream at G37 426 989. At the next gully upstream, a short scramble leads out to the saddle, where there are tarns and boggy campsites. The dome of Kea Cliffs, where there are many more tarns, can be approached from here. From the saddle, a ground trail leads leftwards down through open beech forest and then continues steeply down the spur to G37 431 997, at the edge of Marks Flat.

At **MARKS FLAT,** the northern fringe offers much, much better travel on shingle and short grass than the southern fringe does. The SE sector of Marks Flat is very swampy, with tall tussock. **Bivvy rocks on Marks flat.** The best bivvy rock on the flat is at G37 421 006, just under the 1000m contour, and has a large open area under it facing SE. It is cairned on top and holds about 5. There is a second bivvy rock at G37 417 005 on the true right of both the stream draining Mt Hooker and the Clarke River. It is cairned on top but is not well established or particularly comfortable for that matter. It is about 50m above the river.

There is a third bivvy rock opposite the stream off Mt Hooker on the true left of the Clarke as marked on G37. It is cairned, well built up and established but is small and dark. The 3 person sleeping bench is lower than the entrance.

There is also a huge boulder at about G37 411 002 further down the Clarke just below the bush edge on the true left about 10 to 20m above the river. It is about 50m downstream from where the river seriously begins to drop, and is easily picked up along the riverbank. Although this has not been used, there is a considerable dry area under it, about 10m by 5m. The losses are that it is slightly sloping and noisy, but hey, that's not so important when it is hosing down.

Times: Saddle Creek confluence to Marks Flat, either route, about 5.5 hrs; In the reverse direction, about 4.5 hrs.

LOWER OTOKO PASS Marks Flat to the upper Otoko Valley

The Clarke enters Marks Flat through a gorge. Routes from the flat begin on both sides but join half way and continue as one on the true right. Alternatively, the Solution Range itself can be traversed to almost Mt Gow, before descending to the Lower Otoko lake outlet.

On the **true right** about 150m before the Clarke gorges, a waterfall descends to the flat. Climb tussock and light scrub slopes between the fall and the river to about G37 439 007 and the 1100m contour. Head to the right, NE, up a small creek to the spur on the corner overlooking the gorge and sidle across scree slopes at about the 1280m contour. Descend up valley under bluffs to about the 1200m contour and climb back up into a gully at G37 446 010. Things don't look very attractive above here. Where the gully becomes difficult a reasonable route exists out to the east (right looking up). This leads up a tussock shelf, just above bluffs, where there should be 1 or 2 old cairns. This section is a key to the route. Follow the tussock spur up, gaining 100m altitude, sidle easily across the slopes on the true right of the Clarke and climb to the pass. This route is more direct.

On the **true left,** a variation exists via the Solution Range. Follow up the stream from Marks Flat at G37 439 002 and then the spur on the true left of it. This leads quickly through the scrub to the tussock. An easy sidle now leads across to reach the Clarke River at G37 447 009. Further travel is cut off by bluffs on the true left, and the river must be crossed to the true right, to join the above route in the gully at G37 446 010. Note that low level routes on the true left closer to the Clarke are effectively cut off by scrubby bluffs directly above Marks Flat.

The Lower Otoko Glacier finishes as a lake, with bluffs cutting off access around its fringes. From Lower Otoko Pass, climb about 60m up to the NE, around a knob onto a flat spur and follow it along almost 1.5km to G37 454 034, at the 1480m contour. Descend to the lake outlet, initially picking a route down small bluffs and tussock ledges, but mostly following old morainic debris. Take care, but travel is not difficult. The bouldery outlet stream can be followed down on the true right to the gravel flat in the head of the Otoko. Rock bluffs and a waterfall prevent the true left being used. Alternatively, a good option is to sidle from the outlet stream around above the scrub and descend the lower part of the stream draining Upper Otoko Pass. The gravel flat at G37 455 049 was a lake until about the 1980s.

In the reverse direction, once at the lake outlet, climb up the moraine to the east. Sidle along the bench beginning at the 1480m contour heading south. Descend to the pass and sidle down the Clarke on the true right. A careful recce may be needed to pick up the route down a tussock shoulder to the shelf leading into the gully at G37 446 010. A couple of cairns should be visible. On the true right below here, stay up and sidle easily under bluffs, cutting out onto the shoulder overlooking Marks Flat at about the 1240m contour. Alternatively below here cross to the true left at G37 447 009 and sidle easily out to the Solution Range.

Times: Marks Flat to Lower Otoko Pass, about 3 hrs; Pass to Otoko gravel flat, 3 hrs.

MCCULLAUGH CREEK Monro Flat to the headwaters

McCullaugh Creek can be entered on the true left. Start off near the stream and head directly up through the forest. Small bluffs and plenty of fern in numerous little creeks makes travel slow and arduous. From a shoulder at about the 860m contour, sidle across towards the stream on a good deer trail. (These do not help much lower down, unfortunately). Once above the gorge, at about G37 374 999, travel becomes reasonable in or close to the stream, but care is required to stay on a good line. Generally, stay on the true left. Some scrub in the valley floor can be bypassed by climbing up a sidestream at G37 373 003, sidling above scrub briefly and dropping down the next creek again at G37 372 006. Short grass campsites can be found at about G37 372 008 on the true left in the upper basin. For the crossing to the Paringa, see the Paringa Valley notes.

Time: Monro Flat to the upper flats, about 5 hrs.

ZEILIAN CREEK Clarke Valley to the headwaters

Zeilian Creek is badly gorged. Do not use it for access to the flats and basins of upper Zeilian Creek from the Clarke Valley. Instead, follow the good, reasonably open leading spur downstream from the confluence of Rough Creek and the Clarke up to bushline. Alternatively, the leading spur upstream of Zeilian Creek can be followed. Continue up small folds in the tussock ridge to the flat area 200m south of pt 1407m.

Descend west through humps and hollows into a basin at the 1300m contour. A descending sidle NW leads to a neck of bush at G37 307 989. Cross it into short scrub and tussock slopes beyond. Continue to sidle just above the 1000m contour to the next patch of forest, the upper most in the valley on the true left at G37 304 992. Descend to flats in the valley floor. Grass flats extend above and below here in Zeilian Creek, with good campsites available. Scrub at G37 298 993 can be sidled to the east. For crossings, see the Moeraki and Paringa Valley notes.

Times: Clarke to the upper Zeilian, about 6.5 hrs; going down, about 5 hrs.

THE ROARING BILLY

Most parties using this valley are hunters, who fly in. Crossing the Haast River here is seldom feasible. The cableway is locked. The old permolat marked route into the hut from the Haast is very steep initially, some markers have been removed and it is overgrown. After about 1.5km the river flattens and travel becomes easier with small flats scattered up valley. Roaring Billy Hut (6 bunk, open fire, DoC cat 4) is incorrectly located on G37. It is at approx G37 148 949, on the true left at the edge of the bush on a small flat, and is in good condition (2004).

Crossing the Thomas Range. From Roaring Billy Hut, head upstream, keeping to the true left (in the forest) until the first major flats are reached. Cross and ascend the steep narrow spur that descends SE from pt 1390m. The going is quite good apart from one very narrow steep section where packs may have to be passed over a boulder (plenty of trees to hold onto). The Thomas Range is easy going (with tarns) along to a saddle between pts 1396 and 1379m where it is possible to camp. Descent into the Thomas Valley is straight forward (but watch for holes in the scrub/tussock zone). It is also necessary to weave between some small bluffs in the bush.

THOMAS RIVER

The Thomas is popular with hunters, an occasional fisherman and the less occasional tramper. Crossing the Haast is a major obstacle to valley access. Most fly in, or jetboat from Haast. If the Haast is extremely low, as it occasionally gets in winter, it may, with extreme care, be crossable a little upstream of Thomas Bluff, but only in abnormal conditions. If necessary, the true right can also be followed from the Haast roadbridge.

From the Haast, the marked route on the true left of the Thomas for the first 2km is in poor condition. Either follow up the riverbank, or an old grassy flood channel beside the forest on the east side of Law Flat. This channel leads back to the river and a few red and white markers in the bush lead along the riverbank. A second more recent flood channel is then followed further upstream.

Markers head into the bush 100m before the top of the channel as marked on F37 and quickly lead to an area of flood and windthrow damage, where the markers aren't easy to follow. If you lose it, take the easiest line close to the river up to the start of a flood channel at F37 024 914. Follow up the greasy boulders to the top of the flood channel at F37 027 917.

A good marked route on the true left leads from here up to the hut. The last stretch to the hut climbs along the edge of a terrace spur further from the river than the map indicates, before crossing a stream and descending to Thomas Hut (6 bunk, open fire, DoC cat 4) which is in good condition (2004).

The river has been held back by an old landslide below the hut, forming long deep pools. Tree stumps project from fine gravels upstream. The river is normally crossable about 10 mins above the hut. The riverbed for a long way below the hut is very greasy with big boulders, usually making crossing impractical.

From the hut, there is an old permolat marked route for some distance upstream on the true left of the Thomas. This can be difficult to follow through swampy flats just beyond the hut. Further up valley, the marked route has some short digressions to the true right, but remains primarily on the true left and ends before the gorge (opposite pt 458m) is reached. Cross. This gorge is sidled on the true right, traversing past pt 458m and descending to the river again at about G37 115 990. Cross, and continue in fairly open forest on the true left upstream. Spurs onto the Mataketake Range generally offer open beech forest travel once the valley floor is cleared. On most spur crests the bushline is relatively free of scrub.

Times: Haast River to Thomas Hut, about 2.5 hrs; Hut to valley head, at least one long day.

HAAST PARINGA CATTLE TRACK

Before Haast Pass Highway (SH6) was completed in 1965, a benched stock track led down the West Coast to Haast. A section of this route between the Moeraki River and Waita Creek remains. The

NZFS cleared and marked this track in the 1980s. For a while it became quite overgrown, but DoC has recently done a good job of recutting and clearing it again right through to Coppermine Creek, and it is planned to maintain it to this standard every few years.

This is a great bush trip, especially for those with an interest in bird and plant life, accessible yet not heavily used, and well within the capabilities of an average tramping party. There are also tussock tops with tarns on the Mateketeke Range that can be accessed on a fine day. Care needs to be taken at one or two slips and streams, but it is pretty straight forward.

ROAD TO BLOWFLY HUT

The entrance to this track is at a small parking area and DoC sign about 8km south of Lake Paringa on SH6 (near pt 112m on G37). The track is benched and graded (part of the old Haast-Paringa Cattle Track), as it winds in to meet the Moeraki River. This section of track is in good condition and a very pleasant bush walk in its own right. Red mistletoe blooms in January along the track and *Dawsonia superba*, NZs largest moss, forms patches by the track. Kaka and Blue Duck are frequently seen or heard here. A turnoff sign just before the swingbridge over the Moeraki River (locally known as the Blue) indicates the track up this valley on the true right. The Cattle Track continues beyond the swingbridge for 10 mins to Blowfly Flat and Hut (8 bunks, stove, DoC cat 3, also called Blue River Hut, and Jack Farrels in the past).

Time: Road to Blowfly Hut, 1.3 hrs.

BLOWFLY HUT TO COPPERMINE CREEK HUT

Climbing gradually, the benched and graded track provides wonderful travel to Maori Saddle Hut (14 bunk, stove, DoC cat 3). Powelliphanta snail shells (protected) can often be seen on the ground. The track winds in and out of gullies close to the Alpine Fault, which keeps one or two slips, where rock is very finely crushed, from revegetating.

One such slip (marked on the map) is at Robinson Creek. Descend the open slip of the true left creek to the forks. Cairns and white permolat markers on the true left here indicate where to climb up about 30 or 40m to the track formation again which sidles on through cutty grass back into the bush. There is a small grass campsite at the edge of the saddle, just NE of Robinson Creek by the track at F37 065 012.

The track continues to wind along the slopes through thick forest, slowly descending into lush beech forest on alluvial flats where pleasant mossy streams flow. The track joins an old road formation at F37 016 004, near the start of a long straight heading north. For those going the other way, there is a DoC sign at the junction to indicate where the track leaves this road. A very gentle descent leads to open flats, past a couple of private buildings and on to Coppermine Creek. Coppermine Creek Hut (8 bunks, wood stove, DoC cat 3) is in rough farmland on the true right of the creek as marked on F37, painted green. It is popular with hunters.

Times: Blowfly Hut to Maori Saddle Hut, 5 hrs; Maori Saddle Hut to Coppermine Creek Hut, 8 hrs.

COPPERMINE CREEK HUT TO THE WAITA ROADBRIDGE

From the hut, markers lead down the flats on the true right and cross to the true left at F37 008 026. Passing through an open stand of young kahikateas they lead to a 4WD track which is followed until just below the Waita/Coppermine confluence. Gravel flats now lead down valley. Cross as necessary, following either bank out to the road. A bridge over Maori River allows access out in high water conditions on the true left of the Waita all the way to the road.

If heading up valley, park at the 4WD access 100m from the main road on the true left of Waita River, where there is a DoC sign. Be careful not to block farm access. Follow either bank, but be sure to pick up the 4WD track where it starts 100m below Coppermine Creek on the true left of Coppermine and the Waita River.

Time: Coppermine Creek Hut to Road, 1.5 hrs, either way.

THE MATAKETAKE RANGE

This range offers excellent views and plenty of tarns. Great 2 to 5 day trips can be planned here. The range is covered in tussock and is all relatively easy to traverse in fine weather. Don't get caught up there in mist though. Many spurs can be used on and off the range by experienced parties.

Access is easiest from the Moeraki end of the Haast-Paringa Cattle track. Follow the track up from Blowfly Hut to Whakapohai Saddle. The track then sidles up from the saddle and crosses Wrong Creek. About halfway to this creek, an old benched track leads off to the south, following the spur up from G37 135 058. This track is overgrown in places, but provides a reasonable route to the tops. The track, which was put in for mining mica, stops a few 100m before the bushline. There is some old tape beyond that.

Another route to the tops leaves the Cattle Track and follows the last tributary of Whakapohai River before Maori Saddle is reached. When the creekbed becomes choked with fern and logs, sidle out on the true left and climb the ridge to bushline, about 1 hr from the track. Lake Dime is about 20 mins away. The spur off pt 1105m on the true right of Wyllie Creek is easily followed to the Thomas. It is open and has little scrub at the bushline. There is no hut 1km NE of Mt Smith as marked on G37 Ed.1. The Mataketake Range can also be crossed on a bush saddle between Mt Clarke and Rainytop, crossing from the Moeraki to the Thomas.

MOERAKI (BLUE) VALLEY

A track and two huts make this one of the more accessible West Coast valleys. It is sometimes combined with a crossing to the Clarke River over Zeilian Pass. The huts and tracks in the valley have all had maintanence done on them recently by DoC.

ROAD TO TOP MOERAKI HUT

Access to the valley is along the Haast-Paringa Cattle track from SH6 near pt 112m. Keep an eye out for a small carpark area by the road marked with a DoC sign, as it's easy to miss. A good track leads to the signposted junction where the valley track leaves the Haast-Paringa Cattle Track on the true right of the Moeraki River.

The valley track leads up to the flats, crossing deeply channelled creeks and several swampy open areas. Entrances and exits are marked, but the trackline isn't always accurately shown on G37. Good grass flats are reached about 20 mins below the hut. Follow around the grassy corridor as shown on G37 back towards the river, keeping an eye out for markers. They lead on up valley through the scrub. Beyond the scrub, they lead back to the river. For the last few 100m cross a minor side branch of the river, follow up river shingle, and climb up the bank to Horseshoe Flat Hut, (6 bunk, open fire, DoC cat 3) located on a grass flat.

The track up valley heads up past the hut toilet and later travels under wonderful podocarps and beech, rich in moss and liverwort. Permolat and more recent orange plastic markers continue on the true right to an open flat. From the top of the flat cross to the true left of the Moeraki River, where markers will be seen. Follow up the flat on the true left for 200m, and pick up the track into the bush.

■ View down the Moeraki Valley.

Following the river edge as before, the track here is also fast and easy travel under the trees. It leads to the bouldery edge of the true left hand branch well above the forks and not far below the hut. A crossing of this branch here is fine in normal conditions, but it could quickly become impassable. From the stream, approach the hut from slightly above, not below. Heading down valley from the hut, once across this stream, look down valley for a chainsawn log. The track enters the bush near here, but markers may not be obvious from the stream. Top Moeraki Hut, called Middle Head Hut on G37, (6 bunk, open fire, DoC cat 3) is also in great condition.

Times: Road to Blowfly Hut, 1 hr 20 mins; Road to Horseshoe Flat Hut, 4 hrs; Horseshoe Flat Hut to Top Moeraki (Middle Head) Hut, 1 hr 50 mins.

ZEILIAN PASS Moeraki Valley to Zeilian Creek

This crossing is unmarked, but one of the easier crossings of the Hooker Range. Reasonable bush skills are still required. From Top Moeraki Hut, follow the bed of the South Branch of the Moeraki River up to forks at G37 253 021. If sidling here, be sure to descend to the river by the 500m contour, as up valley beyond this, steep slopes make returning to the river difficult. Above the grid reference forks mentioned, the true right (main) creek becomes confined in a messy cataract. Follow up the open true left creek for about 200m from the forks until an easy entry to the bush is found. Sidle through open beech to the bush edge in the true right creek again at G37 255 017.

The basin above here is thick with fern, scrub and *Hoheria*. Travel is a mix of stream bed and sidling on whichever bank is easiest, but its not too bad. Eventually the stream becomes very confined just before a big boulder. A dry channel on the true left here leads around an island upstream.

Then follow a gravel creek bed on the true right side of the valley up into the tussock, from about the creek junction G37 260 014 to almost the 1100m contour. A fairly easy tussock sidle from the creek leads across to the range at about G37 266 009, and 40m higher than the saddle. Follow the range crest for about 400m to the western side of the saddle where the descent into Zeilian Creek is less steep. A boulder 100m to the true right of Zeilian Creek at the 1040m contour offers good lunch shelter. See Zeilian Creek in the Clarke Valley notes for further information.

Descending from the saddle into the Moeraki, follow the range crest east to about the 1160m contour. Then sidle north to the first stream with continuous gravel and open leads going on down into the scrub of the basin itself. From the bushline, sidle through beech forest on the true left to the creek downstream. This rejoins the main stream at G37 253 021. Follow the stream on down.

Time: Top Moeraki Hut to upper Zeilian Creek, about 6 or 7 hrs.

MIDDLE HEAD BRANCH Top Moeraki Hut to pt 606m flat

From Top Moeraki Hut a track leads across to the Middle Head Branch. White permolat markers indicate a poor crossing of this stream. A marked route on the true right continues up past a bivvy rock to the flats at pt 606m.

A saddle in the head of this valley is occasionally used **to cross into Serpentine Creek** in the Paringa. This seldom used route has some scrub and bluffs to negotiate. Heading into the Moeraki from this saddle, it is recommended to descend under bluffs to beech on the true right, or even go down the creek to the right of that. Heading into Serpentine Creek from the saddle, sidle left in tussock across to a spur at G37 294 030 and descend it to forks in Serpentine Creek at about the 500m contour. The bushline on this side is relatively scrub free, but there is a 20m scrubby bluff about a third of the way down through the bush to get past.

THE PARINGA VALLEY

The Paringa River is clear and blue in summer, draining only small amounts of ice on Mt McCullaugh, making it an exception to many other West Coast rivers. However, the glacial Otoko waters discolour it before it reaches the road. It is also unusual in not descending any gorges from the headwater forks. Forests in the valley are varied, being close to the beech gap boundary. DoC may recut and mark from the Otoko Confluence up to the Tunnel Creek rock bivvy at the bushline this summer, probably to a marked route standard.

ROAD TO TUNNEL CREEK HUT

The lower flats in the valley are farmed by Mr Tony Condon, (Ph 03 751 0895) whose permission should be sought to enter the valley. This is usually given, but be careful not to disrupt stock. With his jetboat, he may also be able to assist with transport up to the forks. The Waiatoto River Jet (Ph 03 750 0780) can also take parties up to the forks on request. Alternatively, for those on foot, either bank can be followed to the confluence. If the river is not easily crossed, use the true left to enter the Paringa and the true right to enter the Otoko, preventing any major river crossings. If the river is easily crossed, following the riverbed from flat to flat is faster.

On the true left of the Paringa from the roadbridge, follow a 4WD track across flats to Filleul Creek. Continue up a minor river channel for 1km to an extensive gravel flat. There are two bush flats eroded by the river and then a bluff to be sidled to reach the confluence by Stew Creek. Muddy cattle trails help along the bush flat river banks. The bluff can be sidled close to the river without climbing above 50m, but it is a bit of a bash. There are some recent orange permolat markers and older white ones which may be of limited help, but they couldn't be called a marked route.

Condons Hut is in a clearing on the true right of Stew Creek as marked on G37. It is locked. Permission from Tony Condon is required to use it. The track up valley begins near here on the true right bank of Stew Creek and is only lightly marked at present (2003) with white permolat. Stew

■ Looking across the head of the Paringa Valley from above the saddle to McCullaugh Creek.

Creek is followed for a few hundred metres before the track heads inland. Take care to keep following these markers as they wind through a succession of clearings in the middle of the bush flat some distance from the river. They eventually lead back to the river at about G37 294 082.

The track now follows near the river all the way to Tunnel Creek Hut (6 bunk, open fire, DoC cat 3). The hut is on a small grass clearing by the river. Note that Serpentine Creek splits into 2 channels as it approaches the Paringa River and the track crosses each separately, about 5 mins apart. Both branches carry about the same amount of water. Tree-fall and washouts at the Serpentine Creek channels make it necessary to clamber up banks to refind the track, but this is not difficult.

Times: Road to Condons Hut, about 3 hrs; Condons Hut to Tunnel Creek Hut, 3 hrs.

Parties need to be reasonably experienced at travelling off track in bush and on the tops to use the following routes. Some of this country is very rough and requires careful judgement.

CROSSING FROM TUNNEL CREEK HUT TO MCCULLAUGH CREEK

From the hut, a short track crosses a creek ditch and continues up the river bank through forest to more extensive flats. Cross to the flat between Tunnel Creek and the main Paringa. Here, markers beginning on the true left of Tunnel Creek lead up the spur onto pt 542m and continue to the bushline, 100m WSW of the bivvy rock. This marked route is getting hard to follow in places, especially at the 600 to 700m contour, where it passes through an area of windthrow with lawyer in it, but it will be maintained. The track goes directly up the face to the narrow ridge at G37 338 039. It's especially important to follow or pick it up again when descending. The excellent bivvy rock is in tussock towards the NE side of the tussock plateau, and faces NW. It sleeps about 6.

Head south from the bivvy rock through open beech and then climb to bushline to avoid scrub. Sidle SE into a stream and continue to a small tarn at G37 347 030. Continue SE into the basin at 1100m and follow up a tussock gully with old deer trails to the range at G37 362 022.

The initial descent into McCullaugh Creek is very steep on hard slopes with very short alpine vegetation. There are a couple of options. Travel up to 300m west along the range crest before descending steep tussock slopes back into McCullaugh Creek. The spur at G37 360 018 has also been used, but is steep short tussock, particularly towards the bottom and requires care. The crest of the range has a short eroded piece at G37 360 022 that some will prefer to traverse with a rope on.

The Paringa Valley from near Power Knob.

Alternatively from G37 362 022, a poorer option is to follow animal trails down shingle and short tussock spurs, crossing small gullies to the main gully, usually snow filled, below the saddle. This route is exposed and slippery. The gully can then be followed more easily down to the valley floor at G37 363 018. Be aware that snow in this gully is mostly avalanche debris from bluffs above. See Clarke Valley notes, P 225 and McCullaugh Ck notes P 228.

Times: Tunnel Ck Hut to biv rock, 4 hrs (2.5 hrs down); Biv rock to head of McCullaugh Ck, 4 hrs.

OTHER ROUTES FROM THE PARINGA

On the west end of the McCullaugh/Paringa pass there are small tarns at about the 1500m contour. It is possible to traverse the main range from this saddle to Clarke Pass, but at parallel snow and rock gullies at the top of Douglas Spur, a rope and ice axe may be necessary for a small sidle on the Clarke side. The range crest itself for 100m at this point is broken and not a packing route.

OUTPOST ridge can also be traversed from the Clarke River to the Main Range. A steep but relatively easy descent on vegetated slopes follows to the Paringa/McCullaugh Pass.

CLARKE PASS has a tarn on it. The descent from the pass to Rough Creek is straightforward, but Rough Creek isn't. The descent from the pass on the Paringa side is as follows. Once in the Paringa basin, climb high through tussock on the true right and descend to the Tunnel Creek junction by the obvious spur. Do not attempt to follow the Paringa river down to the valley floor. Another saddle is sometimes used west of Mt Chesney, involving a steep descent through bush to the Tunnel Creek Junction.

A saddle can also be crossed from **ZEILIAN CREEK TO SERPENTINE CREEK** in the Paringa. The tussock spur at G37 287 007 is steep but reasonable travelling up to the range from Zeilian Creek. Follow the range crest east across the saddle (at pt 1282m) for a km then sidle NE across the slopes of Mt Zeilian to G37 306 010 at the 1240m contour. Now head for the spur on the true right of Serpentine Creek at G37 302 020. This descends north as a prominent spur past waterfalls in the creek to about the 460m contour. Follow down beside the creek to the Paringa.

See the Moeraki notes for crossing from Serpentine Creek to Top Moeraki Hut.

Tunnel Creek Hut.

A HIGH LEVEL ROUTE FROM MARKS FLAT TO TUNNEL CREEK also exists, but requires good alpine skills, equipment and a fine day. From G37 418 008 at Marks Flat, climb the spur to G37 411 015 (this is also the approach route for Mt Hooker). Descend to Murdock Creek where a reasonable crossing exists at G37 400 016. Climb west to gain a major shelf via a steep tussock gully at G37 398 014. Continue west to a higher shelf, then climb up tussock to gain the south ridge of Mt McCullaugh. Climb snow slopes to about the 2000m contour, then traverse NW to cross the west ridge of McCullaugh at G37 376 030.On the northern side, traverse west on rock ledges onto a snowfield and a notch at G37 373 029 above a steep ravine dropping to McCullaugh Creek. Traverse west then NW (keeping high) on the southern side of the ridge below the Buttress (1870m), to avoid ravines on lower slopes. Continue to sidle down, crossing the last ravine at G37 353 031. Descend to the tarn at G37 347 030 and continue to the marked rock bivvy. Allow 8 or 9 hrs in either direction.

THE VALLEY OF DARKNESS

Leave the river at about G37 304 087 on the true left, climbing and sidling through thick ground fern and bush. Continue across slippery rock slabs, returning to the river at about G37 315 077. A good ground trail still on the true left leads along, just above the river, through grassy clearings to a lovely camping flat at about G37 340 070. Beyond here, the best route into the head of the valley appears to begin up the creek falling from pt 1683m. Follow it to the scrubline, then sidle beneath the bluffs.

THE OTOKO VALLEY

The Otoko has an attraction for bad weather. Both sides of the Otoko can and have been followed from the road to the gravel flats in the head, but travel is very rough in sections. The true right is usually followed, and offers better travel. Route options to the Otoko Paringa forks are described in the Paringa section. On the true right, there are cattle tracks through the bush where the river cuts in at G36 287 123, and another from the flat at G36 287 106 to just above the Otoko/Paringa confluence and the grass flat upstream.

PARINGA FORKS TO REYNOLDS CREEK

Continue up flats on the true right past the new hut (locked, Tony Condon) and cattle yards marked on G36 Ed. 1. There is fierce nettle (*Urtica ferox*) in shrubland and forest around here. About 500m up valley from the hut, a stream confined in a gravel gut enters the Otoko on a distinctive bend. On the map, this bend has gravel cliffs marked by the river. Carefully pick your way into this gut and follow it down to the river. From there, if the river isn't up too much, it is normally possible to follow along the base of cliffs to easier going at Swinde Creek, 15 mins from the bend.

Continue along flats and around the riverbank for just over a kilometre to the next bend (G36 337 107), where easy access is barred by boulders. Climb onto the river terrace via a fresh washout and join the old track, difficult to follow in places, which continues to Reynolds Flat (actually a series of flats) taking about 40 mins. The corrugated iron and concrete chimney base remains of an old burnt out NZFS hut can still be seen here.

Time: Road to Reynolds Creek, about 6 hrs; Old hut and yards to Reynolds Creek, about 2 hrs.

REYNOLDS CREEK TO HEAD

Beyond Reynolds flats there is an old, blazed, roughly recut route (the old horse track) that may be picked up on the main terrace above the river or from the cairn where it cuts out of the open, bouldery creek at G37 362 098. This may be followed with care to where it drops to the riverbank at G37

370 096. Continue along the riverbank for 300m to the next major (deep cut) side stream and climb from the upstream (East) corner of the stream and sidle on mixed terraces/slopes 50 to 150m above the river. Signs of the old blazed line may be seen, especially for the last 30 mins before Stag Flat, but it is difficult to follow (2000). **Stag Flat** offers good campsites.

From Stag Flat, follow the river edge for about 500m until the river splits. River conditions will dictate then whether to sidle from here 50 to 100m vertically above and keeping well away from the river in sometimes thick bush, or follow small flood channels and river terraces (the island is fair going) up to the top of the island where a conspicuous large, vegetated boulder bars further riverbed travel. If the latter, then now also leave the river, climb 50 to 100m above it and sidle. The going is reasonable to the wide, clear avalanche channel of a side stream and for a few hundred metres beyond. This is followed by a difficult slow stretch for about 1 hr, negotiating a forested boulder field.

As the gradient of the river changes, cut out to the river at a grassy clearing (with a good campsite at G37 413 071), beyond which travel is easier close to the river. Some cross here to the true left, following good leads along clear side streams but there is also a messy terrace to cross opposite Harker Torrent. Alternatively (and probably still best), continue along the true right bank to the large gravel fan of **Harker Torrent.** Ascend it and sidle upstream back to the river. Generally, the best option from here to the gravel flats in the head is to link up patches of bush, which are more open. However, some scrub bashing is inevitable. The river is easily crossed at the gravel head flats on fine shingle. The lake once here is now infilled.

Times: Reynolds to Stag Flat, about 4 hrs; Stag Flat to the head, about 8 hrs; Allow 2 long hard days from the road for fit, experienced parties.

For crossing to Marks Flat over Lower Otoko Pass see the Clarke Valley notes. For crossing to the Landsborough directly over Upper Otoko Pass, see Landsborough notes. (This crossing is a poor and difficult route, in this direction especially). Climbing parties have traditionally accessed **Mt Dechen** via the big, snow couloir near Mt Matheson. Be aware of avalanche potential here, particularly in winter and spring. An alternative approach from the head of the valley is via the spur at G37 467 043 and a sidle west of Mt Gorden to the narrow ridge leading up to the McCardell Glacier, depending on snow conditions.

THE MAHITAHI VALLEY

This is a rough catchment that few venture into. It is more often used to finish rather than start a trip, and partly this is a reflection of the difficulties and slow travel involved, particularly in the upper valley. It is described from the headwaters at Mueller Pass out to the road.

MUELLER PASS Zora Creek to the Mahitahi

North of Mueller Pass, the Zora Valley slopes are steeply eroding moraine walls. South from the pass, small bluffs and steep tussock slopes are negotiable up a variety of routes (ones further south tend to be easier) from the large terrace at the 1040m contour, H36 547 106. SW of Mueller Pass on the Hooker Range there are exposed campsites and a small tarn at about the 1480m contour. The Mahitahi Valley gently reaches up to Mueller Pass from a lush, scrub and tussock basin. Follow tussock slopes down on the true right of the creek draining the pass. There are heavy old deer trails in places. Just above the 1300m contour, cross a stream draining from the north. Continue down the next spur on the true right also.

From H36 537 113 best option is to follow deer trails sidling across tussock from about the 1260m contour down to the stone fields at H36 530 118. From here, the next section is horrendously

The Mahitahi River above the Edison River Junction.

thick and scrubby with no obvious line and the editor would love to hear of a better route. Head down open creek leads towards H36 523 119, where the main river becomes travellable again. Boulders block the creeks in places on the way down, and the scrub is very bad.

(Alternatively from H36 530 118 (the stone fields), a better route may exist closer to the bluffs on the true right past H36 527 121 and across a gully to the open gravel stream bed at H36 523 123 which offers good going back to the Mahitahi River). In reasonable conditions, from H36 523 119 the river stones can now be followed through a corridor of thick scrub to tiny flats (only room for about 2 tents) on the true left opposite Uaroa Creek. Names: The peak pt 2034m was first climbed and named Crystal Peak by the Marie Byles party (NZAJ 1935).

Times: Zora to Mueller Pass, 1 hr 20 mins; Mueller Pass to Uaroa Creek, about 2 hrs 45 mins.

UAROA CREEK TO THE EDISON RIVER

Situated one creek up from Uaroa Ck on the true right of the Mahitahi, between the 680 and 700m contours, there is an excellent bivvy rock at H36 509 129 that sleeps 6. This has been used intermittently since the 1930s. From Uaroa Creek to the Edison forks the river drops quickly. It is very rough, bouldery and hemmed in by scrubby forest. Very capable parties in fine weather may descend the boulders much of the way, sidling as necessary on the true right until G36 492 123, then crossing. On the true left, sidle onto a bush terrace and cross it, descending to the Mahitahi about 100m before the forks. A good dry river channel leads through this last section almost to the Edison. The Mahitahi water here is clear. The Edison is slightly discoloured with glacial silt, but is usually crossed easily here at the junction on gravels.

Going upvalley, a good variation that mostly avoids river boulder chaos is described. On the true left, 100m past the Edison junction, climb to a forested terrace100m above the river. Follow the terrace upvalley, cross an open side stream near a small flat (about G36 489 123), then keep within sight of the main river. Cross the river about 15 mins later at the first good ford. On the true right, climb onto a nearby forested terrace (G36 493 124), then upvalley, climb onto a narrow forested moraine spur leading to the first landslip. Climb 150m up this and cross to the second open slip. Enter the bush on steep slopes and sidle, keeping well above the river to the next slip. Sidle diagonally up this and reenter bush continuing on a steep sidle which levels and gives access to the river opposite Uaroa forks.

Time: Uaroa Creek to Edison River, about 4 hrs.

EDISON RIVER TO THE MORSE RIVER

There are grass campsites on an old slip on the true right of the Mahitahi, opposite the Edison. Right at the junction there are also a couple of bivvy rocks at the forest edge behind scrub between the two rivers. From the Edison, continue along gravel beside the Mahitahi on the true left. About 500m down valley cross to the true right where a gravel washout stream enters the river. Boulders and a bit of bushbashing follow down valley. There is tin from a past hunters hut at G36 468 133. At about G36 461 135 a huge rock landslide across the river begins that extends down valley on the true left for 1km. Cross easily on shingle to the true left and follow these open rockfields down valley.

Return to the true right before crossings become too bouldery and the river gradient too steep at the lower end of the rockfields. Travel on the true right is then fine until the spur down at G36 441 142. This can be bypassed with some difficulty on the true right by climbing high, but at normal flow, it is much easier to cross the river twice. From the rockfields, the true left can also be followed through big boulders and second growth down to the flats beginning at G36 440 141.

River travel is now reasonably easy. Two crossings, one at a scrubby island in the river G36 434 143 and the other back to the true right at the end of the flats on the bend also helps. From here, at G36 425 141, climb up on the true right to the edge of a bush terrace, and follow the high edge overlooking the river downstream to the 'biv flat'. Bits of an old blaze line, never more than 150m from the river, lead along the edge of this second, higher terrace. The river is confined in greasy boulders, drops quickly, and doesn't become good travel again until the 'biv flat'. Don't be tempted away from the terrace edge overlooking the river by the bush flats. They are full of mossy gullies, logs and offer only slow, complex travel. The bivvy marked on the map is gone. From the 'biv flat' continue down valley by the river on the true right to the Morse confluence.

Time: Edison River to the Morse River, 7 to 8 hrs.

MORSE RIVER TO THE HIGHWAY

Small thin grass and scrub flats on the true right run along the riverbank downstream from the Morse. Just below the stream on the true right below the Morse, pick up an old bulldozed line that stays near the bank down valley. This is washed out in places. Keep by the river. The old musterers hut with a verandah across the river on the true left opposite Plateau Creek is in fair condition. Keep on the true right.

There are several options when flats near SH6 are reached:

1. Cross the river to the main road.
2. Continue down the bank, being careful with electric fences, to the main road bridge where there is a small picnic carpark.
3. Follow the road out to the Condon Homestead at Mahitahi and then the short road out to SH6.

For those heading up valley, contact Mr Daryl Condon, (ph (03 751 0877) who has freehold land and runs cattle in the valley, for access permission. He may also be able to help parties bypass electric fences upvalley, too. Follow a 4WD track, washed out in places further in, and then the riverbed on the true right to the 'biv flat'. Then follow the terrace bush edge overlooking the river on the true right to more flats. Continue up valley, cross and use the open slopes of a massive landslide on the true left then continue up the true right again towards the Edison. The true left may provide easier travel for the last 500m.

Time: Morse River to the Road, 5 to 6 hrs.

MAKAWHIO (JACOBS) VALLEY

This is an isolated and seldom visited valley. An awkward pass in the head requiring alpine skills and equipment leads to the Troyte branch of the Karangarua. The Troyte is also very difficult to access. These valleys are only suitable for fit and experienced parties. Cattle are farmed on the lower flats by John Sullivan (ph 03 751 0828). Parties seeking access to the valley should contact him for permission.

HIGHWAY TO MISTY CREEK

Follow the road opposite the school on the true left of the Makawhio River up valley. Continue along grass flats to the bush edge. From the bush edge, boulder hop up the true left to Greer Creek. Just beyond Kini Creek on the true left there is a small bluff, but it is easily passed on this side. (Don't be tempted to cross the river to pass it, as crossing back above the bluff is deep and difficult). If the river is up, some bush sidling will be necessary, but normally travel by the river on the true left is straight-forward. There are campsites along the river bank here.

Beyond Greer Creek, good travel along the river bank continues on the true left until about 500 to 600m before Jumbo Creek, where the riverbed closes in and travel becomes rough. Climb out here on the true left and sidle up valley on open bush terraces with deer trails assisting at about the 200m contour. At about G36 470 208, travel up valley deteriorates, with thick fern, fallen trees and steep sided creeks to contend with.

Between two marked creeks there is a rock bivvy at G36 473 203, clearly visible from up valley as a huge lump of rock poking out of the bush. It is necessary to descend to near river level to bypass a bluff about 300m up valley from the bivvy rock. Continue sidling across several rough gullies then more open bush leads to Misty Creek. Misty Creek enters the Makawhio at G36 484 187 and drains from Mt Stratford to Mt Butzbach.

Times: Highway to bush edge, 2 hrs; Bush edge to Greer Creek, 3 hrs; Greer Creek to Misty Creek, 8.5 hrs.

MISTY CREEK TO RELIEF FLAT

From Misty Creek travel is slow in thick bush. The river is little better, with frequent obstacles blocking progress and only short sections of good travel. Stay on the true left. Relief Flat is at H36 508 176 on a prominent bend in the river and offers good campsites.

Time: Misty Creek to Relief Flat, 6.5 hrs.

RELIEF FLAT TO HEADWATERS

From Relief Flat, follow the true left river bank where possible upstream to the gravel flat of the old Makawhio Lakebed at H36 534 161. On the way up there is another small flat at H36 517 172, about 1.5 hrs from Relief Flat. Each of these three flats has formed behind a rise of boulders in the river bed.

Makawhio Lakebed Flat provides good travel. (This flat was a lake in the 1950s but has since infilled). Cross the river at the top end of the Lakebed Flat to the true right. Beyond here, look for a good route up to the base of the bluffs on the true right, preferably before being forced out at H36 543 157. Climb 100 to 120m and follow along under the bluffs through tussock and scrub. The river may be returned to at about the 860m contour. From about H36 557 150, climb out again on the true right up a streambed to the tussock and sidle into the upper basin. There is a campsite at about H36 565 145.

Times: Relief Flat to Makawhio Lakebed Flat, 3.5 hrs; Lake flat to campsite, about 3 hrs.

HIGHLAND PASS Makawhio to the Troyte

There are no easy routes from the Makawhio headwaters. There are two named cols on the Bare Rocky Range leading to the Troyte, though neither is shown on the map; Troyte Col at H36 577 146 and Highland Pass at H36 578 139. Highland Pass has been crossed a few times by transalpine capable and equipped parties.

Depending on the season, ascend avalanche debris from the head of the Makawhio at H36 573 141, then follow up a rocky gully. Higher, snowslopes lead to the pass. Drop onto the Troyte side from the saddle and sidle left down a long sloping shelf covered in snow. Continue down snowgrass and rock into a creek bed. This turns into a waterfall. Sidle further left onto a rock and snowgrass rib overlooking a long snow gully. Follow this snow gully down until it ends in a streambed at about H36 584 141. (There is a bluffy step in this gully which may require an abseil onto a cone of avalanche debris filling the lower part of the gully, making the route partly dependent on snow conditions, but alternatives exist).

The Troyte is renown for its trogs or bivvy rocks. The route out down the Troyte is a bit scrubby and steep in the lower part. Head down a tussock bench on the true right of the Troyte and at H36 592 155 sidle through scrub and steep streams at about the 900m contour to the open scrub shoulder overlooking the Karangarua at H36 595 165. Descend through steep bush to either the Troyte-Karangarua forks or a little upstream in the Karangarua. A permolat route existed here once, but is now long gone.

A transalpine crossing has also been made across the Hooker Range about 1km SW of Mt Townsend, connecting the Landsborough with the Troyte.

Times: Makawhio to Highland Pass, 1.5 hrs; Highland Pass to the Troyte Basin, 2 hrs; Troyte Basin to the Karangarua, 5 or more hrs.

KARANGARUA VALLEY

This is the northern extremity of the guide on the West Coast. A brief route description is included to assist those leaving the Landsborough. The Karangarua is in Westland National Park and the DoC office at Fox maintains an up to date information sheet the *Karangarua Valley Route Guide*. The marked route in the valley was recut and marked by DoC in 2004, but care is still required to follow it in places. The track line shown on H36 Ed.1 is generally correct, although from H36 543 194 it now sidles around the 500m contour for 2-300m before climbing to join the track as marked.

CHRISTMAS FLAT TO LAME DUCK FLAT

Crossing Douglas Pass is described in the Landsborough notes. The old (1957) Christmas Flat Hut was replaced in 1996 by DoC. It has 4 bunks, wood stove, and is a category 3 standard, in neat and tidy condition.

Route markers at the bottom end of Christmas Flat on the true left lead through subalpine scrub and bush near the river to an old grassy slip. Climb up and reenter the bush 60m or so above the river on the downstream side of the slip. The track sidles at about this height before dropping to a terrace and finishing about 40m distance upstream from the Troyte River, close to the Karangarua.

Cross the Karangarua River to the true right and use easy gravel flats to avoid a small bluff just below the Troyte junction. Cross back to the true left again. The track recommences about 60m height above the river on the downstream edge of the slip, H36 589 170. It sidles, then descends to follow through beech forest beside the river for the last 20 mins to Lame Duck Flat Hut (currently very dilapidated, but may be replaced).

Time: Christmas Flat to Lame Duck Flat, 2 to 3 hrs.

LAME DUCK FLAT TO CASSEL FLAT

Below Lame Duck Hut, permolat markers continue down valley crossing Jack Creek near the river. The marked route is boggy for a while, then climbs above the gorge. It crosses several exposed slippery slabby creekbeds above bluffs where care and sure feet are required. At stream crossings, red or orange markers frequently mark the track re-entry to the bush. There is a gravel washout slip to cross about a third of the way down the sidle section that is steep and exposed. A marked route leads up through the bush, across and down to the main track again. A chain hanging down from a tree assists the descent past a small greasy bluff. The track then follows beneath bluffs for about 1km. There is a large open slip at approx H36 544 189 that takes some care to negotiate (steep with smooth rock on the true left side). Near here, the track route marked on H36 has been changed, and now descends to sidle around the 500m contour for 200 to 300m to remeet the old line at H36 543 194.

Where it descends through an open scrubby area on the ridge between Tui Creek and the Karangarua, the track is marked with poles. More poles and markers lead off to the right straight down a scrubby slip to the Karangarua Riverbed. Follow along beside the river to Tui Creek. Continue along the riverbank. Travel is on stones, through patches of bush flat and sometimes on grass flats.

The Douglas (Twain) River confluence marks the start of the main grass flats. In normal summer river conditions, the Karangarua water is clear and blue until it meets the heavily glacial gray Douglas waters. From the cableway across the Karangarua below Regina Creek, the track heads diagonally across the grass flat, crosses Curly Creek and heads up to Cassel Flat Hut (6 bunk, wood stove, DoC cat 3).

Time: Lame Duck Flat to Cassel Flat, 7 hrs.

CASSEL FLAT TO THE HIGHWAY

A large orange disc indicates the start of the marked route down valley. The route is not easy to follow in places. About 1 hr 50 mins from Cassel Flat Hut, the marked route crosses McTaggart Creek and climbs immediately out on the other side.

Further down, a Karangarua flood channel is followed for a short time. The marked route leads out onto a small grass flat at a stream H36 545 276, close to the Karangarua. Watch carefully in the bush to the left for the track reentry from the boulders. It's not far and easy to miss. The track leads across a terrace to the beginning of a grass flat at H36 543 285. The route down to the bridge is now along the flats, river boulders, logs, and cutty grass along the true left until the bridge is in sight. Then watch for the track leading up to the roadbridge.

Time: Cassel Flat Hut to the highway, 4.5 hrs.

INDEX

Bold numbers refer to either chapter titles, or route descriptions.

D

E

F

U

V

W

Y

Z

Captions for the following four pages:

P 252, Mount Hooker above Marks Flat.
P 253, Under O'Leary Pass in the head of the Joe. Looking up Victor Creek to Bernard Peak.
P 254, Olivine Falls at the bottom of the Olivine Gorge. Pyke Valley.
P 255, View across the Dart Valley from Lake Unknown. Chinamans Bluff is on the righthand edge of the photo. The peaks are (left to right) Sir William, Pluto, and the West Peak of Mt Earnslaw.

FURTHER REFERENCE

Publications available from the NZAC

These titles can be ordered through the National Office in Christchurch. See The Climber or **www.alpineclub.org.nz** for a full list.

Moirs Guide South. Robin McNeill. Great Southern Lakes Press (6th Ed 1995). The classic trampers guide to Fiordland National Park, and a companion guide to this book.

Barron Saddle – Mt Brewster. Ross Cullen. NZAC, 2002. Covers from Haast Pass to the Mt Cook National Park boundary. An excellent guide for climbers, offering useful information for other outdoor people in the region too.

The Mt Aspiring Region. Allan Uren and Mark Watson. NZAC, 2001. Comprehensive guide for mountaineers, with useful information for other outdoor people in the region too.

The Darrans Guide. The Darran and Wick Mountains near Milford Sound. Murray Judge and Hugh Widdowson. NZAC, (1st Ed 1990).

Aoraki/Mount Cook. Latest guidebook for climbers in the region. Alex Palman. NZAC, 2001.

The Climber. A quarterly magazine covering New Zealand rock and alpine climbing. NZAC.

New Zealand Alpine Journal. A publication of the NZAC, covering both rock and alpine climbing. Published annually.

Classic Peaks of New Zealand. Hugh Logan, Craig Potton Publishing, 2002. Well illustrated book that includes some peaks in the Guide area.

Titles not stocked by the NZAC

Wandering in the Wakatipu. Becky Reid, Information and Track Centre, Queenstown, 1994. Very useful local guide.

Classic Tramps of New Zealand. Shaun Barnett and Rob Brown, Craig Potton Publishing, 1999. Beautifully illustrated book that includes some tramps in the area.

South Island Weekend Tramps. Nick Groves, Craig Potton Publishing, 2003.

Tramping in the South Island: Arthur's Pass to Mt Cook. Sven Brabyn, Brabyn Publishing, 2004.

True South – Tramping experiences of the South Island hinterland. Pat Barrett, Reed Publishing, 2003.

Contact information, websites and emails

New Zealand Alpine Club PO Box 786, Christchurch www.alpineclub.org.nz

Canterbury Mountaineering Club PO Box 2415, Christchurch www.cmc.net.nz

Along with NZAC, there are over 20 tramping clubs in the south of the South Island affiliated to **Federated Mountain Clubs of New Zealand.** They each range in membership from a few dozen to several hundred. The full list, with contact details, can be found on the FMC website at: **www.fmc.org.nz.** A few of the main ones are listed below.

Christchurch Tramping Club PO Box 527, Christchurch www.ctc.org.nz

Peninsula Tramping Club PO Box 13-258, Christchurch

www.geocities.com/Yosemite/Gorge/9393

North Otago Tramping and Mountaineering Club PO Box 217, Oamaru

South Canterbury Tramping Club PO Box 221, Timaru http://sctrampingclub.tripod.com

Otago Tramping and Mountaineering Club PO Box 1120, Dunedin www.otmc.co.nz

Otago University Tramping Club Otago University PO Box 56, Dunedin

Wakatipu Tramping and Mountaineering Club PO Box 137, Queenstown

Southland Tramping Club PO Box 41, Invercargill www.fmc.org.nz/southland

Many hunters use the area covered in *Moirs.* Their national organisation is the **New Zealand Deerstalkers Association.** Details of local branches can be sought through the NZDA website: www.deerstalkers.org.nz or ringing the national office at ph 04 801 7367

Maps, Weather and conditions

Mapworld for topo maps, navigational equipment and guidebooks. 173 Gloucester St Christchurch www.mapworld.co.nz ph 0800 627 967

Metphone (pay per minute) mountain forecast general ph 0900-99926

Metfax ph 090077999

New Zealand Met Service: www.met.co.nz

NZ satellite images: www.oneweather.nzoom.com/index.html

Radio: National Programme. Long Range forecast (6 day): 12.30pm daily; Mountain forecast: 4.06pm daily.

Victoria University Met: www.metvuw.com

Australian/NZ situation maps: www.bom.gov.au/weather/national/charts

Also www.geog.canterbury.ac.nz

South Island snow stability information: www.avalanche.net.nz

ABOUT THE EDITOR

Geoff Spearpoint's association with the area started in 1968, when he joined a large club party on a Christmas trip around Mt Hooker. He began tramping initially with school friends, crashing around the Tararuas. Then he joined the Hutt Valley Tramping Club and later on the NZAC in 1974. Discovering a strong, Kiwi outdoor culture he headed off on tramping and climbing trips to places like the Otoko, Waipara and Olivines, inspired by friends like A Heine, J Rundle, G MacCallum and many others. Since then Geoffs had something of a mission for transalpine trips, finding them a very natural way to relate to our mountains and his trips have led into many remote corners in our hills. He began working in the Aspiring region wardening for the NZAC and later spent several years working for Mt Aspiring National Park, based in Makarora and Glenorchy. Geoff left Glenorchy for a seasons fieldwork in Antarctica, while other trips overseas have taken him climbing in Patagonia and on transalpine trips in the Himalaya/Karakoram. Other interests include photography, stained glass and botany, especially the mosses. He also has written a book about tramping in NZ called *Waking to the Hills.* He lives with Barbara Brown at Birdlings Flat on the coast near Christchurch, and they both remain active in the hills. Sometimes on local trips with the Peninsula Tramping Club, and sometimes with other friends to the wonderfully wild regions described in *Moirs Guide North.*

Photo by D Bamford

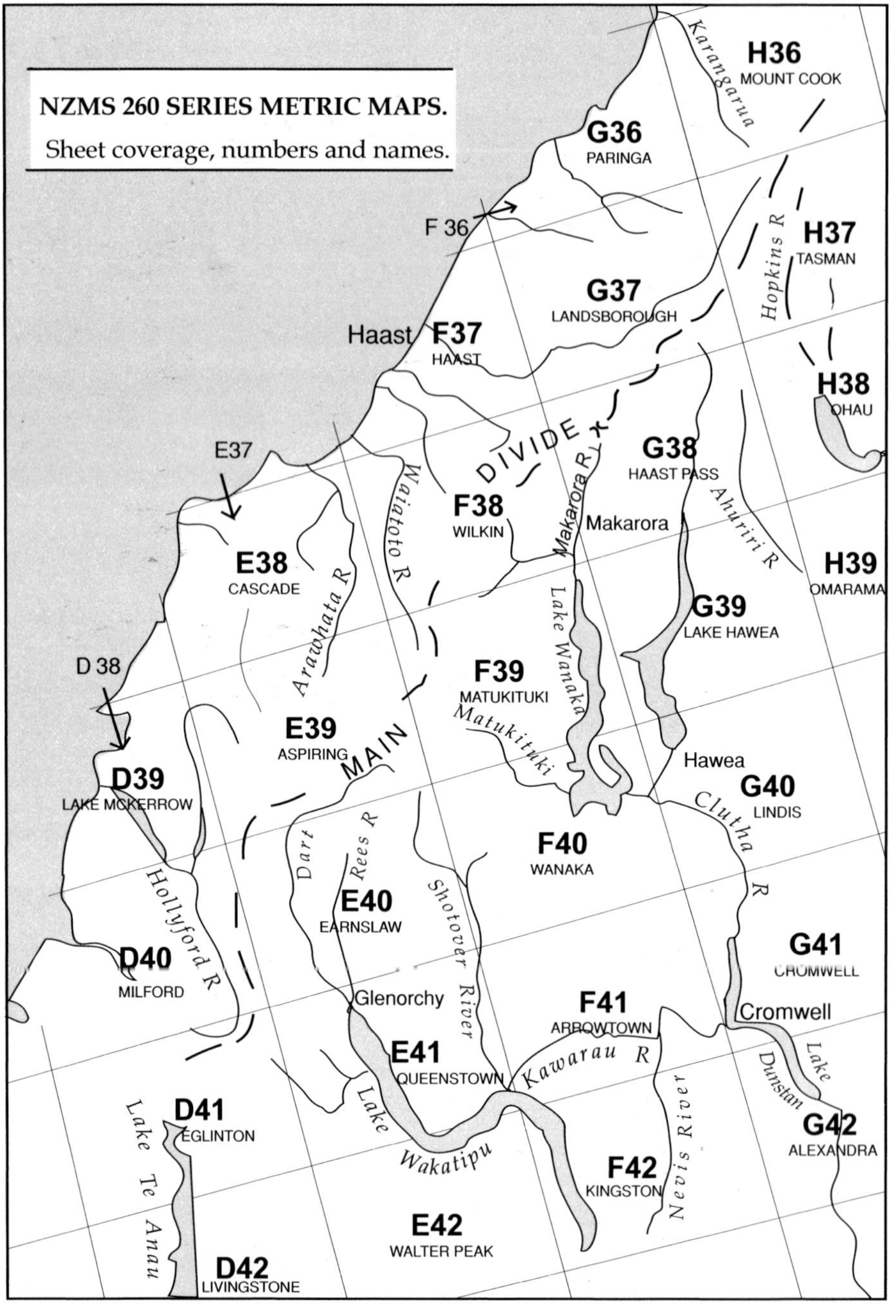

Where only a small land area exists in a grid, it is included on a sheet nearby. Eg, E37 is included on E38 Cascade.